DATE DUE

NO 1 6 '99			

DEMCO 38-296

Ebb Tide in New England

NORTHEASTERN UNIVERSITY 1898–1998

Ebb Tide in New England

Women, Seaports, and Social Change
1630–1800

— ≠ —

ELAINE FORMAN CRANE

— ≠ —

Northeastern University Press

BOSTON

Northeastern University Press

Library of Congress Cataloging-in-Publication Data
Crane, Elaine Forman.
Ebb tide in New England : women, seaports, and social change,
1630–1800 / Elaine Forman Crane.
p.   cm.
Includes bibliographical references and index.
ISBN 1-55553-336-1 (pa : alk. paper).—ISBN 1-55553-337-X (cl : alk. paper)
1. Women—New England—History.   2. Women—New England—Social
conditions.   3. Women—New England—Economic conditions.
4. Harbors—New England—History.   I. Title.
HQ1438.N35C73   1998
305.4'0974—dc21   97-43479

Designed by Joyce C. Weston

Composed in Minion by Graphic Composition, Inc., Athens, Georgia.
Printed and bound by Thomson-Shore, Inc., Dexter, Michigan. The paper
is Glatfelter Supple Opaque Recycled, an acid-free sheet.

MANUFACTURED IN THE UNITED STATES OF AMERICA
02   01   00   99   98   5   4   3   2   1

For Lillian's daughters and granddaughters
Melissa, Andrea, Janet, Mandy, and Joyce

Contents

Acknowledgments

This book has been evolving for at least a decade. During that time, numerous people have supported the project through either their professional expertise or their willingness to explore the topic in one way or another. I am grateful for their support and assistance.

At this point the staff members of the Newport Historical Society are as much colleagues and friends as professional associates, and they have always been extremely helpful to me. My thanks to Dan Snydacker, Ronald Potvin, Bert Lippincott, Joan Youngken, Kate Sexton, and Cynthia Kenney. And to Gladys Bolhouse, who is, no doubt, engaged in a spirited conversation with Ezra Stiles as I write this, I admit her claim that I am a "born-again Newporter."

The legal research could not have been completed without the help of Steve Grimes at the Rhode Island Judicial Archives, and I am indebted to him for his explanations about the Rhode Island judicial system. I am also indebted to the staff of the Rhode Island Archives, particularly Gwen Stearn and Kenneth Carlson, who helped me wade through their voluminous petition collection. At the Massachusetts Supreme Judicial Court, Division of Archives and Records Preservation, Elizabeth Bouvier and Bruce Shaw were particularly helpful. My gratitude is also extended to Professor Bruce Mann, whose suggestions for the legal history chapters resulted in greater clarity and focus.

The staff of other repositories assisted me in a variety of important ways. New England Historic Genealogical Society: Jane Fiske; Essex Institute: Irene Norton, Caroline Preston, Janet Nourse, Prudence Backman; Massachusetts Historical Society: Peter Drummey, Virginia Audet, Aimee Bligh; American Antiquarian Society: Kathleen Major. I also wish to thank all those whose efforts at the New Hampshire Historical Society, New Hampshire State Library, and Division of Records Management and Archives contributed to this project. In addition, Margaret Morrissey and Joseph Copley at the Portsmouth Athenaeum deserve special thanks.

Even non–New Englanders did their part. The Philadelphia Center for Early American Studies, under the directorship of Richard Dunn, acted as a sounding board for one of the chapters at a gathering at The David Library. The American Philosophical Society awarded a legal research grant that enabled me to expand the scope of the book. The National Endowment for the Humanities provided a research grant to ferret out information in Newport, Boston, Salem, and Portsmouth. John Kaminsky compiled the index.

Fordham University has helped in so many ways that it is difficult to list them all. First and foremost, the Director and interlibrary loan staff of Duane (now Walsh) Library: Jim McCabe, Elizabeth Garity, and Charlotte Labbe. Nancy McCarthy, Director of Research, and her assistant, Laura Ebert, were always willing to discuss and offer advice about possible funding sources. Faculty research grants and funded leaves of absence were also ways in which the university signaled its support of this project and I am extremely grateful. My thanks also to the History Department secretary, Barbara Costa, who helped in innumerable ways. My gratitude also extends to Margaret Noonan and Vernon Ifill for their good-natured and usually spur-of-the-moment assistance.

Over time, several History Department graduate assistants have contributed their time to this book, and even though I have not been successful in luring Steve Spishak, Greg Ripple, and Michelle Furlong away from medieval or early modern European history, I trust the experience was beneficial in some way. I will always be indebted to Bernadette Lawler and Oscar Tobar for their computer expertise and for sharing that expertise with me.

I am very lucky to be working with the team at Northeastern University Press. Their professionalism, care, and willingness to include me in what are rightfully *their* editorial decisions has earned my unending gratitude. My thanks to John Weingartner, Ann Twombly, Jill Bahcall, Bill Frohlich, and Larry Hamberlin.

One of the fringe benefits of a New England topic is lobster. And since I am married to a legal expert who willingly accepts lobster in exchange for research assistance, the book is richer for his participation. It has also benefited from the efforts of my daughter Andrea, who as a teenager a decade ago copied lists of names from the overseers' records in Boston. She preferred cash payment to lobster.

ELAINE FORMAN CRANE
August 1997

Ebb Tide in New England

Prologue

$\mathcal{T}$his is a book about today. Set in four seventeenth- and eighteenth-century New England seaports, it attempts to explain, at least in part, the feminization of poverty in contemporary America. Although the book was not conceived with that objective in mind (but rather with the less provocative purpose of analyzing social development in colonial urban communities where women outnumbered men), it soon became obvious that the implications of the saga projected the story to another level. Isolated pieces of information, re-worked into an integrated whole, demonstrated the growing dependence of women on men and the increasingly regulated nature of their lives.

Most historians accept the Whig interpretation of American history as a paradigm applicable to both sexes. The positive, progressive timeline that such a theory postulates is hypothetically gender-neutral and suggests that women as well as men have benefited from the American experiment. In many ways this is accurate, of course, even when we account for the nuances of race and religion ignored by such a glittering generality. Nevertheless, Whig assumptions, though in other ways liberal, are antithetical to the female experience, and this is nowhere more demonstrable than during the two centuries preceding Independence in the New England towns under consideration here.

American society was and is patriarchal in nature—hardly a startling revelation, but the context in which this book should be considered. In the 1960s and 1970s feminist authors embraced this proposition and stressed the "victimization" of women who were subject to the constraints of such a society. Writers coming of age in the 1980s and 1990s moved beyond this approach to accent female agency rather than obedience, female subversion rather than submission, female activism rather than passivity.

I would suggest that the latter focus is tantamount to historical absolution: it lets patriarchy off the hook by suppressing its long-range negative effects. By emphasizing female activism and agency, patriarchy becomes less toxic to female well-being and more a benign force that was outmaneuvered by female adroitness, guile, and persistence. Such an interpretation may be less threatening to the American collective memory than one that underscores oppression, but it distorts history.

Although there can be little doubt that women were central to the development of urban America, and although women have always been activists and agents, their activities and agency have taken place, nonetheless, in a Euro-American world where males exercised the ultimate authority. If women defined their space and exerted power over their lives in the New England seaports, it was within fixed perimeters, not infinite parameters. Since men defined legitimacy and illegitimacy, female agency was by permission only; successful subversion was, of necessity, masked by legitimate behavior. Women engaged in "criminal" activities because of artificially gendered laws or inequitable application of gender-neutral laws. Recognizing the existence of both historical oppression and historical agency, this book attempts to reconcile these opposing tensions: women as subjects, women as authors. At the same time, it charges—on the basis of overwhelming evidence—that at the end of the colonial era, urban women were more dependent and less autonomous than they had been in the founding years of Boston, Salem, Newport, and Portsmouth.

In constructing such a thesis, I could not help being struck by parallels between the development of the archaic state, as analyzed by Gerda Lerner, and the evolution of American society.[1] Lerner argues persuasively that as the state became more powerful, women were increasingly excluded from public activity. She also maintains that women fared better in unstructured, informal societies where governmental institutions were not clearly defined and policy (as well as procedure) remained flexible. The evidence suggests that colonial America followed a similar evolutionary pattern. I do not mean, however, to imply that the words "urban" and "colonial" may be used interchangeably, but rather to acknowledge a process whereby colonial social patterns eventually replicated urban models. I do not even mean to suggest that the New England seaports represent all of urban America. New York, Philadelphia, and Charleston had very different demographic, economic, and religious profiles. Nevertheless, long-distance trade, luxury consumerism, proto-industrialism, legislative authority, and the importation and exchange of ideas all originated in urban settings, and because these factors influenced relationships between men and women, early American towns took on an importance that transcends their numbers.

Moreover, one of the most pronounced distinctions between urban and rural areas in New England was also determined by numbers: the ratio of women to men. My curiosity about communities where women greatly outnumbered men stimulated this book to begin with; my assumption that the tale would be best told by exploring those towns with the most conspicuously imbalanced sex ratios led me to Boston, Salem, Newport, and Portsmouth. In addition, my misguided optimism encouraged me to suppose that female empowerment bore some relationship to numerical superiority, and I originally envisioned a story with a more positive, or at least egalitarian, ending. The sources undermined such convictions, however, and demonstrated both the dedication with which patriarchal forces rallied to the challenges posed by a low sex ratio as well as the ways in which female dependence was exacerbated rather than diminished in the New England seaports.

Quite apart from their distinctive sex ratios, seaports encouraged publicly gendered space to a greater degree than rural communities. By the eighteenth century, stately edifices housed all-male executive offices, legislatures, and courts. Coffeehouses and countinghouses took on a masculine image, while shops and churches emphasized a female presence. The vast number of income-producing opportunities (and the space they occupied) were increasingly limited to one sex or the other.

Because of these interpretive twists, it is also fair to say that this book has been influenced (albeit after the fact) by Judith Bennett, a medievalist whose analysis of patriarchal principles provides a conceptual framework for the evidence I have introduced. In a paper presented at the Tenth Berkshire Conference on the History of Women in June 1996, Bennett explained how a patriarchal society enforces its precepts.[2] She theorized that the exclusion and silencing of women perpetuated control, as did the manipulation of ideology and the development of interacting and reinforcing institutions. Like Molière's *bourgeois gentilhomme*, who was pleased to learn that he had been speaking in prose, I was gratified to have Bennett pinpoint the aspects of patriarchal power that were common to each of the substantive chapters on religion, the economy, and law in this book. Her analysis helped me tie the threads together.

Whereas the introduction provides the demographic context for the following narrative, the first chapter places the story in its chronological context by synthesizing the European experience, and later the Euro-American experience as well, from medieval times through the early modern period. By exploring familial, religious, economic, legal, and intellectual issues in a transatlantic setting, the history of American urban women becomes part of a recognizable continuum rather than an example of an American exceptionalism that was only distantly related to European antecedents.

To parallel and build on the opening chapter, four substantive chapters follow, separately dedicated to gendered messages in the evolution of American religion (chapter 2), economy (chapter 3), and law (chapters 4 and 5). Each chapter shows that, consistent with the European heritage outlined in chapter 1, the earliest Euro-American women had considerable latitude in terms of the work and rewards associated with colony building; each demonstrates an increasing female invisibility and constriction of opportunity over time as church and state building silenced and marginalized women. The final chapter, like the first, refutes American exceptionalism. It returns to the European intellectual legacy, shows its definitive impact on American society, and explains how European precedents and American institutional development combined to thwart any sustained efforts toward female independence in the Revolutionary era.

— ≠ —

Puritanism was egalitarian to the extent that God's plan for salvation favored neither men nor women. In the unsettled founding decades, outspoken women actively participated on committees, judged their fellow church members, joined or withdrew from churches as their consciences dictated, and contributed to the decision-making process. God-fearing women greatly outnumbered men as the colonial era advanced, and their numerical ascendancy paralleled a dwindling role in the formulation of church policy. Even Baptist and Quaker women enjoyed fewer privileges by the turn of the nineteenth century.

Multiple opportunities, a tradition of economic activity, and the expectation of female productivity initially combined to encourage female economic enterprise. And despite the marginalization of women by historians as well as by their colonial contemporaries, urban women actively engaged in a wide variety of mercantile pursuits. Nevertheless, as the urban New England economy became inseparably intertwined with long-distance trade, as a consumer-conscious middle class emerged, as a cash economy replaced the traditional barter system with which it had once coexisted, women's visibility in the mercantile records declined.

Not surprisingly, the New England colonists built a legal structure that coincided with and reinforced their belief system. But before they did so, women (as well as men) took advantage of a legal lapse to maximize their well-being and provide for their futures. Married women commonly bought property; widows alienated entire estates; oral agreements substituted for written deeds. Codification of the law curtailed such transactions, and as the legal system took on the characteristics of its English parent, women were increasingly constrained by its dictates. In some ways Puritan criminal law was harsher than its English counterpart—adultery, for instance, was a capital offense in Massachusetts. The number of people hanged for adultery during the colonial era remained in the single-digit category, however, and although court records verify the vigor with which colonists attempted to eradicate fornication, it was civil law that had the most far-reaching effect on female lives. The establishment and enforcement of civil codes and local regulations restrained female activity through rules from which men were exempt.

Although many aspects of American law were strikingly similar to English law, this is not to say that American urban women were clones of their European counterparts. Factors limited to the American experience influenced the course of events and ensured that there would be variations on the patriarchal theme. The absence of Catholicism as a doctrine in New England, the prevalence of vast tracts of land co-opted for Euro-American use, the subjection of the colonies to imperial law, and the presence of non-European ethnic groups had an impact on the process of gender building.

Yet if an English heritage and New England variables spawned a society that clearly reflected its mixed parentage in terms of religion, the economy, and law, New England's intellectual genes were overwhelmingly European. Attitudes toward marriage and the family, female domesticity and education, friendship between women and men—none of these show any signs of American conditioning or of the more egalitarian impulses that would affect men during the American Enlightenment. In the short run, at least, republican motherhood did not challenge the precepts of monarchical motherhood.

Even in the long run, few countervailing forces were able to modify patriarchal aspirations. By excluding women from control of property, by silencing them economically, politically, and religiously, by manipulating ideology and socializing succeeding generations to perpetuate that ideology, by establishing interlocking institutions of state to reinforce and supervise the structure they created, early American patriarchs prevented early American matriarchs from becoming independent or autonomous.

But the quid for the quo was expensive. Patriarchal efforts to instill female dependence culminated in a financially unstable group of women, particularly in the seaports, where an unbalanced sex ratio created a disproportionate number of never-married, widowed, or semimarried women (whose husbands were away at sea). The number of female names on the poor lists validates the effectiveness of patriarchal policies, but then, as now, the cost of success rankles. Eighteenth-century welfare payments took a disproportionate sum from urban budgets, and women were disproportionately represented among the recipients. Given past priorities, however, it is ironic that after four hundred years of advocating female dependence, the government is now invoking female independence in the name of welfare reform.

Yet female economic instability was only the most glaring end product of patriarchal achievement. The internalization of an ideology that cast doubt on female self-worth, denigrated female autonomy, demeaned female advanced learning, and denied female control of personal assets crossed both class and ethnic lines in the American colonies. This book argues that all women were central to the process of city building, but were persistently and effectively marginalized in subtle and not-so-subtle ways as that process intensified. The resounding success with which challenges to male authority were rebuffed suggests that American women were not positioned to take advantage of the egalitarian forces unleashed by revolutionary rhetoric. It would take another half century before a feminist consciousness solidified in the United States, and more than a century beyond that before some of the most basic issues of a patriarchal society would even be addressed, much less resolved.

~ INTRODUCTION ~

The Demography of Four Towns

*A*lthough the New England seaports shared many features, in some ways each town developed a distinctive flavor that travelers quickly noticed and denizens even more quickly affirmed or denied, depending on the nature of the description. Thus, although urban dwellers were in general "more civilized" than country folk, Alexander Hamilton, a Scottish-born physician, found that Bostonians excelled in urbanity.[1]

Largest of the ports, Boston appeared even more populous than it was. Hamilton compared it in size to Glasgow, which contained between twenty thousand and thirty thousand people, although, in fact, Boston could claim only about sixteen thousand inhabitants in 1744. It was "a considerable place for shipping," with merchants' warehouses lining the water's edge at the northern end of town. Adjacent to the Statehouse were walks for the merchants where they met each day at one o'clock—presumably in imitation of the London exchange.[2]

To protect its interests, Boston was better fortified "than any port in North America." Religious diversity marked the town, but religion was more "speculative" than "practical." The inhabitants were just as diverse, but they shared certain characteristics and opinions. To "cheat" and "cozen" a neighbor was perfectly acceptable; to avoid church service was not. Bostonians were hospitable but "disingenuous and dissembling." The town's cultural opportunities and elite society caught Dr. Hamilton's attention as well. Quiet streets belied nightly activity as gentlemen and ladies met for music and balls. They attended dinners wearing full dress and powdered wigs, a concession to a rising class consciousness in this old Puritan town. Book auctions took place on a regular basis, with customers bidding against each other for *Pamela, The Fortunate Maid*, and Ovid's *Art of Love*. The town abounded "with pretty women who were also free and affable." Indeed, Hamilton noted that

9

among them was "not one prude." Shallow conversation at teatime was limited to "the meaner sort," while among "politer caballs of ladys" such gossip had become unfashionable.[3]

If Boston was the epitome of culture, Newport, Rhode Island, was "the most delightful spot of ground . . . in America," according to Hamilton, who compared it to "one intire garden." Here too the inhabitants carried on "a good trade," and in addition built "a great many vessels." They made "good cheese." Newporters were known for their privateering activities as well as for "chicane and disingenuity." They had "little regard" for English law, and duties went uncollected because customs officials feared "the fury and unruliness of the people"—even as they opened their palms for "presents." Despite their proclivity for lawlessness, Newporters were "civil" and "courteous," in their way. Hamilton noted that townspeople were not as observant of Sundays as in other parts of New England, nor were they "so strait laced in religion." Here, too, women drank afternoon tea.[4] Curiously enough, Hamilton made no mention of one of Newport's most distinguishing features: its slave trade and the by-product of that trade, a large African American population.

Portsmouth, New Hampshire, Dr. Hamilton recorded, had between four thousand and five thousand inhabitants and was a seaport town "very pleasantly situated close upon the water." Another midcentury traveler noted that Portsmouth contained "4 Principal streets," which met at a crossroads and "from which one can see the country on every side."[5] Clearly, Portsmouth did not compare to the metropolis of Boston. Hamilton quickly perceived that Portsmouth's trade in fish was outshadowed by the tall pine masts carried to England for use by the British navy. No balls, book auctions, or chicanery here—merely a smallish seaport whose claim to fame rested on the one item indispensable to Britain's seafaring ambitions.

In its early days, Salem, Massachusetts, was a rough-and-tumble town, far less genteel than Boston, a community that had few rivals in terms of drinking and violence. By the mid-eighteenth century, however, such behavior was much less perceptible, if Dr. Hamilton is a credible reporter—and its confrontation with witchcraft a thing of distant memory. In 1744 Salem was "a pritty town," with a good harbor for small vessels. Wharves and warehouses dotted the shore. Its houses were well built, and in addition to trade, Salemites engaged in the cod fishery. Although a small upper class strove for gentility, the town was not known for its cultural amenities.[6]

— ⚡ —

In the beginning, there were more men than women in these port towns. For every three men sailing to New England in the first decades of colonization, two women made the crossing. In Virginia the ratio of male to female immigrants was anywhere from three to one to six to one. Over the following decades Mother Nature showed no partiality toward native-born males, and thus the population became more balanced, although in the Chesapeake and Carolinas men continued to outnumber women throughout the colonial era. In Pennsylvania, where there was a great influx of Scotch-Irish immigrants in the mid-eighteenth century, the sex ratio was also high.[7]

On the northeastern seaboard, however, social and economic developments fostered a strikingly different demographic profile, the result of which was a low sex ratio—more women than men. In the seaports, over the course of time, people became dependent on the ocean for their livelihood, and most of the inhabitants earned their living through commerce-related trades. The jack tars of the community spent considerable time at sea, while merchants and shopkeepers distanced themselves from the water by selling dry goods. Other townspeople distilled rum, wove ropes, built barrels, or loaded ships. More men than women were engaged in these mercantile activities, but many women earned their livelihoods in a number of other seafaring enterprises such as sailmaking, candlemaking, or baking.

Although the eighteenth-century world was fraught with hazards, it was clearly safer to plow the land than the sea. Those men employed as sailors were more at risk than those whose livelihoods kept them ashore, and depending on the nature of the voyage, weeks could stretch into months for the six, perhaps seven, mariners who faced nature's whimsy aboard an average-sized coasting ship. Each time the ocean claimed such a vessel, its wrath simultaneously created a pool of widows. In the spring of 1768, twenty-four ships from Marblehead sank with 170 men and boys on board, leaving the town with 70 more widows and as many as 150 "fatherless children."[8]

Yet those on shore might remain unaware of the fate of vessels on which loved ones sailed. Indeed, if a ship disappeared, a woman could hover between marriage and widowhood for months or even years. When John Draper of Newport died he left not only a widow but four daughters, all of whom, like their mother, had married mariners. Of the four, only Elizabeth could still claim a husband: Rachel was a widow, and Mary and Sarah were wed to men who had been missing "for some years past and unheard of," and who were "supposed to be lost at sea."[9]

War casualties, resulting from Indian hostilities or European squabbles into which Americans were drawn, also helped to create demographic imbalances in several seaport towns, as did the infectious and epidemic diseases that claimed a disproportionate number of male colonists. Massachusetts lost about six hundred men fighting against King Philip in 1676, and many more fighting for Queen Anne between 1702 and 1713. Boston's male population plummeted after the Cartegena campaign in 1740–1741, and yet again as a result of the expedition to Louisbourg in 1745, when "thousands of young men were lost by sickness." According to Governor Francis Bernard in 1763, the latter toll "affected the encrease of the people" for nearly two decades.[10] In Newport, the Reverend Ezra Stiles noted that "from January 1, 1760 to January 1, 1761 . . . there died 210 Persons, of which 24 died at sea." If this proportion of deaths on the high seas remained constant, it could easily explain the difference in numbers between men and women. At the same time, Stiles recorded the appalling number of Rhode Islanders who died in the French and Indian War.[11]

Whatever the combination of reasons, by the Revolution white women drastically outnumbered white men in Boston, Salem, Newport, Portsmouth, and other smaller towns on the New England coast. The imbalance occurred at different times in the various communities, with the most striking disparities noticeable, not surprisingly, in the aftermath of war.[12]

Circumstantial evidence indicates that Boston's population not only had evened out over the course of the seventeenth century but also had shifted in favor of women by the early years of the eighteenth. Before the turn of the century, Boston was said to be "full of widows and orphans." In 1692 Cotton Mather alluded to "vast numbers of poor widows in every Neighbourhood."[13] Unfortunately, most of the figures that represent Boston's population for the first half of the eighteenth century are imprecise, since no reliable census exists before 1742. Historians have calculated the approximate number of inhabitants by multiplying the number of polls by 4 or 5½, the number of families by 5 or 6, the number of militia by 5⅓ or 6, or the number of houses by an equally speculative number. This means we really do not know exactly when Boston's population peaked or what that figure was, nor can we be sure at what date women started to outnumber men.

A facetious letter to the editor of the *Boston Gazette* on 12 August 1734, accompanied by a "bill" for a lottery to dispose of "distress'd Virgins" in

Great Britain, suggests that Boston shared Britain's surplus of women. The author of the letter pointed out that "such a scheme [the lottery] would be of no less advantage in this part of the world, since the circumstances of our young women in point of marriage . . . do unhappily resemble those of Great Britain." Indeed, this "declining condition" was said to be most visible in the "metropolis"—presumably Boston.[14] According to the writer, Britain's solution to its own demographic disaster would be equally applicable to Massachusetts Bay and would bring "Great Numbers of our single men and Batchelors . . . to Matrimony." The implication is that marriage was retarded not only by a dearth of men but also by the reluctance of the relatively few eligible males to take on the obligations of matrimony. Satire aside, the demographic reality would not surprise contemporary historians and sociologists, who have come to expect such a response to a low sex ratio.

The count of Bostonians made in 1742 showed a population of 16,382. Although this figure was not broken down by sex, it is likely that the imbalance between women and men had made its appearance long before that date. The Boston Selectmen, who kept records of such things, reported at the time that "there is about 1200 widows included in the above number of Souls," which suggests that the tables had already turned by that year to the point where people were taking notice.[15] In 1752 another census of the town projected 15,731 people—down from the previous decade—with a corresponding loss in the number of male polls.[16]

Speculation yields to certainty with the Massachusetts census of 1764/5. By the time the census takers completed their chores, the sex ratio for adult whites was .81, or 122 women for every 100 men. The next complete census of Massachusetts was taken in 1790, at which time Boston's population had increased to over 18,000, but the sex ratio showed no signs of repairing its balance. Indeed, the ratio based on the entire population had dropped to .80 (from .93 in 1765), which means that the adult sex ratio was precipitously skewed—perhaps somewhere around .70.[17]

Fourteen miles to the northeast, in Essex County, Salem's sex ratio showed the same characteristics as that of Boston. As a result of war and disease, Salem's ratio for the entire white population dropped from .95 in 1754 to .83 in 1764. The figure for white adults was .79. In actual numbers, there were 1,335 adult females, but only 1,050 adult males. The American Revolution had an even more devastating effect on Salem than the Seven Years War in terms of male survivors. Among the hardest hit were those in the sixteen- to thirty-year bracket. In 1785 there were 148 young women in that age group for every 100 men. It is difficult to gauge the impact of the war on those aged between fifty and seventy, but for whatever reasons, there were exactly twice as many women as men in that group in 1785. In 1790 the sex ratio for the entire white population was .87, and among adults that figure drops to .77, or 129 women for every 100 men.[18]

Newport's imbalance appears to have been caused by its participation in the Seven Years War. So heavy were the casualties that the adult ratio dropped from 1.04 in 1755 to .80 in 1774. Unfortunately, the worst was yet to come. By 1782, after having been shelled by one combatant and occupied by both, Newport's adult sex ratio stood at .57. In 1790, the whole white population was .79, and since the number of males had grown disproportionately to females, the adult sex ratio would probably have become less distorted in the intervening years.[19]

In 1767 Portsmouth was approximately the same size as Salem, but population figures from that year indicate a total white sex ratio of .91, which was more balanced than Salem's. Although only the male population was broken down by age, if we assume that the childhood sex ratio was nearly even, then calculations indicate that the adult imbalance was more perceptible: .85, or 117 women to every 100 men. Using the same yardstick, by 1773 there were 129 women to every 100 men, and in 1775, 127. The sex ratio for the entire population for those two years was .86 and .88.[20] There is no census for Portsmouth in the years immediately following the Revolution, but in 1790, when the sex ratio for the total population was .86, it is likely that the adult figure hovered around .76, which would mean that for every 100 men there were 130 women.[21]

It is difficult to know what numerical considerations were given to New England mariners off on voyages. On Bermuda, an island colony where seafaring was also the basis of the economy, the census takers were careful to note whether their calculations included men at sea. There, at any given time, between one-fifth and one-third of the adult males were absent from home, a factor that exaggerated already existing perceptions of demographic disaster.[22] In New England, an estimate of 20 to 30 percent may be too high, considering other employment options and relative lack of competition from the black population for whatever jobs were available. Nevertheless, no matter how many men may have been at sea, their absence on a daily basis further widened the already striking numerical gap between men and women.

The New Hampshire census lists for 1767 and 1773 appear to be the only ones that separate women and men into married and unmarried categories, and it is not surprising to find that Portsmouth had the lowest percentage of married women in the colony. Thirty percent of the females in that town entered the bonds of matrimony, while in the rest of the colony anywhere from 31.7 to 38.8 percent of the women were so situated. There were also nearly twice as many widows in Portsmouth than elsewhere in the colony.[23] In 1767 and in 1773 approximately 10 percent of all females had once been married and were now widowed. Between 14 and 15 percent of the unmarried females were widows in those years, and if we eliminate nine hundred girls under sixteen from the total number of unmarried females (assuming them to be approximate in number to boys under sixteen), it appears that one-third of the adult unmarried women were widows in both years.

It would be instructive to compare Portsmouth with other towns, but only Salem vaguely lends itself to such comparisons. There the figures indicate that in 1754, 12 percent (205) of all females were widowed, and that in 1785, after the Revolution, although the proportion of widows had dropped to 11.5 percent, their numbers had risen to 419.[24]

With little more to go on than the scanty references to widows in Boston noted earlier (a count of widows in Boston in 1742: 1,200, of a total population of 16,382), all we can conclude is that widows represented a greater proportion of the total population there (7.3 percent) than in Portsmouth (5–5.3 percent) or Salem (6 percent). If the population were balanced, 1,200 widows would have represented 30 percent of Boston's adult female population. Since the population was probably severely skewed by this time, it is more likely that one-quarter of Boston's adult women were widowed, which must have severely affected the economic viability of the town. Although some widows died and many marriages took place during the remainder of the 1740s, so many male Bostonians were struck down during the Louisbourg expedition in 1745 that the *Boston Gazette* could still report 1,153 widows in 1751.[25]

Twelve hundred widows in Boston in 1742 and who knows how many other single women; 235 widows in Portsmouth and perhaps another 450 of marriageable age; and 205 bereaved women in Salem in 1754, more than double that number thirty years later. The other seaports probably claimed the same proportion of unmarried women. The likelihood of a first marriage in any of these communities was possible but not necessarily probable; the chance of remarriage was slim.[26] As Robert Wells demonstrates, single men in Portsmouth did not rush to the altar despite the surplus of marriageable women. Anywhere from 37 to 40 percent of the men between the ages of sixteen and sixty in that town chose to remain legally unattached—which confirms anecdotal evidence from Boston and supports the contention of some sociologists that men are less likely to marry in a society where women predominate because sexual activity is as readily available outside marriage as within.[27]

Where census data include the names of household heads, it is possible to determine the proportion of female-headed households. It is important to distinguish "households" from "families" because any given household was likely to include people who were not members of the nuclear family. Even though in eighteenth-century terms an indentured servant or slave might be labeled a family member, this tends to confuse the demographic profile of a community by mixing related and unrelated people.

The percentage of female-headed households appears to correspond with the proportion of single women in the population as a whole. Thus, in Boston in 1695, 6.8 percent of the households were headed by women (almost all of whom were widows), but a century later, female-headed households had soared to 20 percent of the total.[28] In Newport, another community that allows us to trace this phenomenon over time, female-headed households in 1774, 1782, and 1790 constituted 20, 24, and 21 percent of the total number of households. Of the 242 female heads of households in 1782, 168 were widows. These percentages are roughly equivalent to the rate of female householding in preindustrial European communities.[29]

In societies where the sex ratio was balanced or nearly balanced, women were less likely to find themselves heads of households. In Yarmouth, Massachusetts, also on the coast, only 8 percent of the households in 1790 were headed by women, while in Brookfield, Worcester County, that figure was 6 percent. In the New Hampshire communities of Rochester and Concord only 3 percent and 1 percent of the households were represented by females, whereas 14.5 percent of Portsmouth households were headed by women in 1790. Providence, Rhode Island, is a puzzling exception to the rule. There were slightly more men than women in that town in 1790, yet women headed 13 percent of the households. It is likely, therefore, that although there were equal numbers of men and women in that town, there was also a large pool of unattached women. Rhode Island being the sort of place it was, however, it is not impossible that the census takers in Providence "overcounted" the number of men in order to enhance their position in the Rhode Island General Assembly.

Households headed by women were generally smaller than those headed by men. In many cases this was because a woman became head of family only in the absence of an adult male, whereas in male-headed households, additional adult women and men were likely to be residing there as well. In addition, female-headed households had fewer children, although nearly 54 percent of the approximately 325 female-headed households in Newport contained children under sixteen. What is striking about the Newport census figures, however, is that in only two of the white households was a single adult woman raising a male child under sixteen. Twenty-one households contained only female children under sixteen (thirty-four girls altogether) and twenty-two households included boys and girls (thirty-six boys, twenty-six girls), but single women raising male children without sisters are conspicuously absent from the census. Indeed, the vast majority of female-headed households with children also contained additional males or females over sixteen (129 and 175, respectively), although it is difficult to say whether they were older brothers and sisters, indentured servants, or unrelated adults.[30]

Where census records identify heads of households by sex, an interesting pattern emerges. Women appear to cluster together on many streets, more than as if by chance. Three, four, sometimes five households in a row claimed female heads. In Newport this was most visible in poor neighborhoods and most striking among black female heads of households. This pattern was still evident in the 1790 census.[31]

Such a residential pattern was not limited to Newport or the eighteenth century. The Boston tax assessment of 1687 (which is neither in alphabetical order nor by amounts owed) shows women's name clustered on a number of pages, while they are only randomly separated on others. On some pages not a single female name appears, yet others have many. If this tax list was drawn up by residential district (as it was in Newport), it is clear that women were more heavily represented in certain neighborhoods than others.[32]

Boston's tax valuation list of 1771 confirms this pattern. Unalphabetized, this tabulation of potential taxpayers shows that women were far more strongly represented in certain areas of Boston than others. Furthermore, of the approximately 188 women counted on the list, 142 were rated as heads of households, of whom 99 lived alone and 43 claimed lodgers. Forty-six women lived as tenants in other households, 44 of which were headed by men. Of those on the valuation list, women were slightly less likely than men to be given tenant status (24 percent versus 28 percent), and male tenants were slightly more likely than female tenants to have a female landlord (10 versus 4 percent).[33]

The 1790 census lists for Boston and Salem also show more women living next door to each other than one would expect in any random sample where they represented a small proportion of the heads of households. The Portsmouth enumeration of 1790 is the most interesting in this regard, however.[34] Unlike Boston, Salem, or Newport, most of the names (83 percent) are in alphabetical order. Few women in this group are listed as heads of households (6 percent). But the last 154 names are unalphabetized, and of this number, 87 (56 percent) are female. Many of these names are clustered. Free blacks were also located in this section of the census, and their names are similarly listed together. In Newport the unalphabetized list of 1774 was a street census—a house-to-house count in different sections of town. Was this also true of Portsmouth as far as the last 154 names were concerned? Were female heads of households more likely to be found in a certain area of town?

As we learn more about female networking, we may find that single women deliberately chose to live near each other for a variety of reasons. Midwives and relatives attending predawn deliveries might have preferred company en route; women who frequently attended late-evening quilting parties may have been similarly motivated. If Sarah Osborn's friends were indeed available to help her "in any wise," it is likely they lived close by.[35]

A skewed sex ratio meant fewer marriages, fewer children, and a gradually aging population. The one exception to this—on paper, at least—is Boston, where the 1764 census shows the highest proportion of children under the age of sixteen in the Bay Colony. As Robert Wells suggests, this does not necessarily mean that these children were the products of legitimate unions, but rather that the high child/woman ratio resulted from a large number of young indentured servants or from illegitimate births.[36] Combined with female economic instability, it meant a large pool of children who would grow up in poor households.

The white childhood sex ratio presents a somewhat different picture from that of the adult. In Newport in 1755 and in Boston in 1764, there were slightly more boys than girls under sixteen. We cannot determine what happened to Boston's childhood sex ratio in the following years, but Newport's dropped to .95 in 1774 and .93 in 1782. Salem, however, increased from .90 in 1764 to a surprising 1.01 twenty years later. In Portsmouth, only males were categorized by age, making it impossible to calculate the childhood sex ratio.

The most salient point to be made concerning census figures for the non-white population is that males in pre-Revolutionary Boston, Salem, Portsmouth, and Newport outnumbered females by considerable margins. Not every census separated the African American and Indian populations by sex, but where they did, the pre-Revolutionary sex ratio was uniformly high. An enumeration of slaves in Boston in 1754 showed 647 males and 342 females, for a ratio of 1.9. In that same year, Salem counted 47 males and 36 females (1.30). Of the 811 "Negros and Molattos" in Boston in 1765 (total population 15,520), 510 were male (sex ratio = 1.69). In Salem in the same year, the total population was 4,254, and of that number more than twice as many blacks were male: 117 men and 56 women.[37] In 1767 in Portsmouth, 124 black males outnumbered 63 black females (1.97), and six years later there were 100 black males but only 60 black females (1.67).[38]

Newport's census follows a similar pattern and has the additional advantage of being broken down by age as well as sex. Of the African American population in 1755, the figures show 400 adult males, 341 adult females, 248 boys, and 245 girls, reflecting a high sex ratio among adults but not among children. The 1774 census indicates that the number of black adults had risen to 454 males and 403 females, but the youth population had dropped to 204 males and 185 females under sixteen.

The number of African Americans in Newport declined considerably by the end of the war owing to emancipation legislation and war losses, and in 1782 the census takers reported only 159 males and 188 females above sixteen—numbers that also show a striking reversal of the sex ratio. This turnabout was also evident among African Americans under sixteen in 1782: 96 males and 112 females.[39] The Newport census distinguished between blacks and "mulattoes" in 1782, and both adults and children in this category show more females than males as well. There were 11 males and 16 females under sixteen; 6 males and 18 females above sixteen.

Figures for American Indians are spotty: 21 male and 16 female Indians in Boston in 1765, and none reported in Salem in that year. Portsmouth does not appear to have counted its Indian population, but in Newport's 1774 census the small number of Indians is broken down both by sex and by age. Of 35 Indians over sixteen, 31 were female; there were 8 males and 3 females under sixteen. Even these numbers saw a drastic reduction by 1782, with the census taker reporting only 11 adult Indians (5 male, 6 female), and 6 children under sixteen (4 male, 2 female).[40]

The Newport manuscript census for 1774 shows eighteen households headed by black women. It is not at all certain that these were free blacks, however, since nearly one-third of them carried the last names of some of

Newport's affluent slaveholders: Richardson, Wanton, Tillinghast, Honyman, and Townsend. Other surnames were unusual for Newport—Beard, Jack, Sutton, Secater, Goree—and it is tempting to conclude that they were probably free. Households of the former group were interspersed among the merchants and tradespeople in the center of town, while the latter families were more likely to be found on the fringes of the city.

Half of the households headed by African American females in Newport in 1774 had three members and were thus quite smaller than average. One had five members, another four, and the rest one or two. Indians were almost always integrated individually within white households.[41]

Nearly 30 percent of Newport's families owned slaves in 1774; Indians were scattered among other families. Given this demographic layout, it is likely that there was less need for white female servants (either indentured or wage-earning) than there would have been if fewer families owned blacks or Indians. As a result, this employment opportunity was less available to white women than it would have been in rural areas or other communities with a smaller number of African Americans.

— ≉ —

Between the early seventeenth century and the end of the eighteenth century, the New England seaports underwent dramatic demographic change. Boston, Salem, Newport, and Portsmouth all originated with male majorities, only to see that plurality dissipate in favor of females as war, disease, and shipwrecks took their tolls. The feminization of these New England seaports was accompanied by and perhaps even responsible for other changes over time. As subsequent chapters show, the churches in each of these towns eventually claimed a disproportionately female membership, and each community endured an increasing number of female poor. How this profile affected the ongoing process of community building is explored in chapters 2, 3, 4, and 5, but before turning to the New England seaports themselves, it is appropriate to trace those aspects of European social development that would influence the direction of women's lives in the New England towns. The impact of European religious, economic, legal, and intellectual forces cannot be overestimated, and the unfolding story in chapter 1 is merely a preamble to the succeeding chapters, where the New England religious, economic, legal, and intellectual experience confirms that history does indeed have a way of repeating itself.

~ CHAPTER 1 ~

The European Connection

Margret Weston's Story

*M*argret Weston and her husband, Francis, were among the Salem settlers who arrived with Winthrop's fleet. They were West Country émigrés, as were many of those who first set sail for Massachusetts Bay. By 1633 a growing number of former East Anglians had also made Salem their home, and the rivalry between the factions—thought to have been lost at sea—surfaced again on this side of the Atlantic. Church doctrine divided the groups, as did differences arising from the "disorderly" departure of some brothers and sisters from their church in Rotterdam. As a result of these controversies, the Westons were unable to shake off their European past.[1]

Initially, Francis and Margret Weston were comfortably settled in Salem. Francis was made a freeman in 1633 and subsequently elected deputy from Salem in 1634. The couple received a sizable land grant in 1636.[2] Yet both had misgivings about church policy in Salem, and the factionalism that arose appears to have stemmed from long-simmering European doctrinal differences, which Francis insisted on airing in 1637. And although magistrates, elders, and pastor directed their ire at Francis for creating a "damnable" schism, Margret was drawn into the fray by events taking place outside the church walls—events for which she was held accountable by the same church authorities who confronted Francis. Though initially unrelated, the simultaneous attacks on Francis and Margret suggest that church and state in Salem were nearly as intertwined as they had been in Europe, protestations to the contrary notwithstanding.

While Francis Weston was defending his disparaging comments about church policy, William Pester sued Francis and Margret Weston for defamation. That the suit was really directed at Margret is indicated by her solitary challenge of three prospective jurors: Jeffrey Massey, Edmund Batter, and Anthony Dike, *all of whom were substantial citizens and two of whom (Massey and Batter) were members of the First Church of Salem.*[3]

Because these prospective jurors as well as "others also" were "offended" at Margret's effrontery, and because they were prominent church members who were antagonistic to the Westons anyway, "the case of . . . Sister Weston was brought before the church."[4] *Why had she challenged the jurors? the elders asked Margret. "She did think it her liberty," the scribe recorded in the church minutes. Admitting such a right, Weston's interrogators insisted that she must have "just cause" nonetheless. One of the prospective jurors "was all one with the party against her," she maintained, hinting at a cabal that transcended this particular squabble. Margret implied that these men were open to bribery, or "temptation," as she put it. "Gifts blind the eyes of the wise," she reminded the church tribunal, suggesting that considerations other than the facts of the immediate slander case might determine its outcome.*

The church authorities seem to have been unsure of what action to take. They were unwilling to exonerate Margret but equally unwilling to deprive her of long-standing English procedural rights. Thus, when the authorities found only that she had waited too long before confronting the jurors and could determine only suspicions of wrongdoing rather than actual cause, Margret Weston "was referred to the next church meeting."

If the church eventually dealt harshly with the Westons, the records fail to say so. Nevertheless, in the general weeding out of malefactors following the Hutchinson upheaval, the couple was sent packing. In addition to their controversial behavior, the Westons had been supporters of Roger Williams. It was appropriate, therefore, that they went to Rhode Island, where they were counted among Williams's "loving friends and neighbors," all of whom were a step further removed from the European controversies that had dominated their lives far longer than they anticipated.[5]

— ✻ —

In some ways, the current historical debate over the status of medieval and early modern European women echoes the *querelle des femmes,* that ongoing Renaissance and Enlightenment dialogue about the nature, worth, and role of women. Contemporary discourse accepts the judgment of the early modern era that in fact women have souls, are rational, and should be educated, but modern historians are less unanimous about related issues: the implications of Reformation theology, the manipulation of female rationality, and the content of female education. Furthermore, there is considerable and ongoing disagreement about whether women were more advantaged or disadvantaged by the economic trends of the fifteenth to eighteenth centuries, and whether the effects of the Enlightenment were negative or positive. The status of women within the family as well as their autonomy outside of it has also stimulated controversy.

Some historians, moreover, question the framework of the debate: Should lives be described as becoming better or worse? Does an examination of gender roles require value judgments at all? Those who are inclined to answer these questions in the affirmative are then led deeper into the maze: What conditions must exist, what standards should be applied, in order to justify one conclusion or another? To compound the problem, historians have ceased to think of history as a linear phenomenon, but rather as one that more approximates a stock market chart, with peaks and valleys to be explored as separate entities.

Yet even a recognition of historical fluctuations does not preclude the propriety of a general assessment of change over time. Not only is it appropriate to ask whether long-range trends are marked more by continuum or transition, but if one argues for the primacy of transition, it is equally proper to inquire whether historical patterns suggest an enhancement or diminution of women's status over the four-hundred-year cycle from 1400 to 1800.[6] Indeed, it is difficult *not* to ask whether short-term swings (taken collectively) show a slow appreciation or decline in the status of white women—status as defined by the degree of autonomy, independence, personal decision making, and influence over others that these women could exercise. None of these personal attributes are absolute, of course, and all are imbued with different meanings in different eras. Nevertheless, even if hierarchy, deference, and dependence reflect the worldview of seventeenth-century men and women alike, it is also true that within those constraints men were more independent and autonomous than women.

Historians of American colonial women have explored topics parallel to those of their European colleagues, and they share similar misgivings about the various analytical approaches to these issues. At the same time, American historians have only rarely considered their evidence from a transatlantic perspective, which, if examined in such a context, would affirm the continuity of trends that determined the quality of life for women on both continents. Early American women and men were shaped—and would continue to be shaped—by a western European collective memory even as the North American continent wielded its influence on their lives. The European background at least as far back as the Middle Ages must be understood as a legacy that had a profound and ongoing effect on the development of gender relations on this side of the Atlantic. Past was indeed prologue. And if one accepts the proposition that the experience of white women in the American colonies was a continuation of events set in motion centuries earlier in Europe, it becomes easier to understand the story as it unfolds during the two centuries following the settlement of Salem and Boston.

This chapter is an overview of some of the most recent and important writings about European women during the Middle Ages, Renaissance, and early modern era. Collectively, they argue powerfully and persuasively that over time women lost ground in the arenas that most influenced their lives: family, religion, the economy, law, and education. This is not to argue that the starting line was imbedded in a golden age, but rather to emphasize the persistence of trends over time. Early medieval women may have enjoyed little power and even less authority, but the position of women in 1800 was in many ways more, not less, circumscribed than it had been hundreds of years earlier.

For many reasons, Euro-American women who settled in New England at the beginning of the seventeenth century started off on a more level playing field than the one they left behind. Their experience and intellectual heritage notwithstanding, the new American environment offered opportunities that had ceased to exist for women on the European continent. Thus the evolution of gender roles in an urban New England setting was simultaneously affected by a European past and presence, a geographical area previously unsettled by Europeans, a more diverse ethnicity, and (most decisive in the long run) the evolution of stable, structured, and formal American institutions.

WOMEN AND THE FAMILY

The basic social unit in Europe and in what would become the New England colonies was the family, and women and the family were bound together in a symbiotic relationship that was regulated by nature, economic conditions, church doctrine, and law. The relationship of the family unit to other social institutions changed over time, and historians appear to agree that the status of the wife and mother shifted according to the importance of the family within the community. Her role was inextricably linked to the role of the

family, and her autonomy and power (limited in the best of times) was pro-
portionate to the autonomy and power of the family as a socioeconomic
group.

Historians of Europe have noted that in the ninth and tenth centuries
the family enjoyed great prestige and authority, a phenomenon that coincided with the rise and fall of Charlemagne's empire and the accretion of
power by aristocratic families during that time. A fusion of the public and
private spheres in the early Middle Ages reinforced familial authority, and as
it did so, it enhanced the authority of women. During this feudal period,
aristocratic women had considerable power in and out of the household, as
the noble family acted as a unit to determine the administrative, legal, and
military functions of landed property. Daughters and wives exercised control
over real property, since it remained in their hands (rather than in the hands
of prospective or existing husbands) unless the women willed otherwise. Increasingly, women appeared as chatelaines, in charge of landed property and
castles with judicial and military rights that had been confirmed by the Car-
olingians. Legislation eliminated unilateral divorce by husbands, ensuring
that women had less to fear from unexpected male whims.[7]

The family as a governing body had lost much of its hegemony by the
twelfth century, as kings and princes siphoned off public power by creating
institutions apart from the household to act as administrative units. According to feminist historians, this division and the increasing strength of
the bureaucratic state worked to the detriment of women. These scholars
suggest that as the domestic and public spheres were separated in this way,
women's status and power dwindled proportionately. Since women were
bound to the family or domestic sphere, and the family no longer retained
its privileged position, women's role was commensurately constricted. Furthermore, as access to political power became associated with the individual
citizen as opposed to the family in the late Middle Ages, citizenship was increasingly defined as a male prerogative.[8]

In the early modern era, the family continued to decline in importance
vis-à-vis the state, as the process of state building reinforced the monarchy
at the expense of the family. Moreover, the growth of governmental absolutism in the seventeenth and eighteenth centuries closely coexisted with an
intensified patriarchalism—which in turn stimulated parallel developments
within the family and further weakened women's position therein. Just as the
monarchy seized power from the family and took a patriarchal/hierarchal
stance toward its subjects, so too did the familial patriarch exert greater au-

thority over his kin and household.[9] If the eighteenth century was not quite the turning point that Joan Landes suggests, it was still a century that reinforced public/private opposition and continued to foster a gender identity that associated women with home and family, thus foreclosing extrafamilial options for women at a time when such economic and political opportunities were eagerly embraced by men.[10]

The link between urban medieval women and American colonial women may seem tenuous, but in some ways New England women of the early seventeenth century had more in common with their European ancestors than with their American descendants two centuries in the future. If it is true, as some theorists maintain, that a low incidence of political organization meant a higher status for women, then the status of medieval women may have had more than a little relevance for early American women, who initially settled in communities where political consolidation was in its formative stages. During the first decade of settlement, the inclusive New England family exercised considerable suasion over community decisions, creating a short-term niche for itself from which it would recede as all-male governmental units became firmly established as the locus of power.[11]

KEEPING FAITH

When the first English Puritans set sail for North America, they left behind not only a rich mélange of Protestant sects but also a Catholic tradition that continued to mold European society as it had done for a millennium and more. An old Catholicism and a young Protestantism coexisted—albeit uneasily—in Europe, and the absence of such strong competing faiths in New England would profoundly affect that society in its formative years, particularly in terms of gender.

One of the most striking differences between the two faiths was that Catholicism ranked celibacy over marriage in the hierarchy of virtue, a point that rankled Protestants on both continents. More importantly, Catholic women as well as men could take advantage of the celibate state, either as female religious or in specific instances without taking vows. And some did so, even if they could never perform certain Catholic rites or attain priesthood.

Catholicism offered a number of opportunities to women in the early Middle Ages, at a time when royal or aristocratic families controlled Europe and women used their authority and money to appoint bishops and abbots and to influence religious policy. Between the mid-seventh and mid-eighth centuries, female and male saints shared center stage in England and France. In addition, abbesses acceded to positions of responsibility and power, as the female monastic movement and the communities founded under it reached their zenith in the seventh century. The double monastery, composed of religious men and women and usually headed by an abbess, flourished with thousands of people and vast territories under its control. Wealthy women, able to devise property, liberally endowed churches and monasteries with dower lands and inherited property.[12]

Moreover, throughout the centuries, convents offered a convenient alternative for a small number of elite Catholic women whose parents chose to provide for their daughters' future in this way. By donating money or property to the Church, a family ensured a daughter's security at less cost than a dowry. This route also consolidated familial assets to a greater degree than if that wealth was dissipated through marriage to a second family line (not to mention a third or fourth if a family contained several eligible daughters).[13]

European women supported convents financially, received education in them, and occasionally spent their widowhood in the care of nuns who ran such institutions. Convents, as well as monasteries, contained libraries that were available to the daughters, as well as the sons, of local gentry. Among this elite class there was an acceptance, perhaps even an expectation, of female literacy, as liturgical literature, devotions, books of hours, and romances were absorbed by a small female readership.[14]

Some women entered the convent willingly, others under protest—but all could begin or continue an education unencumbered by the responsibilities of family life. Given the status associated with celibate life in Catholic doctrine, these women became esteemed members of the community, even if their numbers never amounted to more than a small fraction of the female population. As members of an order, Catholic women could nurse, teach, preach, write, and translate. They could be abbesses and prioresses, with uncontested supervisory and managerial authority—not to mention the ability to forge political and financial relationships with powerful men. Such a life provided dignity, autonomy, and a sense of female community that must have been enhanced by the absence of daily contact with males. Less affluent women might enter convents as servants or workers, and the convents in turn provided a means for some women to earn a dowry.[15] Before the Church attempted to enclose them, these women reached out to the larger community and provided aid to the poor, disabled, orphans, and others who were unable to help themselves.

The Beguine movement offered an alternative to European women who sought a godly life outside both marriage and the convent. The Beguines were urban religious women who pooled their property, lived as families, and pledged themselves to chastity. These women, who devoted their lives to good works, were most prominent in northern Europe, where their vigorous activities attracted the greatest attention in the thirteenth century.[16]

In the late eleventh century the Church began to dissolve the double monasteries, and from that point forward the Church made consistent (if sporadic) efforts to enclose female religious. At the same time, secular women seemed to have had less control over money with which to support female monasteries. By the end of the twelfth century double monasteries under the leadership of abbesses were a thing of the past, while endowed cathedrals and universities began to replace the remaining monasteries as centers of learning. These stately and prestigious institutions, designed to train priests, were closed to women.[17]

A tendency to discourage religious women in the eleventh century became a trend in the early thirteenth century, with limitations on the number of nuns and a prohibition against the formation of new orders. In the future, women were to be associated with (and under the control of) existing male orders. Neither convents nor independent orders, such as the Poor Clares, escaped incorporation by male orders—even when the male orders themselves were less than enthusiastic about the merger.[18]

Between the eleventh and fourteenth centuries the Church also stepped up its efforts to enclose women who had formerly been free to perform their good works outside the convent walls. Religious women were reluctant to give up their autonomy, and the Beguines, despite a decline in their numbers by the fifteenth century, did not disappear altogether. In 1566 Pius V ordered the cloistering of all professed nuns, and although there was both resentment of and resistance to the edict, even the Ursulines, which had been founded as a teaching order in 1535, became a regular cloistered order in 1667. With the arrival of the Reformation, convents themselves came under attack. Most were degraded and disbanded in areas where Protestants held sway, although some continued to exist by professing to a Lutheran conversion—much to the chagrin of both Catholics and Protestants.[19] Thus, by the time of the Reformation, Catholic women wielded somewhat less power and authority than they had during the early Middle Ages, and their autonomy had eroded as well.

— ♯ —

On the face of it, aspects of the Protestant Reformation were favorable to women. Central to its doctrine was the "priesthood of all believers," which incorporated the idea of personal salvation, personal conscience, and an individual relationship with God, unimpeded by hierarchy or other male intervention. The Bible and liturgy were translated into the vernacular, and reformers placed emphasis on the ability of both men and women to read the Holy Book. Since mothers were entrusted with the elementary education of children, their own proficiency became a matter of some concern. Men and women raised their voices in congregational song, and communal activities were shared by both. Since Protestantism placed great emphasis on the family, reformers urged cooperation, companionship, and love within marriage to a greater degree than before. Men were urged to treat their wives with respect and to eschew physical abuse. Divorce, at least in theory, became an option. Its very challenge to religious hierarchy contained the potential for defiance of other superior/inferior relationships. By the mid-seventeenth century Protestantism had paved the way for female preachers in Britain.[20]

Pregnant women or women in labor would also have been reassured that Protestantism was in their best interest if they had been aware of the mortality rate of Catholic women in childbirth. By the mid-eighteenth century midwives in Catholic areas were required to baptize a miscarried fetus and to perform a Caesarian on a pregnant woman who had died, also for the purpose of baptizing the fetus. Although these practices alone should not have affected the maternal death rate, some historians maintain that they led to a decreasing concern for the health of the mother and child. A study of one German community between 1650 and 1800 in which Protestants and Catholics were neighbors but were delivered by midwives of their own religion showed a significantly higher postpartum death rate among Catholic mothers and their newborns compared to Protestant women and their infants.[21]

The Protestant Reformation never intended to equalize the relationship between men and women, however, and while it opened certain doors to women, it shut others. The attack on and closing of convents in the areas under Protestant control dislocated a great many women who had found comfort, community, and satisfaction even after the Church insisted on the cloistering of female religious. Women who had been placed in convents against their own inclination were, no doubt, delighted with the turn of events, but others only reluctantly abandoned communal life as they were forced to return to households that may have been ambivalent about taking them in.

The worship of female as well as male saints was abolished under Protestantism, thus undermining the female presence in all aspects of the reformed religion. Even Mary had a far smaller role to play in Protestant theology, and surely the loss of Saint Margaret, the patron saint of pregnant women, must have been disturbing to a great many women who had taken spiritual comfort in her during labor and delivery. Protestant women were also denied the opportunity to participate in public festivals and religious processions where, at one time, women had been quite visible. Protestantism may have challenged the Church hierarchy, but in so doing, it reinforced the hierarchal household by instituting the husband and father as its religious head. The most recent research suggests there was no sharp break between Catholic and Protestant family doctrines.[22]

For whatever reasons, as Natalie Davis points out, Calvinist women never published as much as their Catholic counterparts. This may have had to do with the upper-class bias of learned Catholic women and the essentially middle-class nature of Protestant converts, but it is apparent that intellectual creativity never reached the same level that it had in the older female Catholic tradition.[23]

For all the advantages that the Protestant Reformation supposedly offered, individual women rarely converted to Protestantism in the sixteenth century. For the most part, conversions were family affairs, and female converts without male Protestant kin were rare indeed. It is difficult to say whether women did not find Protestantism as attractive as it professed to be, or whether unattached women feared to face the persecution that accompanied conversion without the support of male relatives, but whatever the reasons, their numbers were small. The largely middle-class constituency of Protestantism drew disproportionately on widows and women with skills or trades of their own, such as dressmakers, small merchants, midwives, or hotelkeepers.[24]

European Catholics and Protestants did not live together happily ever after, but they lived together, and that proximity may have worked to smooth the roughest edges of persecution once toleration became acceptable to all but the radical fringes of both religions. In short, each offered an alternative to the other; each beckoned people away from the excesses of its competitor. And each knew that the other stood in the wings, ready to woo converts to the opposing faith.

— ⚹ —

This was not the case in New England. Not only was Massachusetts Bay at least theoretically devoid of a papist voice, but the Puritans who settled the colony were more closely aligned to the left branch of the Reformation than to mainstream moderates. The raison d'être of the colony ensured the absence of overt Catholicism in its founding decades, and although the nonpresence of the old faith had an impact on both men and women, in some ways the void affected women more profoundly than it did men.

Puritan doctrine and a high sex ratio conspired to make marriage the only choice for New England women. And Puritan doctrine virtually ensured certain marital tensions that would have been absent in a Catholic or Anglican environment. In the North American setting, the husband and father, rather than the priest (or even the minister), was theologically responsible for the entire household, a burden that added considerably to his list of responsibilities. Furthermore, Puritanism had a more restrictive admission policy than Catholicism, and although the Puritan churches promised equal access to visible sainthood, standards were high and the acceptance rate low. It is not clear how often a wife was accepted for church membership before or to the exclusion of her husband, but surely such occurrences must have undermined the theological role relegated to males as heads of households. From this perspective, and because public recognition of spiritual excellence bestowed esteem upon women, one can only wonder if—or how—husbands might have exerted their authority at home in response to a public rejection of worthiness. Despite Protestant assertions of female spiritual equality, a stronger commitment to hierarchy and patriarchy within the family probably overcame any egalitarian tendencies.[25]

Although relatively few women entered convents in Europe, Catholicism offered respectable alternatives that were unavailable to New England women. This is not to say that given a choice many New England women would have turned from the secular world; it is simply to note that it was not even an option. It is not even to say that more than a handful would have consciously chosen a life of good works in a teaching or charitable order that did not require vows; it is merely to point out that in Boston, Salem, Newport, and Portsmouth that choice never existed. It never existed for members of the Puritan churches, obviously, but neither was it a viable alternative for those whose aspirations toward visible sainthood were eternally thwarted.

The absence of female communities may also have retarded the formation of a feminist consciousness on this side of the Atlantic. No orders, no convents, no convent schools, no models of independent women working together and being governed by a woman. No tutelage in the art of raising money from the sale of gold and silver embroidery or illuminated manuscripts. New Englanders had rejected one of the traditions that helped to establish group identity in Europe. Women would join church committees and establish a multitude of networks as time went on, but their very informality only emphasizes the absence of a structured and collective female identity that was highly visible in a Catholic country, such as France.

Thus the Puritan family had no competitors; New England women no role models besides wives and mothers. Indeed, the fact that so many women married in the founding decades of New England may have created great expectations in and about all women, expectations that persisted yet could not be met as the sex ratio shifted in urban New England and not all women married. The lack of alternatives to marriage placed tremendous emphasis on the family as an institution in American society—perhaps more so than in the western Europe it left behind.

On the other hand, the lack of options may not have worked as much of a hardship in New England as it would have in Europe, because one of the factors propelling women toward convents—the cost of dowries—was of little relevance here. Moreover, the vast amount of land, Indian rights notwithstanding, made partible inheritance a common phenomenon, and there was initially little need to prevent a daughter's share from being alienated from her birth family.[26]

It also appears that some of the more radical Protestant sects—precisely those that were most appealing to women, such as the Quakers—were more easily tolerated in Europe.[27] They were never fully accepted (a surge of female preachers in England during the 1640s paralleled a surge of witchcraft accusations directed at women), but in the 1650s it was Cromwell, and after him Charles II, who encouraged the Bostonians to adopt a more moderate position toward dissenters. It is an interesting postscript that the last large-scale witchcraft executions in England preceded Salem by seven years, and that witchcraft epidemics died out all over Europe in the early 1680s.[28] In the English outposts, where Puritanism was strongest, witchcraft accusations continued into the eighteenth century.

GENDER AND ECONOMIC DEVELOPMENT

European precapitalist society functioned through what historians label the "family economy." Wives, daughters, and sisters contributed to the economic well-being of the family (indeed, they were equally responsible for its survival) through household production and marketing of various items. The historical record confirms that between 1400 and 1800 economic changes simultaneously generated and reinforced the separation of what has been labeled public and private spheres, and as the disintegration of the family economy took place, factors inherent to a rising capitalist economy and patriarchal state precipitated a decline in women's economic status. The changes took place over many centuries, but the pattern that emerges from an examination of the long-term historical chart leaves little doubt of its direction. When the saga is extended to seventeenth-century North America, where conditions more nearly approximated an earlier stage of European development, women's opportunites appear to be commensurate with a less advanced system that offered slightly better opportunites for participation and contribution. Yankee ingenuity being what it was, however, it did not take long to reach that state of development where American women would become less privileged members of the economic community.

— ✻ —

Throughout fourteenth-century Europe, urban women were clustered into housewife-associated activities and light crafts. In Exeter, England, women processed and marketed food, cloth, and hides; they also brewed and sold ale. They were less likely to be found as purveyors of high-priced imported products such as wine and spices, or necessities such as grain, and they were less visible as skilled processors of bread or meat. They were involved in candlemaking and worked as spinners, weavers, tailors, hosiers, and dressmakers. The English silk industry was almost entirely in the hands of women, and clothmaking itself was one of the chief occupations of English women between the fourteenth and the end of the eighteenth centuries.[29]

In medieval Montpellier women proliferated in the food trades, the textile industry, and precious metalwork; unlike women in Exeter, who were not formally apprenticed, they entered into contractual relationships in such industries. In Montpellier women would also be found in the silk finishing industry. Wives and widows participated in the luxury trades that required capital and commercial organization, and to this extent enjoyed resources

less easily obtained by never-married women. Here women were involved to
a greater degree in agricultural trading: grain, grapes, and livestock. Absent
from legal, medical, and political positions, a few women engaged in local
banking activities as borrowers and lenders. Women did not partake of the
spice trades (although this was not true elsewhere) and, for reasons associated with their family obligations, did not act as traveling merchants.[30] And
although women's occupations varied somewhat from place to place, all
women were subject to the time constraints placed on wives and mothers.
Women, far more often than men, earned income on an irregular and sea-
sonal basis.

In Lyon, as elsewhere, family survival depended on women's economic
participation, and among provisioners such as butchers, hotelkeepers, and
tavernkeepers, historians have found numerous examples of joint husband-
wife ventures. Silk making was a family enterprise, and one in which wives
as well as husbands worked at the looms. Female apprenticeship was not
unheard of in Lyon, as Natalie Davis's example of pinmakers demonstrates,
and women appear as barbers and printers even though only men received
formal training. Women also worked as artisans in the textile and clothing
trades and were amply represented as cord makers, dress and glove makers,
wimple makers, and lace makers. They unwound cocoons and wove and
threw silk.[31]

Thirteenth- and fourteenth-century Parisian women were also heavily
represented in the luxury fabric industry. They were the chief spinners and
weavers of silk and prominent in the not-so-luxurious production of linen.
They were comparatively less prominent in the woolen industry. Their variety of employments and presence in shops and households outside their own
homes suggests to the historian David Herlihy that medieval women occasionally participated in occupations that distanced them from the authority
of the male head of household.[32]

Because women were so heavily represented as food sellers and retail
traders, city governments often appointed them to positions as inspectors
and overseers. Nevertheless, their high visibility in the trades and as retailers
in the urban marketplace should not obscure the fact that domestic employment was the primary occupation of women in urban early modern Europe,
and that two-thirds of all servants were female. In the same period, hospitals,
orphanages, and infirmaries were staffed mainly by women.[33]

Despite their vital contribution to the family and local economy, female
workers were usually marginalized, as measured by either status or compen-

sation. With few exceptions they performed the less skilled tasks necessary for production, and their wages reflected the low esteem accorded their labor. Furthermore, historians assume that husbands had the final say over the distribution of family income, although the evidence for this assessment is less than compelling.[34]

Guilds were integral to the European urban economy, and although under certain conditions women might be found in these organizations, it would be too much to argue that their power was greatly advanced by such associations. Most women were unskilled, and their labor inappropriate to guild formation. Accepted as widows of guild members, women were in subordinate positions and rarely admitted to full membership on their own application. Female guilds existed only on the continent: in Rouen, Paris, and Cologne, seamstresses, spinners, lingerie makers, and boutique keepers were among those so organized. Even here, however, it was the family production unit that enhanced women's status and made access to craft organizations easier. And even in female guilds decision making was circumscribed, since only in the early modern period were members permitted to elect their own officials. A prime example of too little, too late: by the eighteenth century guilds were disappearing altogether in England and France.[35]

ECONOMIC DECLINE

While historians of Europe disagree over whether women's experience was marked more by continuity or by change, they generally concur that little happened between the high Middle Ages and the nineteenth century to improve women's economic status. An increase in household income, or the upward mobility of family members (for whatever reasons), could translate into greater prosperity for women whose identity and well-being were linked to others, but there is little evidence that individual women, as autonomous workers, made any notable gains over the centuries. Indeed, it seems that during this period women on the whole not only became less visible but also experienced a significant loss of autonomy. This assessment crosses both class and what passed for national boundaries, and although the time frame differs from place to place, the basic story line is remarkably consistent.[36]

The preponderance of evidence suggests that over time women suffered a constriction of economic opportunities. Where women's work was essential, or where an expanding economy reduced competition for jobs, this was less evident, but the general pattern is unmistakable: the role and status of working women, and particularly those of the housewife, were diminished slowly and definitively, particularly in the early modern period.[37]

This phenomenon appears to be particularly true for women in prosperous families, who began to withdraw from productive labor at this time, while women from poorer families found themselves shunted into the lowest positions offered to wage labor. Women in urban centers were particularly vulnerable, as they were excluded from occupations in which they had once been prominent.[38] Rural women, as well as men, began to realize that agriculture could not sustain a family, causing both men and women to turn to day labor, a movement that eventually created a wage labor force. In the case of women, those workers were likely to become spinners or servants.

The presence of women in guilds—never great to begin with—diminished, as a series of restrictions created difficulties for wives who acted alone and widows who sought to act in their husbands' stead.[39] Because most urban trades and industries were organized and regulated by guilds, and the skills necessary to the production of goods were limited to members of such associations, women became increasingly marginalized and relegated to lesser, unskilled tasks, which paid lower wages. In late fourteenth-century Cologne hat makers forbade wives, daughters, and female servants to help in the trade, and in 1461 the Bristol weavers imposed similar restrictions. Although it is difficult to determine whether practice was consistent with these established rules, it does appear that by the fifteenth century most of the guilds contained only male members.

All-female guilds took longer to exclude women, but by the fifteenth century many of the women's guilds in France had disappeared or had merged with larger organizations. Since English guilds appeared on the scene later than those on the continent, women may not have had the opportunity (or perhaps the desire) to organize themselves independently, but the end result was the same. The London silkworking industry, once dominated by women, eventually succumbed to male control in the sixteenth and seventeenth centuries, at which time men formed a guild to protect themselves and simultaneously exclude all women but widows of guild members. Forbidden from entering apprenticeships as widows, women became less visible as barbers and apothecaries. If, in bad times, male apprenticeships were limited in number, female apprenticeships were almost totally eliminated in sixteenth-century Lyon.[40]

If, as Martha Howell asserts, a high labor status is associated with the control of economic resources or the production, distribution, and consumption of goods, then Howell is right to conclude that as the family lost its central role in this process, women's status declined commensurately.[41] And if status is associated with esteem, then the status of the family increased if the wife was less visibly employed. To the extent that they shopped, bought, and consumed, women were integral to the formation of a middle-class capitalist society, but their activity as consumers further confirmed the different roles men and women would play in that evolving society.[42]

For many reasons, authority over resources passed into fewer and decidedly male hands, and as it did so, the housewife lost her market value. The inability to compete for investment capital was central to the problem. Industries such as brewing, once a female preserve that provided a small income from neighbors and friends, became male dominated by 1700 as brewers served regional networks rather than local markets. Increasingly, the domestic sphere was identified as female, and as other income-producing options contracted, housewives became a labor pool of spinners who would contribute to the production of cloth for export as part of the new mercantilist order. The division of labor intensified as urban males (unlike their rural counterparts) ceased spinning at adolescence.[43]

It is difficult to assess whether the disparity in income between men and women, which was fairly substantial at all times, actually increased over time. Some historians imply as much, while others do not address the issue except to note that in general, women could expect to earn no more than three-fifths or two-thirds of male income. Whether men and women ever received the same wage for the same task is debatable, although some historians argue that if it happened at all, it would have been in the Middle Ages rather than later.[44]

Although differences in earning power may be ascribed to the nature of work itself (the abundance of spinsters kept wages low), it is also true that as women were displaced from higher-status trades or professions, their income suffered as a result. Thus, if women invested in long-distance commerce in the sixteenth century, dwindling access to capital forced them out of middle-level trade after that date, further accelerating their inability to accumulate income. In addition, English women, subject to the law of coverture, were hampered in their ability to borrow or otherwise obtain the necessary capital for investment.[45]

Although historians generally acknowledge these shifting economic patterns, there is some question about the causes of such change between the fifteenth and eighteenth centuries. It is not so much that scholars dispute the variables offered in explanation, but rather that they disagree about the relative importance of each factor. What seems to be clear, however, is that the interplay of factors, rather than any specific one, resulted in a reshuffling of relationships that worked more to the benefit of men than of women.

If patriarchy never existed, women might still have been tied more closely to childrearing than men by virtue of their ability to provide sustenance for infants and young children. That issue aside, their rhythm of life has been tied to domestic responsibilities, a historical continuity that is hard to challenge and that usually impedes physical, not to mention upward, mobility. An adherence to the demands of a regulated and inflexible workday was all but impossible. Thus, when production for home use and small-scale marketing were the only demands made on the family economy, women could participate in the creation and distribution of goods, but with the expansion of the commercial market, husbands appear to have taken control and were accepted as the representative of the productive unit.[46]

Centralization of political authority and a growing pool of landless males also contributed to a decline in female participation and visibility. As a trade or craft became associated with politics by either direct action or through the appointment of guild members to city councils, women were edged out of such organizations. Concurrently, as journeymen became more fearful of wage labor and a competitive job market, guilds and craft associations found other reasons to close their doors to women. And as women turned to less prestigious employment opportunities, new restrictions were imposed. As property accumulation—and the ability to pass it on to legitimate heirs—took on added importance, women were excluded from such decisions.[47]

Professionalism also had a negative effect on women's status in early modern Europe. As the professions took shape, the imposition of educational standards and licensing requirements effectively barred women from occupations in which they had once engaged.[48]

COLONIAL VARIABLES

Given the tenacious grip of prescribed gender roles and the association of European women with specific domestic tasks and trades, it was unlikely, if not impossible, for that tradition to wane, much less expire, on this side of the Atlantic. Nevertheless, it is not too much to suggest that the conditions of the New England experiment in the seventeenth century were potentially favorable for female economic advancement even within the domestic setting. As it turned out, however, a combination of European legacy, American environment, and the expectations of the colonial-mercantile system eventually limited rather than advanced those opportunities, particularly in towns and what would in time become cities.

In Europe women were closely affiliated with cloth production as well as food processing and marketing. Indeed, cloth manufacture was the leading industry in East Anglia, the region of England most responsible for populating New England.[49] Nevertheless, even though small-scale domestic textile production existed in New England, large-scale importation of woolen and linen cloth from old England prevented the early development of an industry that might have benefited colonial women, their families, and thus the community.

Ten years after the settlement of Boston, woolen cloth represented 80–90 percent of English exports, and although that percentage declined over time, England still exported vast quantities of woolen and linen cloth to its North American customers throughout the entire colonial period.[50] The absence of sheep would have been a rather severe drawback to the production of woolen cloth, but New Englanders were importing the animals as early as 1620, and since these creatures appeared to have taken their charge to go forth and multiply as seriously as their owners, Rhode Islanders were producing extraordinary amounts of wool by the end of the seventeenth century.[51]

That the British were determined to limit the production of woolen cloth in the colonies is demonstrated by the 1669 statute forbidding the British colonies to produce woolens for export even to a neighboring colony, a law that was reinforced by the 1699 Wool Act, which allowed wool manufacture for local sale but prohibited the export of colonial woolen cloth.[52] The Navigation Acts, therefore, disproportionately affected gender roles in ways that historians have yet to analyze.

What is puzzling about this scenario is that England was perpetually short of yarn in the seventeenth century. So desperate was the need to furnish the English textile industry with yarn that more than half the value of Irish imports to England came from wool and woolen yarn, for which the English paid good prices.[53] Here was an opportunity for England to feed its hungry looms and for American women to engage in a lucrative enterprise. Such a compatible scheme even fit within the guidelines of mercantilism, but this combination, beneficial to both parties, never materialized.

Americans also grew flax—as evidenced by the exportation of flaxseed— and the fibers of the plant could have supported a thriving linen industry. But England also exported sizable quantities of linen cloth, and thus only small amounts of linsey-woolsey (a flax-wool combination) were locally produced for domestic consumption.[54] If wishful thinking could have produced a silk industry in the colonies, Americans would surely have had one, but luxury fabrics had no place in the American economy. Thus, large-scale textile production, an important means through which European women participated in the domestic economy, was all but closed to American women. Moreover, American women were less likely than European women to be integrated into textile production, since American males monopolized the weaver's craft on this continent more so than in Europe.

Throughout New England, women were involved in small-scale food production and distribution in much the same way that their mothers and grandmothers had been in Europe. At the same time, there is little evidence that beer production, once a female-dominated home industry (and a source of income) in England, ever contributed much to the family economy in the colonies. Americans grew barley and drank beer, so the beverage must have been brewed, but the evidence says little, if anything, about the manufacturing process or whether urban housewives routinely bartered this staple item along with butter, cheese, and eggs. In any case, beer production does not appear to have enhanced the family economy as it did in Europe.[55]

Although a few guilds existed in seventeenth-century New England, female labor was affected more by their absence than their presence. In Europe, craft guilds were training grounds, and although relatively few women were members of either mixed guilds or all-female associations, their existence did provide access to skilled, higher-status work. More explicitly, they legitimized female participation in a particular trade or craft. For the few American women who might have been advantaged by such associations, the lack was a loss.

In New England, Boston shoemakers, coopers, and possibly tanners were organized into guilds in the seventeenth century, but their records are too sparse to determine either sexual composition or what role, if any, women played among their numbers. For all we know, women may have been associated in some capacity with the few organizations that received charters. Apprenticeships were open to girls as well as boys, but since the variety of trades that accepted female apprentices were more limited than in Europe, so too were the range of apprenticeships themselves.[56]

More important, however, is the fact that without a strong guild system, economic and political decisions were made elsewhere. Moreover, whatever training originally existed in this labor-starved economy was conducted under the auspices of a family that was not bound to guild regulations. Where gender roles were weakened by a less defined economy, women may have received experience in high-status trades that were closed to them in Europe by the seventeenth century. Men and women never competed on an equal basis, but the existence of a society that was not dominated by guilds opened economic doors at least for a short while.

On balance, the absence of guilds should have enhanced the position of American women, especially if it is true that female economic opportunity was greatest where guilds claimed the least control.[57] Combined with a weak political and economic structure and a scarcity of labor, a large unregulated work force should have benefited women on this side of the Atlantic, as it had in Europe many centuries earlier. Not only would the difference in economic status between male and female have been minimized as the family economic unit (rather than the guild system) served as the primary training ground, but local politics might have been less gender defined as well.

As long as the family was central to production and marketing, women were likely to have had a more substantive role to play than they would when the family lost its control over all aspects of production and long-distance marketing became a male-dominated activity. Women's place in the economy of Newport, Rhode Island, in 1686, when Edward Perry shipped a cargo of flour from there to Elizabeth Perry in Boston, was very different from women's role in Newport in the 1770s, when the putting-out system thrived and the merchant Aaron Lopez supplied raw materials to some three dozen people, mostly women, who produced cloth and garments for him to sell locally or export abroad.[58]

Similarly, if the road to political authority in Europe wove through highly organized guild organizations, and such a structure was absent in the colonies, then power (if not authority) may have taken a detour here. This is not to say that women would have had considerable input in political decisions, but it is possible that their voices were heard (or at least their hands were counted) in the formative period of Massachusetts Bay, in ways that would cease to exist as American society became more structured, centralized, bureaucratized, and capitalized.[59]

European historians are divided over whether a bullish or bearish economy offered more employment opportunities for women. Susan Stuard maintains that in medieval society an expanding economy encouraged female participation, while Mary Prior found that between 1500 and 1800 economic downturns forced more women into the labor market either as substitutes for or as additions to the male providers in their households.[60] Chronology may be the important variable here, as the movement toward wage labor made job competition all the more fierce, and the different findings are a reminder that a higher participation rate is not necessarily tantamount to greater advantages. Whatever the relative weight of various factors, the European female wage labor force grew throughout the eighteenth century, at the same time that domestic service was becoming increasingly feminized. Both factors would have an impact in the American environment as the availability of land on the eastern seaboard constricted and the maturing colonial economy showed signs of following in the footsteps of its European parent.[61]

If, as Gloria Main's rural New England account books indicate, greater numbers of women were being hired in the two decades before Independence, this phenomenon may also indicate patterns similar to ones that emerged in Europe many decades earlier. There the feminization of agriculture, as Merry Wiesner describes it, was a reflection of the hardships suffered by artisan families in towns where wives were forced into agricultural work to supplement family income. New England rural landholders would have been as pleased as their European counterparts to hire proportionately less expensive labor.[62]

UNCOMMON LAW

The evolution of the law of property, as applied to women, also contributed to female economic instability. Before the second millennium, European women had more access to and control over property than they would in later centuries. Throughout the early Middle Ages their ability to acquire property by marriage or inheritance increased through the Germanic practice of the bride gift and morning gift. The bride gift, bestowed directly by

the groom upon the bride, was usually an unencumbered piece of real property that became hers to alienate at will. A morning gift, of some value, followed consummation of the marriage. There is also some evidence that
women benefited from inheritance customs that allowed them to inherit
movables (such as furniture) as well as immovables.[63]

In the late tenth and eleventh centuries women began to lose what gains
they had made, as fewer deeds gave wives outright ownership of property
that they in turn could dispose of as they wished. In 1037 German women
were excluded from inheritance of fiefs, and in the twelfth century the practice of the morning gift was abandoned in favor of the Roman dowry, a gift
from the family of the bride to the prospective husband.[64]

From the twelfth century onward, towns began to outlaw all but the Roman dowry, on the assumption that it was a fair substitute for what had
originally been a share of patrimony. In the next century most European
countries began to pass primogeniture laws, or other laws that favored males,
while the Normans went a step further and permitted parents to exclude
daughters from patrimony altogether. These legal changes coincided with a
decline in female economic independence, both within marriage and during
widowhood.[65]

In tenth-century France husbands and wives managed their own property separately, without the interference of their partners. Such female independence gave way to joint ownership in the eleventh and twelfth centuries,
any egalitarian aspects of which dissolved by the thirteenth century as the
father/husband increased his authority over the entire estate in order to as-
sure the devolution of undivided property. By the sixteenth century any act
a married woman performed without her husband's authority was non-
binding.[66]

As Roman law wended its way throughout western Europe in the early
modern era, women's economic viability suffered proportionately. In England after 1660 women were less likely to be named executors, and the bequests of husbands to wives decreased as well.[67] English equity courts, once
attentive to the needs of women through the sanctioning of separate estates,
became in the eighteenth century the forum in which dower rights were
eroded and replaced by jointure (a guaranteed annual payment to a widow).
A prenuptial jointure agreement barred dower in any existing property or
any acquired during marriage, an arrangement less advantageous to women
than dower itself. Nevertheless, the application of the contract theory to marriage encouraged the payment of "pin money," a fixed annual sum paid to a

wife during marriage. Although this practice came under attack for its potentially liberating effects, weakened versions were upheld by English equity courts.[68]

Notwithstanding such devices, however, by the eighteenth century French and English women had largely lost what independent legal rights they had once enjoyed, including the right to dispose of their possessions. And as propertied women in France were excluded from local political participation, there remained no one to speak on issues that affected their economic interests. In England the borough custom, recognized in common law as the right of a married women (with her husband's consent) to independently own property for trading purposes, fell into disuse, and by the end of the early modern era "feme sole" merchants could be found only in London.[69]

If, in an alleged thirteenth-century partnership of equals, some partners were a little more equal than others, no pretense of equality even existed after the sixteenth century. In the absence of a marriage contract to the contrary, husbands had complete legal control over their wives' assets. In the absence of an equal share of patrimony or access to high-status, high-income jobs, the alternatives left to single women were few. Moreover, their independence was discouraged: early modern laws prevented unmarried women in Augsburg from establishing their own households. In the sixteenth and seventeenth centuries, statutes provided unmarried women with guardians over their financial affairs.[70]

— ≠ —

By the time English emigrants sailed for the New England colonies, English common law contained strict rules governing the relationship between women, men, and property. Unmarried women could buy and sell both real and personal property, enter into contracts, conduct business, and devolve property through wills. Once a woman was married, however, this autonomy ended, at least in theory. What this meant, legally speaking, was that unless special provisions were made to the contrary, a married woman no longer controlled property that currently belonged to her or would belong to her in the future.

At the same time, laws governing married women were originally designed for a society where real property was finite and where there was a long-standing tradition of paper documents that not only validated the transfer of property but also confirmed events that impinged on that transfer. English law required registration of births, marriages, and deaths as well as the transfer of property by written record.

But the New England settlers of the first decades resisted a paper trail. Their societies were so unstructured, local government so immature, Puritan doctrine so strong, that births were recorded in Bibles, and marriages only inconsistently. Deaths were etched in the memory of those left behind rather than in local records. Time and again authorities would pass laws requiring inhabitants to make offical record of life's defining moments. The colonists were slow to comply. Their unwillingness may hamper efforts at historical accuracy, but it offered married women opportunities to circumvent the most restrictive aspects of common law.

Few would deny that the dearth of written documents and a reliance on memory caused confusion in the courts. The widow Jane Walford remembered in 1667 that her husband, Thomas, had given his daughter, Elizabeth Savidge, a piece of marshland "aboute 9 yeares before he dyed" and "it was comonly Called Bess Savidges Marsh." Thomas's grandson, John Homes, recalled that his grandfather "tooke a stone" to mark the boundary. Other witnesses corroborated details of the gift.[71] But was that gift of marshland a legal conveyance if the transfer was merely oral? How did one prove entitlement to property if a birth went unrecorded? If a marriage was never registered (as required by law), did the couple need a divorce to dissolve it? If one or the other remarried in such circumstances, would that constitute bigamy? These interrelated questions—and their answers—had considerable effect on urban women in colonial New England as the century evolved.

The New England legal narrative follows the European declension model, but the story contains different episodes, which only corroborate one of patriarchy's salient characteristics: its amazing creativity. No bride gift in Boston, no morning gift in Salem, no fiefdom in Newport, no "pin money" in Portsmouth—even in the beginning. Instead, what appeared to be an unlimited supply of land and a reliance on oral agreements combined to enhance female opportunity for a short time. Once New Englanders established codes and applied common law constraints, the tale becomes more familiar. The means to the end may have been different; the end was not.

A LEARNING EXPERIENCE

Before the Renaissance, if a woman received any education at all, such learning usually took place either at a convent or at home under the watchful eye
of a private tutor or a progressive father. Either way, these alternatives were
limited to a small number of affluent women. The curriculum varied somewhat, but accomplished women were expected to read, write, and be familiar
with the Latin and Greek classics. Religious education was integral to any
female course of study, as were such skills as needlework and drawing. Although learned women were not an anomaly even as early as the Carolingian
age, few women were able to claim even the most rudimentary knowledge
before the Renaissance.[72]

The various reforms that swept through western Europe throughout the
Middle Ages and resulted in constraints on women also restricted educa-
tional opportunity. In England, Latin ceased to be taught in convents, and
by the fourteenth century bishops were forced to write to English nuns in
French instead. By the fifteenth century French died out as well, leaving only
English as the language of correspondence.[73]

Nevertheless, a few individual women continued to receive an extraordinary private education, and among them was the woman celebrated as Europe's first professional female author and feminist, Christine de Pizan.[74]
From de Pizan's *Book of the City of Ladies*, composed in 1404–5, through the
early nineteenth century, supporters of women would press for female education on the assumption that uneducated women would always be subservient to men. The *querelle des femmes* (or woman question), which de Pizan
initiated, revolved around the capacity of women to be educated, and although the issue would not be settled for several centuries, the winds of
Renaissance humanism propelled the arguments forward.

Municipal schools with female teachers accepted girls as well as boys in
fourteenth-century Florence, and Dame schools could be found throughout
England by the late Renaissance. Schoolmistresses and female pupils appear
in French and German records as well. Continental authors such as Corne-
lius Agrippa, Erasmus, and Juan Luis Vives were translated into English in
the first half of the sixteenth century, and although none of these writers
advocated sexual equality (and all of them praised the "female" attributes
that linked women to domestic responsibilities), each sanctioned female education.[75] In short, any evaluation of the Renaissance must conclude that,
though the record varies according to time and place, female education in

general continued to be spotty and rudimentary, and expressions of support were not matched by any sustained efforts to improve female educational standards.

It was the Reformation that eventually became the driving force behind female education. Since all believers were urged to know God through the Bible, Protestantism required literacy of both men and women. As usual, this doctrine was more advantageous to men than to women, since the quality (and quantity) of education varied with sex. Nevertheless, Luther's efforts led to girls' schools in Germany and Geneva, and King Gustavus Adolphus of Sweden instituted an educational system that claimed universal literacy before the first half of the seventeenth century.[76]

At the same time, Catholics attempted to combat the spreading threat of Protestantism by expanding the number of convent schools on the continent, a movement not supported by Henry VIII, who closed all English convents and their schools in 1534.[77] In response to the new proliferation of continental convent schools, however, boarding schools for women began to appear in Protestant England in the seventeenth century. Their mission: to ensure that daughters of the merchant class obtained the necessary training to become gentrified wives. Education for young women continued to emphasize religion and domestic duties, rather than self-fulfillment, although the latter was, of course, an unavoidable by-product.[78]

By the end of the seventeenth century an increasing number of sharp-witted English and French women had entered the literary fracas over women in an attempt to advance female educational opportunities. The literacy rate of women rose in the seventeenth and eighteenth centuries, yet the gap in that rate between men and women of the same class widened concurrently. Even greater was the disparity between men and women at more advanced levels of achievement, particularly in terms of Latin, the classics, and scientific knowledge.[79]

Yet if British women lost proficiency in Latin, their facility with English improved, and their appetite for the written word increased. Books directed at a female readership escalated in number, with "how-to" titles leading the list, and romances, history, and biography not far behind. Religious literature was not neglected, but such offerings were usually not aimed directly at women, even though females were considered the greatest beneficiaries of devotional books and pamphlets.[80]

Thus, by the time the first boatloads of settlers turned their prows toward Massachusetts Bay, Englishwomen could claim many intellectual advances.

It is equally true, however, that Anglicanism had severely weakened the Catholic educational tradition, and despite the Protestant emphasis on literacy,
no public education system existed for middle- and lower-class Protestant
girls. As far as the lesser sort were concerned, the charity schools that flourished in France by the end of the sixteenth century would have no parallel in
England until a century later.[81]

Middle-class Puritan emigrants were caught in a bind: they advocated
universal education for their purposes, but they had no appropriate institutional model to recreate once they reached North America. New Englanders
would establish a system of public education and Dame schools soon upon
arrival, but they made no particular effort to educate the females among
their numbers beyond elementary levels, and only sporadically at best. Since
higher education for women was not one of their priorities and flexibility
not one of their strong points, they would take no notice of the Englishwoman Mary Astell's *Serious Proposal to the Ladies,* which was published
at the end of the seventeenth century and created considerable controversy
in England. Astell proposed a communal retreat for women where they
would retire to contemplate, pray, and most important, study. One historian
calls Astell's innovative institution a "Protestant nunnery" and likens it to
the American female colleges that were, alas, 150 years in the future.[82]

THE URBAN SETTING

An urban environment offered women opportunities that were not as readily
available elsewhere. For those seeking employment, the potential for wage
labor was greater in the larger towns and cities of Europe, even if women
faced competition for jobs from a growing number of landless men. Shunted
into sex-segregated positions with low wages, young women still found domestic employment a viable alternative to a rural life (or no job at all), and
before the end of the Middle Ages, household service had become the most
important female occupation. Spinning also provided a meager income for
many women—so many, in fact, that in the seventeenth and eighteenth centuries the terms "unmarried woman" and "spinster" became synonymous.[83]

In urban areas women were also heavily involved in marketing, particularly the necessities of life. Indeed, markets came to be viewed as a particularly female domain where they sold, among other items, food and beverages
that had been produced at home. Women ran other retail establishments,

boardinghouses, and taverns. Not surprisingly, they found employment there as cooks, cleaners, and laundresses—jobs that were extensions of their traditional female roles. Furthermore, the city offered greater educational advantages for women than the countryside, and thus the female literacy rate in both France and England was higher in urban areas than it was elsewhere.[84]

Urban society also produced female networks unlike the ones that existed in rural Europe. Urban circuitry included shopkeepers, landladies, tavernkeepers, guildworkers, and servants: young women, middle-aged women, and elderly women who interacted on a daily basis and were keenly aware of the politics, economics, and volatility of city life. Information traveled quickly through these channels, far more speedily than it did outside the city walls.

Less affluent women were particularly magnetized by the city, not only because of job opportunities but also because poor relief existed there on a scale unmatched in nonurban areas. Indeed, women made up the largest proportion of charity cases in the cities. Early modern Warwick was not the only community where poor women outnumbered poor men two to one, and unemployed single women posed the greatest threat to any town's financial well-being. Systematic programs to combat female poverty were nonexistent, and when women threatened to become public charges, a variety of governmental agencies, charitable groups, and convents provided alternatives to starvation or prostitution. In the late eighteenth century, *ateliers de charité* supplied poor women with textile work in factorylike settings.[85]

As early as the later Middle Ages, those responsible for the town's pocketbook began to worry about the cost of supporting such a large number of indigent women and devised means to safeguard their limited funds. City councils waived the rules for needy women by allowing them to hawk goods as an alternative to public charity. During the sixteenth century some communities chose to resolve the problem by excluding unmarried women from their environs altogether. Moreover, an unmarried, unemployed domestic servant was not free to turn down a prospective job. Should she do so, she too would be forced to leave the city.[86]

As attractive as the bustling town might have appeared to single women, female independence was compromised to the extent that authority over resources was tightly concentrated in male hands, a factor that permitted the strict enforcement of gender codes. In addition, some historians argue that the concentration of power in city and state governments not only encour-

aged patriarchal attitudes toward women but also offered unparalleled opportunities to regulate female behavior. If this is so, the example was not lost
on New England patriarchs.[87]

Demography, economics, and politics are inextricably linked, and the
European urban environment was shaped over time by the vagaries of these
components acting either separately or in unison. Thus by the year 1200 female longevity, war, and the Crusades had conspired to distort the sex ratio
and shift it toward a plurality of women. Seaports were particularly hard hit
in the succeeding centuries, as commerce expanded and emigrants sailed off
to settle the New World.[88] By the late Middle Ages there were only 83 to 91
men for every 100 women in many of Europe's great urban centers. London's
sex ratio at the end of the seventeenth century ranged somewhere between
.77 and .87 (77–87 men for every 100 women).[89]

More important, the sex ratio dictated that some of these women would
remain unmarried, a situation that presented problems on two counts: as
independent women they would not be under the control of a male head of
household, and given their economic fragility, they might threaten the financial vitality of the city. The worst fears of patriarchal Europe materialized
when, in the fourteenth century, an economic downturn helped to propel
the number of unmarried women upward to a point where they constituted
a substantial group in Europe for the first time.[90] Just how substantial that
group was is hard to gauge: estimates of the proportion of European women
who were unmarried at the time of their deaths vary widely. They range from
5 to 40 percent between 1550 and 1800, although demographers and historians agree that the high point occurred somewhere between the onset of the
Reformation and the mid-seventeenth century, after which the rate dropped
appreciably. In the following decades, despite a continuing sexual imbalance,
new job opportunities allowed more couples to marry—and marry earlier—
than had previously been the case. By the end of the eighteenth century
approximately 10 percent of the adult population was made up of never-
married women.[91]

For the purposes of this analysis, it is not necessary to distinguish between the number of unmarried women in the population at any given time
and the number of women who would never marry during their lifetime,
except to say that the two cohorts are not interchangeable, and that the best
estimates suggest that between 10 and 15 percent of northwest Europe's population in the early modern period never married.[92]

The category of female heads of households is another indicator of independent urban women, and this segment of the population ranged from 15.4 percent in Paris in 1292 to 18–28 percent in the German cities of the fourteenth and fifteenth centuries, to 10–20 percent in Reformation Germany.[93] Whatever the numbers, however, individual women and urban households headed by women were always at the bottom of the economic ladder. Indeed, unmarried women frequently shared lodgings to make survival easier.[94]

— ≠ —

Initially, the American colonies could claim no cities at all, much less thriving entrepôts or great cultural centers. Nevertheless, as urban communities evolved in New England, it took relatively little time for the problems that beset the aging European cities to infect the young American seaports as they expanded and developed after 1630. By the end of the seventeenth century that seemingly endless supply of real estate had dwindled to the point where America was producing its own company of young, landless males, a demographic feature that would eventually affect the marriage rate and the distribution of property between the sexes as it had in Europe. In the eighteenth century at least two of the more important New England towns (Boston and Newport) thought themselves worthy of the title of city, as the sex ratio swung from a preponderance of males to one with strong female majorities. As in Europe, many of these women were disproportionately poor. Some would never marry, and only a small proportion of unattached women had the marketable skills to produce enough income to attract the attention of the tax assessor.

Only dimly perceived as an urban problem until the end of the seventeenth century, financially disadvantaged unmarried women had fewer options in America than they did in Europe. The convents that had housed, trained, and otherwise cared for poor women were hardly viable alternatives in Puritan New England. Charitable institutions had been secularized during the Reformation, and although many such institutions in Europe had once been run by women, this was no longer the case. Similarly, almshouses and poorhouses, when they became necessary, were usually under male control in New England.[95] Overseers of the Poor were invariably male; the persons they oversaw were disproportionately female. And although there was a seemingly endless demand for servants, Americans were increasingly attracted to slave labor, competition that neither women nor men faced in Europe. The textile industry, which absorbed so many European women, was all but absent in New England, and thus income from that source was severely curtailed as well. The United Society for Manufactures was Boston's answer to the *ateliers de charité,* but this attempt to employ poor women in a linen manufactory met with a variety of problems from the time it opened in 1751 until its demise in 1758. American women, like their European counterparts, resisted a regulated workday unsympathetic to their unregulated domestic obligations.[96]

Historians, though well aware of Boston's economic sluggishness and population stagnation in the mid-eighteenth century, have not explored the effect of the extremely low sex ratio on both these trends. Whatever the reasons for Boston's dislocation, however, Americans could not call on European precedents that might have enhanced female economic vitality through education and training because those precedents simply did not exist. As a result, the New England towns fell back on time-honored methods designed to relieve the plight of poor women. That this tradition kept women dependent at the same time that it attempted to alleviate their distress is hardly coincidental—nor is it any more coincidental that the genesis of the feminization of poverty on this side of the Atlantic may be found in the New England seaports of colonial America.

The European connection would have a great impact on the relationship between men and women in the American colonies. American family organization and its link to the governing polity, religious convictions, economic development, legal structure, and intellectual pursuits originated in the European setting discussed in the preceding pages. How each of these was replicated, yet modified, in the urban New England context is the subject of the following chapters.

~ CHAPTER 2 ~

The Sin of an Ungoverned Tongue

Sarah Osborn's Story

A *Londoner by birth, Sarah Haggar sailed for New England with her family in 1722, when she was eight.[1] They eventually made their home in Newport, Rhode Island, where Sarah remained for the rest of her long life. A rebellious streak—and love—prompted the eighteen-year-old to marry Samuel Wheaten, a sailor, despite her parents' admonitions. Wheaten died at sea scarcely two years later, leaving Sarah "poor" and with a child to support.*

The following years must have been difficult for the young widow, but as Sarah later recalled, at the end of 1734 the "widow's God" rescued her by creating a teaching job for which she was qualified by her own education. Sarah would run her school almost continually for four decades as the number of students multiplied. Informed at one point that it was "unreasonable" for her to keep so large a school, Osborn responded that if so, it was only "reasonable" that she "should be able to Live Comfortably by a smaller"—and she threatened to raise tuition.[2]

The 1730s were a time of soul-searching for the widow Wheaten, a time when she constantly wrestled with her personal piety. In 1737, however, as religious revivals gained momentum, she joined the First Congregational Church. Sarah Wheaten's reputation as an intelligent, pious, and capable woman must have spread, because in 1741 "a number of young women, who were awakened to a concern for their souls," approached her and proposed the creation of a female religious society if Wheaten "would take care of them." The twenty-seven-year-old widow "joyfully consented."

The death of Sarah's brother and the temporary failure of her school "business" tested Sarah's "resignation" to God's will. Hoping to remain in Newport, she rejected offers to keep a country school, but alternatively "knew not what to do." God intervened once again, and Sarah accepted a job as shopkeeper in return for room and board.

In 1742 Wheaten married Henry Osborn and in so doing became the mother of three additional sons. If by entering into this second marriage Sarah Wheaten Osborn had hopes of improving her financial condition, she was destined for disappointment. Her husband's tailoring business declined, his health deteriorated, and she found herself the main breadwinner of an extended family. For the next half century Sarah Osborn saved money by teaching school and saved souls by leading Newport's female religious society. On the side, she drew chair seat designs for a "Gentlewoman."³ Despite these undertakings, her income must have been small; together, the Osborns earned too little to be counted among Newport's taxpayers. No matter: religion was Sarah's main occupation. Several months after her marriage, she and "a number of young women" formed a second female religious society in Little Compton.

Sarah Osborn became a well-known, respected, and influential religious figure in Newport. Although her memoirs are couched in pious, submissive language, it is evident that she wielded extensive authority through the prayer meetings held at her house in the mini-Awakening of 1767. Not only did she host the ongoing female society, but on other evenings of the week boys met for "instruction and blessing," children learned their catechism, slaves and free blacks received schooling, and young men and women as well as "heads of families" attended for "prayer and religious conversation." The "throng" that gathered around Osborn "for counsel and prayers" in her modest house on Church Street eventually numbered over five hundred regulars. Bestowal of blessings? Adult male attendees? More than five hundred supporters? Somewhere Ann Hutchinson was smiling.

Osborn anticipated criticism from those who resented the acceleration of her power and authority, and she admitted that her "fears" were often alarmed. Alarmed or not, she never retreated from the religious niche she had carved out for herself, and she defended herself admirably when scolded for "moving beyond" her "line" as a woman. In response to a stinging letter from the Reverend Joseph Fish of Stonington, Connecticut, Osborn claimed she was merely "a Servant that Has a Great work assigned Him" by the "Power of christ." Could she refuse such an assignment? Hardly. On the surface, her letter is deferential; on a more subtle level it is a firm, even rebellious, assertion of intent. "God will in no wise suffer me to be a Looser by His Service," she added reverently—or irreverently perhaps, as a warning to Fish.⁴

Whether Fish and her other detractors backed off or whether Osborn was simply undeterred by criticism, the schoolmistress and religious leader persisted in her endeavors. According to Samuel Hopkins, from 1770 until the British occupation "the church, both male and female, used to hold their monthly meetings at her house." Osborn claimed that their prayers, which continued during the war years, were responsible for the "deliverance of Newport."[5] Sarah's female religious society survived her death in 1796 and thirty years later was officially renamed the Osborn Society.

THE WORLD THEY LEFT BEHIND

Given John Winthrop's negative attitude toward learned women, there is some irony (perhaps even a hint of providence) in his crossing the Atlantic on board the *Arbella*. Arbella Stuart, cousin to James I and claimant to the English throne, was born in 1575 and became one of the last highly educated English noblewomen of her day. The daughters of Henry VIII had received a classical education, but Elizabeth had no daughters to instruct, and by the time James ascended the throne in 1603, English upper-class society was perceptively less receptive to learned women. James himself was outright hostile, and in this intellectual climate, Winthrop was a product of his time.[6] Similarly, although Winthrop and his company aboard the *Arbella* looked forward to building a city on a hill where this radical wing of the Protestant movement could worship as they chose, their vision was, in fact, shaped by the English world they had left behind.

That world had been fragmented by bitter religious controversy. Catholics and Protestants denounced each other on a regular basis, while Independents, Lollards, Levellers, Baptists, Ranters, and Quakers all sought converts to their particular version of the truth. To ensure that its own vision prevailed, the Church of England employed persecution as well as persuasion. As a result, English male heads of households found it prudent to maintain outward conformity to the Anglican Church, while many of their wives privately observed Catholicism at home. Indeed, women made up a large proportion of the recusant population, and although they were harassed and fined if they did not attend Anglican services, the domestic nature of their lives permitted a private adherance to Catholicism that was not available to men.[7] Not surprisingly, Catholic and Protestant women of all sects lived side by side, and in community after community Catholic women might have Protestant or Dissenting husbands, Catholic husbands Protestant or Dissenting wives.

Thus, a world of things Protestant and things Catholic defined the collective memory of that first generation of New Englanders. They fervently believed in the faith that drove them to Massachusetts, but the ways in which they attempted to construct their new world depended on which portion of the English religious montage resonated most powerfully.

In terms of gender, Puritan women could take some comfort in their enhanced importance within the family, as ministers elevated the status of wife and mother to a new plateau and extolled the idea of love and companionship between husband and wife. Protestants respected lay piety, and thus the virtuous, devout wife had a significant role to play within the household.[8] At the same time, however, they may have begun to realize that Puritan tradition increased the authority of the husband as well, since Puritan women were urged to seek religious clarification from their husbands, whereas neither Catholic men nor women were expected to interpret doctrine on their own.

Nevertheless, since both Catholicism and Protestantism insisted that devotion to God's will superseded obedience to a husband's authority, European women of both denominations had taken advantage of this legitimized defiance of spousal rulings. In sixteenth- and seventeenth-century England, Catholic women invited priests to hold mass in private homes despite the danger to and opposition from Conformist husbands. If God commanded a Protestant woman to prophesy, she was required to do so, "yea, though the Husband should forbid her."[9]

To complicate the collective memory, European Protestants and Dissenters did not speak with one voice, especially where women were concerned, and arguments continually erupted over the acceptability of female participation in church governance. If the Separatist Henry Ainsworth limited women's role to silent, physical attendance at all deliberations, John Robinson insisted on public confession by females as well as the right to "reprove the church, rather than suffer it to go on in apparent wickedness" in the absence of male activism. Robinson was the pastor of the Separatist congregation that eventually made its way to Plymouth, Massachusetts, without him, and although they waited patiently without a minister for a number of years, Robinson was to die in 1626 without ever rejoining his flock. Nevertheless, from all accounts his spirit continued to influence the fledgling colony across the Atlantic.[10]

Although the Great Migration slowed during the English Civil War, communication between England and America continued unabated, and most New Englanders were undoubtedly aware of the radical sects that proliferated in England once censorship declined under Cromwell. Englishwomen took advantage of this more tolerant atmosphere by preaching, publishing, petitioning, prophesying, and admonishing the government. Some radical sects even allowed women a role in church governance. None of this was lost on New England women in the decades before the Restoration.[11] And although New England women were required to consciously reject religious tenets that conflicted with the Puritan belief system, Puritans were hardly unaware of alternative doctrines. Memories of the English Baptist tradition intruded on the Puritan consciousness, for example, if only as a reminder that voluntary adult baptism offered women as well as men a meaningful measure of personal choice. These aggressive Dissenters (and their potential threat) were part of the Puritans' religious legacy, and vociferous New England women would openly draw on the Baptist alternative in the 1640s.

Although Puritan leaders eschewed Baptist doctrine, they still recognized Baptists as misguided Protestants. Conversely, colony leaders rejected Catholicism in its entirety—or so they thought. In reality, however, Puritans could hardly erase the collective memory of a Catholic past. And as Puritan women shared that communal knowledge of what was left behind, they must have realized what effect the absence of Catholicism had on gender and the development of American society. True, the dissolution of English convents had taken place toward the end of the 1530s, but a late-middle-aged Puritan woman emigrating to Salem in 1629 was likely to have had a grandmother for whom a convent was a realistic (and empowering) substitute for the familial social unit that legitimized and relied on male authority.

Furthermore, by the time English Puritans had begun to emigrate to Massachusetts, their countrywoman Mary Ward (1585–1645) had already established eight unenclosed religious houses on the continent—an effort that Pope Urban VIII rebuffed. But other English Catholic women belonging to various orders opened similar houses in Europe where at least three hundred young Englishwomen were schooled in Latin and Greek, French, local languages, mathematics, geography, and astronomy. Moreover, Ward's work was not confined to the continent. Much to the chagrin of the English authorities, she continued her teaching and missionary work in England even after her order was suppressed in 1631. She spent her last years in Yorkshire, a hotbed of Puritanism.[12]

Puritanism in New England foreclosed such educational opportunities. It advanced female education by demanding a basic level of literacy to facilitate Bible reading but at the same time discredited higher learning for women. The absence of convents also foreclosed the administrative experience and empowerment achieved by the women who directed such European establishments. When the sex ratio shifted in the New England seaports and adult women began to outnumber adult men by increasing margins, it was hardly worth remembering that European convents had been—and were—a refuge for surplus women.

Puritan women strongly adhered to their faith, but one can only wonder at the strength it must have taken to disassociate themselves from the symbols of Catholicism. Removed to a remote corner of the world where the agonies of childbirth filled women with as much dread as it had in England, to what spiritual source could they turn for comfort? Although saints had been expunged from the Puritan pantheon, it may have been more than a respect for royalty or a function of family naming patterns that Mary remained the most popular name for New England daughters from 1650 to 1750. Whether this pattern honored the Virgin Mary, a patron saint of childbirth and motherhood, or Mary Magdalene the penitent sinner, no matter. How deliciously rebellious if, in fact, New England women chose this ambiguous way of amending a belief system with which some undoubtedly were at odds. Elizabeth (the second most popular nonbiblical name) was not only the virgin queen, who personally represented ambivalence about the marital state, but a niece of Saint Anne (mother of the Virgin Mary) and a member of the Holy Kindred, or Jesus' extended family.[13]

Some practices allowed to Catholics, Lutherans, and Anglicans must have been difficult for Puritans to abandon even as they opposed them. Midwives from these other denominations were free to baptize infants facing imminent death, a rite Puritans found to rest on shaky scriptural ground, and thus "repugnante" to "the worde of God." Yet many godly New England communities lacked a minister for the first years of settlement. What was the state of such an infant's soul, and how would a parent react to the death of an unbaptized child? The answer seems to be that since infants continued to die, the practice of private baptisms continued to live, and although it never became "custom" in New England, in 1717 the Reverend Benjamin Colman admitted that he occasionally "met" with private baptisms either performed or supported by "the Dominion of the Gentlewomen."[14] It appears that New England women made peace with Puritanism on their own terms.

Churching, a ceremony welcoming a woman into the church after childbirth, was also rejected by radical and reforming Protestants on the grounds that it demeaned women. Puritan women said little about the practice, but the fact that sexual intercourse was prohibited in the weeks prior to the ceremony suggests that women themselves may have favored the practice as a means of contraception as well as a way of taking control of their bodies. Thus, Protestant doctrine notwithstanding, 93 percent of the women in one London parish were amenable to the churching ceremony.[15]

The fact that the religious denominations most vigorously proscribed by the Puritan fathers contained elements attractive to Puritan mothers says something about the nature of New England society. Catholics, Baptists, Quakers, and Anglicans left room for female self-worth because they did not demand complete submission of the self to patriarchal authority. Puritanism made that demand on both men and women, and although Puritan men could eventually regain authority through marriage and domination over their wives, Puritan women had no such opportunity. But competing doctrines allowed a measure of personal judgment that might have been attractive to women. Catholics offered an alternative to marriage, Baptists a choice of voluntary submission as adults, Quakers a more participatory role, and Anglicans an ability to reclaim the self through works. The memory bank of early New Englanders was active in the first decades of settlement, and Puritan women withdrew their accounts as necessary.[16]

Is it entirely coincidental that Roger Williams, who flirted with Baptist doctrine for a short time, "had so far prevailed at Salem, as many there (especially of devout women) did embrace his opinions"? And, conversely, is it surprising that later in the century Cotton Mather, who reflected the most conservative Puritan attitudes toward women, felt that no man was as much the object of female "Venom" as he?[17]

— ⚹ —

The European legacy extended to the physical structures in which Dissenters met. English Puritans gathered secretly in private houses—conventicles by definition—and the term "meetinghouse" (as distinguished from "church") appears to have been a New England invention, since neither the Separatists nor Puritans built meetinghouses in England before 1642. Unauthorized assemblies in private homes probably privileged women to the extent that this was space over which they exerted some control. Indeed, within the confines of her home a woman could hardly have been silenced. Given this tradition and the colonists' immediate needs, it is likely that New England Puritans also met in private houses for the first decade of settlement. Congregations were slow to gather in many places, and few records survive for meeting-houses built between 1632 and 1640.[18]

When New Englanders began to construct meetinghouses, they drew on an English tradition that conflated secular and religious purposes. The distinction between churches and market halls was blurred in England, and settlers emulated this model in Massachusetts. Town officials conducted everyday business in meetinghouses: Thomas Lechford recorded an election held at a Boston meetinghouse in 1642. Shops lined the sides of the Charlestown, Massachusetts, meetinghouse in 1651. As gathering places for every pursuit, such structures dominated community life.[19]

The temporary fusion of secular and religious functions within a single physical structure had far-reaching implications, since it testified to the merging of public and private spheres. Women and men mingled inside and outside the meetinghouse for a variety of purposes, all integral to a well-ordered New England town. Theoretically, Puritans may have propounded the separation of church and state, but their collective memory and daily routine argued otherwise. If Perry Miller is right and few people could grasp the idea that church and state could be distinct entities, the reality of New England life placed women directly within the public sphere and invested them with a status that was elevated by the powers and authority of the church itself.[20] The communal nature of religion and its importance to early New Englanders, the participation of women in the marketplace, and the open (rather than secret) exercise of religion made the gendered notion of a public/private dichotomy meaningless.

The external and internal design of the meetinghouse was also a carry-over of the European church tradition, with a few modifications reflective of doctrinal differences. In an effort to thoroughly disassociate themselves from Catholic tradition, New England meetinghouses eschewed the towers and spires of European cathedrals. Because the Puritans elevated the sermon liturgically, they emphasized the pulpit physically. The seats faced the pulpit rather than the communion table, an innovation that tended to reinforce the importance of the minister as opposed to the sacrament.[21]

Seating patterns also relied on a European tradition that separated women and men—not because of the ancient belief in female impurity, but because of a sixteenth-century fear that amorous attachments might be stimulated by the proximity of male and female congregants. In the 1600s Londoners appear to have initiated a trend toward family pews, although in the countryside, segregation of men and women was more likely to have prevailed. Change was slow to come, and it was not until the nineteenth century that English men and women were integrated in family pews.[22]

In seventeenth-century New England the general rule seems to have favored separate seating. Configurations might differ, but the most frequent pattern finds young men and "maids" separated in the galleries, while adults were segregated in main floor pews. Church elders and the elderly received preferred treatment in front pews, as did the widows of former ministers. In Portsmouth, boys and girls under fourteen sat in the men's and women's galleries; those above fourteen but not yet considered adult sat in the rear of those galleries.[23]

By the eighteenth century the evidence is slightly more ambiguous, with an occasional hint that segregated seating might have been optional and that the idea, at least, of family pews had been introduced to New England churches. On 1 April 1722 Samuel Sewall recorded that he sat with his new wife "in her Pue," and a week later that he "introduced her" into his pew and "sat with her there." And although men and women sat separately in the First Church of Boston at least until the Revolution, in 1731 some progressive church members made a motion to add pews "for men and their Families to sit in." Nevertheless, in the overwhelming majority of cases where records survive, males and females sat apart from each other until the nineteenth century. Blacks appear to have been segregated by race and occasionally by sex as well.[24]

Apart from reducing the potential of sexual misbehavior, segregated seating had the advantage of making it perfectly clear (in terms of sex) who was participating in church discussion or transactions and who was not. From the vantage point of the pulpit, or indeed other pews, it would have been easier to distinguish female voices and raised hands—assuming that was of some interest—if men and women sat separately. And if the family became more, not less, patriarchal over time, integrated seating would have been compatible with a family unit where a husband and father had become more, not less, authoritative and responsible for the behavior of his dependents. This does not negate the possibility of a companionate marriage but rather puts it in its hierarchal perspective.

THE WORLD THEY CREATED

The founding of a New England town was not necessarily synonymous with the gathering of its church. Salem and Boston manifested their godliness by forming churches almost immediately, while Newporters dragged their feet for nearly five years before formally establishing the First Baptist Church. Settlers trickled slowly into Strawberry Bank (or what would become Portsmouth), and although there is evidence of houses and traders in the early 1630s, it was not until the spring of 1640 that the inhabitants granted funds for a "parsonage house," "chapel," and fifty-acre "glebe," in language reminiscent of an English world dominated by Anglican parishes.[25]

Yet whether the formalities were instantly observed or considerably delayed, the gathering of a church must have been a momentous occasion, given the strong religious convictions of the first generation of settlers. Indeed, even though historians, like the contentious ministers about whom they write, engage in vituperative interpretive struggles, there is a remarkable consensus concerning the extraordinary influence of religion on virtually every aspect of New England life.

The evidence also leaves no doubt that women were deeply involved in the process of church building from the moment they affixed their signatures to a church covenant. In 1629, 47 men and 33 women signed such a document in Salem, and when Bostonians gathered their first church in 1630, 64 men and half as many women recorded their names. More than three decades later, 27 women and 24 men signed a similar document, which led to the founding of the First Church of Beverly, Massachusetts—a spinoff from the earlier Salem congregation. Ezra Stiles noted that 12 sisters and 10 brothers were the "Founders" of Newport's Second Congregational Church in 1728.[26]

If religion was vital to New England life, and women an integral component of the church polity at that moment in time when the first generation actually believed in a brave new world, then acceptance of and participation by women could only have enhanced female self-esteem and sense of purpose. Yet our perception of women's role in the various religious institutions has been shaped more by ministerial sermons and pamphlets than by a close examination of the internal organization and operation of the churches.[27] And although clerical literature tends to illustrate widely shared social values, such writing reveals little about the way women functioned in a world controlled by such values.

It is true that the New England ministers were as demanding as the God they served. As the spiritual leaders of the community, they were also the arbiters of morality, which meant that they played no small role in setting standards and exacting behavior that conformed to such prescriptive guidelines. In this effort they were assisted by a variety of parishioners whose exertions served to broaden the definition of "salvation." In short, if churchgoers could not be absolutely certain of their own state of grace, the very least they could do was save other people from themselves and one another.

Since congregants and communicants alike fell into temptation, it required constant attention and certain punishment to prevent those offenses that would try God's patience. Such prevention was time-consuming because the list of crimes was endless. Drunkenness, theft, wantonish (or unseemly) behavior, lying, cruelty toward children, adultery, assault, profanity, and fornication were only a few of the sins churchgoers might commit and for which they would be held accountable by their brothers and sisters. The Society of Friends added to the list compiled by its spiritual antagonists, and thus claimed the right to oversee members who married out of meeting, engaged in the slave trade, or carried arms.

Those who judged also imposed sentence, although the range of penalties that could be dispensed by the church was limited. Blandishments, admonishments, warnings, withdrawal of fellowship, and excommunication were the only means by which churches could keep unruly members in line. The latter two were no small matters to be sure, but perhaps of less concern than the civil penalties for similar infractions.

The obligations of church membership also included consideration of more mundane issues: admission of new members, assessments, the minister's salary, building and repairing the meetinghouse, selling church property, and supporting the poor. From time to time it was necessary to choose a new minister, a process that varied considerably from church to church. Given this potential range of church-related activities and the opportunities they provided for influencing the course of events, what were the actual boundaries of or constraints on female participation? How did they share in the dynamics of church organization? What authority did they have and what decisions did they make? How were their lives affected and how did they affect the lives of others through the church?

The answers to these questions not only are inherently important but take on a potentially greater significance in the context of a distorted sex ratio: numerically speaking, women dominated the church.[28] Evidence from Massachusetts and Rhode Island suggests that throughout most of the colonial period, women dramatically outnumbered men as full members and probably as congregants. In a sense, the church fathers brought this upon themselves because membership in the New England churches was not gender selective, nor was there any overt attempt to limit the number of female members. Ministers knew that God favored men in the human hierarchy, but since salvation itself was gender neutral, it would have been unseemly to exclude visible saints from church membership on the basis of sex. Thus we are left with a paradox, albeit not a surprising one: an extraordinary number of women acting as the rank and file of an institution where men exerted the ultimate authority.

Yet even if such sexual imbalance was common in England by the mid-seventeenth century, it took longer for the same disparity to manifest itself in colonial America.[29] During the first half of the seventeenth century the sex ratio among church members in New England was more or less balanced, and it was not until after 1650 that the number of female admissions soared out of proportion. By the end of the colonial period, nearly 70 percent of those admitted to the churches were female. In terms of numbers this meant that of Increase Mather's 144 visible saints in 1678, a full 100 were women. Between 1664 and 1718 Newport's First Baptist Church recorded the admission of 57 men and only 17 women, but between 1718 and 1776, 42 men and 68 women joined as members. By 1708 Newport's small congregation of Seventh Day Baptists claimed 29 women and 12 men, and a little over a decade later, 17 women and 4 men were admitted to the First Congregational Church in that town. Newport's Second Baptist Church appears to have had the greatest disparity, however: in 1731 a list of members showed 53 men and 119 women, while forty years later, one-third of the church was male, two-thirds female. A report from Salem's East Church in 1718 showed 26 women and 10 men.[30] By the middle of the eighteenth century, the demographic imbalance in Boston's churches resembled the sex ratio of the town itself. The skewed ratio of Newport's churches, however, preceded the rising proportion of women in the larger community.

To sort out (and perhaps even resolve) some of the issues relating to female participation in the dynamics of organized religious life, one must inevitably turn to the records of individual churches and the documents that present the ordinary problems and biases of historical research. They were written by men, they are scattered and sketchy, and they do not detail female activity. Moreover, little survives for the founding years of the Puritan churches. But all this is secondary to the unique ambiguity arising from inconsistency of language, the dubious meaning of words and expressions that have changed over time, and the all too easy assumptions by historians based on the vagueness of seventeenth-century phrases.

Did "brethren" mean just brothers, or brothers and sisters? Did "church" mean the entire religious community? Just the communicants? Male communicants alone? When Martha Foxwell was "summoned before ye congregation" in 1651, was she reproved by men and women alike? When an issue was resolved by the "Joynt Consent of the Congregation," who was involved in that decision? And when a matter was decided by the "silent consent of the church" or by "silentiary vote," should one assume the acquiescence of both males and females? Did a "unanimous vote" mean unanimous or male-unanimous?[31]

To rely on twentieth-century definitions would be a mistake; our attitudes toward the colonists have been clouded by nineteenth-century historical distortions. Furthermore, to assume that the eighteenth century can speak for the seventeenth would be as bad; there were critical changes in the meaning of words over the course of 150 years. To seek answers from seventeenth-century English precedent merely adds to the confusion, since various congregations defended different practices.[32] Thus, it is not altogether clear whether "brethren," "congregation," and "church" refer to men and women or men alone.

Only on the few occasions when entries and documents clarify a word do they become male specific. Thus, in 1685 the Topsfield Congregational Church noted that "there was a contribution by the Church," and then added in parentheses, "that is male-members in full communion." In 1719 Benjamin Colman equated the "church" (outside of Boston) with "male communicants." And when the brethren raised a question in Boston about the definition of the congregation and its powers in 1742/3, a committee of the First Congregational Church reported "that by the Congregation ought to be understood only such male persons as give their constant attendance on the publick worship . . . and who . . . duly assist towards the Support of the Gospel Ministry."[33] Yet one can only wonder why the issue arose to begin with, and why the record keepers felt compelled to define these words. Is it possible that it was not a foregone conclusion that "church" and "congregation" were always synonymous with "male"? Was there a time when the words were understood to include both men and women? Was this a response to the disproportionate increase in female membership during the Great Awakening?

The uncertainty of the language makes the simplest questions difficult to answer. At the most basic level, we should know whether the presence of women can be documented at meetings where issues were considered and decisions reached. Yet it is often impossible to tell who attended meetings because surviving minutes frequently begin with ambiguous words that changed only to indicate the particular community. At an assembly of "the inhabitants of the Sixth Parish in Ipswich," or "of ye inhabitants belonging to the meeting house" in Byfield, it is unclear whether those inhabitants were composed of men and women or men alone. Indeed, we are just beginning to fully understand the word "inhabitant."[34]

The most we can say under the circumstances is that in the early years of Massachusetts Bay women were present at some church meetings, although their presence is attested to in offhand and indirect ways. John Fiske, minister of the Congregational Church in Wenham, Massachusetts, noted in his diary for 1648 that "Brother Fiske's wife being present at the time she was desired to speak." The same year Fiske mentioned that "after the Church meeting" Sister White visited Sister Read and related to her "somewhat of the proceedings of the church," which she could have done only if she had been present. At a business meeting of the First Church in Boston in 1668 a motion was made for certain "dissenting brethren" to absent themselves and "when they were departed, some of their wives continued in the Church," an obvious confirmation of female presence.[35]

In the following year, during a heated controversy in Boston's First Church concerning accusations against the Reverend John Davenport, "they put forth all the sisters, not suffering them to be present, as if their consciences were not to be considered in satisfaction." A week later, when tempers had cooled somewhat, "Mr. Allen [Rev. James Allen] offered something towards the satisfaction of the sisters, who had bin excluded last church meeting." The implication of these remarks is that it was somewhat unusual for women to be excluded from meetings where controversial issues were being debated, that the sisters had complained, and that Rev. Allen felt obligated to "satisfy" the sisters as well as the brothers. In December of that same year, "the first church in Boston had a church meeting where the sisters were particularly warned to be present."[36]

Although the records are few and often fragmentary, there is no evidence that women were systematically excluded from "business" meetings in the founding decades of the Massachusetts Congregational churches. In the eighteenth century, however, the few surviving documents emphasize either their absence or their silence. At Trinity Church in Newport in 1725, business was conducted after announcing that "the majority of males of the Church Congregation" were in attendance. In 1771 Ezra Stiles recorded the presence of the "Sisters" during a business discussion, and although "one of them spake once . . . the Brethren only voted." And in the same year, "At a Meeting of the first Baptist Ch and Congregation," thirty-two men attended—but no women, confirmation of Susan Juster's thesis that women suffered a declining visibility in the evangelical churches of the revolutionary era.[37]

The question of female presence is compounded by the controversy over female speech and the various interpretations of scripture on that point. In 1 Corinthians 14.34–35 Paul admonishes the brethren: "Let your women keep silence in the churches: for it is not permitted unto them to speak; but *they are commanded* to be under obedience, as also saith the law. And if they will learn anything, let them ask their husbands at home: for it is a shame for women to speak in the church."

Strictly interpreted, the Apostle's words posed a quandary for the Congregational churches, because a public profession of faith was a key element of church admission. In Boston, John Cotton took a conservative approach to this issue in 1633 and "desired his wife might . . . be admitted a member . . . but withal requested, that she might not be put to make open confession etc. which he said was against the apostle's rule, and not fit for women's modesty; but that the elders might examine her in private." This policy seems to have gained general acceptance, and by 1641 Thomas Lechford could report that in Boston women usually confessed in private to elders and a "private assembly" of men and women, and then listened while the minister read their testimony aloud.[38]

Conversely, Salem, a comparative bastion of liberalism, originally afforded women the privilege of public confession, if only (and inexplicably) "upon the week days." In explanation, the Reverend John Fiske (whose Wenham congregation originally emanated from Salem) reminded his flock that "this kind of speaking is by submission where others are to judge." A personal revelation did not "argue" or "impart" power to women (which would have been unacceptable) but rather gave the whole church the opportunity to judge a woman's "meetness," which could not be accomplished "if she speak not herself." Fiske knew full well that not all churches agreed with his interpretation and that frequently women would dictate their professions to a church officer, who would subsequently read them aloud. Thus, Fiske was not taken by surprise in 1656 when, after his move to Chelmsford, his new church agreed that "the officer should repeat and declare the relation of the women of the church." One church after another adopted this policy, and as Mary Dunn has observed, by 1660 silence had been imposed on women in the matter of the relation.[39]

While the silencing of women had some connection, no doubt, to the dramatic escalation of female admissions following the Restoration, some women may have been grateful to let a written expression of faith speak for them. It may have been an anxiety-producing experience, and even though men were encouraged to make a "publick relation," they too occasionally asked to be excused from these exercises. Such was the case in Dorchester in September 1672 when some young men agreed to join the church if they "might have ther relation read in wrighting." Their request was not to be taken lightly, given the general shortage of male church members, and it was granted. Similarly, in 1705 the Plymouth elders agreed that by forcing men to make "a personal and oral Relation" it might "hindr the growth of the Church." And in a concession ordinarily limited to women, they voted that men could submit their relation of faith in a document that would be publicly read by someone else as long as the writer "owned" it.[40] The difference between women and men was that women did not seem to have any choice in the matter.

Yet, despite Paul's injunctions, the Puritan fathers allowed for exceptions that depended, not surprisingly, on what was being said and where those words were being expressed. On a nonconfrontational basis, women made motions in the church, as when Mrs. Stoughton requested of Rev. Mather and the church that her children might be baptized, since she was a member of the church by her parents' covenant. And Rev. Fiske implied that motions were "attended to" whether they were proposed by men or women so that "any brother or sister" might be "satisfied."[41]

On the other hand, female prophesying (a more emotive and authoritative form of speech) turned out to be as controversial in Massachusetts Bay as it had been in Europe. Although the covenant written by the minister of Salem's First Church in the late 1630s allowed women to prophesy there, in Boston this practice was restricted to the clergy. As a result, Sarah Keayne, a member of the First Church of Boston, was admonished in 1647 for "hir Irregular prophesying in mixt Assemblies."[42]

First Corinthians 14 was also waived so a repentant woman might exhibit regret in front of an audience. In 1692 the Danvers brethren advised Sister Mary Sibley that if she was convinced that she had acted "sinfully" and was "sorry for it," they would willingly listen to expressions of remorse from her "own mouth." The danger, of course, was that some women might take such opportunities to add insult to injury—as one Plymouth sister did in 1689 when called upon to offer public apology. Instead she carried herself "offensively"—and presumably vociferously.[43] Despite the potential for unexpected diatribe, however, female speech was encouraged as long as its context was submissive, contrite, and nonmenacing—in short, under distinctly unfavorable conditions.

Ann Hibbens must have sensed her disadvantage during excommunication proceedings in 1640 and attempted to use the biblical restriction on female speech to improve her situation. Through one of the brothers, she questioned the "lawfulness of a women's speaking in the church" and requested a stay until the "next Lord's Day" so that with God's help "her scruple may be removed." John Cotton recognized a delaying tactic when he heard one: "It hath been answered already by our teacher that it is lawful for a woman to speak when she is asked a question."[44]

VOICES OF AUTHORITY

Despite the vagueness of many of the church records and the deliberate qualification in others, we may be certain that women not only were present and outspoken at a variety of church meetings but were involved in the decision-making process of many churches as well. That participation included, but was not limited to, the formal expression of choice we know as the vote. Votes brought in new ministers and members, and conversely, votes discharged both clergy and communicants. Sometimes the latter process was at the behest of a minister or other church member who requested his or her own dismissal; at other times a member was involuntarily removed as a result of moral transgressions.

The choice of a minister and fellow church members was crucial to the image and strength of the church itself. In some churches women participated in the selection of a minister; in others they were denied any voice in the matter. In some congregations they voted for admission of new members as well as in disciplinary proceedings; in other congregations they were not permitted to do so. The nature of the records are such, however, that it is impossible to say with any precision how many women voted or what they voted for. Most documents frustrate the reader with a paraphrase of the following resolution—this particular one referring to the choice of a minister in 1732: "The Congregation were called together and allowed the Privilege of a written vote." But who made up the congregation in this instance? Men? Men and women?[45]

English precedent is not helpful because historians differ in their reading of relevant documents. Anne Laurence maintains that the English radical sects allowed women a vote in the congregation and for elders, deacons, and ministers. Patricia Crawford's survey, however, suggests that in many such congregations women were disqualified from voting. Controversy and ambiguity followed the Dissenters across the Atlantic, and although John Cotton was elected to lead Boston's First Congregational Church in 1633 "by all the congregation testifying their consent by erection of hands," such language is not conclusive of an all-inclusive church polity.[46]

Of the Congregational churches in Boston, the Brattle Street Church (or Fourth Congregational Church) has the most interesting history as far as female voting rights are concerned. Quickly labeled "the Manifesto Church" for its statement of governing principles, it stood to the left of its sister churches in terms of doctrine. Not content to practice without announcing what he preached, the twenty-six-year-old minister, Benjamin Colman, encountered "differences and troubles" (not to mention the wrath of the Mathers) after he published his Manifesto in November 1699. Article 16 of this document was the heart of the controversy: "We cannot confine the right of chusing a minister to the Male communicants alone, but we think that every Baptized Adult Person who contributes to the Maintenance, should have a Vote in Electing."[47]

Increase Mather responded immediately and testily to this heresy with a lengthy pamphlet entitled *The Order of the Gospel* (1700), in which he argued against Colman's proposition. "If all that Contribute have power to Vote in the Election of a Pastor, then many women must have that Priviledge, for they may Contribute to the Maintenance. But this the Apostle allows not of. 1 Cor 14 34, 35."[48]

The particular apostle in question was Paul, but Mather's citation did not support his position. A lesser scholar than he could have reasoned that even if chapter and verse prohibited speech, a woman could lift her hand or sign a document to record her choice and still remain the Lord's obedient servant. Mather was on safer ground when he reminded Colman that the synod that met in Boston in 1662 explicitly declared "that the power of voting in the Church, belongs to Males in full communion, and that others are to be debarred from that Power."[49] Furthermore, the question was not only one of gender. Perhaps more important was the implicit issue of non-communicants outvoting communicants when the former greatly outnumbered the latter.

Colman lost no time answering Mather in *The Gospel Order Revived*. The good minister stood his ground by avoiding the gender issue altogether and limiting his remarks to the rights of communicants versus non-communicants. Colman pointed out that the Bible itself negated Mather's argument because in the "first ages of the Church, Pastors were chosen by all and only their flocks." And he dismissed Mather's stronger claim—that of the synod's determination—and the "Law of the Land" by cavalierly asserting that the rules did not apply to Boston, and even if they did "as they were done by men, so they may be altered and undone by the same men, when they please."[50]

The Reverends John Higginson and Nicholas Noyes of Salem were also among those who expressed their hostility to the Manifesto. Their objections were twofold, one based on gender, the other on democratic tendencies—both of which had the potential propensity "to subvert the ministry," as well as grace, order, and liberty. "Females," the penmen reminded the Brattle Street supporters, "are certainly more than males, and consequently the choice of ministers is put into their hands." Equally distasteful was the thought of allowing baptized adult noncommunicants a role in the electoral process, since they clearly outnumbered communicants and were likely to "make worse work in all the churches than we are willing to say."[51] Thus Higginson and Noyes explicitly rejected the idea of democratic rule, an undesirable side effect of Congregationalism to which Mather only alluded.

At the same time, it is difficult to know what actually transpired within the walls of the Brattle Street Church. In a 1719 letter to Robert Wodrow, Colman explained how ministers were selected by the various Massachusetts churches. Outside of Boston "the Church (which is to say, the Male Communicants at the Lords table)" nominated a pastor and then the entire congregation confirmed or rejected him. But the law left Boston "to their liberty or former usage," which meant that the communicants independently selected a minister and then advised the congregation of their choice without permitting "a second Vote of Concurrence." Colman eschewed this implicit elitism, and remarked that his congregation "practice[d] otherwise." But did "otherwise" include women?[52]

The most persuasive evidence suggests that even if women did exercise a limited franchise in a few of the Congregational churches in Massachusetts

Bay, such participation was tenuous. The First Church of Plymouth counted only male votes before the turn of the eighteenth century. In 1686 the elders and brethren voted for an additional deacon "man by Man," and in 1693 "voting could be by lifting up of hands, sometimes by silence, sometimes calling upon every brother one after another to speak his minde." At a meeting of the First Congregational Church of Boston in May 1731 "the male-members" voted to raise the salary of the minister. And after the brethren of the Eighth Church of Boston discussed an issue to their satisfaction in 1742, "each man declared himself Ripe for a vote."[53]

In Boston's Trinity Church in 1735, the proprietors and benefactors voted that in the future only pew owners could vote for the minister, church officers, and "all afairs in the Church." As a result, Mary Marshall and Ann Wroe joined the brethren who selected a minister in 1746, although their presence only confirms the dearth of eligible female pew owners.[54]

In 1629 the First Congregational Church of Salem announced that it would allow "every member (being men)" to have "a free voice of their officers etc.," although at least one other Salem church eventually developed a more permissive tradition. A 1783 list of the proprietors of the East Meeting House who voted that "their Interest Be Incorporated for the Settlement and Support of a Gospel Minister" included twelve women out of a total of eighty people.[55] Yet twelve was a small proportion of the whole.

An examination of church records in Newport, Rhode Island, suggests that practices varied as much there as they did in the Bay Colony. At the only Anglican church in Newport, women could not vote, and Stiles admitted in 1771 that as far as the Congregational churches were concerned, he "never knew or read of the Sisters voting: they often stay with the Brethren and see and hear what is transacted, but dont even speak in the Church."[56]

But in the Baptist churches—which claimed seniority in Newport—women voted. And it is in these Baptist churches that one can see the conflicts and challenges that arose as a result. The earliest documented evidence is from the records of the Seventh Day Baptist Church. In a move to allow the Baptists at Westerly some autonomy in 1708, the Newport affiliates agreed that their comrades in spirit could be "a distinct Congregation by themselves . . . provided the brethren and sisters at Newport [that] were not present att said meeting do consent thereto." When the members of the Second Baptist Church called Gardner Thurston to the ministry in 1758, forty-six women were included among the seventy-four subscribers.[57]

Yet Ezra Stiles suggested that the question of women voting was being debated at the very time he was putting quill to paper, and his remarks imply that men became uneasy if women voted as a group on specific issues. "In a memorable controversy" in 1747 or 1750, "the *Sisters generally voted*" not to dismiss Elder Eyres. This did not sit well with Mr. Green and other men who objected that "it was done by the Sisters vote." To emphasize his point, Stiles also related a story about the sisters who voted for the admission of Mr. Manning to the Baptist Church in Providence even though "it was not agreeable to Elder Windsor." Since it did not escape Elder Windsor's notice that the women had voted as a bloc, he "asked the opinion of the next Baptist Association, *whether the Sisters had a right to vote in Chh Meetings*."[58]

Although it was plain to Stiles in 1771 that it was a "practiced Principle among the Baptists of the Colony . . . to admit the Sisters to equal votes in the Chh meetings and this by *Lifting Up* of Hands," it was just as clear that only "some few of the aged Sisters" continued to avail themselves of the privilege, while "the younger sisters keep their places and say nothing. . . . Probably their Voting is growing into Disuetude—so that the usage may be intirely dropt in another Generation." His prophecy was correct, at least for one Baptist church. At a Second Baptist Church meeting in Newport on 29 January 1801 seven men and twelve women outvoted six men and one woman. Although the outcome would have been the same if only the men had participated, the potential risk of women casting the deciding ballots was too great. Later that same meeting, "it was Voted the Sisters Be Excluded from Voting to Govern the Church."[59]

While the Baptists seemed more willing than either Congregationalists or Anglicans to extend a share of church governance to women, it was only the Quakers who even approached equality. In Newport, for example, it is clear that Quaker women were expected to vote on a wide range of issues and otherwise participate in the running of the meeting.

The meeting minutes of the Society of Friends in Newport begin in 1676 and continue throughout the eighteenth century. From the earliest years there were men's meetings, women's meetings, and mixed meetings, which gathered weekly, monthly, or quarterly. Here, as elsewhere, the language is ambiguous, because while the women's meeting seems to have excluded men, the men's meeting was not necessarily devoid of women. The minutes of the gathering, which begin with the words "at a Man's Meeting . . . the 27 day 1680," go on to explain that "the men and women being together did agree that it will be of service to meet the next monthly men and women's meeting at the Eight [h]our."[60]

The women's meeting did not merely rubber-stamp the men's meeting. While some "weighty matters" were referred to the men's meeting for discussion, women elected their own elders and committees, collected and disbursed money, and denied "unity" to women who breached the rules of the Society. Both the men's meeting and the women's meeting had separate incomes, both passed judgment on marriage proposals, and both could make unilateral decisions.[61]

Outside the Society of Friends, the issue of female participation intersected with issues of class. There was a great deal of difference between allowing female proprietors or pew owners a say in church governance and extending that same privilege to female church members and congregants. Trinity Church in Boston could afford to let female proprietors vote because there were so few of them. And even if women were included when the proprietors of the North Brick (Seventh Church) agreed to let all persons vote who had purchased places in the meetinghouse, this was hardly risky business. Only two or three women were ever mentioned in the records as purchasers.

Opening the decision-making process to include either female communicants or congregants meant giving all women (not just elite women) a disproportionate say in church matters. Thus, even if his own church was an exception, Benjamin Colman could say of Boston generally that women were allowed "no share in the government of the Church." In fact, women held no positions of authority outside the Society of Friends, with the possible exception of the widow Mary Gammidge of Gloucester, who was elected "Saxton" of the Fifth Parish in 1757 and who remained in that office until 1767, when Thomas Dresser replaced her as "Parish Clark and Saxton," at the same salary.[62]

Whether or not women actually cast votes on specific issues, the fact remains that voting is only one means of participation, only one manner of expressing an opinion or choice. A course of events may be influenced by procedures other than the franchise, and power may be exercised in the absence of formal authority. Issues related to church membership, for example, provided a setting hospitable to female influence. At John Fiske's church in Chelmsford in 1656, both "brethren and sisters" were invited "to be present" when testimony concerning the "life and conversation" of a prospective member was given. Should there have been objections to the person who was being propounded, there is no reason to assume that the sisters would have remained silent.[63]

The procedures in the First Congregational Church of Essex were more complicated, but the result was probably the same. The pastor and ruling elders examined the candidates and read the relation of their experiences "to the Church in the Public Congregation." At that time, if the Church "have no objections against the candidates which they signify by a vote, such persons are to stand propounded a fortnight from that time; and public notice is given when they are propounded that if any member of the Church wants further satisfaction respecting the persons propounded, they have an opportunity to seek it, by conversing with them in private."[64]

Thus, even if the vote by "the Church" was limited to males—and the evidence on this point is inconclusive—circumstances would still have permitted women to gain "further satisfaction," should they have desired to do so. Furthermore, if anyone was privy to information about the principles or morals of the people propounded, they were requested to come forward and share that information. In short, even if women did not vote on membership in the common sense of the word, they could still "vote" by imparting information that would prejudice the outcome one way or another. Theoretically, therefore, this process assured women a role in selecting voting members of the church, thus providing them with indirect church governance.

One may infer that theory translated into reality in this instance because the testimony of women as witnesses was taken seriously in membership as well as in disciplinary proceedings. Although only men voted in the First Church of Salem, the "sisters" were expected to give testimony in support of people proposed for membership, and in the Wenham Church in 1663, the testimony of two women and one man provided the information that determined Sarah Fiske's admission. In 1685 in the Second Church of Boston, Goodwife Fuller was excommunicated for "drinking to excess" on the testimony of four women and two men. In similar fashion, when Rev. Blinman of Gloucester had a grievance against a member of John Fiske's church at Wenham in 1646, he produced female as well as male witnesses to support his case. More than a century later, Brother Samuel Maryott was charged with railing or speaking disrespectfully of the elders. He denied the charge, but "by the evidence of Sister Ann Sabin and Ann Cartwright" the members of Newport's Seventh Baptist Church church concluded he was guilty and admonished him to repent.[65]

The common act of renewing the covenant required a decision by churchgoers. Although the church elder in Dorchester reminded the congregation in 1676/7 that "they weer . . . not to be admitted to the Lords table, nor

Voteing in the Church," but only "to declare ther willingness to subjection to the government and discipline of Christ in and by his Church," this issue demanded the consent of the female members of the church and congregation. Indeed, approximately two-thirds of the respondents were female. The emerging idea of a compact or contract based on the consent of the governed—one of the basic doctrines of modern Anglo-American political theory—was not confined to men, at least not in the colonial churches.[66] Nevertheless, its egalitarian tendencies as they affected women should not be overemphasized: the same compact theory could and would be used to justify female submission within marriage on the grounds that women chose to enter such a relationship.

In Plymouth some months earlier, the same scene had been enacted. A paper was read concerning members in full communion, after which "the church was called upon to manifest their consent thereunto by standing up, which all both Elders and Brethren and sisters did." The pastor then spoke "to all the children of this Chh" and read a paper in which they agreed to "owne our interest in the Covenant. This being read the Pastor called upon all the adult children of the Chh to manifest their consent unto, which they readily did all of them both males and females by standing up."[67] The concept of government by consent consists, at least in part, of an agreement to abide by the rules of a particular body, be it secular or religious. It is not likely that women formulated the rules of such institutions or consistently chose the people who did. Nevertheless, they played an active (rather than passive) role by agreeing to be bound by those rules, and in this sense they were part of the decision-making process. It is not too much to say that the process may have fostered a sense of inclusion among women as well as a heightened self-worth.

By the mid-eighteenth century a church might have offered a constitution as well as a covenant for the approval of members and congregation. In 1746 the First Congregational Church of Essex published "Articles of Faith and Discipline," which outlined, in great detail, the qualifications and election procedures for church officers, requirements for admission, duties of the pastor, and points at which the church took exception to the Cambridge Platform. Eight men signed this document, after which other people—presumably communicants—were asked to ratify it. Thirty-two white women and twenty-five white men did so, along with two black women and two black men. The same number of men and women agreed and consented to the church covenant in 1746, and other names were added to both lists in the following decades. Between 1750 and 1773, ninety-one women and thirty-six men signed the document. Presumably, this was an important decision and a meaningful ritual for all concerned.[68]

Such experience with covenants, renewals, and constitutions provided education in self-government and even encouraged women to strike out on their own. Thus, when a number of pious women approached the twenty-seven-year-old widow Sarah Wheaten in 1741, she agreed to help them form a religious society in Newport and act as their spiritual advisor. At its height the society claimed over sixty members, most of whom belonged to the First Congregational Church.[69]

To formalize its creation, each member of the society signed a compact that outlined rules of conduct and that provided for future signatories. Articles relating to membership, meeting times, financial considerations, confidentiality, and behavioral oversight and admonishment were carefully recorded, as were provisions for the removal of impenitent, scandalous sinners. Osborn remained the head of the society "by unanimous consent," while other matters were left "to the discretion and decision" of the majority—a concession to democratic principles.

That this group directly affected church politics is borne out by the fact that in 1770 Osborn and her society were instrumental in calling the abolitionist Samuel Hopkins to the ministry of the First Congregational Church. This event occasioned severe unrest because it pitted Osborn against those who were either opposed "or only luke warm" in their support of Rev. Hopkins's candidacy. "Mrs. Osborn and the Society of her Meeting are violently engaged and had great Influence." Indeed, they prevailed.[70]

Osborn and her group were hardly unique in their ability to influence a ministerial appointment, although they were among the most overtly partisan. Another sequence of events, recorded in the Danvers church records, suggests the more subtle ways in which women's opinions became decisive factors in the selection of a pastor. In 1695 eighty-four persons from Salem Village (seventeen young men, twenty-nine householders, six male and eleven female communicants, five freeholders, and sixteen female non-members) sent an "instrument" to the elders of several churches meeting at Cambridge. The signatories expressed their frustration at their internal conflicts, laying blame on the Reverend George Parris. In their reply, the elders urged Parris's removal.[71]

Within the month the elders received another paper, this time subscribed to by 105 persons: twenty-four female and twenty-nine male householders,

and twenty-five male and twenty-seven female church members. In a somewhat surprising rebuff to the elders, the villagers claimed that they had had
too many ministers already and that they had decided to retain Parris.[72]
Clearly women were participating in decisions that affected the future of the
church. It is difficult to determine how often women were involved in issues
of this nature, but there is no reason to assume, given the existing evidence,
that their opinions were unsolicited or perfunctorily accepted. Indeed, the
women of Danvers were helping to select their minister just as surely as if
Parris was among several contenders on a ballot.

Serving on an investigative committee whose members visited parishioners charged with infractions of church rules or who otherwise had difficulties was another means of exerting power over the lives of others. In the
founding decades, at least, Congregational churches occasionally appointed
women to such committees, while the Quakers consistently refused to excuse
women from this obligation. In the Society of Friends it is likely that female
committees visited women and male committees visited men, although the
women's meeting judged the marriage suitability of both partners. If the importance of the occasion demanded it, both female and male delegations
might make separate reports.[73]

Although the extent to which Quaker women participated on these committees sets them apart from women in other churches, Quaker women
seemed less than eager to act as "visitors." In 1773 the women's meeting had
difficulty finding enough women willing to serve in that capacity. "Lydia
Chase and Sarah Howland . . . concented to fill the station of visitors for a
time hopeing thereby others may be incouraged to assist or releive them—
Amy Thurston and Dorcas Earle boath decline it for the present." After serving for a year, Howland dropped out on the grounds that she was not "in a
situation to perform such a weighty Service."[74]

In the first decades of the eighteenth century, the Seventh Day Baptists
of Newport also named women to committees to visit parishioners who
strayed from prescribed behavior. The issues might have involved fornication, excessive debts, or a combination of problems, and the committees
would subsequently report their findings to the Church. No records suggest
whether the committees' functions included recommendations, or whether
they were merely investigative. In any event, whatever information they provided influenced the lives of their fellow congregants.[75]

Female Baptists and Quakers were also more likely to keep books and
handle money than their sisters in other churches. Several of Elder Crandall's

congregants—all female—presented "an account of money" to him in 1718. Many decades later, "the meeting house was painted which cost twenty dollars the money collected by the women and young people of the church." Female members of the Society of Friends consistently collected and disbursed money, neither of which was an insignificant task, since collection implied recognition as representatives of the church, while allocation of funds included decision-making authority. Payments were made not only to the poor, but for current expenses: to Thomas Leach £1/6, for a wool bed 6 shillings, and in varying amounts to saddlers, for ferriage, butter, or clothing. Sixteen shillings went to "the woman Carter that helps the widow Stapleton." So important was record keeping to the Quakers that they dipped into their limited funds to pay a secretary "for writing the meeting."[76]

A QUESTION OF POWER

The churches, like all other institutions in colonial America, provided a setting for the usual power contests. It was another arena where men and women struggled for control over their own lives while they simultaneously made decisions that determined the path other lives would take. Because of its commitment to self-government, however, the congregational form of church polity raised multilayered questions about authority that were difficult to resolve. Majority rule became an issue because the congregation eventually outnumbered communicants by a great majority, and even worse, the feminization of the churches meant that women outnumbered men by appreciable margins. Under such conditions, how could a small group of men retain control over the single most important institution in New England? Alternatively, what powers did the majority have to restrain the minority and prevent the total submission of the former?

Given the unplanned demographics, the most important means of control employed by the church leadership was systematic suppression of female speech.[77] Although this approach to social control was hardly innovative in the seventeenth century, the concept could claim a special justification in the Bible Commonwealth because it rested on the biblical authority of 1 Corinthians. As a result of Paul's injunctions, the church fathers were able to define the limits of female speech, which meant that women could be punished if they exceeded those boundaries. Punishments ranged from admonition to excommunication, depending on the infraction, and were meted out for a variety of reasons, the most severe of which were imposed when a woman challenged male authority.

At first, Ann Hibbens was only admonished for charging that "sundry of the brethren" who were joiners set "extortionously . . . high rates upon their worke." When she persisted in her accusations, however, and did not "[hearken] to her husband at home," she was excommunicated. Although Ann Hett tried to drown her children, her excommunication was based on additional charges: "for blasphemous speeches against God . . . and likewise for her stubborne unruliness with her husband." To link the latter two accusations meant equating God with husband, a parallel with which at least some members of the Puritan colony were comfortable, even if doctrine demanded that God's word took precedence over a husband's demand. Hett's only recourse was repentence, at which time she was reinstated. The lesson was clear: submissiveness protected church membership; assertiveness threatened it.[78]

Other women learned the same lesson. Judith Smith received a sentence of excommunication for persisting in lies "in the Congregation," and when Phillip Harding (wife of Robert) challenged the censures heaped upon Ann Hutchinson, Harding was cast out "for speaking evill of Authority both in Church and Commonweale"—this on the testimony of two male witnesses. In 1669 Mary Wharton was excommunicated "for reviling of her husband and striking of him," while three years later Mercy Verin was cast out "for uncivill Carriage with Samuel Smith and bad language to her husband."[79]

In 1649 Goodye Shelley suffered excommunication for slander and "conceived Jealousyes." She condemned the Brethren "many times . . . that they delt not with her in a way of God." And when Sister Weston challenged two male jurors in a civil case, they were offended enough to bring the matter to the attention of the church, where she was severely reprimanded for the affront. We will never know whether it was disorderly singing or refusing to labor that cost Sister Hogg her church membership in 1657, but there is little doubt that when Mrs. Clark was charged with slander, she was excommunicated for "the sin of an ungoverned tongue."[80]

A strong assault on the ministry by an indiscreet woman might even warrant interference by the civil authorities, who could mete out a more severe punishment. Thomas Trusler's wife was fined in 1644 for saying that their teacher, Mr. Norris, taught the people lies, and "that there was no love in the church and that they were biters and devourers." In her defense, she responded that "before she came to New england she knew that men were not the foundation of the Church." Two years later, Thomas Oliver's wife had good reason to wish she had never said that "all ministers were blood-thirsty men," because the court sentenced her "to be tied to the whipping post with a slit stick on her tongue."[81]

Mrs. Phelps had her choice of a fine or whipping when she insisted that Mr. Higgeson "sent abroad his wolves and his bloodhounds amongst the sheep and lambs, and that the priests were deceivers of the people." The widow Mary Hamond went a step further in 1682 by protesting that "going to hear the minister preach [was] the way to hell," but she was only admonished for these reproachful words—perhaps in deference to her age.[82]

It did not always take such harsh words to evoke a strong response from the authorities. Mrs. Coats was admonished in July 1646 for pointing out that "Christ was circumcized on the eighth day, and that then he was not baptized." Why this comment precipitated punishment becomes clear when, in the same month, two women and a man were admonished "for offensively with drawing from infant baptism." Rhode Island was becoming a Baptist stronghold at the same time, and the combined attack on the clergy and receptivity to Baptist indoctrination must have been threatening to Congregational leaders in Massachusetts Bay. On the other hand, it did not take much to threaten them. The wife of William Edwards was admonished "for striking a man and scoffing at his membership."[83] Presumably, this meant something other than church membership.

Voices emanating collectively from groups of women could seem even more threatening to the Puritan patriarchy than the words of individual women. Clerics in mid-seventeenth-century England frequently denounced women's meetings because they appeared to represent the exercise of authority; George Fox, even though he encouraged such meetings, still maintained that women were to be silent in the church and subject to their husbands. Initially, English Baptists discouraged women from speaking anywhere but in female associations.[84]

Female meetings came under attack in Boston during the Antinomian controversy in 1637, when a synod resolved "that though women might meet (some few together) to pray and edify one another; yet such a set assembly, (as was then in practice in Boston,) where sixty or more did meet every week, and one woman (in a prophetical way, by resolving questions of doctrine, and expounding scripture) took upon her the whole exercise, was agreed to be disorderly, and without rule."[85]

The surviving records do not tell us whether the suppression of female speech stifled criticism and encouraged silence, yet women must have known that they would pay a hefty price for asserting themselves. If silence and sub-missiveness were the twin keys to a harmonious relationship with the church authorities, women may have either consciously or unconsciously chosen that path. In the Quaker meetings this translated into the expulsion of re-calcitrant males for a variety of transgressions, whereas women who con-sistently gave satisfaction by submissively condemning themselves were retained as members in good standing. And although the First Church of Boston almost always forgave and forgot after appropriate expressions of re-morse, the brethren of the First Church of Salem were not as quick to agree to the reinstatement of a female transgressor unless contrite actions matched contrite words.[86]

Whatever issues may have sparked patriarchal concerns, efforts to silence women were successful. Church-related documents record fewer female voices as the seventeenth century progressed, although the motivating forces that precipitated the decline were not limited to speech alone. It is likely that the increasing number of female church members after 1660 exaggerated the threat that outspoken women seemed to pose, and the cacophony of English female voices at midcentury only reinforced perceptions that women were the source of civil unrest. Witchcraft accusations escalated precipitously in both England and America during this period as officials on both continents conflated aberrant women with unnatural affairs of state. After linking the prevalence of witchcraft and "strange opinions" to events in England, Ire-land, and Scotland, the magistrates of Massachusetts Bay ordered a day of humiliation.[87]

If women were censured for loose tongues, their loose morals were also a source of some concern. Men defined disorderly conduct; men stipulated the rules by which women were determined immoral. As a result, women were disproportionately charged with fornication and excessive drinking. Al-though men were occasionally brought up on fornication charges and often chastised for imbibing excessively, it is clear that women bore the brunt of these accusations.

Whether this numerical distortion was discriminatory is another matter altogether. Seventeenth- and eighteenth-century records do not tell us whether men or women were the heavier drinkers, nor can one assume that exactly the same number of women and men were fornicators. One peripa-tetic male and several compliant females could produce a legitimate imbal-ance in the sex ratio of sexual offenders. It may also be that women were accused more often because they—and not their husbands or lovers—were under the care of the church. But if seventeenth-century women were also treated more harshly than men in the civil arena, where the sex ratio was considerably more balanced in the seventeenth century, the case for discrimination becomes more powerful. Accusations of immoral conduct then become, like the suppression of speech, a means by which the church leadership exercised control and domination over women in a society where good or bad reputations enhanced or undermined power relationships.

Women may have been acceptable witnesses in such proceedings, but in most cases, particularly as the colonial era reached maturity, men rendered decisions about guilt or innocence. In the Congregational churches, the committees that visited accused women quickly became all-male groups, and male "brethren" condemned the transgressors. In such a setting, female witnesses may have been hesitant to alienate men who might one day pronounce judgment against them. Thus, as supportive of other women as they might have wished to be, self-interest may have influenced testimony. As far as men were concerned, however, today's male witness or defendant might be tomorrow's judge, giving the brethren reason to think twice about treating one of their own too harshly. This is not to say that men were never admonished or warned to repent: they were, but in far smaller numbers.

Once cast out of the church, repentance was the only path to a restoration of church membership, and it required a submissiveness that women were required to show to the church's satisfaction. In 1727 Sarah Merrifield, a member of the First Church of Christ in Ipswich, having committed "the odious sin of Fornication . . . was ordered to abstain from coming to the Lords Table til upon her Manifest [Humiliation] and Repentence the Chh should see meet to Restore her." And although Abigail Kippins confessed and repented "drinking and Fuddling to excess" in 1681, the brethren were not satisfied with her "poenitent words without works" and she was admonished. It took Kippins seven months to apologize to the satisfaction of the brethren.[88]

Despite disadvantages, women still had considerable leverage because of their numbers. Most important, they could independently request dismissal to another church, and in a variation of the same theme, they were not automatically dismissed with their husbands. Although some ministers "conceived" that women were "supposed to go with their husbands," in practice women acted according to conscience, and while it may have been desirable for married couples to worship together, it was not compulsory. As the elders at Salem concluded, "Tis satisfaction enough that she be a member of another church."[89]

Dismissals were usually granted with a minimum of fuss. In 1677 the brethren of Boston's Second Church "consented that sister [Baker] should be dismissed to the Church in Dorchester." The desire for consensus and harmony was strong enough in most churches that even a rebellious sister would be granted dismissal if she chose to leave, and on many occasions the act would have been welcomed by the rest of the church. Women may also have voted in the dismissal procedure, a conclusion suggested by an incident in 1696 when several brethren and sisters in Danvers were dismissed to another church by the consent of "a full or universall vote at the motion and desire of sd Brethren and sisters." At the same time, dismissal was not automatic. When Sister Blake asked to be excused to another church, several votes were taken before a narrow margin approved her request.[90]

The issue, which was as much political as religious, became more complicated when a group of men and women asked for dismissal in order to form a new church. Although the reasons for the request were not always clear, the numerical disparity between the sexes usually was. In 1667, 27 women and 23 men requested dismissal from the First Church of Salem to form their own church in Beverly. And when the Marblehead members sought to separate from the First Church of Salem in 1684, 14 men and 36 women made the appeal. The First Church shrank in size again in 1713 when 27 women and 13 men petitioned for a new church, and once again in 1718 when 26 women and 10 men chose to depart. This time, the First Church voted to meet on 25 December "to consider the request of our Brethren etc. in the Eastern District to be Dismissed and recommended from this Church in order to their being Constituted a Distinct Church." (The sisters appear to have been the "etc.") It is not likely that the remaining brethren received the petition with any enthusiasm. Spiritual considerations aside, an erosion of members diminished a church's assessment base, which meant that any decision to renounce affiliation and create a new polity had to be considered seriously by all parties. Moreover, since the minister had already been selected by the time the splinter group petitioned the First Church in 1713, it is likely that women had some say—perhaps even a determining one—in the choice.[91]

Although, as Laurel Ulrich points out, geography undoubtedly played a role in the decision to form a new church, internal conflicts and disagreements with the minister or ruling elders might persuade any number of people that their interests were better served at another church. Such was the case when dissenting members of the First Church of Boston seceded and formed the Third Church in 1669. The original dissidents (at least on paper) were the brethren—twenty-eight of whom had requested dismissal in 1667. The petition was not granted, and the remaining brethren of the First Church did everything possible to convince the sisters (many of whom were married to the seceding brethren) not to defect. First Church elders refused to permit the women to take communion with their husbands at the Third Church, which was a mistake, because had this request been granted, the women implied they would have remained at the First Church. When the sisters finally presented a petition for dismissal in January 1669/70 (on scriptural grounds), Elder Pen pocketed it for three days and, in the interest of procrastination, demanded that each woman submit a separate request of "two or three lines." Two weeks later, when "after much agitation" it was "put to vote," the sisters were denied dismissal. The dissenting brethren never received permission either, but both men and women left anyway, and the rebuff only served to impede rather than halt the formation of the Third Church.[92]

During the Great Awakening, Samuel Mather, an Old Light opponent of the revival, left the Second Church of Boston—which had been the church of his father, Cotton, and grandfather Increase. With a group of his supporters Mather formed the Tenth Church of Boston in 1741/2. That the opinions of his female constituency were not to be taken lightly was made obvious in their petition for dismissal: "We the Subscribers, from a hearty Dislike of the Proceedings against our dear Pastor Mr. Mather ... and from the Benefit which we have had ... from his Ministry, think it our Duty to withdraw and continue with him." Seventy-one women signed the petition, 8 had second thoughts, and 63 were finally dismissed. Twenty-nine men also requested permission to follow Mather, leaving 80 men and 181 women in the Second Church. The Second Church had lost 25 percent of its membership.[93]

If a woman chose to remain within the folds of her church despite her discontent, there was little she could do to seek redress. Aggressive speech brought stiff reprisals, and a Massachusetts law requiring church attendance meant that she risked fines if she absented herself. Women did take that chance, however, and the Essex County Court records indicate that women were called to account for their absences more frequently than men, a suggestive indicator of social control even if the disparity is merely a reflection of the disproportionate numbers of male and female church members.[94]

CHURCH MEMBERSHIP AS OPPORTUNITY

Despite the patriarchal and hierarchical nature of the church, membership and participation offered women political, organizational, and financial opportunities. Such cumulative experience was at once public and prestigious, and although not all women shared the benefits of these opportunities, all women saw female friends, neighbors, and kin accumulating skills that, whether they realized it or not, added to their competence just as they did for men. Women attended joint business meetings, held independent women's meetings, kept books, saw to the use and disbursement of funds, had oversight of poor parishioners, and took their place on visiting committees that refereed behavior. Indeed, women on visiting committees could and did vote to admonish men as well as women, which, when added to their role as civil witnesses, gave them some leverage over male behavior. They chose their church minister and fellow members.

Given the range of permissible activities, it is conceivable that women joined the churches in such disproportionate numbers not because of an overload of piety genes but because their ability to influence was maximized in this corner of the public arena. If this interpretation is even partially accurate, then it follows that women had a stake in the power struggle between church and state, because as the power of the church waned and that of the all-male state rose, women lost personal power in the process.

At the same time, liberty of conscience (even within its narrow New England confines) was liberating for women. Albeit reluctantly, women were permitted to join churches separate from their husbands' place of worship, a decision that ever so subtly hinted at an independent female identity. Most women joined evangelical churches alone, without spouses or other family members.[95] The most immediate danger to such permissiveness was that it legitimized opposition to one's husband and in so doing undermined the patriarchal order, just as female admonishment of men turned hierarchy on its head.

How all this played out is evident in Rhode Island, where Roger Williams, women, and the devil appeared to have entered into a conspiracy. The problem arose initially when women interpeted Williams's stricture "that no man should be molested for his conscience" to mean women as well as men, and then "claimed liberty . . . to go to all religious meetings" despite spousal objections. John Winthrop reported in his journal in 1638 that "because one Verin refused to let his wife go to Mr. Williams so oft as she was called for,"

Williams's adherents demanded Verin's censure. "One Arnold," however, argued against this liberal construction of liberty of conscience, and insisted that "when he consented to that order, he never intended it should extend to the breach of any ordinance of God, such as the subjection of wives to their husbands." In the ensuing debate, "one Greene" reminded the brethren that "if they should restrain their wives, etc., all the women in the country would cry out of them, etc"—a comment that suggests how broadly women perceived female religious liberty.[96] It also appears that although Verin walked away uncensured, Williams and his followers prevailed on the more important issue—the rights due to female conscience.

When a similar issue arose in Massachusetts in 1656, the results were much the same. The General Court insisted that Joan Halsell had liberty to go to "publicke meetings on the Lords and lecture days, or at other times . . . without interruption or disturbances" from her husband George.[97]

The opposition of a woman to a husband's error in word or deed was not only legitimized by church authorities but demanded by them as well. In 1725/6 the First Baptist Church of Newport refused to allow Mary Vaughn communion until she acknowledged the "Evil" she had perpetuated by "countenancing her husband in the breaking of a bargain or covnant between him and Lawrance Clark."[98] In short, church officials expected Mary Vaughn to repudiate her husband's actions. Vaughn's husband, John, does not appear to be a member of the First Baptist Church, and this episode suggests that the church could intercede between husband and wife even when one was a nonmember. From the standpoint of a patriarchal society such intercession could backfire, since it supported and encouraged female independence. Indeed, the danger of female assertiveness was that once women got the hang of it, they could use it to challenge church as well as spousal authority. Not only did women capitalize on this potential, but they did so on Saint Paul's terms: in silence.

Female muteness in the face of criticism was taken as strident rebuttal to the charges and clear evidence of unsubmissive behavior. Women embarked on this route at their peril, because in almost every case their refusal to respond to charges resulted in excommunication until they yielded. In Boston in 1669 the church asked Brother Negus's daughter to answer fornication charges, "but her mother would not suffer her to come forth into the Congregation."

In Newport the church withdrew from Sarah Langworthy after she refused "to hear the church when Required." A comparable fate awaited Mehetable Telford, who "neglected to hear the Church" when accused of adultery. Susanna Spensebe erred by absenting herself from worship and engaging in unchristian, scandalous conduct. As she refused to answer these charges in front of the church, she was ejected from it. Similarly, in 1771 Mary Sanford complained against Elisabeth Potter, who closed her ears to the complaints and was therefore "set aside." In Cambridge the church called the widow Elizabeth Champhey to answer charges in 1774. When she refused to appear in front of the all-male committee, she was suspended from communion.[99] Clearly such recalcitrance and self-assertion was costly. Nevertheless, the price—excommunication—was part of an exchange that ended in a standoff for both parties: church authorities could not force a woman to submit, but her membership remained in purgatory until she did.

Quaker sympathizers, although known for their occasional loud and disruptive behavior, also used silence and absence as protest against Puritan principles. Although both men and women could be counted among the dissenters, more rebellious women than men displayed their nonconformity by refusing to come "to the publicke meeting to heare the word preached on the lords day." Group presentments to the court for such behavior show eight women and five men in November 1659, several wives in June 1660, two men and three women the following November, and thirty women and eleven men in June 1661, all of whom were either fined or whipped. Attendance at "a disorderly Quaking meeting" might also bring imprisonment.[100]

In other circumstances, female silence could be interpreted favorably by the authorities, even if they misjudged the intent of the women involved. In a hearing before her congregation, Ann Hutchinson apparently contradicted herself on a doctrinal point. According to John Winthrop, "there were diverse women also with whom she had dealt about the same point, who (if their modesty had not restrained them) would have born witnesse against her herein (as themselves after confessed)."[101]

Winthrop's comment is open to several interpretations, the most likely of which suggests that in this instance, like some others, women were capitalizing on silence for their own ends. First, it is possible that the women were indeed too modest to testify, which, given other evidence about female Bostonians in the first half of the seventeenth century, is unlikely. Second, they really supported Hutchinson, did not want to testify against her, and in refusing to do so on the grounds of modesty, actually manipulated Winthrop. Third, they saw which way the wind was blowing and decided to ally themselves with Winthrop, without actually testifying against Hutchinson.

Fourth, they in fact turned on Hutchinson, which would have been surprising given the long-standing and widespread support she received among women. Whichever interpretation is nearest the truth, however, their silence was effective.

A MATTER OF MONEY

The sex ratio of New England seaport towns affected the economic vitality of its churches. Although married women had the advantage of a husband's income, they frequently lacked control over their pocketbooks. Moreover, in a community where many men earned their living at sea, women could count on those wages only periodically and at erratic intervals. Independent unmarried women were, paradoxically, in the most precarious financial situation, usually eking out a living in the needle trades (tailoring, sewing, spinning, knitting, or weaving) or as landladies or shopkeepers. Such economic fragility seriously undermined the day-to-day operation of the churches.

Whatever privileges women lacked in colonial America, they had the unassailable right to be taxed. They may not have voted on the minister's salary, or on the amount of a pew tax, but they were expected to contribute to those items nevertheless. If the language of church documents is occasionally imprecise, the clarity with which record keepers defined "his" and "her" obligations is a striking counterpoint to the vagueness with which less vital matters were discussed.[102]

Disproportionately few women owned pews or parts of pews, but even when they did, they were frequently unable to make the stipulated periodic payments. Although "the widow Vibert [had] a title to her pew," she was "Incapable of Paying Contribution." Husbands usually held title to their wives' pews and paid the assessments thereon (even if they never saw the inside of a church themselves), but even so, the disproportionate number of single women without such support threatened the economic vitality of the church. At the Seventh Church in Boston in 1764, eight women and two men owed back assessments, and five years later, most of these same people were still "difisent in their contribution" and owed "doble" what they should have paid in 1764.[103]

Some churches assessed everyone equally, while others recognized the inability of certain people to meet their obligations. In the First Congregational Church of Newport in 1753, assessors were chosen to determine the amount each person should pay toward the minister's salary "according to Circumstance and Ability of the Owner or Seaters." In recognition of the disparity between male and female income in 1792, the church in Truro, Massachusetts, voted to have male members contribute sixpence and female members fourpence for one year in order to pay the church's arrears.[104]

The church and vestry of King's Chapel in Boston voted a pew tax of fifty-two shillings per year in 1723, with forfeiture of the pew as penalty for nonpayment. But in recognition of reality, the wardens and vestry announced that if any person, through misfortune, should be "unable to pay the Same," he or she could be "Relieved." At Trinity Church in Boston in 1780, wardens were advised to consider the case of widows and other persons unable to pay the tax on their respective pews and to make such abatements as circumstances required.[105]

The imbalance in the number of female church members, plus their inability to contribute as much as their male counterparts, created problems for the church in general and the minister in particular. The proprietors of Boston's Seventh Church were forced to call a special meeting of "purchasers and constant hearers" in 1730 "to agree or advise what may be done to advance the Contrebution." Apparently outgo continued to outpace income, because four years later the proprietors admitted that contributions still came "very much" short of supporting the pastor and "the charges of the Society." Communicants were bound to support the ministry, but what they did not have they could not share, and in February 1728/9 an extra collection was taken in Boston's Brattle Street Church and distributed among the pastors who were having trouble making ends meet.[106]

In a very real sense, the ministers were dependent on women more than on men for their livelihood. A clergyman's standard of living could easily rise or fall depending on the proportion of women in his congregation and what resources they commanded. Shreds of evidence indicate that women added to ministerial wardrobes, and abundant documents testify to the food they donated to his table.[107]

Nevertheless, in terms of the larger picture, the problem could not be solved because as the sex ratio became increasingly skewed, the churches found themselves saddled with an increasing number of people who not only were unable to contribute their share of assessments but also drained the church of its limited resources. Communicants and congregants alike could expect constant supplications for funds to supply "the poor . . . with wood and other necessaries of life." Women, as we have already noted, took a disproportionate share of those funds.[108]

Poverty affected church attendance. In 1778 Quaker women were asked to raise money for the relief of people "whose circumstances in life are so straight they have not wherewith to appear at meeting with decency." And in Plymouth in 1782 Patience Burgess pleaded that it was poverty and "want of suitable clothes" that prevented her from attending church.[109]

Although historians have interpreted women's reaction to inclement weather as reflective of a culturally constructed innate timidity, it is possible that some women were simply too poor to own the proper winter outerware. The Third Church of Boston minutes record that on 24 February 1717 "a violent storm of Snow [made] our meeting very thin especially to women." And in February 1767 "by reason of badness of weather there was only 1 woman friend present" at the Quaker monthly meeting in Newport, although the men's meeting contained a larger group. William Bentley of Salem recorded in his diary that 9 December 1786 "was so stormy and cold the snow so deep, that few were out at Church and no women."[110] While some women may have stayed at home to prevent their long skirts from trailing in the snow, and others may not have wanted to expose small children to the severe weather, a few may have lacked a cape warm enough for the walk back and forth.

Women who relied on the benevolence of the church for their financial support may have developed a sense of dependency that had far-reaching implications. In most cases men voted to take up the collection, and in most of the churches, deacons were responsible for distributing the largesse, either on the "Advice of the Ruling officers" or at their own "Discretion." With their well-being at stake, one wonders how assertive these women might have been, or whether, in such circumstances, they would have risked antagonizing the church fathers.[111]

The process worked two ways, of course, since ministers could ill afford to alienate their congregants. A few—very few—women were able to exceed their basic financial obligations to the church, and a minister was in no position to offend these women any more than he could offend the wife of an affluent citizen (who may or may not have been a member of the church). A pious and contented churchgoer might leave "a considerable Legacy" to the church, as Mrs. Anne Mills did in 1728/9. Like Mary Norton, she might even donate the land on which a meetinghouse could be built. A woman with positive thoughts about her church might contribute "a Silver Cupp" so the sacrament could be celebrated with elegance. She might persuade her husband that even if good works did not promise salvation, they did no harm.[112]

Yet New England women may have been conscious of the need to support each other as well as the church. If Ann Mills left a legacy to the church, she also left one to a group of people that included at least a dozen women and perhaps three men. And the widow Martha Pitman deeded two-thirds of a pew in the Newport Second Congregational Church to Peace Clark, "her heirs and Asigns Forever"—which meant that Clark was free to dispose of it as she pleased. The pew originally belonged to Martha's father, and the subsequent events show how property could eventually end up in nonfamily female hands.[113]

DECLINING VISIBILITY

The theme that winds its way through two centuries seems to be that women's role in the church declined during that period of time. If this is true, we are faced with the same paradox that is evident in the economic world: increasing numbers coinciding with decreasing visibility. Moreover, the two spheres (secular and religious) intersected where the growing number of women who were unable to support themselves leaned on both church and state for the necessities of life. Both institutions took economic responsibility for these women, but at the same time, they created an ever larger pool of dependent women. Only the Second Baptist Church of Newport ever tried to provide employment, rather than an outright dole, in an attempt to help the poor support themselves. In May 1739 members decided to employ the needy of the church "with some convenient work when they stand in need thereof, and pay them faithfully."[114]

Although the records are incomplete, it appears that over time women less frequently exercised a voice in the affairs of the church. Whether the transition from informal private worship at home to institutionalized religion in a meetinghouse played a role in silencing and marginalizing women can only be conjectured, but the simultaneity of the events suggests that the two may indeed have been interrelated. What is certain, however, is that the aggressively assertive women of the seventeenth century had few counterparts in the eighteenth, and if women attended business meetings in the early years of settlement, their absence from those forums was the rule rather than the exception in later decades. Public professions of faith, probably confined to Salem initially, died out altogether by the late seventeenth century, as women limited their confessions to private audiences.

John Fiske mentioned women on fewer occasions after his move to Chelmsford in 1656, and a century later, Ezra Stiles remarked on what he perceived to be a long-term trend in the Baptist churches in Rhode Island. His prophecy that the decline of female participation would continue was confirmed at the turn of the nineteenth century, when the Baptist Church arbitrarily disenfranchised the sisters. On the eve of Revolution in the Congregational churches in Newport, women no longer voiced "Consentment" to the admission of new members, although Ezra Stiles hinted at the inequity of such proceedings. "Upon the principle that there can be no vote unless every Brother consented, the Consent of every Sister may be required."[115]

In New England's youth, Puritan women had responsibility for teaching young children at home. As the Congregational churches became more firmly established, however, they gradually usurped the religious training of children. In the 1660s and 1670s, Gerald Moran argues, ministers increasingly became the catechists of choice, thus diminishing the role of women in childhood education.[116]

Even in the Newport Friends Meeting there is some evidence of changes that resulted in a loss of authority for women. In 1775 the Newport Women's Meeting debated "whether it may not be useful for the Women to prepare Certificates for women friends who traval in the Ministry or assist therein." They approved the less authoritative latter plan, acquainted the male members of their decision, and received word from the Yearly Men's Meeting some months later that in the future women should assist (rather than initiate) the preparation of such documents.[117] A small matter, perhaps, but the fact that this procedural change emerged from the women's meeting may hint at a shift in the way women perceived their role within the larger Society.

As late as 1778 the women's meeting unilaterally chose their own elders, yet in 1782, when Catherine Almy was nominated by the women's meeting, it was only after she had received "the concurrence of the men friends" that she was "chose to that place." Until 1769 the women's meeting appeared to act substantially independent of the men's meeting. In that year, however, they agreed that "for the future" they would "acquaint" the men Friends with those taken under or put from their care. The records indicate that for the next decade the women's meeting abided by that decision, first denying unity to members of their own meeting and only then acquainting the male

Friends with their decision. In July 1781 the quarterly meeting retreated still further from that modified position and advised that "the women shou'd have the assistance of our brethren in a meeting capacity" whenever a member was received or disowned.[118]

But it was not merely procedural modifications that signified changing relationships between men and women. Cavalier attitudes reflected diminishing respect as male Friends treated their female counterparts on a less egalitarian basis and with less consideration. The Newport Women's Meeting records that in the spring of 1775 male Friends decided to hold a subsequent meeting at East Greenwich "and neglected to confer with the women thereon or acquainting them thereof which has thrown some difficulty in our way respecting attending it." Clearly exasperated and angry, the women adjourned their meeting to confer privately in hopes of resolving the issue.[119]

With the exception of the Quakers, women were less likely to be members of visitation committees as the colonial era matured. In 1640 Ann Hibbens was criticized for not "hearkening ... to the brethren and sisters in private," but a century later there were no women on committees of any kind in the First Church of Boston. Baptist women were appointed to visitation committees in Newport throughout the 1600s and until 1722. But from the mid-1720s on, no women were named to committees at all. At the same church in 1708, twenty-nine women and twelve men signed the yearly letter written to the congregation in Pennsylvania and Piscataway, while in 1753 only a dozen men added their signatures to that annual missive (which was now addressed to the "brethren" rather than to the "Congregation").[120]

Neutral words fade from the manuscripts as the decades pass, and male-oriented words and phrases replace them. "Brethren" stood in for "congregation," and in Boston's First Church, the expression "with the consent of the Brethren" began to replace "the silent consent of the church" as early as 1655–56. Long before the first third of the eighteenth century, the latter expression had been dropped completely. The Third Church began to use the phrase "the Brethren of the Church and Congregation" about 1735, and this same wording becomes noticeable in Boston's Seventh Church by the 1740s. "Brethren" was used consistently in the Danvers records by the late 1720s.[121]

If, in fact, this is a distinct pattern, the most telling support for its existence may also be the most subtle. In other words, the way women were referred to changes almost imperceptibly over time. When women were admitted to the First Church in Boston in 1630 they were listed in such typical

forms as "Elizabeth Aspinall the wife of Willyam Aspinall" or "Henry Gos-
nall and Mary his wife." The identity of a woman may have been linked to
her husband, but each woman was recognized as a separate individual. At
the First Church in Charlestown in 1630, the records read "John Harvard and
Anna Harvard his wife." Less than a century later, however, in the 1720s, a
woman was more likely to be referred to as "the wife of Mr. Stephen Ford"
or "the wife of Mr. John Sprague"—with no first name of her own. On admission lists in Cambridge, women were named as "the wife of John Wyth"
or "the wife of Tho Stacye" even earlier.[122]

In Beverly in 1667 husbands and wives were listed separately with the full
names of each carefully written, but in the years just prior to independence,
far less care was taken to identify the female members of the family. Husbands were invariably listed by their full names, wives either as the "wife of
Jonathan Biles," or simply "Goody Ashby" (with no first name inscribed in
either case). Women lost their identity altogether when they were recorded
as "Jon Herricks" or "Goodman Gile's"—a concession to their existence
without the addition of the word "wife." But even this is less indicative of the
general attitude toward women than the notes made by the Reverend Edward
Tompson, who was pastor of the church in Marshfield, Massachusetts, between 1696 and 1704/5. He recorded the names of each of the thirteen male
members in 1696 and then went on to say, "the number of the Sisters of the
Church was about thirty whose names I cannot recover."[123]

The evolving relationship between the secular and religious spheres over
two centuries also affected women's status. In the early decades of settlement,
the priority given to moral transgressions dictated that they be subject to the
dual sovereignty of church and state. Thus, double jeopardy notwithstanding, men and women were usually held accountable in both jurisdictions for
the same infraction. And rather than mitigating the worst effects of household patriarchy, as Carole Shammas suggests, such cooperation between
church and state reinforced it by working in tandem to corroborate and vali-
date a husband's authority.[124]

In this doubly disadvantageous situation, women were originally positioned to moderate its worst excesses. As long as New England churches set
and enforced moral standards, those women who held public roles as witnesses, committee members, and electors of either fellow church members
or ministers exerted some control over decisions that affected their lives. By
the end of the seventeenth century, however, the ascendancy of the secular

legal system had undermined church authority, and because of women's absence from the former (except as witnesses), they sustained a loss of public
authority commensurate to the loss of religious authority itself.[125]

Moreover, their diminishing involvement in church affairs was hardly
without precedent or parallel. If, as Patricia Bonomi maintains, the eighteenth century saw the growing stabilization of religious institutions, then
the simultaneous decline of female authority in religious matters may be seen
as analogous to their increasingly unfavorable position in civil society, where
a codified legal system had established and sustained male privilege.[126] In
both instances, Gerda Lerner's point that female marginalization corre-
sponds with such stabilization is well taken.

Other, slow-moving cultural changes also had a negative effect on female
independence. As William McLoughlin suggests, eighteenth-century townspeople began to shed their collective identity and subjugation of self (a dual-
ity intimately tied to religious behavior), leaving bare an individualism that
was marked by conflict of interest and disharmony.[127] Such a sequence of
events would hardly have been gender neutral, since the eighteenth-century
pulpit continued to emphasize the subjection of the female self. For a woman
to be personally responsible for her salvation was one thing; for her to be a
wordly, independent, self-interested individual was quite another.

If the issues raised by townspeople throughout New England during the
Revolutionary era were ones that had initially been contested within the walls
of the meetinghouse, women were conspicuously absent as subjects of the
later debate. Earlier matters involving church policy and gender that had
been resolved had no secular counterparts in the war of words that took place
in the 1760s and 1770s. Could married women apply for church dismissal as
individuals? Under what conditions should women be permitted to speak?
Did spiritual equality suggest an entitlement to political equality in church
proceedings? Such seventeenth-century questions about church policy could
have been translated into a civil debate when, in the eighteenth century, the
relationship between white men and the state was being challenged and
transformed. That it never happened speaks to the limits of that debate.

Yet one might argue that it was precisely because of their similarity that
egalitarian issues had to be suppressed in the religious context. Critics of the
Brattle Street plan had noted, quite perceptively, that opening the vote to all
adult communicants and congregants would leave decision making in the
hands of a female majority. It was unseemly in 1699; it was no more seemly
in 1776, although Ezra Stiles's Second Congregational Church in Newport

paused, at least, to consider the undemocratic nature of church governance. Noting that "the Congregations almost thro'out Christendom have lost the power of chusing their pastors," Deacon Moses Pitman added, "and yet all who pay towards the Support of the Pastor have a right to vote in his Call."[128]

Since the logic of this argument propelled its adherents toward untenable conclusions, it was better to avoid the issue altogether, especially since the church itself was not under attack (as it would be in France a decade later), and by ignoring gendered inequities, its patriarchy could be quietly preserved. Consciously or unconsciously, ministers and elders managed to retain minority control of churches whose vast majority was female.

Thus the authoritative voice of the church in the Revolutionary era emanated from the pulpit. The irony was that at the same time, each congregation was expected to carry its minister's words to other members of the community. Those who listened in silence to the sermons had a duty to disseminate the message from church to family, from family to neighbors, from neighbors to tradespeople. If those words were political as well as religious—as they were from Ezra Stiles's pulpit in the mid-1770s—then women, by their very numbers, were in a unique position to influence the course of events by acting as the conduits—indeed, interpreters—of that message.[129]

One final point: given the experience of female societies such as Sarah Osborn's, it is somewhat surprising that no group awareness, no female consciousness emerged from religious circles during the Revolutionary upheaval. Having taken such political excursions on church grounds, what was it that prevented women's groups from expanding their horizons and rejecting marginality? Indeed, it is precisely organizations such as Osborn's that will play a vital role in pursuing women's rights a half century later. The absence of a collective female voice in the maelstrom of the independence movement suggests that by the second half of the eighteenth century, New England women had perhaps forgotten the contentious, demanding, and assertive women of the world they left behind.

CHAPTER 3

Invisible Earnings: Women and the Seaport Economy

Horod Long's Story

*H*orod Long's father died before she entered her teens, and shortly thereafter Horod's mother sent the grieving youngster to London, where she and one John Hicks were secretly married in Saint Faith's church.[1] "In a little while after, to my great griefe," she recalled, her husband carried her off to New England. At the time, Horod was "betweene thirteene and fourteene years of age." They eventually settled in Newport. Around 1644 "a difference" arose between Horod and John, and the authorities allowed them to separate. For her support, Horod was granted the estate sent to her by her mother.

Unfortunately for Horod, John "went away to the Dutch," and with him went most of Horod's estate. As a result, Horod "was put to great hardshipe and straight." She had not been "brought up to labour," she was young, and she "knew not what to doe to have something to live." Because of her circumstances, she tells us, she "was drawne by George Gardner to consent to him" for her "mayntainance." She lived with him, she added, "with much oppression of spiritt, judging him not to be my husband, never being married to him according to the law of the place." Ostensibly plagued with misgivings about their relationship, and "seeing that hee had that little that I had, and all my labour," Horod asked George for a separate maintenance "to live apart from him." Short of that, she implored him not "to meddle" with her, presumably referring to their sexual activities. "But hee . . . always refused."

In 1664, after cohabiting with Gardner for almost two decades, Horod finally petitioned for some sort of legal separation. Her application caused no end of consternation, since the relationship between Horod and George was admittedly ambiguous. Nine years earlier Gardner had been acquitted of "keeping John Hickes . . . wife as his owne,"[2] and in 1665, when Robert Stanton was asked *whether "George Gardner and Horod, his reputed wife were ever married according to the custom of this place," Stanton replied that "one night . . . both of them did say before him and his wife that they did take one the other as man and wife"—a ceremony that would have validated the marriage in England.*

In Rhode Island, however, this was not the way marriages were customarily performed, and Horod was therefore accused of living "in that abominable lust of fornication." For the future, she and George were prohibited from living "soe scandolose a life." Since Horod had already categorically refused to return to George, this resolution by itself worked to her advantage. But Horod, now past forty and with children to support, petitioned for maintenance from George "of that estate and labour hee has had of mine . . . and that the house upon my land I may enjoy without molestation." Twice, now, Horod had referred to the value of her labor. Yet, ignoring both her situation and her supplication and focusing instead on the "fowlness" of their "sin," the General Assembly fined George and Horod twenty pounds apiece.

Sometime between 1665 and 1668 Horod Long, alias Gardner, began living ("in way of incontenancy") with John Porter.[3] Porter's wife, a "poore anciente matron," complained that her philandering husband not only was "destitute of all congugall love towards her" but also had "left her in such a nessesetous state that unavoydably she is brought to a meere dependence upon her children for her dayley suply."

Sympathetic to Margaret's plight, local authorities ordered John to maintain the "aged wife" he had abandoned in favor of a younger woman. Horod, who had probably turned to Porter because she, like most other women, was incapable of supporting herself, was disappointed once again. The court seized all of John's considerable real and personal estate until he "settled a competent reliefe upon his aged wife to her full satisfaction," a scenario that probably encouraged Horod Long Hicks Gardner to seek security elsewhere.

THE SEAPORT COMMUNITY

The intimate relationship between the sea and the seaport was nothing less than symbiotic. Most imported commodities found their way to eighteenth-century port towns courtesy of Father Neptune, a commercial relationship that tied the prosperity of each community to an unobstructed and thriving trade. Twentieth-century cities that hug the ocean are served equally well—or better—by air routes, train tracks, or highway, and thus industrialism and technology have diminished the relative importance of the ocean as an avenue of commerce. Modern seaports are cultural, manufacturing, and service centers (as well as entrepôts), and their well-being is less dependent on proximity to the water than it was in colonial America.

In contrast, the demography, layout, and organization of the eighteenth-century seaport revolved around its harbor, where population and building density were highest. In these towns, merchants erected their fine homes with commanding views of the sea, and shopkeepers clustered near the source of their merchandise. Warehouses and stores dotted the dozens of wharves, their congestion increasing in proportion to the mariners, carters, and draymen who loaded or unloaded vessels and the shoppers who milled about, exchanging news and seeking the best wares at the lowest prices.

Although such traffic may suggest chaos and disorder, there was nonetheless a sense of organization that accompanied these activities and emanated from eighteenth-century constructions of time and space. In a society where food spoilage was a constant problem and people were dependent on their feet or wagons for locomotion, marketing customs differed from contemporary practices. Common sense dictated that perishables be confined to locations most favorable to a speedy sale and widely recognized by both buyer and seller for that purpose. It was expedience, not coincidence, that prompted the Newporter Nathan Beebe to pursue "his baker's business" on the wharf of Mr. George Gibbs, who also ran a bakehouse.[4] By so doing, customers could limit their exertions to a well-defined area. Some markets specialized as well: one in fish, another in meat.

Other considerations determined the location of subsidiary industries. Hogsheads of molasses were heavy, and thus distilleries sprang up near the wharves owned by the largest importers of the sticky stuff. Moreover, some molasses and rum spent little time ashore; most of these liquid assets were quickly processed and reloaded onto ships for export and—with luck—a good return. Lumber, clumsy as well as weighty, traveled only a short distance from where laborers loaded it on Newport's Long Wharf to the nearby workshops of the skilled cabinetmakers. Ropewalks and tanneries needed open space; the peripheries of town offered such accommodations.

Since commerce was the lifeblood of the seaport, town officials, acting with the blessings of common law, took measures to ensure public access to the harbor and wharves. Private property was subservient to public interest, and encroachments that hindered the "privileges of the shore" were not tolerated. With few exceptions, no one could be excluded from waterfront property between the high and low water marks, and once a perpendicular right of way to the water was established by usage, local officials jealously guarded it. In such a setting, men and women, bound together by their common dependence on the profits to be extracted from a mercantile economy, struggled to make the most of what the ocean highway brought to their shores.

The economic structure of the New England seaports reflected the needs and opportunities of time and place. Women as well as men played a significant role in that economy at all times, although the nature of the role underwent subtle changes as the colonies evolved. Not only were women an essential part of a system that required an elaborate and intricate exchange of goods and services, but there can be little doubt that from the earliest days of settlement female productive input was considered crucial to the success of the experiment.

New England colonists emigrated from a society where women were an integral part of the economy in general and a highly visible component of the textile trades specifically. Those factors, combined with the general labor shortage in the American colonies, prompted new settlers to incorporate female labor wherever necessary to promote the general welfare. Thus the General Court sought to forestall a clothing shortage in 1656 by ordering "all hands not necessarily imployed on other occasions, as women, Girles, and Boyes," to "spin according to their skill and abilitie, and that the selectmen in every town doe consider the condition and capacitie of every familie, and accordingly to assess them, as one or more spinners. 2ly ... that every one thus assessed for a whole spinner doe, after the psent year, 1656, spin, for 30 weekes every yeare 3 pound p weeke of lining, cotton, or wooling under the poenalty of 12d for every pound short."[5]

True, the legislation says nothing specifically about the disposition of the thread—whether it was for use within the household, or whether the town officials intended to co-opt it. Yet it was a peremptory demand on female time without any indication that the spinners were to be compensated for their efforts. Indeed, this assessment may even be interpreted as a tax that fell most heavily on women and even children.[6] Nevertheless, implicit in the order was a recognition of the relationship between female productivity and the well-being of the community. Legislation merely codified expectation.

Throughout the colonial period few women remained aloof from economic activities that extended beyond the boundaries of their households—and that tended to make their "private" world public, and "public" private. Indeed, the driving force behind their involvement arose from the nature of the seventeenth- and eighteenth-century American world. This was a world where female hands spun thread, and where quilts, curtains, sheets, towels, tablecloths, and napkins were either handmade or finished by women. If few women wove fabrics, many women turned domestic or imported cloth into wearing apparel and household items, much of which found its way to shop shelves. Early America was also a world without frozen foods, fast foods, or the means of preserving most fresh foods over time. Bread and rum might be purchased on the wharves, but nearly every other edible product was either processed at someone's home or imported from afar (such as tropical fruit). Not surprisingly, therefore, women also sold food, a point most succinctly acknowledged in 1798 by the author Charles Brockden Brown, who queried rhetorically, "do we not buy most of our meat, herbs, and fruit, of women?"[7]

Notwithstanding their role as the producers and distributors of two necessities of life—food and clothing—our perception of female economic participation in colonial America has been distorted for several reasons. Historians must take primary responsibility for this misrepresentation because they have based their assessment of female economic contribution on standards that deny recognition of its worth. Those standards place value on the accumulation of wealth, rather than on the significance of work itself. Individual components of the entire economic enterprise have received little or no recognition because high hierarchal status was determined by the final reckoning: assets that most women could not hope to amass. By this measurement, white men became responsible for and the most visible agents of economic achievement.

It is true that women were less likely than men to run a mercantile establishment or distillery or tavern. And because of the dearth of women in prestigious occupations, because their earning power was limited, historians have turned history upside down. By focusing on the few women who attained visibility through "high" economic status, they have overlooked the many women whose pervasiveness throughout the economy ensured the successful functioning of the mercantile community. Thus, any construction that continues to assume the marginality of women must recognize that those margins encroached on the entire text of urban life. Moreover, women were not merely a support system to a hierarchal order: their skills and participation were central to the very existence of that order.

Female participation in the market economy was, of course, inextricably intertwined with their contribution to the family economy.[8] This was true enough with the assistance of male earners as joint providers, but by the eighteenth century there were many more women than men in the port towns, an imbalance that was exacerbated with every boatload of mariners that left the harbor. Not only did the demographic imbalance cloud marriage prospects for many women (and thus limit one path to greater economic security), but women whose husbands were off on voyages were left to fend for themselves. In practical terms this created a paradox: although women were brought up to be dependent, they had independence thrust upon them, and both married and single women had strong incentive to earn an income.

If most white women acquired money or goods through the needle trades or from the production and exchange of food staples, many more supported themselves or added to the family economy by charging for what would have been unpaid labor if done for the immediate family. Thus, some women boarded or prepared meals for mariners or washed and ironed for other transients. Some mended, cooked, and cleaned for teachers and ministers whose live-in students were too occupied to tend to such chores. Others boarded the poor and infirm for the town and received compensation for so doing. Women also found employment as midwives, wet nurses, and servants. Not always confined to the most obvious gender-related occupations, women also taught school, ran inns and taverns, and sold rum with or without a license. They leased out land, houses, warehouses, horses, and slaves, and they lent money at interest.

Women whitewashed houses, drove milk carts, ran lotteries, ground chocolate, sowed the ground, wintered the town bull, taught dance, and sold dung. They worked as shipwrights, apothecaries, and brasiers or brass founders. Women carted wood or hay, repaired the town highways, and kept the post office. They made buttons and mourning rings in partnership with jewelers and prepared the dead for burial. Women made candles for export, nets for fishing voyages, and ships' bread for slaving ventures. They embroidered chair seats for upholsterers and painted Windsor chairs for cabinetmakers. They retailed the goods imported by merchant grandees and made wigs to cover up their scalps, if not their scalping. Moreover, during her lifetime one woman might have had several occupations. At one time or another, Hannah Pickering Collins of Salem (b. 1708) was a wife, mother, widow, boardinghouse keeper, schoolteacher, and midwife. Between April and August 1761 nearly four dozen children were under her tutelage, and between 1769 and 1773 she acted as midwife for 327 potential students.[9]

Shopkeeping was an important means of income, and among the 133 licensed retailers in Boston in 1737 were 57 women. Another 57 are found on a list of 171 "Persons licensed to sell tea, coffee, and chinaware" in Suffolk County, Massachusetts, in 1755. Thirty-eight women and 57 men held retail licenses in 1765. That women were likely to be merchandisers, if not merchants, is evident from the recollections of Henry Channing, a Newporter whose pre-Revolutionary memories included the following reminiscence: "My father kept a wholesale store on Governor Wanton's wharf, being an importer of goods from England. He kept a large retail store of dry goods opposite the Governor Wanton's house. As it was then the fashion, my mother superintended the store, having one or two clerks."[10]

Various tax assessments place the Channings safely within the confines of the upper middle class, which confirms Henry's notion that Mary Channing's employment was customary rather than necessary. Similarly, Temperance Grant, wife (and then widow) of the merchant magnate Sueton Grant, was counted among Newport's shopkeepers, which also reinforces the idea that even the most well-to-do families tapped every available resource without regard to gender.[11] Equally interesting, Channing's phraseology, "as it was then the fashion," hints that in 1835 it was no longer fashionable for wives to superintend stores.

If few urban women were independently identified as tailors or upholsterers, they were strongly represented in these trades nonetheless, either as individual entrepreneurs or as employees. William Waine, a tailor in Boston between 1728 and 1744, employed women on a daily or weekly basis to sew for him. By the 1770s at least two dozen women were working for the affluent Newport merchant Aaron Lopez, making frocks, greatcoats, trousers, and jackets. In 1769 and 1770 alone, Mary Crandall, Ann Moss, and Elizabeth King together spun nearly eighty pounds of cotton and made four dozen shirts and ten pairs of trousers. Mary Wood delivered over two hundred articles of clothing to Lopez. They completed these garments from material supplied to them without charge (thus eliminating investment on their part), and they were paid either by the piece or for their time on a daily or weekly basis.[12]

Samuel Grant, a Boston upholsterer, was less specific in his ledgers about the people he hired, but his cash payments to Lydia Calley and Abigail Coverly suggest they were in his employ. It would not be surprising to find that women provided the upholstery or crewel work for the wing chairs or sofas Grant sold. Indeed, Sarah Osborne, writing from Newport in 1751, indicated that she was about to work on "cloth" for a set of chairs.[13] Thomas Robinson of Newport was one of colonial America's largest exporters of spermaceti candles, and as such a purchaser of vast amounts of the raw material needed to achieve that end—spermaceti oil. His accounts over two decades indicate that he bought whale oil from various male suppliers and that in addition to exporting candles himself, he sold large quantities to other male distributors—merchants who also shipped candles abroad. Robinson's books, however, are unclear about the process by which the oil was transformed into candles, although the records do hint that women were involved in the process.

Few people purchased oil of Robinson, and those who did were almost always female. Several (Elizabeth Carey, Sarah Cozzens, Mary Shearman, and Abigail Pitman) consistently bought oil in 31½–32 gallon quantities. Only one man (Jabez Carpenter) made regular purchases in comparable amounts, and it is possible that these people were responsible for providing Robinson with candles, especially since Carpenter hired women to spin candlewick for him. Although Robinson's ledgers do not show corresponding payments to the same persons for labor performed, Robinson frequently marked the oil purchase entries "paid," a notation omitted elsewhere in his account books. Robinson's oil buyers may have made candles themselves or subcontracted the work, returning a portion of the finished candles as payment for the raw oil. Whatever arrangements existed, however, it appears that women played an integral role in this lucrative enterprise.[14]

While the foregoing pages have referred to urban women as an undifferentiated group, the discussion has, in fact, focused on white females. The labor of enslaved African American women is more difficult to define, since they rarely appear in merchants' account books, in contrast to African American men, who were portrayed as being engaged in a wide variety of activities and trades. It is likely that female slaves occasionally paid off their master's or mistress's debt with their own "work," as Elizabeth Coggeshall's "Negro woman" did in 1748, but it is equally likely that they labored as house servants. In Newport, black women were found in the more affluent, larger households of merchants, distillers, tailors, shopkeepers, coopers, or bakers, but whether they performed tasks associated with those occupations or were engaged in housekeeping chores is impossible to determine.[15]

"WE DO NOT GREATLY ABOUND IN FEMALE FORTUNES"

If the ledgers of merchants and tradespeople suggest that women were central to the operation of the mercantile community, this is not to say that women were compensated in proportion to their contribution. Despite their wide involvement in the market economy, they made little money, and if they were single, their standard of living would have been commensurately low. It is well established that throughout the eighteenth century women's earning capacity was considerably less than that of men, a disparity that would be slightly reduced in the nineteenth and twentieth centuries.[16]

Notwithstanding this assessment, however, quantification of the earning imbalance remains imprecise. Although hundreds of account books have survived the centuries, and although the pervasiveness of women in the economic life of each community is confirmed by countless ledger entries, exact comparisons are extremely difficult given the nature of the data. Barter coexisted comfortably with cash, making calculation difficult at best, impossible at worst. The problems involved in evaluating the relative worth of eggs vis-à-vis fabric without knowing how many eggs or how much cloth is compounded by the constant use of the generic term "work." Similarly, with no further information beyond the actual exchange it is difficult to compare compensation for stitching a greatcoat with mending a rake. How long did each task take? Out of context, isolated pieces of information remain suggestive rather than conclusive, making comparisons meaningful only if date, task, compensation, duration, and cost are evaluated simultaneously.

There are few examples, therefore, to illustrate the exact difference in earning power between men and women. Nevertheless, exhaustive readings of account books make it clear that in the seventeenth and eighteenth centuries urban trades that attracted men, such as bricklaying, stonecutting, or shoemaking, rewarded workers with higher compensation than occupations that employed women, whose skills confined them, for the most part, to the needle and service industries, and whose "labor" and "work" were compensated at far lower rates than those paid to men. Indeed, no matter what the task entailed, and no matter in what community it took place, men were almost always paid more than women. Thus, by carting two cords of wood or making a bed cord Joseph Crandall and Lewis Buliod were likely to have earned more than Mrs. Boynton, who carded for a spinner. And at two pounds per day for sowing, Nathaniel Rogers's income surpassed that of Mary Steward, who earned eighteen shillings per day for sewing.[17]

The few examples of wage differential between men and women that bear comparison demonstrate the disparity most vividly. They have been drawn from seventeenth- and eighteenth-century account books, and the illustrations are geographically and chronologically compatible. Some emerge from a single ledger. The Stevens family account book from Newport indicates that in 1727, Stevens charged ten shillings per day for his own labor as stonecutter or shoemaker (skilled work), and seven shillings per day for "Phillip's" labor. In the same ledger, for the same year, "Marcy" was paid two shillings per day for "quilting," which also demanded skill and expertise. Twenty years later, the merchant Thomas Richardson (also of Newport) paid Abigail Barker no more than eight shillings per day for tailoring, while during that same year, Joshua Hacker could earn thirty shillings per day for undisclosed (but probably unskilled) "labor." In 1760 both Sarah Nichols and Lawrence Clarke were earning income for what was loosely described as "work." Sarah received £2 per week, while Lawrence pocketed £2½ per day. In October 1774 Josiah Rogers earned £7 per day for undisclosed "work" while the widow Rogers stitched away at £2/5 per day, mending, sewing, and altering.[18]

Men involved in the needle trades invariably earned more than women. For example, the widow Lawton received two shillings for one day's work making a jacket in 1787, while Thomas Manchester made a pair of breeches in the same amount of time and was paid seven shillings for his effort.[19] What the evidence suggests is that in the normal course of events, a white man could expect to earn three times what a white woman could, even if his labor was unskilled and she was a skilled seamstress.

The account books also indicate that although slaves were hired at rates lower than those of white adult males, they were still paid more than white adult females. In 1759 and 1760 different slaves could earn anywhere from £1½ to £3 per day in Newport, while the most Ruth Nichols could expect at the same time was £3 per week. Margaret Brussels earned £1½ per day for "work" in 1768, while in that same year, Lydia Rodman's Negro hired out at £2½ per day. What this meant, of course, is that a woman who could afford to buy a slave could earn more by hiring him out than by working herself.[20]

As a general rule, both white and black males earned more than white females. There were, however, exceptions that complicate the picture and suggest that there may have been changes over time. In Boston in the late seventeenth century (1677–79), Goody Teal and George Thomas each received one shilling per day for washing and starching—labor commonly described as women's work. Throughout the seventeenth and eighteenth centuries a few women appear among the many men who were paid by the Salem, Massachusetts, Selectmen for highway repairs, commonly described as men's work. In each instance, the women were paid exactly what the men received, and it appears that, at least into the 1720s, the daily wages for that chore were comparable to those received by other common laborers.[21]

In Newport in the 1750s, there are spotty records for two chocolate grinders: Elizabeth Robinson and Obediah Brown. The records show that she charged more per ounce for grinding chocolate, but that he ground considerably more than she did and may have given a volume discount, which once again clouds the issue of earning power.[22] Nevertheless, it is of some importance that a man and a woman were both involved in this occupation, since it hints that division of labor based on sex was, perhaps, in a transitional phase. Male tailors were already better paid for the same tasks than their female competitors, but there may have been other occupations where such discrimination was not yet entrenched.

Gloria Main's analysis of rural account books suggests that different trends were at work outside the New England seaports. There is no evidence in the urban ledgers (as there is in rural ones) that the gap between male and female earnings had narrowed in the last decade before the Revolution. And unlike their increasing visibility in rural ledgers, there is considerable evidence of a diminishing female presence in the account books from the port cities. Read in unison, however, rural and urban account books indicate that economic forces at play in one area may have had a far-reaching impact on the other. Between 1755 and 1764 farm laborers and skilled rural craftsmen could expect roughly 2 shillings sterling per day, but unskilled workers in Newport could count on anywhere from 2 shillings 6 pence to 4 shillings per day in 1760. And if rural craftsmen and laborers sufferered a decline in wages between 1764 and 1774, urban ledgers do not corroborate the same downward trend.[23]

Such differences would explain why rural employers found themselves shorthanded in the last decade before the Revolution: male wage earners sought better opportunities in urban locales such as Newport. In contrast, the records show that women in Newport were more likely than men to migrate from the town, and it might be such displaced females who were being hired in the countryside. Colonial New England might also have been experiencing a trend similar to one in some parts of Europe where the demand for female agricultural workers outpaced the demand for male workers.[24]

WHEN MORE MEANS LESS

In the seaports of New England, women were disproportionately numerous and disproportionately poor, although the latter condition fluctuated with marital status. Married women shared the benefits of an upwardly mobile family, but single women lacked the skills, credit, and communal support to compete for anything but a fraction of the economic rewards available to others. And although married women outnumbered single women in all of these communities, there remained, nonetheless, a substantial pool of never-married or widowed women at any given time. In addition, seaports were home to a third category of women: those whose husbands were away for long periods of time, leaving them to shift for themselves.

Whether their husbands were on moneymaking voyages or taken captive during one of the eighteenth-century Euro-American squabbles is immaterial; the implications of any protracted absence are evident in the appeals by the women left behind. Fifteen New Hampshire wives requested government assistance in 1745 because they were "destitute of the help they used to have by the Day Wages of their Husbands on which only they Depended for Subsistence."[25]

Given these demographic and economic realities, New England authorities were caught in a financial vise: the town coffers demanded constant replenishment, but assessors could not depend on the most numerous group of inhabitants to do the job. Thus, after every potential prospect was tapped, local taxation schemes still required occasional adjustment to meet the equivalent of a balanced budget. For example, poll or head taxes were usually limited to men, but in a singular and apparently unsuccessful experiment in 1695 Massachusetts legislators extended the tax to women at half the male rate—an attempt to offset the town's needs against women's meager economic resources. And even if single women with property were theoretically taxed at the same rate as men, the actual apportionment of taxes still left room for selective manipulation. As the Selectmen of Portsmouth, New Hampshire, readily admitted, "we have no certain Rule to rate or Doom Persons by for their Income by Trade or Merchandize, and the assessors informs us that there never was any such Rule in the Town but that they always tax'd the People by guess and the best information they would get of their Circumstances at the time of Taxing."[26]

The "Circumstances" of women as a group were poor, giving ample support to the argument that the feminization of poverty had deep roots in the seaports of early New England. And although the distribution of wealth was unlikely to have been gender neutral during the seventeenth century, the evidence from tax assessments suggests that urban women suffered a loss in economic standing in subsequent decades. The 1687 tax evaluation for Boston lists 1,326 persons who were called upon for financial contributions. Of the total number, 188 men paid only a poll or head tax; they did not have enough rateable property to be assessed for any more than just their person. Out of the remaining 1,138 people, 1,048 men and 89 women were assessed on their property.[27]

That only 7.8 percent of this group of taxpayers were female is not surprising, since most women were married and thus not susceptible to taxation in their own stead. More interesting is the fact that women were assessed almost in proportion to their number: that is, their rateable estates amounted to 7.1 percent of the total property evaluation. Stated another way, the average rate of each woman was 1.5 shillings, that of each man, 1.6 (for calculation purposes, poll taxes have been eliminated). Nevertheless, the 1771 tax assessment for Boston suggests that this near equity of assessed wealth dissipated in the eighty-four years following 1687. The percentage of women who were rated dipped slightly to 7.3 percent of the total number of people rated on property, at a time when the pool of single women who were fair game for the assessors had expanded considerably. Even more significantly, women now contributed only 5.7 percent of the total assessment. In 1771 each female averaged £181, each male £236.[28] If this is an accurate reflection of the distribution of wealth, women had lost considerable economic advantage (compared to men) during the eighteenth century.

We cannot tabulate what proportion of single women were untaxed in either 1687 or 1771, since the number of unmarried women who lived in Boston in those years went unrecorded. In other words, although we know what percentage of men were taxed on property because of the list of polls, we do not know how many women may have been in the pool of potential female taxpayers. We do know that the percentage of women assessed as a proportion of total assessments ranged from 3.6 percent in Newport in 1760 to 9 percent in Salem in 1754, but as in the case of Boston, this tells only part of the story, since the number of single women who were qualified to be rated remains unknown.

The poll tax itself is another variable that affects any evaluation of male and female wealth. If one includes this head tax on males in the calculations, the figures show a far greater disparity between men and women. Yet even though it was usually not a property tax but rather an indiscriminate assessment on male persons, one could plausibly argue that the poll tax was simply another "rate," since men were presumed to have the ability to pay this tax on their persons, wheras women were not. To complicate matters still further, the Rhode Island legislature pegged the poll tax to the amount of property a man owned by requiring that "the poll tax shall be six pence for each every thousand pounds."[29]

However one chooses to calculate the Rhode Island figures, the numbers show that women in Newport were assessed proportionately less than their male counterparts. The thirty-six women who made up 3.6 percent of the 1760 tax list paid 1 percent of the total assessment. Women averaged 17 shillings 6 pence apiece, men £3/7. In 1772 in Newport, 3.7 percent of those on the tax list were female, and they were expected to pay 1.7 percent of the total assessment. No woman was assessed more than £1/7/0, but 167 men incurred liabilities of up to £37/11/0. And although the figures from Salem do not lend themselves to the same kind of comparison, it is notable that in 1754 only 18 (8.8 percent) of the 205 widows in the town were assessed.[30]

Probate records corroborate tax lists. In her study of American wealth on the eve of Independence, Alice Hanson Jones found that approximately 9 percent of colonial wealth was in the hands of women, with men holding substantially greater amounts of property, particularly in New England. Because New England women showed no greater number of sample cases than women elsewhere despite the distorted sex ratio, Jones suggested the possibility that fewer women in New England had wealth of their own than in either the middle colonies or the south. New England itself was not uniform, however, because although Essex County (in which Salem is located) showed female wealth holders as 9.8 percent of the sample, only 5 percent of the inventories belonged to women in Suffolk County (Boston).[31]

Seventeenth-century probate documents from Essex County form an interesting parallel to Jones's findings. While 8 or 9 percent of the inventories and wills belonged to women, the number of female wealth holders between 1635 and 1681 dropped. Indeed, the percentage of wills and inventories belonging to women declined from 9.5 percent to 8.5 percent at the same time that the proportion of women in the population was rising. Moreover, the amount of real property owned by women declined as well.[32]

Taken together, the evidence suggests that women's economic viability dissipated over the course of two centuries. The fact that the colonial era began and ended with Salem women owning 9–10 percent of the total wealth, while the pool of unmarried women who could own property in their own right increased dramatically over that period, suggests that women were losing ground economically. This conclusion is reinforced by Gary Nash, who found that widows were the second most numerous group among the bottom 30 percent of Boston's decedents in terms of wealth, and that their presence at this level slowly increased as the eighteenth century advanced. Between 1685 and 1699 they represented 14.3 percent of this lowest group of wealth holders; by the 1720s that number had risen to 16 percent.[33] Nevertheless, although there is little doubt that widows as a group were economically disadvantaged, it is also true that probate records minimize their standard of living, since any life interest in real property from which they benefited (as a dower right) is not reflected in those records.

Poorhouse records confirm the tax and probate documents, even assuming that any community with an excess of women should show proportionately more women on the poor rolls by virtue of their greater numbers. Moreover, almshouse records and payments to the poor bear silent witness to the exaggerated dependency of women on men during wartime. Between 1759 and 1761, 136 women and 84 men were admitted to the almshouse in Boston, while the years 1768–73 saw a total of 347 female and 287 male admissions. The latter figures also suggest that the number of people who could not support themselves increased as Boston's population stagnated. Although men and women were frequently admitted for the same reasons—poverty and disease—a number of pregnant women sought entrance because they had no other place to go to deliver their children.[34]

Indigent women and men might receive "out relief" instead of being confined to the almshouse, and the surviving records show that here, too, women were more likely than men to receive assistance from the town. By 1677 women, mainly widows, received most of the contributions for the poor in Salem. In that year the Selectmen dispersed money to nine women and three men. A year later, twelve women and three men benefited from town assistance. When the Boston Overseers of the Poor granted their monthly allotments in 1738, thirteen people (eleven women and two men) were listed as recipients. The women generally received ten to fifteen shillings each; the two men each received twenty shillings per month. A decade later, only seven people (five women) were on this particular list, and there was no difference

WOMEN AND THE SEAPORT ECONOMY 113

in payments. The decline in numbers does not indicate a decrease in poverty but rather the opposite, since Boston, like many other New England communities in the 1730s, had built a new almshouse to accommodate the burgeoning number of indigent persons.[35]

By 1769–70 Samuel Whitwell's accounts from ward 2 in Boston show that forty-four women and twenty-five men were unable to maintain themselves without help from the town, and in ward 12 a year later, twenty-six women and twenty-three men found themselves in the same condition. In Boston as a whole, perhaps one thousand or more were receiving financial assistance each year, and from every account it appears that women made up the majority of the cases. The Boston census takers testified to the particular distress of older women when they noted that 1,000 of the 1,200 widows in the 1742 census were in "low circumstances," and the tax assessors reinforced that conclusion in 1751 when they admitted that "at least half" of Boston's 1,153 widows were "very poor."[36]

Even in Newport, by all standards a prosperous community, women were at a disadvantage. Ruth Peckham, director of the poorhouse, had sixteen white women and three white men in her charge in 1774, along with two white males and four females under sixteen. Her household also included one male Indian, two black males, and one black female—a total of twenty-nine.[37] In Newport, as in Salem, Boston, and Portsmouth, women who could not support themselves received a disproportionate share of funds from the town treasury.

Church records also attest to the limited resources women possessed. Each church for which records survive claimed a disproportionate number of female poor, and where records can be traced over time, the number of women for whom the church took responsibility increased as the eighteenth century advanced. Even before the end of the seventeenth century, the Second Church of Boston kept long lists of "poore," noting the amount of money that was doled out to them. Almost all the entries were for "syster," "widdo," or "goody." Many were repeats: there were probably no more than seven to ten different names, but the repetitive entries indicate not only a constant call on limited funds but also the difficulties entailed in breaking the cycle of poverty. In 1734, when the elders distributed money to the poor of the Second Church on Thanksgiving Day, fifty-three sisters but only seven brothers were recipients, a distortion that is excessive even after the imbalance between male and female church members has been accounted for. Boston's King's Chapel responded to the needs of eight women and two men in 1753, but by 1758 they assisted twelve women and six men. The number of poor in Boston's Seventh Church also rose between 1769 and 1774–75.[38]

The number of warnings out (orders to transients to remove themselves from within the town limits) in Essex County, Massachusetts, also measures the ability of women to provide for themselves. Assuming that warnings out were directed, at least in part, toward the economically frail, it is of some interest that at the beginning of the eighteenth century, while the number of recorded warnings was comparatively low, approximately 90 percent were directed toward women. Later decades also brought economic dislocation to men who years earlier would have been able to support themselves and their families, and they began to appear with greater frequency on the lists of those banished. Although Douglas Lamar Jones has shown that after 1743 single males and male-headed families were usually dispatched more frequently than single females or female-headed families, the number of women forced from towns continued to grow in proportion to their inability to find means of support. Indeed, in certain years, such as 1766–67, a far greater number of single women were warned out than men, and in Rhode Island women were constantly in the majority on the unwanted lists.[39]

If there are hints from tax assessments and probate records that the economic viability of women—shaky enough to begin with—declined over two centuries, the question still remains whether women as a group were more disadvantaged than men by forces at work in a maturing urban economy where, among other demographic trends, the once abundant land supply had diminished. Evidence indicates that as the finite amount of land on the eastern seaboard contracted, female access to real property suffered a disproportionate decline. Males became the legatees of choice—a preference that could be sustained, however, only as long as their presence in the population allowed testators to name them as potential heirs.

A decline in available land affected women in different ways, depending on their circumstances. A reduction in the accumulation of real property by women meant less collectible rent—a valuable source of income for women in seaports, where fewer skills meant fewer options that could be translated into cash. In this context it mattered little whether women acquired property on their own, were left property in fee simple, or enjoyed a life interest in it. Rent was rent—but if a dwindling land supply meant that fewer urban men had possession of real property in the eighteenth century, then fewer husbands could devise property to their prospective widows, even if they desired to do so. Moreover, if all male children could not be assured of a real property bequest, it is likely that personal property, which in better times might have been left to women as a substitute for real property, also shifted toward male ownership—reinforcing a domino effect that left women with ever fewer material possessions, not to mention a place to live.

Paradoxically, however, the skewed sex ratio may have mitigated the worst effects of this trend, since the increasingly unbalanced sex ratio meant fewer men were available to receive legacies. Although the study by Alice Hanson Jones found that, compared to women in the middle and southern colonies, New England women had by far the lowest total physical wealth, they nonetheless had proportionately more real property than women in those other regions. The value of that real estate was considerably less than that held by women in the middle and southern colonies, but the pattern itself may suggest another way in which the sex ratio shaped urban society in colonial New England.

James K. Somerville has shown that after 1730 male testators in Salem more frequently left land to unmarried or widowed daughters than they had in the past, a fact that may have contributed to Jones's findings. Somerville also found that after 1750 wives also received a greater share of real property than they had for the previous thirty years.[40] One explanation for this turn-around might be that the colonial wars in the first half of the eighteenth century had decimated the male population to the extent that the effects were reflected in testamentary patterns. Whatever the intentions of testators, these bequests appear to have had little upward effect on cumulative real property holding among women as measured by probate records.

If white women had little property they could call their own, black and Indian women had even less. Most of the blacks and Indians in the seaports of New England were absorbed into households headed by whites. In Newport the names of free blacks who maintained their own residences (1.7 percent of the total population in 1774) are completely absent from the tax lists, a reminder that race as well as sex determined economic status. The Newport census also counted 46 Indians of a total 9,209 inhabitants in that year, none of whom maintained their own households or were noticed by the tax assessors. Most of the 31 adult female Indians were probably servants. In Boston, only five free black households appear on the tax valuation list in 1771, none of which were headed by women. Poverty was egalitarian in Boston, however: the town maintained an integrated almshouse.[41]

"ALL MY DEPENDANCE IS UPON YOU"

Although urban households with multiple income producers were likely to enjoy an adequate or even comfortable standard of living, those headed by single women were just as likely to remain on the fringes of economic viability. Despite the numerous income-producing opportunities in all these seaports, most women earned very little. Moreover, some women could not eke out a living at all. Whether it was because they were overly consumed with child care, were too old, were too frequently struck with the various illnesses that attacked eighteenth-century Americans, or simply did not have the education, skills, or trades to compete in a world that was becoming increasingly complex is irrelevant to the larger question: How did these women survive in a society where they had neither a male provider nor means by which to earn a living? The answer suggests that the economic constraints of eighteenth-century urban society forced many women into a greater dependence on others.

Both law and custom assumed that families were responsible for those members who were incapable of supporting themselves. Sarah Nichols worked forty-nine weeks at two pounds a week to pay off her mother's debt. In such circumstances, a mother was better off with a male offspring, since Ann Sears was able to collect twenty pounds for one month's labor expended on her behalf by her son. That many families were less than enthusiastic about taking over the responsibility of poor or sickly relatives is not to be doubted, and the court records abound with evidence of such reluctance. The children of Mary Stephens of Marblehead refused to support her until a court order forced them to do so. Mrs. Webber and Mrs. Andrews also found it necessary to obtain a judgment. Brothers quarreled over the support of a single sister, and the courts had no dearth of cases concerning children who refused to pay an assessment "toward the relief of their poor decrepid mother." If no sons or daughters were able to help, the town called on grandchildren.[42] It is not that poor men were treated any differently; it is simply that the problem arose more frequently with women.

Semimarried women, whose meager incomes allowed only a minimal standard of living when their husbands were away at sea, had recourse to an additional source of income. They could call on the merchants for whom their husbands sailed to obtain back or prospective pay. In July 1775 Mary Rogers of Newport noted that she had received £103 old tenor "for two months and 2 days wages, due my Husband John Rogers on Board the Brig

Royal Charlotte." Gracy [Walch] informed Mr. Lotrop in 1776 that she was "in want of money," which she hoped he could "seply" her on her husband's account because he sailed in Lotrop's "imploy." And in the same year, Marther Mackloud wrote to the merchant Aaron Lopez for money because she was "in great want," pointing out to him that her husband was in Lopez's "service."[43]

Sometimes needy women had nowhere at all to turn for assistance. In such cases the town reluctantly dug into its pocketbook and took responsibility for the person involved. From birth to death, from a rug and blanket at the lying in to a coffin and winding sheet at the funeral, the town—sometimes with the help of the church—paid the expenses of women unable to provide for themselves. The town officials might give outright cash; the parish might supply food or clothing as needed. The town picked up the bill for medical assistance (including rum) in sickness and abated taxes when necessary. The Selectmen of Portsmouth, New Hampshire, authorized payment for an addition to a woman's house so she could keep her mother and father.[44] Town funds paid families to board their own members if they were unable to do so on their own. Town officials also paid other people in the community to take in ailing or indigent women.

Despite their strong commitment and sense of responsibility, town officials faced problems as the number of poor increased. Given their limited budget, it was expensive to support the indigent in individual homes, whether their own or someone else's. With affluent and middling townspeople reluctant (and ungracious) about paying taxes, it was a strain on the town purse even to abate the taxes of those people in economic difficulty. Thus by the mid-eighteenth century the problem of an increasing number of poor forced the New England seaports to reevaluate their methods of assistance. As early as 1722 the Selectmen of Portsmouth, New Hampshire, "voted that all persons that have any Dependence on the Town shall be put into the Almshouse," and in 1749 in Salem, the town fathers directed the Overseers of the Workhouse "to move all persons there who are wholly maintained by the Town." Newport followed suit in 1760.[45]

The records do not indicate whether the low sex ratio precipitated the removal of relief recipients to a central location. Nevertheless, documents show that in each of the towns women received the bulk of the outlay prior to the policy change by town officials. The Selectmen or Freemen may not have recognized that women were disproportionately handicapped by this decision, and they may not have intended to exercise additional control over those who were institutionalized, but those unfortunate enough to be so stig-matized were stripped of personal independence and decision-making pow-ers and put under the direct supervision of the Overseers of the Poor. The relocation also reduced the income of those who earned money by main-taining the poor in their homes.

It was not necessary for a woman to be confined to a workhouse for her to be dependent on town officials. In Newport the town relied on legislation that permitted officials to regulate the lives of women whose husbands were incapable of providing for their needs. In an effort to prevent these women from becoming town charges, the Overseers of the Poor were allowed to bind out any [male] person who might become a town charge and "to receive his wages and deal them out for the use of his Family . . . as the said Overseers shall judge they or he have occasion for same." Since these wives were likely to have been perfectly capable of evaluating their own needs, the legislation is another example of the dependent relationship between the town mothers and the town fathers.[46]

In 1754 a New Hampshire court permitted John Paige to sell Ann Griffin's real estate in order to support her and prevent her from becoming a town charge, since Griffin lacked family, income, or the means to provide for her-self. Two years later, Reuben Morrell petitioned the court (and was given the right) to sell ten acres of land belonging to Mary Morrell, a single woman who had been "supported principally by Charity of Reuben and others." Pre-sumably, neither woman protested the court's decisions. The widow Peters was deceased and therefore in no position to protest when the Selectmen of Salem distributed her best clothing to the widow Frost and the widow Bush after her demise. Nevertheless, one can only wonder why the decedent's daughter, Mary Cloutman, did not acquire the estate herself, especially since she had cared for her mother before the latter's death.[47]

In many ways, some subtle, some not, the dynamics of the mercantile community interacted with common law traditions and an unbalanced sex ratio to enhance the dependence of women on men and activate the pater-nalism of the latter toward the former. Mary Forrester relied on the charity of Aaron Lopez when she was forced to "make application" to him to help her through the winter, and Lydia Bissell was not far from the truth when she begged for assistance and reminded Lopez that "all my Dependance is upon you."[48]

The dependence of women on men was exacerbated by the establishment of male-headed support organizations. The Fellowship Club of Newport, instituted in 1752, acted as an insurance company for seafaring members who paid dues and whose widows (or wives, if the unlucky mariner fell into enemy hands at sea) were entitled to a refund of all the money that the subscribers had paid into the Treasury, if upon application "the Society shall think them proper objects of their charity."[49] What advantage there was to receiving the principal without any accrued interest or other benefits defies understanding, the more so considering that many individuals lent money at interest to friends, family members, or business acquaintances.

Other policies, designed to relieve ailing or impoverished women, also exacerbated rather than mitigated their dependence. Although workhouses provided spinning wheels and presumably taught unskilled female inmates to spin, that skill was still gender based and effectively relegated women to an employment that provided little income. Alternatively, their taxes (like those of poor men) were abated as necessary or eliminated altogether (unlike male obligations) by informal processes. Female delinquencies were overlooked when the Town Meeting of Newport appointed a committee to investigate reluctant taxpayers with the stipulation that no freeholders were excused from their tax obligations, "women excepted." Echoing European precedent, female hucksters were tolerated; male hucksters were not. And in 1709 it was within the power of the Surveyors of the Highways "to favor such persons as they judge are not well able to work or find workmen [as] poor widows and the like."[50]

A careful reading of the Selectmen's records from Salem suggests that although both men and women were successful in having their taxes abated when their financial situation required it, only women consistently received an outright dole. Each measure reinforced the expectation of female economic incompetence—a sharp change from the early years of the seventeenth century. And deliberately or not, increasing dependence may have acted as a means of restraint: an enhancement, rather than a diminution, of patriarchal control in communities where women outnumbered men.[51]

Surviving account books (almost all of which were kept by men) confirm the patriarchal propensities of mercantile organization. The existence of these leather-bound volumes and the numerous entries relating to women attests to a detailed knowledge of, and therefore the ability to control, female behavior. John Banister's entries for "interest by my wife" meant that little of her business could escape his watchful eye. Thomas Richardson also knew exactly with whom his wife traded and whether her accounts showed a profit or loss. Since he kept the account books, he may have had some say over her accounts.[52]

Richardson also had a running account with one Elizabeth Stafford between 1737 and 1749. Stafford bought shoes, furniture, and other sundries from Richardson and was charged for "a gound" made for her by R. Sandford. There is nothing unusual about these transactions, but they do say something about the relationship of Richardson and Stafford as well as the nature of the mercantile economy. First, Richardson appears to employ women such as Sandford to make clothing for his customers. Second, Stafford's purchases expose her to Richardson's long-term scrutiny, since he was consistently aware of what she bought. Third, she paid her bill in "service" at ten shillings per week (a rate established by Richardson?), which means that depending on the number of hours she worked, she might have paid more for the goods than someone whose labor was valued in excess of ten shillings per week. Joshua Hacker, another Newporter, earned thirty shillings per day for his labor in 1747, and even Abigail Barker could count on as much as eight shillings per day for her tailoring at that time. The Negro Quash traded a day's labor for sixteen shillings in 1748.[53]

Yet the news out of the eighteenth century is not all bad, and one entry in the ledger book of the Newport farmer and stone supplier Jonathan Easton allows a more positive assessment of women's economic position in the mid-1700s. On one page of Easton's account book, he computed the money owed to Ruth Nichols for work done over a period of 49½ weeks. He paid her, according to the final tally, at the rate of sixty shillings per week. But what makes this entry of more than passing interest is the fact that "60/" was written over an original entry of "40/" and the whole debt was recalculated at the higher rate.[54]

Although in this instance only a flight of fancy permits speculation that Ruth Nichols refused to work for less than sixty shillings per week, there is evidence that women were occasionally able to negotiate their wages. In the infancy of settlement, Elizabeth Estick supported Mary West's demand for twenty shillings because she was "a very diligent woman," even though Goodman Canterbury disputed both the amount and West's qualifications. And when Mary Drue "signifyed to some of the Brethren" of the Second Baptist Church in Newport that "she thought her pay was short," they counteroffered with a higher rate for sweeping the meetinghouse in the hope that "she will Except of the same."[55]

THE INVISIBLE WOMAN

Given the pervasiveness of women in the colonial market economy, it is somewhat ironic that until recently, historians have all but ignored their existence. On one level, this omission is explained by historical ratification of an ideology that devalued women's work. That is, nineteenth- and early twentieth-century historians have applied their own attitudes about female labor (which were shaped by industrialism) to a time when that labor took different form and perhaps even meaning. On another level, the evolution of industrialism during the nineteenth century may have conditioned historians to focus their attention on merchant magnates and international trade rather than on the economic infrastructure of the eighteenth-century seaport. Thus, from 1869 forward, the standardized national product and income statistics exclude female household labor, home repair, and home dressmaking from its series of figures.[56]

Charles Brewster, author of *Rambles about Portsmouth* (1873), explained his emendation of a local tax list: "We have before us an Inventory of the Polls and of the Town of Portsmouth in 1727. . . . It is the best record extant of the names of the citizens of this town at that time. . . . The names of some widows who were reported as taxpayers—and a few names which were not legible, have been omitted." It is not known how many other nineteenth- or twentieth-century historians have shared Brewster's cavalier attitude toward early records, but the possibility of such editorial policies poses a problem for contemporary historians who depend on quantifiable data to explain the social structure of a community. The published version of the seventeenth-century Salem town records does not hint that women maintained or repaired highways. Yet the manuscript version of the Town Records indicates that once in a while women were, in fact, paid for just such work—and at the same rate as men.[57]

The removal of female names is destructive of accuracy, but even without the Portsmouth or Salem deletions, the lists are problematical insofar as they compile only those people whose incomes and estates are weighty enough to merit inclusion. Another tier of people earned enough income to sustain themselves but not enough to warrant the tax assessor's attention; many were women, whose invisibility was thus compounded.

At the same time, some of these same people, once thought irretrievably lost to history, surface in other documents such as court records, where, for example, one woman will petition for a license to sell "cyder" and another will plead poverty as a defense to selling "strong drink . . . without license." The only reason we know that Mary Willoughby ran a shop is because she brought suit against Elizabeth Lennit for breaking into it. Similarly, Susanna Mills may have been a receiver of stolen goods, but she was also a spinster. Unice Coudry earned too little money and no place at all on any assessment list, but Jonathan Easton rescued her from historical oblivion when he recorded in his ledger the four pounds she earned by making two gowns.[58]

The law itself also reinforced female invisibility. In theory, common law restrictions prevented married women from making contracts, thus creating a need to disguise a wife's activities by subsuming her transactions under her husband's name. Thomas Richardson acknowledged his wife's "adventure" to Saint Christopher in 1723 or 1724 as well as the "sundry accounts" owed to her in 1725 and her "new account" for a voyage to London. Nowhere, however, did he indicate that she was an apothecary who imported pills and other medicines to sell to doctors in Newport. In the same way, John Banister set aside a page in his ledger for accounts relating to "interest by my wife," a nondescript reference to her trading activities.[59]

Sometimes entries are misleading. Between 1716 and 1722 John Briggs of Boston boarded Deborah Jacob, daughter of David and Sarah. The account reads in the name of David Jacob, but it was Sarah, "wife of sd David Jacob," who paid the debt with, among other goods, cheese, eggs, and eighteen pounds of candles. All eight transactions in the account between Briggs and Mr. Joseph Kent were with the latter's wife.[60]

Sometimes records are straightforward statements of a male acting in behalf of a female. Thus, Joseph Lambert and Thomas Mason settled an account for their mother, Stephen Webb for his wife and mother, and John Ives in behalf of four women. But more frequently the reference is vague: one account between two men—John Clarke and John Tompson—indicated that the transactions between 1745 and 1758 concerned Tompson's debt of nine years' rent. Payment, however, was "By her account for work" and "by her note of hand." Who was the "her" in this case? Between 1753 and 1761 Clarke also conducted business with one Paul Rivere, where the transactions were described as "by her account," or "by cash of her daughter," leaving the reader ignorant once again of the identity of "her"—although not of "her" role.[61]

Female invisibility took many forms in ledger books, some of which border on the demeaning. Samuel Ingersoll's "Account of my fish sold and to who" included the names and titles of a dozen men. The remaining fish were sold "to a woman." John Chaloner, a merchant and shopkeeper, listed both male and female customers by name, and all male customers by occupation. Most of his female clientele (with the curious exception of schoolteachers) were designated by marital status, even though they may have carried on trades as well. His entries fail to indicate that Sarah Peckham and Alice Gould were Newport shopkeepers, or that Phoebe Battey was a well-known tavern-keeper.[62]

The height of invisibility was reached in Thomas Robinson's account book. In his very detailed ledger, he designated by name all the men with whom he conducted business (Samuel All, Jack Sanford), and the slaves he employed (Pompei Scot, Cudgo), but when he paid a worker for spinning cotton, the only book entry was the task ("to spinning cotton") and the amount paid (£1/4/0). Since women did most (if not all) of the spinning, the absence of a woman's name suggests that this merchant, at least, did not value the individual contribution each woman made to his economic well-being. Yet the number of accounts that were credited with the labor of spinning "linnen yearn" or "spining candlewick" silently acknowledge female economic contribution while, paradoxically, they deny credit to any particular woman. In addition, if Mary Prior is right and our very identity is defined by the work we do, what does Robinson's omission say about female identity in eighteenth-century America?[63]

If seventeenth- and eighteenth-century account books have hidden the economic input of women, other documents have obscured female participation as well. It is clear from the Salem, Massachusetts, Selectmen's records that indigent people were boarded in private homes at the expense of the town. In 1709 Edward Bishop collected six pounds from the town treasurer for keeping Anna Dolliver for six months, and a year later Selectmen ordered George Felt "to be given a note for what is due to him for keeping Mary Elsy." During the same year, Benjamin Putnam contracted with the town "to keep Dorothy Good with meat, drink, washing Lodging and Clothing etc. for 1 yr," for which he was to be paid forty shillings.

The question, of course, is whether these women were placed in the homes of single men, or whether these were families. Unseemly conduct between George Felt and the widow Mary Elsy (who was "non composmentis") was unlikely even if Felt was unmarried, but the situation was more complicated with Dorothy Good, since we learn that in 1722 Nathaniel Putnam took Dorothy Good's "Bastard Child" to apprentice. The question is, who actually cared for these women, and whose invisible work was responsible for the income? Not surprisingly, women appear to have been the caretakers. The town may have paid the "sd Edward Bishop Sr.," but if our perception of gender roles and division of labor is at all accurate, it was probably Sarah Bishop, his wife, who bore most of the responsibility for keeping and maintaining Anna Dolliver with "suitable meat, drink, cloathing washing and lodging."

Elizabeth Good was in David Judd's "keeping," but when the treasurer allowed widow Good "a homespun gown and petticoat, as well as 2 cotton and linen shifts" in 1723, they were delivered to David Judd's wife. Moreover, whose home was homespun spun in? George Jacobs earned money by keeping Nicholas Bartlett. Toward this end, Jacobs was supplied with fabric for shirts and a jacket, stockings, "a pair of plain shoues," buttons, and "thred." It is reasonable to assume that Mrs. Jacobs (or a neighbor), and not her husband, turned that fabric into wearing apparel.[64]

The historical paradox is that the evidence to rescue women from economic invisibility is most readily obtained from the same account books of colonial merchants, tradespeople, and artisans that have just been so roundly criticized for their failure to detail women's work. Isaac Stelle, the Newport bakehouse operator, is a good example of a person whose accounts partially redress the historical balance. So meticulous were Stelle's entries that one can picture him bent over the ledgers, carefully entering the debits and credits in their respective columns. Sometimes Mr. Stelle paused between entries, however, and while engaged in thought, he scribbled on the flyleaf of his account book. Most of the doodles were meaningless notes or numerical calculations, but on one particular day, something provoked him to enter a single word on the inside cover of his ledger book. The word he jotted was "women," underlined twice for emphasis, and followed by no fewer than seven exclamation points.[65] Although it is impossible to reconstruct the reason or meaning behind that amusing notation, Stelle's account books in general—and those of his predecessors and contemporaries—are invaluable tools in reconstructing the economic relationship between women and men in the colonial seaports. They hold the key to the urban economy because they reveal what work men and women performed, and how much each was paid.

ECONOMIC AGENCY

On the basis of the number of women who appear in the account books, it is evident that the self-reliant household where a woman made all the necessities of life for herself and her family is largely an exaggeration of the nineteenth-century historical imagination. Not all women spun and even fewer wove. Instead, they purchased thread and fabric from those who did or from those who sold such items. And as the eighteenth century advanced, many seem to have bought their finished clothing in exchange for cash or bartered goods.

At the same time, the family economy in an urban setting provided both need and opportunity for every able hand, linking it inextricably with the market or commercial economy. In this setting, household members worked cooperatively in joint ventures to provide the maximum standard of living for all concerned. Andrew Tucker caught fish in the ketch *Adventure;* Mary Tucker "made" (salted?), "carried," and "sold" them. According to Isaac Stelle's ledger book, his wife, Penelope, was an active partner in the Newport bakehouse operation, and Martha Leuby made, mended, and washed leather goods alongside her husband, Thomas. Nathaniel Ridgeway, a Boston tailor, ordered scissors, fabric, and other "sundries" delivered to his wife between 1756 and 1759, suggesting that Mrs. Ridgeway was associated in some capacity with the tailoring establishment. And when Ebenezer Frost of Boston petitioned for a liquor license, it was to open a shop "with the Assistance of his wife." Henry and Hannah Dyre ran the Boston almshouse together between 1738 and 1742, and she took over "support of the House" when he died in the latter year.[66]

John and Dorothy Farnham rented out wharf space to sloops and schooners, and although James Barnard contracted with John Farnham "at £5 pr annum," Captain Samuel Stroud and Mr. James Bishop dealt with Dorothy Farnham for "wharffage" of their vessels. Portsmouth residents Walter Abbott and his wife sold "wine and Liquors"—one of many husband-and-wife teams who ran taverns, boardinghouses, and retail establishments with different chores assigned to various family members.[67] One of the best examples of a family enterprise was the printing establishment of James Franklin. A brother to the more famous Franklin, James removed to Newport in 1726 with the warm encouragement of Boston's officials. After his death in 1735, his widow, Ann, and their children continued the business, and Ann Franklin's own imprint appeared on various publications. It is because women had experience in these businesses as wives that they were able to run them as widows.

Sometimes widows took on new partners, as did Elizabeth Mumford, who advertised that she was continuing the shoemaking business of her late husband in association with John Remington, who had worked previously with her deceased spouse. Yet a husband's former business partner might resist an ongoing association with his widow, a reluctance suggested by a petition from Jane Willson, who informed the Rhode Island General Assembly that Henry John Overing had "for sometime refused to carry on the Business of Sugar Boiling with your Petitioner and she is entirely unable to carry it on alone, so that the will of the Testator [James Willson] cannot be complyed with." Alternatively, then, a widow might lease the family business after a spouse's death and enjoy rental income from the property. The tanner Joseph Wight hired a tanyard from the widow Hannah James, whose former husband was likely to have been the original owner.[68]

It is not at all clear, however, that married women working in partnership with their husbands thought of themselves as surrogates, or that they subscribed to the notion of deputy husband, Cotton Mather notwithstanding. A "deputy husband," Mather maintained in 1692, kept "good orders in the House" when her husband was "out of the Way." Yet Mather's female parishioners may not have endorsed such a definition, any more than they endorsed Mather himself. Laurel Ulrich's interpretation of this concept also implies "permission" to act under certain circumstances (in contrast to the assumption of an ongoing right), and in an urban environment with a distorted sex ratio such a construction may not be applicable.[69] Moreover, the family economy required cooperation; given the assertiveness and independence displayed by women in the records it is entirely possible that husbands and wives (if they considered the matter at all) recognized mutual responsibilities rather than authoritative hierarchies. Catherine Davis partitioned a cellar in a house she rented, and although her husband shared that cellar space, Catherine made it perfectly clear that "she had partitioned it for her own use."[70]

It is evident from account books that the labor of wives diminished debts that were recorded in their spouse's names. James Carter's account in James Taylor's book indicates that a debt of eighteen shillings was paid off in part "By work his wife Don," as well as by cash from both Carter and his wife. John and Elizabeth Legros kept a running account with the merchant John Touzel of Salem. They bought pork, for example, in 1733, and were credited by Touzel for "work about my son cloths"—work that seems to have been done by Elizabeth Legros.[71]

Similarly, Joseph Boarman was charged by John Hovey of Ipswich for combing and weaving yarn, and he was credited in turn with various food products and spinning two pounds, twelve ounces of wool yarn. It is likely that Boarman's wife or daughter was responsible for that payment, even though neither was specifically named. Walter Fairfield discharged his debt to Hovey by making bricks, laying a floor, plastering a wall, boarding, and clapboarding. His account with the weaver Hovey was also credited with a half pound of linen yarn and spinning six pounds of flax yarn, for which a female member of his family was likely to have been responsible. Joshua Buffum of Salem recorded that William Banes was a "tennant in my house" whose rent in 1703 was paid in part by "work by his wife."[72] The somewhat vague word "work" or equally ambiguous phrase "work done" suggests that the wives in each case added to the family income, but the specifics of that work went unrecorded.

Women's labor may have been interchangeable with that of their husbands, or they may have been involved in different enterprises altogether. Dorothy Jones and Jane Barnard sold coffee and chocolate in separate public houses in 1670, while their husbands were involved in other activities. The wives of Thomas Richardson and John Banister engaged in trading ventures that differed from their husbands' in magnitude and content but are evidence of female participation in long-distance commerce nonetheless. Mary Cranch ran a boardinghouse and sold dry goods while married to the mariner John Cranch.[73]

Lemuel Crandall's wife, Mary, worked for the merchant Aaron Lopez as a spinner, and Sarah Jacobs, wife of David, helped pay for their daughter's schooling by bartering eighteen pounds of candles, cheese, and eggs. In 1723 Thomas Amory recorded that he bought and received of William Young eighteen pair of women's gloves, which he took for his "wife's use." Since even the most affluent and fastidious colonist was unlikely to need eighteen pair of gloves at one time, it is probable that Amory's wife intended to retail them—possibly in connection with a funeral. Both Rebecca and Captain Isaac Holmes ran accounts with Amory, and she appears to have dealt in wine, rum, fabric, and plank in her husband's absence. Abigail Adams engaged in small trade with goods her husband sent her from Europe.[74]

Ledgers also demonstrate that wives commonly engaged in financial transactions for the enterprises in which the family was involved. Thomas

Richardson of Newport rented a house in 1747 to Abigail Barker, and Barker, Richardson noted, "settled with my wife." Richardson's wife also collected rent from Sarah Johnson. Similarly, Thomas Dean's ledgers show that Mrs. Mary Dean collected debts from [Thomick] Proctor, Nath Richardson, and Samuel Webb. Mrs. Dean also lent twelve shillings to James Collins.[75]

In Boston, Rebekah Partridge "Received of William Wain £5 12 sh . . . on account of [her] husband Samuel," and in Salem, the merchant John Touzel noted in 1733 that Thomas Makintyer was indebted to him because of the thirty shillings Touzel's wife "paid" Makintyer. In 1686 Jane King borrowed twenty pounds from Thomas Maule "for the use of [her] husband Nicholas King," while in 1694 Joan Pembrook acknowledged that she received settlement "in full of all accounts between him the said Maule and my husband Elkanah Pembrook." Captain Estas How had an account with the bakehouse proprietor Isaac Stelle, but it was to How's wife and to his "wife's order" that payment was made. John Banister's accounts show a number of receipts from women who collected their husbands' wages.[76]

The frequency with which wives lent and received money, and the circumstances surrounding these fiduciary relationships, implies that women were well aware of the income-producing potential of their families, as well as their financial status. More than just agents, messengers, or deputy husbands, women were involved in cooperative ventures that affected the wellbeing of their families no less than the efforts of their husbands. Implicit in such arrangements is the idea that many women must have enjoyed some degree of literacy. In addition, handling money and recording transactions required at least elementary math and accounting skills. By twentieth-century standards, barter may have been a primitive means of exchange, but it required a sophisticated understanding of equivalents and the ability to convert goods and services to a common denominator. How much rum equaled a dozen eggs? How long should Widow Davis nurse a patient to pay her shoemaker's bill?[77]

Given such evidence, it also appears that the common law restrictions that prevented married women from entering into contractual arrangements were not quite as ironclad as they theoretically might have been. When Mr. Collins obligated himself to Mrs. Dean, they each recognized a contractual agreement, even if no formalities were observed. The only reason that John Touzel could collect on Thomas Makintyer's debt was because each understood the binding nature of the agreement between Touzel's wife and Makintyer. Although ship captains about to embark on long voyages occasionally

left their wives with powers of attorney to ensure the legality of their spouses'
actions, similar documents constructed by husbands-in-residence have not
surfaced. Common law notwithstanding, the number of informal agreements involving women suggest a willingness by the participants to honor
their "contractual" commitments.

Furthermore, an even closer reading of the records suggests that many
women kept the account books for family mercantile enterprises, a fact that
is demonstrated by their testimony in court when controversies arose over
payment for goods. If Samuel Holmes of Newport was on record as having
sold goods to William May, the bill was signed and attested to by Rebeckah
Holmes. Similarly, John and Joanna Chapman boarded Nicholas Migood in
1722 and 1723, but it was Joanna who signed the accounting for "bord, washing and lodging, makeing of shirts and licor," done and sold at "sundry
times." Payment by Migood included items to benefit the entire family: tobacco, a casement, and gardening, as well as specific compensation in cash
paid to Joanna's "dawter" for sewing. Through the barter of such goods and
services the entire family contributed to its well-being, and in return, the
family stood to gain both individually and collectively. Migood was a ship
carpenter, and the "casement" (either a window frame or small cupboard)
upgraded the family's residence. Gardening may have been at Joanna's behest
in compensation for washing or food preparation, and the Chapman's
daughter received a monetary return for her efforts.[78]

Peter Treby was a Newport sailmaker whose wife(?), Mehetabel, kept the
accounts in what were probably well-organized ledgers. As a result, she was
able to attest to the accuracy of the running exchange between Rebecca May
and Treby when May sued Peter for a thirty-six-pound note. Indeed, Mehetabel herself may have shared the work involved in "making [two] Bed Bot-
toms" for May as well as the duck and bed sacking that accompanied them.
After examining the accounts presented by litigants Treby and May (the latter's receipts having been made on small pieces of paper that were burned
upon payment), an inspection committee set a twelve-pound value on the
remaining debt, a sum representing one-third of its face value.[79]

This case demonstrates not only the centrality of female participation in
mercantile activities but also the growing importance of record keeping as
disputes over debt increased. In a controversy over the amount of wages
promised to a servant, Martha Church testified that she kept accounts of
"sevll mens name and time of their Comeing to work att hammersmith in
the Summer 1719." Because Church recorded only what she said and omitted

the rate of payment, the dispute was first resolved in favor of the plaintiff, who then lost to the defendant on appeal. Thus, even if women who kept accounts were no less integral to the market economy than those who produced goods or loaded ships, the growing sophistication of the economy and the increasingly intricate nature of long-distance transactions would eventually displace many female bookkeepers as accounting became professionalized.[80]

— ≠ —

If it is possible to compensate for the constant invisibility of women in colonial America by a more thorough analysis of the historical record, it is more difficult to account for a related phenomenon that occurred during the eighteenth century and may be described as a declining visibility, or conversely as an increasing invisibility. In short, there is little doubt that fewer women appeared in the records as the eighteenth century advanced. This does not necessarily mean that women were less involved in the market economy, but rather that their economic participation was recorded in a different fashion or simply ignored with greater emphasis. At the same time, this trend is paralleled by a similar decline of female visibility or activity in other urban institutions such as the church and law, and thus was more likely to have been part of the same ongoing social phenomenon experienced by European women.[81]

The evidence that prompts this assessment and comparison is also contained in the various account books that have survived the centuries. In the seventeenth century female names proliferate; by the later decades of the eighteenth century they are curiously absent. Joshua Buffum, a late seventeenth-century wheelwright and carpenter from Salem, was one of many artisans whose ledger confirms that he commonly dealt with women.[82] A century later, account books showing a persistent female presence are rare.

Robert Gibbs, another example, ran a general store in Boston between 1660 and 1708.[83] Transactions were mainly in the form of barter, and women supplied him with merchandise such as yarn, eggs, or gingerbread, which he, in turn, would sell. In this early ledger there were as many accounts with women as with men—a ratio that would not be sustained as the eighteenth century advanced. More important, where husband and wife each purchased items from Gibbs there were separate entries for each name, a distinction also unlikely to be perpetuated in later decades.

Peter Burr's account book from 1695 to 1699 also documents the many women who bartered for the sundries Burr kept in his shop and whose accounts were just as extensive as Burr's male customers. By the middle of the eighteenth century, however, these individual transactions appear less frequently. Instead, merchants' ledgers show women "charging" on their husbands' accounts. Husbands gave their wives "permission" (frequently in writing) to buy against credit or to purchase sundries.[84]

In similar fashion, Walter Newberry's shipping accounts between 1673 and 1688 document a number of active female merchants in the Caribbean and New England. In 1686 Newberry shipped "flower" from Newport to Boston on the account of "Edward Pery," but delivery was to be made to "Elizabeth Perry" or "to hir assignes." In 1723 Richard Partridge and Martha Hall had a joint account with the merchant Thomas Richardson, and the same ledger showed Margaret Newbury sending a consignment of goods to Walter Newberry. Samuel Ingersoll, a merchant who was active in Salem between 1685 and 1695, also recorded many trading ventures in which women participated. Ingersoll carried fish and tobacco from Mrs. Mune, small amounts of oil, shoes, skines (skins?), and pines (pins?) from Mrs. E[dwards] as well as a bag of hopes (hops?) and a yard of lace from Mary Chatwell. Several other women, including a Mrs. Shute, sent off tobacco with the hope that it would be sold to best advantage. Ingersoll also referred on other pages to a Mr. Edwards and a Mr. Shute, suggesting that some of these entrepreneurs were married women acting on their own.[85]

Entries such as these were rare later in the eighteenth century. The transition, or decline in visibility, shows up in a variety of sources. Take, for example, the account book of the Boston tailor William Waine. His receipt books run from 1728 through the 1770s. In the early years, although there are more accounts with men than with women, women's names are interspersed throughout. Starting with the 1760s, however, fewer and fewer women's names appear, and by the 1770s there are none at all. The ledgers of Jabez Carpenter, who was also a tailor, indicate the same trend. The entries begin in 1755 and continue to 1774. In the former year he had accounts with forty-nine women, in the latter year two, with a constant decline in the intervening years. In his ledger, the reduction of women's names becomes most obvious in the middle and late 1760s. William Redwood's account book suggests much the same pattern. His transactions cover the period 1749–62, and he had accounts with twenty-one women in that period of time. Most of these transactions took place in the early 1750s, and by 1762 only two women were left with whom he conducted business.[86]

Benjamin Greene's records corroborate Carpenter and Redwood. Greene was a Boston merchant as well as a silver- and goldsmith. His surviving records run from 1734 to 1782. Between 1734 and 1753 he had accounts with twenty-three women, but between 1764 and 1782 only six women are represented in his records. The same holds true for Peter Verstilles. He was a small merchant or shopkeeper in Portsmouth, New Hampshire, in 1754–55, and he eventually moved to Boston in November 1757. In the nine-month period between December 1754 and September 1755, he recorded far more accounts with women than there subsequently were in Boston in the twenty-one-month period between November 1757 and September 1759.[87]

ACCOUNTING FOR THE TRENDS

Claudia Goldin's economic history of American women begins in 1790 and focuses on the nineteenth and twentieth centuries. Her conclusions, however, are directly linked to the eighteenth century, where trends, set in motion decades earlier, forecast the future. She argues that between 1790 and 1860 the number of female heads of households with occupations "declined modestly over the 70-year period" before subsequently rising again. Furthermore, she cautions that the eventual upturn was "only the rising portion of a U-shaped process" that had been two centuries in the making and that the market activity of adult women probably declined from an even higher participation rate at some point in the past. It is likely that Goldin's hypothetical decline is what has been herein described as the increasing invisibility of urban women in colonial New England.[88]

There can be little doubt that these patterns are somehow related to the maturing of American society and the growing complexity of the commercial economy. Although the precise nature of that connection remains elusive, it is probably part of an emerging market capitalism that altered the New England seaport economy in such a way as to reduce female participation and further sap female economic viability. Thus two separate yet interrelated issues require explanation. First, why did women become less visible? And second, what factors in the evolution of the American economy might have eroded female vitality? Although few historians have probed such questions in the past, current research has begun to address these issues.[89]

Mary Prior notes, for example, that in family industry the profits belonged to the entire family, even if they were theoretically vested in the head.

If this arrangement existed in fact, the unity of capital and labor (as a feature of the domestic economy) was a combination favorable to women. Peter Hall traces the steps by which that unity was undermined. He argues persuasively that the family as a mercantile unit declined as capital was disengaged from it, mercantile operations were specialized, and partible inheritance (another feature advantageous to women) discouraged. Although Hall does not apply his findings to gender roles, his conclusions imply that under these circumstances women would have been excluded from various aspects of the mercantile enterprise, which in turn would account for their declining visibility. This interpretation presumes that the sequence of events that Hall describes actually began earlier than he indicates.[90]

C. Dallett Hemphill tackles the gender issue directly by arguing that increasing specialization hampered women because as husbands acquired skilled trades—as in the case of a gunsmith or cooper—the participation of wives in the production process waned. Indeed, women's presence in the market economy may have declined as early as the late seventeenth century, when, as Carol Karlsen maintains, women who had turned domestic activity into profitable business enterprises were discouraged from engaging in such activities. Witchcraft accusations served as a strong deterrent to productive initiative.[91]

Another reason for the disappearance of women from the market economy may have been related to difficulties in obtaining credit by the middle of the eighteenth century. Easy credit had been available in the seventeenth century, when merchants needed craftspeople and other laborers; by the eighteenth century this incentive was no longer necessary. Whether women benefited by easy access to credit is debatable, but it is likely that a restrictive credit policy affected them adversely, as did the periods of economic dislocation such as the one following the French and Indian War. According to a study by Bruce Mann, promissory notes replaced book debts by the mid-1700s, a move that formalized lending procedures and imposed a stronger obligation to pay.[92] Since the economic fragility of women impaired their ability to repay loans, it is possible that their declining visibility reflected a perception of women as bad credit risks.

Furthermore, a dwindling land supply conspired with a surge of dislocated males to provide workers for expanded market production. This market favored males, as employers showed preference to those members of the family who demonstrated skills and were free, at the same time, to work in the manufactories that were beginning to dot the urban scene. Thus, the progressive separation of home and production for income that Claudia Goldin holds responsible for the decline in female proprietorships and occupations after 1790 may have begun decades earlier.[93]

Increasing evidence suggests that urban women in colonial New England were more economically vulnerable on the eve of the Revolutionary era than they had been one hundred years earlier because of developments that were gendered in their effects.[94] For example, the transition from a barter system to a cash or monied economy was more disadvantageous to women than to men. Barter assumed standard weights and measures: if a quarter weight of common bread was worth five shillings, it would have been traded for that, no matter who was involved in the exchange. Thus, if Mrs. Witherspoon swapped an equally standard measure of distilled rum for that bread, she was probably compensated measure for measure. But once Mrs. W. was paid in cash for labor performed, there was room for discrimination. A value judgment could be made on the worth of needlework versus carpentry, or midwifery versus blacksmithing. Moreover, since male tailors were compensated at a higher rate than female tailors, it appears that Christine Delphy is correct and that it is female labor that was devalued, not the nature of the work itself. Barter may have been cumbersome, but it had the potential of being a more equitable compensation in terms of gender.[95] Moreover, it put women in possession of negotiable goods. The evolution of a cash/credit economy left women with less room to maneuver, economically speaking.

The attempt at regulation of wages in labor-starved New England may also have affected men and women in different ways. Local control was established early on, and in the seventeenth century towns appear to have achieved modest success in imposing a scale of maximum wages on tradespeople and laborers. The legislation imposed fines on employers who gave and employees who accepted excessive wages. Under these regulations, women stood to gain because enforcement prevented a spiraling income discrepancy between men and women by keeping male wages down. Richard Morris found that wage and price fixing disintegrated in eighteenth-century Massachusetts, and that the system of internal regulation broke down.[96] If this is true, male earning power may have increased disproportionately in the later colonial period.

Similarly, the earlier colonial pattern where earning packages included room and board was more favorable to women than one where wages were the sole compensation. Female earnings could not buy the same standard of food and living accommodations that women enjoyed as live-in servants. The shift from indentured servitude to a wage-earning economy was well under way by the middle of the eighteenth century and may partly explain the increasing inability of women to provide for themselves. Wage-earning women were often subject to merchant employers who hired them for needle-work under the increasingly popular putting-out system and who preferred to pay by the piece rather than by the day or week. Such methods worked to the benefit of the employer, since no matter how long it took to make the item, he paid only a predetermined amount. As the putting-out system—protoindustrialization—expanded, therefore, it added to the accumulating disadvantages women faced.

In many ways, the quest for refinement and gentility had gendered over-tones. The demand for material goods stimulated the importation and pro-duction of consumer wares, but eighteenth-century urban women were neither importing nor producing most of the commodities that fed the pre-industrial economy. Some molded candles, others drew patterns on canvas for embroidered chair seats, but there is little if any evidence that luxury goods in high demand such as teacups, mirrors, mahogany tables, or silver sugar tongs were either imported or crafted by women in appreciable quanti-ties. Most urban women lacked wheels and looms and thus could not meet the increasing demand for fabrics. As Carole Shammas convincingly demon-strates, Britain had successfully thwarted an American textile industry, even if Govenor Francis Bernard overstated the case when he reassured the Board of Trade in 1763 that "the Inhabitants of the trading Towns . . . have their whole supply of Cloathing from Great Britain."[97] Nevertheless, the absence of viable woolen and linen industries shut off employment possibilities for women, even if the compensation for such work would have been small. Imported fabrics allowed New England women to sew many of the fine gar-ments with which genteel Americans adorned themselves, but their remuner-ation for so doing did not permit their own ascendancy into the ranks of the people they clothed. And unlike their rural counterparts, urban women did not produce dairy products in any quantity for the market, thus further lim-iting their ability to trade.

The literature on consumerism has been more than persuasive that com-modity acquisition defined status, but it has only hinted at the gendered nuances of that hot pursuit of property. Married middle-class white women might enjoy the benefits of improved housing, but unmarried women in the New England seaports could not aspire to the same living standards. The "shared expectations" of middle-class whites for "personal advancement" could not be shared by those who had no expectation of such advancement.

If refinement was determined by housing accommodations and other material signs of gentility, single women without property were in danger of being relegated to the ranks of the unrefined and ungenteel. How could the burgeoning number of servant women present themselves as "worthy and acceptable" if gentility did not extend to servants' space in the late eighteenth century?[98]

If, as T. H. Breen argues, the status of eighteenth-century Americans depended on commodities, he is implying that those who could not buy such amenities were reduced in status, a condition that disproportionately affected urban women. Packaged respectability was beyond the reach of those for whom the purchase of everyday necessities proved difficult enough. In 1763 Margaret Brussells earned thirty shillings (Rhode Island currency) a day for her work, but one quart of milk cost her six shillings.[99] Dancing and singing lessons would not have been in her budget.

Ironically, eighteenth-century women were thought to be imbued naturally with the qualities associated with refinement: gentility, delicacy, and sensibility, an association that should have mitigated (if not obviated) the need to purchase material objects for the same end. Nevertheless, any interpretation that attributed respectability to inherent tendencies rather than to purchasing power would have frustrated the flow of trade, and thus its logic was drowned in the myriad of goods flooding the marketplace.

At the same time, to identify purchasing with power is too glib an equation. Even if women had a strong say in the consumer products that filled the home (and this premise is conjectural to begin with), the sum of those goods does not necessarily add up to enhanced power. What influence was tucked into the secret compartment of a desk from the workshop of John Goddard? What authority steamed from a Wedgwood teapot? Although the deliberate diversion of purchases from one tradesperson to another could theoretically affect the material well-being of the purveyor, such economic clout presupposes affluent customers or consumers engaged in collective action. The reality of furniture maker Job Townsend's ledgers suggests another scenario, one where most customers were male, and where women bought small, less expensive pieces of furniture or took chairs, tables, and chests to Townsend for repair.[100] Rather than reflecting an image of power, it is more likely that the fashionable Chippendale mirrors reflected women who had internalized appropriate female behavior and who were both creating and acting out stereotypical attitudes about women, among which was the notion that gentility begins at home.

Furthermore, women would be responsible for gentrifying the home just as the home was being displaced as the locus of authority and, as Richard Bushman observes, decisions, production, and handshakes took place elsewhere. If middle-class virtue rested in part, at least, on a work ethic, the household had become marginal in terms of productive performance. In short, as middle-class white married women gained control of the household, the significance of the household declined. Indeed, the new bourgeois values associated with gentility resulted in a negative attitude toward "working" women.[101]

Yet some women, both married and unmarried, did work outside the home in the post-Revolutionary years. When Jacques-Pierre Brissot de Warville visited Boston a quarter century after Govenor Bernard posted his letter, he took note of a competitive spirit that, he said, "created factories for spinning hemp and flax, which provide a good occupation for young people . . . and which supply a particularly suitable occupation for women left idle by the long voyages of their seafaring husbands or by other accidents."[102] More than a century after the Massachusetts General Court had called on otherwise unoccupied women and children to spin for the public good, both groups were still inextricably linked to a skill that thwarted the devil's plans for mischief but left little room for economic mobility.

The separation of home and production had other ramifications, no less gendered. If business was conducted elsewhere, not only did women lose the opportunity to learn trades and skills, but their familiarity with the financial aspects of commercial activities was also reduced. In such circumstances, women would have been less likely to keep books or take responsibility for family business accounts as they had in the past. In their former capacity as receivers of rent, payments, wages, or fees, as shopkeeping wives of merchant traders, women had access to cash. Self-esteem and sense of participation aside, once their role as family financial officer was eliminated, whatever economic independence they possessed dissipated as well.

Increased consumption encouraged borrowing, contracts, debt, and ultimately an increase in litigation. But married women were excluded from the new economic order by the legal system itself; they could not make contracts (and thus borrow money based on enforceable obligations), nor could they sue or be sued independently. Thus, female access to capital and credit was curtailed at the moment in time when such access was necessary to take advantage of new economic opportunities. As Marcus Rediker acknowledges, long-distance trade required capital concentration, large sums that were often created by merchant partnerships.[103] Women were precluded from engaging in such cooperative ventures. Shut out of the public network by legal constraints, a woman's husband became her sole banker. And as their quasi-partnership dissolved because of circumstances beyond her control, she became more dependent on him for "support," a marital relationship that nurtured the seeds of hierarchy and patriarchy and that paralleled the way in which the new industrial order would be organized. If in medieval Europe married women who were long-distance traders took advantage of family capital accumulation to further their own interests, eighteenth-century American women were not supported in the same way.

However the story unfolded, one thing is certain: if women were central to the economy of early urban America, that economy was no less central to their lives. Economic changes threatened their public visibility and economic standing, and they moved into the era of independence more dependent and less equal than they had been in the past. To counter with the argument that most white American women shared in the prosperity of an expanding economy by marrying upwardly mobile men is merely to emphasize their inability to arrive at material well-being on their own. Yet they themselves were a manifestation of the new upward mobility because the same dependence and indolence that corrupted men were positive female attributes. A successful middle-class husband relieved his wife of "work," and thus her nonproductivity became a measure of his success. She was at "liberty" to create a virtuous home, paradoxically "free" from the excesses of a luxury-seeking consumer society, and committed to the republican family rather than liberal individualism.

Moreover, whatever role the Enlightenment played in encouraging individualism and self-awareness, women were less affected than men by those heady intellectual currents. For women, a diminishing public presence and a faltering economic status culminated in a submissiveness that would inhibit any feminist potential in the Revolutionary era and preclude any but the most modest achievements for the next half century. Thus, even if it is inaccurate to say that the seventeenth century was a golden age for women, it seems apparent that the eighteenth had less luster than we once imagined.

~ CHAPTER 4 ~

A Severe Legislation

*In the temperate latitude . . . women have not been
deprived of their liberty, but a severe legislation has,
at all times, kept them in a state of dependence.*
—TOM PAINE (1775)

Mary Polly's Story

When Mary Polly's tailor husband left Portsmouth for an extended trip in 1714 (perhaps in connection with his duties as post rider), he gave his wife power of attorney to act in his stead.[1] Because of his long absence and her lack of income, she was "necessiated" to sell a "certain Lott of Land" for "the Suport of her family." The buyer, Samuel Hinks, who may also have been a neighbor of Mary and Edward Polly, "Suplied her with money and other necessaries as she had Occasion . . . and She gave Possession" of the property to Hinks. Mary Polly had a deed of sale drawn up but, for reasons she never articulated, delayed execution of it.

Edward Polly died before returning to Portsmouth, and by the time Mary heard of his demise sometime before July 1715, she no longer retained power to execute the deed. Owing to her newly acquired (and presumably unexpected) status as a widow, however, she did retain a one-third life interest in that property, since she had not legally consummated the sale. Mary did not remain a widow for very long, and "Sometime after She was married again, to one Woolet." Unfortunately, it was Mary's bad luck to be attracted to peripatetic men, and once again her husband "went out the Country," never to return.

Meanwhile, the status of Hinks's property remained in limbo. He had already paid forty-one pounds of the fifty-five-pound purchase price, and Mary appeared quite willing to complete the transfer. According to Samuel Hinks,

139

Mary told anyone who asked that "she had sold" the property to him. But Mary complicated matters by dying before the property was legally conveyed to Hinks. And although "sufficient witnesses" were willing to come forward to attest to Hinks's "possession of it," the New Hampshire General Assembly refused to confirm the transaction initiated in April 1714 by Mary Polly. Hinks's petition to that body received a cool reception, since "the heirs of Edward Polly" (Mary and Edward's children) contested his claims. Unable or unwilling to rule on the matter until it could be presented to the governor, the General Assembly postponed a decision from April 1719 to their fall session, and then again until the spring of 1720.

The final decision rendered by the governor and council reflected the complexities of common law rules governing married women and the ambiguities that women could seize upon to make unfavorable laws work in their favor. Neither Mary's children nor the governor considered Mary's transaction a bona fide sale. Thus, Mary's heirs were given first claim on the property, but in fairness to Hinks, the ruling required them to return his £41/16/10 downpayment. If they refused to repay Hinks, the court allowed Hinks to complete the purchase on the original terms by paying Polly's heirs the remaining sum due: £13/3/2.

Mary Polly's procrastination worked in her favor. The delay allowed her use of the property until her death. Had she signed off on the sale before her husband's death, she would have relinquished her dower rights in the parcel and Edward Polly would have controlled the proceeds had he returned. At his death, creditors would have had first call on whatever money remained from the sale, and neither she nor her children would have gained from the profits. It is likely that the value of the property increased between 1714 and 1720, which meant that either Hinks or Mary's heirs would obtain real estate that was worth more than the original purchase price of fifty-five pounds. Since Mary's heirs took the trouble to challenge Hinks's alleged ownership, they probably returned his money and reclaimed the property. It is not impossible that this is what Mary Polly intended all along.

— ⚹ —

On one level, Tom Paine was right: the colonial legal system, like the English model from which it sprang, furthered the development of inegalitarian gender relations. If, however, Paine meant that a particular code of laws, enacted at the onset of the colonial experiment, had "at all times" subjected women to such "dependence," he miscalculated the historical time frame. Evidence suggests that law and gender maintained an unstable relationship at the beginning of the seventeenth century, and that it took at least a century of evolution for that match to produce the state of dependence Paine perceived.

Although the colonists transported weighty legal baggage across the Atlantic, the first settlements in the Bay Colony were societies where legal procedures were flexible, codification nonexistent, and the application of law subject to discretionary justice. Whatever effects this may have had on men, such a combination had an unanticipated—and unintended—impact on women by affording them somewhat more autonomy than they had enjoyed in England. And rather than being "frightened" by such autonomy, women seized unplanned opportunities to advance themselves.[2] Given their cultural and common law backgrounds, however, lawmakers and jurists were not likely to encourage such autonomous behavior, and in the century following 1630 colonial leaders constructed a legal system that constricted female independence as it thwarted their personal decision making. Few laws were aimed at women directly, although those that were drafted with such intention demeaned and discriminated. Nevertheless, even seemingly neutral laws influenced men and women differently, and their uneven effect emphasized and reinforced distinctions as people acted out their lives.

This is not to argue an ephemeral golden age for women that evaporated as the colonies developed. Nonetheless, as codes proliferated and local resolutions were promulgated, as court decisions multiplied and the English common law filled in the gaps, legislators and judges created public and private patriarchies that effectively negated any advantages that legal elasticity and frontier fluidity once offered. The impact of a growing body of legislative and judicial pronouncements on estate matters, property, divorce, education, and economic opportunity not only marginalized women and contributed to their increasing public invisibility but also laid the foundation for the feminization of poverty in the seaports of colonial New England.

FEMALE AUTHORITY

Given these persistent trends, it is more than a little paradoxical that the same judicial system legitimized female power and clarified female authority. In the legal world, gender roles were turned upside down: the judicial system sanctioned unsubmissive behavior and rewarded undeferential women. Indeed, in the theater of the court, women engaged in role reversal as a matter of right. A suit by its very nature is an assertive act, an appeal even more so.

Furthermore, married women petitioned not only as individuals but also on behalf of their husbands. Significantly, they acted as attorneys for their spouses in cases of some importance, confirming the notion that they were taken seriously as litigators or their husbands would not have appointed them to begin with. And as their husbands' attorneys, necessity demanded that they be familiar with the details of the case.[3]

Wives with errant husbands also had a legitimate public role to play. They could—and did—petition the courts for a reduction or curtailment of their husbands' sentences. To be sure, the role was one of supplicant, but the outcome was surely as important to those concerned as one where the rules of litigation invested women with more authority. Women petitioned to have their husbands released from prison or their fines abated or their sentences reduced. The court removed the rope from Jenken Davies's neck at his wife's request, and upon the petition of Hannah Ballantine, the court reversed a sentence mandating the severance of her husband's ear from his head. The court denied Elizabeth Fairechild's petition to have her husband's neck un-noosed, but upon her application, granted the family permission to resettle elsewhere.[4]

It is somewhat strange that these husbands did not petition in their own names and even stranger that husbands rarely petitioned for mitigation of their wives' sentences. It is not likely they were precluded from doing so, since such pleas occasionally surface in the records. And one can only hypothesize that female petitions were a strategy to engage the court's sympathy for a plea from an innocent and distressed wife rather than from an already convicted husband, but this possibility does not address the absence of petitions from husbands whose wives had been sentenced for a variety of infractions.[5]

Although the very nature of a petition positioned lawmakers to treat it as a request, in fact such importunities could be persuasive, demanding, and even threatening, especially if there were multiple signatories. When officials imprisoned midwife Alice Tilly for what appeared to be contempt of authority in 1650, several petitions, signed by both men and women, urged her release. One remarkably humble document addressed to Governor John Endicott, Deputy Governor Thomas Dudley, and the rest of the General Court was signed by 130 not-so-humble female Bostonians.[6]

In response, the court admitted that it was "no small greife" to be "so often pressed . . . by so many women heretofore, and now also by so many men." Nevertheless, given the circumstances (and the fact that Tilly lacked contrition), it would have been a violation of their consciences to grant her a full rather than a partial pardon. In the view of the authorities, Mrs. Tilly sought "a compleat victory over magistracy" not only by her own "cariage and speaches" but by her "urginge others thus still to petition for her." There was, after all, "as much need to uphold magistracy in theire authority as Mrs Tilly in her midwivry." With such reasoning the General Court rebuffed the petitioners and, in so doing, confirmed the limitation of petitions as a political tool. Nevertheless, it is equally clear that despite the submissive tone of the petitions, the magistrates of Massachusetts Bay could not ignore the collective voice of so many women and, feeling threatened, responded by re-asserting their authority.[7]

Petitions with multiple female signatures (or with male and female signatures) were extremely rare in the seventeenth century and almost non-existent in eighteenth-century Massachusetts and Rhode Island. Yet individual women as well as men were authorized to use this method of expressing their grievances and obtaining relief. Women petitioned for (among other things) new trials, estate reckonings, division or sale of property, power of attorney, child support, divorce or maintenance, cancelation of bonds, remission of fines, abrogation of indentures, and to have claims allowed. And they did so with the understanding that "justice is the Right of Every Honest person."[8]

Women must have been judicially savvy whether or not their petitions were written with the assistance of counsel. Some may not have been able to read their own petitions, and others could barely affix a signature or mark, but it is unlikely they were ignorant of the contents of documents that so directly affected their lives. In an appeal to the General Assembly of Rhode Island in 1731, Grizel Cotton argued in her case against the town of North Kingston that "Reason and Justice" taught that no property "shou'd be so taken away for Nothing." By prevailing, Cotton's understanding of her common law rights was confirmed, as was the power that arose from her authority to petition. Similarly, when Experience Briggs appealed to the Rhode Island General Assembly in 1744, she did so despite the "Ignorance" of her attorney, and with the conviction that she "was in the right of the case."[9]

Despite the potential for redress and the rate of success, however, women exercised this judicial remedy far less often than men, even if it was available to them on an equal basis. In the half century between 1725 and 1775, fewer than 8 percent of Rhode Island petitions to the General Assembly were from women.[10]

Judicial power invested with authority was not limited to the institution of a suit, an appeal, or the right to petition. As litigants in civil cases or as defendants in criminal proceedings, women as well as men were entitled to challenge prospective jurors, a right that offered some protection in a forum where they might be subject to discrimination and bias. In theory, women should have retained the right to challenge jurors throughout the colonial period, although the silence of the records makes confirmation of such challenges impossible. At the same time, the cultural climate of the eighteenth century may have made women hesitate to confront male jurors in such a manner, and it is conceivable that this prerogative fell into disuse over time. But in the seventeenth century, at least, neither color nor class prevented the exercise of this right: when Anna, a black servant, was accused of infanticide, "she had liberty yet objected not against any of the Jewry."[11]

If jury challenges enhanced the possibility of a fair trial for women, the process of arbitration, which served as an alternative means of dispute resolution, may have leveled the playing field still further. And if David Konig is correct that in seventeenth-century Essex County each party to the controversy could select a negotiator sympathetic to his or her cause, arbitration maximized women's chances of a fair hearing over that of a judge and twelve-man jury. Arbitration in seventeenth-century Rhode Island corroborates Konig's findings: when Sarah Reape confronted Samuel Reape over a debt, they agreed to a negotiated settlement that would bind both parties, "and in order to Reach a Composure did in the present Court nominate and choose fower persons for arbitrations."[12]

In rare instances, women not only challenged those men who would judge them but were also invested with authority to judge males. On at least two occasions in early eighteenth-century Rhode Island, women served on inquest juries where a husband had been accused of murdering his wife. Twelve men and twelve women were appointed to a "jury of inquest" to consider the evidence in Jeremiah Meecum's case, where he was suspected of inflicting the head injuries that mortally wounded his wife and sister-in-law.

That extensive female participation provoked controversy is evident from one of the surviving documents relating to the murder of William Dyre's wife a few years later: "theire is a generall Dissatisfaction of the people of the Towne [Newport] that theire was not a jury of men as well as women, upon the Body of Hannah Dyre." The records are sparse, but it appears that Hannah's body was exhumed and that an inquest jury composed of men subsequently examined her remains. Whether female participation on such juries was confined to a small number of cases where husbands were suspected of foul play or whether women played a more extensive role in the inquest process is unknown. Suffice it to say that either way, they were authorized to determine the fate of males in capital cases. Meecum and Dyre were both hanged.[13]

Women also confronted men in less dramatic courtroom situations. Once the county court bestowed upon the widow the title of executrix or administratrix, that power entitled her to sue for debt and defend the estate from attack. Such actions were, no doubt, time-consuming and annoying, but they authorized women to take assertive postures toward men and to deny their demands, attitudes that were discouraged in any other arena. These challenges even crossed class lines when a cooper's widow dunned a distiller for barrels he never paid for, or a sailor's relict sued a merchant for her husband's back pay. Mary Johnson, a Boston widow and administratrix of her shopkeeper husband's estate, sued William Cheney (a "gentleman") and John Sheppard, "Esq.," for trespass and debt. She collected even after Sheppard appealed.[14]

Not only did women challenge men by suing them for debt, but in recognition of their defiance, men sued them in turn "for refusing to deliver" sums of money. Women emphatically testified against male opponents and aggressively appealed unfavorable decisions. Indeed, if a woman lost in the lower courts and appealed, she was, in effect, protesting a verdict decided by men in authority. And in prosecuting an appeal, she, like her male counterparts, was engaging in risky behavior, because an appeal was expensive: the appellant was obligated to post security for costs.[15]

It was as witnesses, however, that most women came in contact with the judicial system, and historians concur that their testimony was given equal weight by the jury as it wrestled with evidence in any particular case. Here, too, they were authorized to testify for and against men as well as women; and here, too, they exercised power when such testimony brought about a decision for or against a particular person.[16]

— ≠ —

Euro-American law was color blind to the extent that the system afforded members of minority cultures the opportunity to act authoritatively in a variety of formal or quasi-legal settings. A Pequot woman translated negotiations between a sachem and the General Court. A mulatto wife and mother contracted to indenture her son to a white family on the express condition that he "be learnt to Read."[17]

Blacks and Indians also had recourse to the courts, which often served them equitably—if one accepts the proposition that Anglo-Americans had rightful jurisdiction over them to begin with. In the seventeenth century an Indian defendant in a felony case might be afforded a jury that was half Native American and half white. Sexual chastity of female Indians was respected at least to the extent that authorities whipped a young white man "for soliciting an Indian squaw to incontinency" after she and her husband "complained of the wrong." The courts and legislatures entertained petitions from blacks and Indians just as they did from whites, and throughout the colonial period, non-white women could bring successful suits for debt against the most affluent white Rhode Island merchant.[18]

Furthermore, the few cases where African American women achieved freedom as a result of lawsuits highlight a rare potential of the legal system. Mary Auternote of Boston proved that she was a "Free Woman" and therefore "ought to have her Liberty and Freedom according to Law," a point with which the court concurred. And a Massachusetts freedman, Titus, took his wife's owner to court when he reneged on a promise to free her, "pretending she is still his slave" after Titus had paid him twenty pounds. The Supreme Court of Judicature eventually awarded Dinah her freedom.[19]

The most telling stories concerning race, gender, and power, however, must have been those that involved the founding saints and the female sachems. From what we know about John Winthrop, we may conclude that he was a patriarchal figure whose rejection of female assertiveness was surpassed only by his convictions regarding female inferiority. Yet Winthrop and his colleagues were confronted by a number of Indian women who had powerful, authoritative leadership roles within their communities, and who were less than deferential to the leaders of the Bay Colony. Squaw sachems, as they were called, figure prominently in the early records of Massachusetts. In 1637 a "squa sachem" was among those who consented to the sale of Indian land to the inhabitants of Concord and Charlestown. Three years later, the town of Cambridge agreed to give a female sachem a coat annually for the remainder of her life, while in 1641, the townspeople agreed to supply her with "so much corne as to make up 35 bushels, and 4 coats for the last year and this."[20]

According to Winthrop, in March 1643/4, four or five sachems, including the "squaw sachem Mascononoco," volunteered to put themselves and their subjects, lands, and estates under the government and jurisdiction of Massachusetts. Although it was not unheard of for women to sign covenants, much of the wording of this particular one is similar to an earlier oath constructed for the residents of Massachusetts—a document likely to have been devoid of female signatories. Yet Mascononoco signed the covenant in her capacity as chief. She, along with the others, presented the court with wampum and in return received a coat and dinner.[21]

The Massachusetts Bay leadership also negotiated with female leaders in an effort to mediate a settlement between warring tribes. Their skills (and tempers) were sorely tested as they tried to reconcile the Nipmucs and the Narragansets after the former refused tribute to the latter and the female leader of the Narragansets, Watowswokotaus, sent 126 men into Nipmuc country to take by force what had been denied by pride. In the process of arbitrating the dispute, the Massachusetts Bay Council summoned the sachem in her capacity as the widow of Meexano and mother to the deceased sachem Scutabee, "being at present in cheefe power . . . in the Narganset Country." Never referring to her by name in the letter, but always in relation to her male relatives, the Puritan magistrates revealed their disdain and their hope that Watowswokotaus's "present" power would be shortlived. For a while the Narragansets refused to appear "to make out their right" to the General Court, which probably frustrated the governor and council still further and encouraged their belief that only "a meete man or men" were qualified to be tribal chiefs.[22]

What must have run through the minds of these good Puritan gentlemen, as they were forced to negotiate with (and even defer to) a female sachem? Did they separate the monarch from the woman as they did with Queen Elizabeth, or were they grievously peeved that they were required to deal with her at all?

The founders of Massachusetts Bay were also anchored to beliefs about the roles of combatants and noncombatants in wartime, a mentality that affected their attitudes toward and treatment of Native American women. The Puritans had left a Europe embroiled in the Thirty Year War, and although Great Britain was not directly involved, Protestantism most assuredly was. In this context, the devout Dutch Protestant Hugo Grotius published his treatise on the law of war and peace, which affirmed the widely held notion that warring parties were obligated to safeguard the innocent, a category that included women and children.[23] In wartime, women had absolute immunity from attack unless they acted in place of a male. Sparse evidence hints that the Indians quickly absorbed this cultural attitude and used it to their advantage by sparing the lives of militarily useless Englishwomen and redeeming them for militarily useful female Indians.

At the same time, Indian rules of warfare did not preclude the killing of women from enemy tribes. A combined force of English and allied Indians attacked a Pequot fort in 1637 and slaughtered two sachems, 150 warriors, "and about one hundred and fifty old men, women, and children."[24] It is possible, albeit unlikely, that the English participated in this massacre: two months later, when an all-English company surprised another Pequot settlement, the soldiers "put to death twenty-two men" and reserved two sachems for exchange, but "all the rest were women and children" and thus were spared and divided up among the English and their Indian allies.

When assaulted by a group of male and female Indians, the English were not reluctant to return fire, but they appear to have tried, at least, to abide by the rules of what they considered to be civilized warfare. Unhampered by such European-born legalities, however, Indians recognized the warring capacity of female Indians by treating them as combatants, a practice of which the English took note. When the Narragansets killed eleven members of an enemy tribe, Winthrop was quick to record that it was six men and five women.[25] The point, of course, is not which rules of warfare were more "civilized" or "gender neutral," but rather that the English, by applying European standards to the Indians, were confirmed in their belief that Indians were savages, heathens, and barbarians.

INEQUALITY UNDER THE LAW

Despite access to and participation in the judicial system, women suffered from disadvantages that worked unequal hardships on them as the seventeenth century and state formation advanced. Whatever the exact literacy rate of early America at any given time, women were more likely to be illiterate than men, and the implications of this disparity become evident in various legal settings. In 1650, for example, because of "the inconvenience of taking verbal testimonyes," the Essex County Quarterly Court ordered that all testimony be given in writing to the jury. Since the regulation required juries to return such depositions with their verdicts, historians stand to gain by the order, but not mid-seventeenth-century witnesses who were incapable of putting quill to paper. A person could ask a family member, friend, or neighbor to record testimony, but in the end was forced to rely on the good faith of the scribe, since an illiterate deponent could not read back what she or he had signed.[26]

As property disputes increased and debt cases took up an increasing amount of the court's time, it was advantageous for litigants to keep clear and accurate records. Court documents suggest that wives and widows were often responsible for family business accounts, but those records did not always meet evidentiary standards. When Rebecca May, a Newport widow, sued Peter Treby for a thirty-six-pound note, the court appointed a committee to inspect the accounts of both plaintiff and defendant.[27] The committee found that May was literate, albeit not disposed to record transactions in systematic fashion. The disposition of her case confirms that women were disadvantaged in the courtroom if their written evidence was insufficient to convince a jury. It is also possible that women would be reluctant to sue altogether if they realized that they could not produce account books that employed modern bookkeeping techniques.

If women experienced more hardships than men as they negotiated the judicial system, it was not only because of their educational background but also because their economic viability was inferior to that of males. Thus the gradual imposition of fees for various steps in the legal process may have affected women and men disproportionately, and once filing fees were levied on Massachusetts petitions in 1648, it may have required more effort for women to pay the established rate than for the brethren of the community. Across the border and nearly a century later, the Rhode Island House of Deputies received Patience Hull's petition "without money" in recognition of her status as "a poor widdow."[28] Similarly, it was costly to prosecute an appeal, since the court required a bond for that process, and it is possible that financial considerations deterred some women, at least, from appealing a case—a situation that would have been exacerbated in Boston, Salem, Newport, and Portsmouth, where low sex ratios enhanced the number of women whose discretionary income was severely constrained.

The growing complexity of legal issues and the resulting rise of the legal profession meant that women as well as men had to resort to attorneys to prosecute a case successfully. More often illiterate, less often affluent, women were handicapped in terms of technical knowledge and the ability to compensate a lawyer. Yet, as the legal process became as important as the merits of the case, attorneys could mean the difference between winning and losing. Insufficient pleas, unserved papers, obscure legislative clauses, untimely processed writs, and default judgments required expertise to argue and skill to defend. Occasionally a woman appeared alone to argue a technicality, as Lydia Machewn of Boston did when she asked the court to quash an indictment because "it is not laid out that she entertained lewd disorderly persons knowing them to be such."[29] Machewn was successful, but it is unclear how she knew the grounds on which to plead, and it is unlikely that she or anyone else would have had recourse to such information without the assistance of counsel.

Married women were also hampered by their need for powers of attorney to transact business in their husbands' stead, whereas husbands usually needed no such legal instrument to act for their wives. For women to recover debts, lease real estate, or act for a mentally incompetent mate required powers of attorney, which in turn entailed a petition to the appropriate court or General Assembly. And to submit a petition for any reason was an expensive proposition by the mid-eighteenth century. In Rhode Island the fee was four pounds.

Thus, the eighteenth century saw alterations in the judicial process that reduced female participation on many levels. It was not so much that laws changed as that social, economic, and intellectual currents combined to modify behavior, and together they worked to minimize women's presence within the legal system. With more property at stake as the eighteenth century advanced, administratrixes and executrixes had more reason to sue aggressively on behalf of an estate—at precisely the same time that female aggressiveness became a less desirable attribute. Whether this attitude influenced husbands to bypass their wives as executrixes when they drew up wills (or local officials to circumvent widows as administratrixes) is unknown, but the declining number of widows acting in such capacities is well documented.[30] Women were also far less likely to act as attorneys for their husbands in the eighteenth century and more likely to act in concert with a son or other male relative in issues involving property.

Fewer female witnesses appeared in court proceedings as the economy diversified and disputes arose in arenas from which women had been excluded. Women could not testify to what they had not seen. By the mid-eighteenth century 90 percent of civil litigation was between males, and women were rarely involved in issues other than estate matters. After the Revolution (in the 1790s), women appeared in civil court even less frequently and almost always in estate controversies.[31] Indeed, there is little in the court records of that decade to suggest that women were in business at all—a far cry from the seventeenth and early eighteenth centuries.

Women petitioned less frequently in the third quarter of the eighteenth century than they had earlier, dropping from 10.6 percent of all petitions between 1725 and 1750, to 5.9 percent between 1750 and 1775. The process of arbitration also underwent change, and instead of each party choosing referees, the court appointed arbitrators with the consent of the parties.[32] For a woman who might have suffered from a biased all-male jury had the dispute gone to trial, the more recent innovation was less advantageous than it had been when she had the right to select a negotiator.

So certain were mid-to-late eighteenth-century scribes that women had little or no place within the legal system, that their hasty formulaic language betrayed their attitude. On a number of occasions the word "he" was mistakenly recorded for the word "she" when the party involved was clearly female.[33] But the most subtle reminder of women's declining visibility is found in the Newport, Rhode Island, Town Council proceedings, where early in the eighteenth century the minutes of this judicial body opened with the salutation: "To all persons to whome these presents may come greeting," neutral language that alternated with "To all Christian People" or "To all People." By the mid-1760s the minutes began with the phrase "To all Men," further evidence of the process of female marginalization that had been taking place throughout the eighteenth century.[34]

SKIRTING THE LAW

Although Puritans were committed to biblical law, they were also heavily influenced by English precedent. And because the common law on which the Puritans relied contained such restrictive rules governing married women and widows, because a strict application of these feme covert and dower guidelines severely constrained female autonomy, women sought opportunities to circumvent a system that was stacked against them. Initially, women compensated for their legal disadvantages through illegal or quasi-legal ploys. In the final analysis, however, they were unable to overcome the obstacles designed by a society dedicated to patriarchal order.

Aware of their intellectual lineage—and the legal progeny it would necessarily spawn—women in the newly founded settlements quickly adopted the principle that in certain civil matters (and especially in relation to the accumulation of property), no law was better than common law. They knew from long experience that even if recorded wills and deeds ensured an orderly, honest devolution of property, such documents protected male and female interests only in proportion to the gendered principles of that society. As a result, both women and men found it expedient to enter into oral (rather than written) agreements of sale, a manner of transferring real estate that rested on dubious legal grounds, but was particularly beneficial to married women or widows who would have been otherwise restrained from such sales by common law prohibitions.

The decade of the 1640s confirmed that such unconfirmed transactions represented the best opportunity for female mobility even if the 1641 Body of Liberties offered legally sanctioned alternatives to the rule of thirds pertaining to dower. Under the Liberties, if a husband had not left his prospective widow "a competent portion of his estate," she could apply to the General Court and "upon just complaint" she would be "relieved."[35] Yet, whatever lawmakers may have had in mind in 1641, the vagueness of that statement gave way to a more explicit pronouncement in 1648 when (on paper, at least) the officials of Massachusetts Bay retreated from the expansiveness of their previous wording.

The 1648 compendium of laws promised a widow that dower would include a life interest in one-third of the real property her husband owned at any time during marriage, free of any debt that he may have incurred during that marriage. She was also entitled to interest in one-third of the personal property he possessed at death, although his debts were to be deducted before she could claim her share.[36] Compatible with common law standards, such a distribution could hardly have been an incentive to women who had enjoyed, alienated, wasted, deeded, or converted entire estates for nearly two decades.

The Massachusetts General Court openly acknowledged what must have been a widespread problem as early as 1637 when it advocated "that some course be taken to cause men to record their lands"—which would have been all to the good if that august body had actually meant men, rather than men and women. That they were more concerned with conveyances by the latter became clear in the preamble to a 1649 act, when they explained that they had found, "by two often experience," that wills were neither revealed nor proved and recorded, and that administration for the estates of intestates was not usually sought, much less granted. The real rub, however, was that "the wives, children, kindred, or freinds of the deceased . . . doe enter upon the lands, and possess themselves of the goods, of the said deceased, and the same are many times sould or wasted, before any creditor[s] . . . know . . . how to recover their just debts."[37] Thus, to the chagrin of lawmakers, widows had been enjoying their deceased husbands' entire estates without a by-your-leave, in violation of every tenet of common law dower. Worse, they seem to have habitually alienated both personal and real property and kept the entire proceeds—rather than the thirds to which they were legally entitled—to the detriment of creditors.

In an effort to resolve a situation that threatened saintly control of property distribution, the Massachusetts magistrates repealed the 1648 personal property clause barely a year after it had been enacted, and in 1649 stipulated that county courts would now disburse any personal estate to the widows in such measures "as they [the courts] shall conceive just and equal." The legislators gave no reason for the deletion other than to note that it appeared "not so convenient as was formerly conceived," although by implication, widows stood to gain by conforming to the new law. And although the potential for a minimal allocation of personal property by mean-spirited jurists was ever present, in fact such discretionary justice in the following decades frequently provided the widow with a major part—if not all—of the movable estate.[38]

Nevertheless, enterprising colonists were not convinced that their best interests would be served by such a law, and with their typical disregard for inconvenient legislation, they continued to "imbezill" property while authorities clamped down on technically illegal conveyances.[39] Under the law of 1649 heavy penalties lay in store for people who did not enter wills into probate or deliver estate inventories, or who sold property to which they were not legally entitled. For men, compliance with the law may have been incommodious, but for widows it had far more serious implications—and the demographics of the community suggested that the legislation would affect them most directly.

To clear title after the fact, parties to such nefarious transactions usually threw themselves on the mercy of the General Court, which assumed the power to confirm or deny the legality of these prior sales. This body almost always validated "clandestine" bargains that were subsequently recorded, thus salvaging the seller's proceeds and buyer's title, but the threat of a rebuff remained a disturbing possibility, especially if the sale had been in clear violation of a will. As a result, many people still considered circumvention of the law their best option, and in 1652 the General Court once again attempted to curtail transactions that rested on "a verball bargaine" by warning that no sale would be "good in law, except by deed in writing."[40]

Authorities also attempted to combat this problem on a local level, and in 1660 Essex County magistrates mounted an attack on "divars within this Jurisdiction" who engaged in clandestine conveyances that rested upon "unsarten bargins or salles."[41] Their demand for written, acknowledged, and recorded deeds met with the usual lackadaisical response.

Writing itself may have been a sticking point for some women, whose literacy rate as a group was considerably lower than that of men and whose formal schooling often ended after mastering elementary reading skills. Presumably, lawyers could both read and write, but they were expensive and, more important, were still regarded with great hostility—as were the filing fees that attested to the legality of recorded documents. Thus, the requirement of a written deed may have imposed a heavier burden on women than on men for reasons other than rights to the property itself.

For a combination of reasons, therefore, Massachusetts authorities continued to be plagued by illegally consummated sales. As a result, in 1657 they were still confirming (albeit with great reluctance) all transactions made "in the infancy of these plantations," while simultaneously offering a five-year grace period for the recording of deeds—with sanctions to follow the moratorium. Despite law, imprecations, and threats, however, decades later widows were still petitioning for confirmation of previously unrecorded sales.[42]

Widows found themselves in an extremely precarious position by the growing movement toward application of and adherence to property law. If they attempted to sell in violation of the law they might be forced into a reduced price because of the risk—that is, if they could find a buyer to begin with. If they sought permission either to acquire more property than a will allowed to them or to alienate some (or all) of it, they ran the risk of denial or being otherwise constrained by Boston's Selectmen or the courts.[43] Either way, their efforts to turn a profit and provide a livelihood for themselves and their children would be seriously undermined if the Massachusetts authorities made good on their threats.

Married women (or femes covert) were also governed by restrictions that prevented them from alienating property. The 1641 Body of Liberties empowered the General Court to waive such prohibitions, but married women appear to have been just as reluctant as widows to seek permission for the conveyance of real property.[44] Thus, both groups of women stood to lose if the General Court succeeded in applying common law standards to property transactions.

There was, however, one loophole in the rules and regulations governing femes covert that was potentially advantageous to law-abiding widows. If a woman came to marriage with real property of her own, or if a husband and wife purchased property in both names during marriage, the wife retained, in addition to her dower rights, fee simple title to such jointly owned property after the death of her spouse. In theory, such property could not be attached to satisfy either spouse's debt, and that rule should have applied to all married women of the first generation of settlers who received original land grants.[45] Yet in practice widows appear to have had difficulty asserting their rights to property held in joint names, even in those rare instances when a deed formalized the transaction.

In 1677 Mary Feild requested that the Suffolk County Court consider "her necessities and her being a joint purchaser of the lands in Boston whereof her ... husband dyed seized as appears by the Deed thereof" and grant her power to sell one-half of the property "for the payment of her husband's debts and her own maintenance."[46] The court granted her petition, but the request itself is puzzling. Apart from the issue of how a married woman could be a joint purchaser (since femes covert were prohibited from making contracts), if she, as a widow, held title to the property in fee simple, why did she find it necessary to ask permission at all? And if the property was sheltered from her husband's debts, why was she selling it to satisfy those debts?

Susannah Amsden's situation was similar, and her story suggests that by the beginning of the eighteenth century widows were finding it difficult to maintain themselves, especially if they had young children or were aged, disabled, or incapable of earning an income, or if the property provided an inadequate income. Financially strapped, the widow Amsden petitioned to sell some property, a move her in-laws resisted. In an effort to persuade the authorities, both Mrs. Amsden and her neighbors testified that "the whole of the Real Estate" left by Amsden's husband "was purchased by them after their marriage together"—and thus was hers to sell.[47]

The legislature granted Mrs. Amsden's request on the grounds "that the Estate was acquired by the joint Labour and Industry of the Petr. and her ... late Husband during their marriage." By granting permission to sell, the government was actually clearing title to the sale, which was, after all, the heart of the matter. Yet Susannah Amsden expressed her pique at being unnecessarily forced into the role of a supplicant against her will. When she eventually sold the property she covenanted that she was seized of the estate in her own right and made no allusion to any authority conferred upon her by the legislature. From her perspective, the alienation of jointly acquired property by widows needed no stamp of approval by a higher authority.

Mr. Amsden's other heirs pleaded ignorance of his widow's plight and offered thenceforth to assist her. In response Susannah noted acerbically that "My Brethren were pleased to say that they were not Informed neither sensible of my wants; which I believe true, for their kindness was not so much, as to be willing to be inform'd or sensible of it—though it is evident I was in great want."

Even when the parties agreed that marital property was jointly amassed, the court did not always support the widow's claims. According to her depositions and will, Mary Ward "alwaies" had "a hand in geting of the estate." The Joint "labour and care" of Mary and her second husband, Benjamin Ward, "for about forty and five years" produced a sizable inheritance that unfortunately was buried in litigation for over a decade after Mary's death in 1667. And even though the appellant's now deceased mother "by her care and industry was helpfull in getting part of the said Estate," the court found against Mary Ward's son and in favour of Benjamin's heirs by his first marriage, a decision that suggests that a wife's economic contribution was not as highly regarded in the courtroom as it was in the abstract.[48]

If a widow could not or did not assert that her deceased husband's estate was acquired through joint effort, she had little claim to anything more than her dower share if he died intestate. And although widows—if they appeared in civil court at all in the eighteenth century—were likely to be involved in estate matters, the records show no widows demanding more than their thirds on the basis of jointly acquired property. Over time, therefore, widows amassed less, alienated less, and devolved less.

BUILDING PATRIARCHY

Although the construction of a patriarchal society was furthered by a strict application of the law, and married women and widows became petitioners who required permission to alienate property (for reasons that did not apply to men), in actual fact county courts frequently awarded widows the entire real estate or a substantial portion of it, at least for the first two-thirds of the seventeenth century. Authorities also permitted widows to sell the estate of their deceased husbands (in part or whole) if they so desired, regardless of whether the former husband had expressed compatible intentions through a will. Such decisions, based on discretionary justice, transformed these bodies into equity courts that handed down decisions favorable to women in the hope of encouraging them to abide by the law.[49]

Yet with the evolution of the judicial system women increasingly came under the scrutiny, supervision, and sway of male authority figures in ways that men did not. By the last third of the seventeenth century, the law required women not only to seek permission to buy or sell property but also to accept oversight by male officials as the price of that permission. In 1668 Mary Wharton's estate was "to be secured and improved" by the Selectmen of Boston, while in 1681 the General Court appointed two men to "direct and assist" the widows Russell. In 1674 the court permitted Ann Hitt to sell part of the estate she was administering "with the advice and consent of sureties," and Elisabeth Rogers, Mary Symonds, and Ann Sheffield were required to obtain "the advice and consent" of their respective county courts (Ipswich, Essex, and Suffolk) before engaging in any transaction. Whether it was advice or consent (or both), whether it was one man, two magistrates, a committee of sea captains, or an entire court, women were more likely to be dependent on public authority than they had been at the beginning of the century.[50]

There were other disconcerting pronouncements and decisions as the century evolved: Elisabeth Rider, abandoned by her husband with five small children to support, could sell the house and land left to her by her father only as the Boston Selectmen "shall judge meet." Mary Scarborough could sell the house and land of her late husband only if "hir husband that shall be" agreed to bring up the children. Similarly, after Jonathan Negoos wed the widow Lugg and educated the children of John Lugg, "the inheritance of the house and land of . . . John Lugge [was] confirmed on him, and the power freely to dispose thereof graunted to him." Surely this turn of events was not in Jane Lugg's best interest.[51]

The problem was that the rules of the game changed as the seventeenth century advanced. As women's ability to exercise independent judgment waned, the transition was accompanied by related developments that jeopardized women's economic well-being. A close examination of estate distribution in the last third of the seventeenth century shows that by the 1670s courts were far less likely to allow a widow to alienate an entire estate (either retroactively or prospectively) than they had been earlier in the century. Instead, the courts permitted widows the use and improvement of the entire estate for their lives, and sanctioned the sale of estate property only under narrowly defined conditions that emphasized a shift in priorities. Thus, widows were to pay off creditors first and then put the remaining "overplus" out to advantage, of which proceeds the widow would receive one-third and the children two-thirds.[52]

The legal shifts that precipitated a decline in women's financial status did not occur in a vaccuum but were intimately connected to late seventeenth-century economic trends. The expansion of production and trade and the growing acquisition of property combined to increase the debt load of seventeenth-century New Englanders. Debt satisfaction always preceded the distribution of personal property in Massachusetts, but when debt was minimal, legislators and jurists could demonstrate their generosity by awarding widows a sizable portion of their spouses' estates. As debt mounted, however, authorities bowed to the demands of creditors who took the position that the satisfaction of estate debt superseded the right of women to a comfortable maintenance.

When widows initially petitioned to sell real property from the decedent's estate, it was for the support of themselves and their children. By 1670, however, petitioners had begun to include estate debt as the primary reason for their request. Whether their financial situation actually dictated such action, or whether their pleas were designed to arouse a court sympathetic to creditors, no matter.[53] The flexibility of the court and the generally discretionary nature of the decisions meant that if the court granted permission at all, and the value of the property being sold exceeded the debt, widows might have ended up with surplus income over which they had some control—at least until 1692.

The 1692 law for the "Distribution of Intestate Estates" not only enhanced creditors' rights at the expense of widows but also diminished the ability of widows to allocate the remaining proceeds. Debts came off the top, and then the probate judge distributed any "surplusage" (or remaining goods and estate), both real and personal, subject to the rule of thirds. This was a clear retreat from 1648, when a widow was entitled to her share of real property free of her husband's debt.[54] More important, the 1692 law required the judge to distribute the property as dictated by the legislation. No longer could he exercise discretion and award her more than her thirds.

By the intestacy law of 1692, widows who inherited heavily indebted estates could be shorn of everything but their thirds in real property, a situation that negatively affected not only the amount of property they acquired themselves but also their ability to pass it on to whomever they pleased. Moreover, in an effort to resolve any ambiguity in favor of creditors, a subsequent insolvency law in 1696 distributed a widow's thirds among any remaining dunners after her death. Only her necessary bedding, utensils, and household implements were exempt from creditors' demands, and the 1710 law specifying these items only validated a practice that seems to have existed for some time. These laws go a long way toward explaining why a widow's share of property shrank after the initial years of settlement.[55]

A 1719 Massachusetts statute gave creditors the right to act even more aggressively. Instead of waiting for a reluctant widow to sell real property, a creditor could collect the rents from an encumbered estate to satisfy the debt. In case of forced sale, the law also required the executrix or administratrix to divide the entire proceeds among the creditors, and although the widow retained her right to thirds, one can only assume that it must have been difficult for her to pay for housing and the other necessities of life on such a reduced income.[56] Certainly her standard of living must have declined. In the 1720s the number of petitions by widows requesting to sell indebted real property escalated. Since such petitions were now uniformly directed to the Massachusetts Superior Court of Judicature (instead of to the county courts), the proceedings depended on more impersonal relationships—male judges and female petitioners who were unknown to each other—a situation that reflects the interconnection between hierarchy and patriarchy.

— ≠ —

When Rhode Island legislators spelled out their intentions vis-à-vis dower rights, their laws followed a pattern roughly similar to that of Massachusetts, with some variations on the theme. Nevertheless, the usual caveat applies: Rhode Island legal codes often had little connection to the practical application of the law. Moreover, there is little surviving evidence from seventeenth-century Rhode Island that allows speculation about property accumulation by women. Rhode Island authorities required all grants of land to be recorded in a "State Book" in 1644, but admitted at the same time that there had been unrecorded resales, some of which were concluded by settlers who had left the jurisdiction. Under such circumstances, if anyone could demonstrate proof of purchase by writing, bargains, contracts, or other testimony, the property could be recorded in the "State Book."[57]

Although a 1663 law reiterated that "all Devises and Bequests of Land"

were to be in writing, surviving documents hint that women such as Goody
Powers were taking advantage of lax enforcement procedures to manage estate property contrary to "the Law of the Colony." Yet it was not until 1711
that the Rhode Island legislature admitted in euphemistic fashion that "in
the beginning of settlement" deeds, grants, and conveyances "were weakly
made"—a practice that threatened title. Presumably, these conditions had
afforded women the same window of opportunity to act independently as
they had in Massachusetts, and the Rhode Island Assembly hastened to make
good those titles upon prior "uninterrupted peaceable possession for twenty
years." Since "he, she, or they" gained fee simple title, the legislation was
particularly meaningful to women.[58] Nothing in the act prejudiced the rights
of femes covert, a protective device that safeguarded dower rights even in the
absence of specific references to them.

Public officials in Rhode Island were strangely taciturn about dower
rights during the seventeenth century. As early as 1647 each Town Council
had authority to make an equal and just distribution of a decedent's estate.
A 1663 statute gave intestacy administration of "personal estate" to the
widow, who was responsible for submitting an inventory to the Town
Council—a body that would take on increasing authority over women's lives
as the century moved along—but there was no hint as to what her entitle-
ments might have been. No one spelled out the meaning of "personal estate,"
either, although in later decades the legislation clearly distinguished personal
property (meaning movable goods and chattels) from real property. A 1718
statute for the distribution of intestate estates allowed a widow one-third of
her husband's personal estate forever, and one-third of the real estate for life.
This law was repealed in 1728, although for all practical purposes the widow's
status remained unchanged.[59]

At the turn of the eighteenth century the General Assembly passed legislation that permitted English law to fill the gaps in the Rhode Island codes.
Subsequent lists of such statutes in 1749 and 1767 indicated that Rhode Island
supposedly relied on the Statute of Merton Concerning Dower, by which
a widow was entitled to one-third of all land her spouse possessed during
his lifetime, and the intestacy statute of 22/23 Charles II, chapter 10, which
awarded her one-third of his personal property.[60]

So much for the law. More to the point, how was it applied, if at all?
Unfortunately, a strange evidentiary silence sets Rhode Island apart from
Massachusetts Bay. Few seventeenth-century hints of property distribution
remain, few suits at law by malcontents, few petitions by widows (before the

third decade of the eighteenth century) to sell estate property for debt. And yet there are suits by administratrixes and executrixes to collect estate debt. Femes covert could be barred from their dower shares only with their consent, but there are no cases to suggest how, when, or who applied this rule.[61] Neither is it clear whether the 1718 law that deducted debts before dispersing dower was a change from previous practice. Given Rhode Island's casualness about the law, it also remains uncertain whether in the ten years between 1718 and 1728 the provisions of the 1718 act were even enforced.

Yet if widows in Massachusetts either took or were granted possession of property far in excess of thirds during the seventeenth century, it is likely that Rhode Island women were no less acquisitive. In 1681 Joanna Reape of Pawtuxet petitioned the Rhode Island General Assembly because she had been left desolate by her husband. In response (and in one of the few extant examples of property distribution), the General Assembly ordered her husband's estate sequestered for her use "during her naturall life." Her son and son-in-law were to take possession and collect rents for her, which limited her autonomy, but her ability to enjoy the entire estate was consistent with similar practices in Massachusetts at that time.[62]

From 1663 onward, Rhode Island law permitted widows and other heirs to administer only the personal estate of an intestate decedent. Responsibility for the division of such decedent's real property was vested in the Town Council until 1770, when a new statute gave an intestate's heirs the right to petition the Inferior or Superior Courts for partition of the estate. But here again the records are silent. If the widows in Newport were required to petition the Town Council or the courts for partition of their thirds, if they were required by the General Assembly to seek the advice and consent of the Newport Town Council prior to selling property, such requests are conspicuous by their absence.[63] References to thirds appear only when property was contested and litigated, leaving one to wonder whether Newport widows were usually left to enjoy whatever real property their husbands had owned, if it was unencumbered by debt or controversy—Merton notwithstanding.

It is also possible that during the seventeenth century Rhode Island widows enjoyed that property free of prior debt. Nevertheless, by 1718 creditors' rights had taken precedence over widows' prerogatives, just as they had in Massachusetts, and a law of that year permitted the Town Council to distribute the estate only after debts had been deducted from it. By midcentury widows were forced to turn over all goods and chattels from an insolvent estate to creditors "saving her apparel, and such Bedding and other household goods . . . necessary for the upholding of life." At her death or remarriage even this modest property would revert to any hovering creditors. If the personalty did not cover the entire debt, the Supreme Court of Judicature could authorize the sale of real property by the executrix or administratrix, once again exempting the widow's right of dower. By 1769 the right to initiate a sale no longer belonged to the widow or the court. A new statute made real property liable for debt, and if a creditor levied execution of a judgment, the sheriff was obliged to sell as much real property as necessary at vendue to satisfy that debt.[64]

Petitions to the Rhode Island General Assembly indicate that women took such threats to their well-being seriously. Dinah Cahoon feared that if creditors attached the estate, the property would "be sold for much less than the true value." Under such conditions, "the whole estate would be destroyed." Furthermore, property seized in a wife's "own right" should have eluded the creditor's grasp, but for whatever reasons Ann Tyler petitioned the Rhode Island General Assembly in 1773 to sell such real estate in order to pay her husband's debts. That she sought permission to alienate what was rightfully hers reinforced the link between male oversight and female property holding just as it had in Massachusetts.[65]

— ≠ —

Given the circumstances of their existence on the North American continent, it is not surprising that free African Americans were subject to Anglo-American property law, but it is mildly disconcerting to realize that within a half century of settlement, Indian leaders over whom the European settlers had gained jurisdiction engaged in land transactions that conformed to Anglo-American estate and dower law. Thus, when a number of the leading Indians "gave" a large tract of land to their overseer, Daniel Gookin, in 1679, the signatories acted in gender-defined capacities in accordance with English law. Assoaske, widow of Josiah Nowel, signed the deed on behalf of her children and with her new husband "consenting." Sarah Oonomog agreed to the gift as "sole executrix" of her late husband Oonomog, and Elisabeth affixed her mark as "the only daughter and heire of Solomon, deceased."[66]

Sarah Oonomog was the widow of the late ruler and sagamore of an Indian plantation near Marlborough. As such, the Suffolk County Court conferred "liberty" upon her "to sell and allienate unto any English person" her late husband's real property of something under one hundred acres, provided that "major Gookin and Mr Elliot consent and approve the bargain on behalfe of the Indian woman." By such tactics the English accumulated parcels of property from Indians of high standing (to the detriment of their heirs), while at the same time they prevented Indian women from acting any more independently than English women.[67] Presumably, Indian women were in no better position to decline such sales than were Indian men.

English dower law affected Indian land transactions as well. When Thomas Awassomoag conveyed two thousand acres to Edward Rawson, Awassomoag's wife, Abigail, renounced all her rights "by way of dower or otherwise," and both signed the document with their marks. The concept of English dower was alien to Indian culture, and "otherwise" was no small matter, since Indian custom treated women on a more egalitarian basis than did English law.[68]

By the eighteenth century Indian women were no better off than Anglo-American women with regard to estate property, and in some instances worse. In 1741/2 the widow Hannah Speen, a Natick Indian, petitioned to sell twenty acres of land that she held in her own right, and she requested permission to do so for payment of debts contracted for the maintenance of her children and for the more comfortable support of her family. The Massachusetts legislature granted her petition, required her to pay off any debt, and then to put the rest of her assets in the hands of an Anglo-American male overseer, where it would be improved for her future necessities and the comfort of her children. In similar circumstances, Anglo-American women—not overseers—usually had responsibility for the overplus, and in this case, Indian women fared no worse than Indian men, who were also required to petition in order to sell real property.[69]

— ⚏ —

Assessing the relative status of women over time is essentially a historical balancing act. Widows were precariously positioned, yet most women were not widows and their economic stability was assured, however temporarily, by marriage to the middle-class tradesmen and mariners who emptied a pint now and then at one of the many pubs in Boston, Newport, Salem, or Portsmouth. And surely there were many widows who were left solvent, and some even in great comfort.

Nevertheless, economic stability could be transitory. We will probably never be able to reconstruct the accumulation of wealth and transfer of property by married women in Massachusetts and Rhode Island in the first decades of those colonies' existence, but there is reason to believe that the autonomy they possessed both as femes covert and as widows provided them with better financial health than their great-granddaughters would enjoy generations later. In addition, the number of landless men who could claim only personal property was increasing in the seaports, and that demographic factor, combined with laws that granted creditors a decedent's entire personal estate, contributed to the economic decline of eighteenth-century New England widows.

To make matters worse, laws that were designed to ensure female economic viability appear to have withered from disuse over time. The 1648 Body of Laws indicated that a wife could renounce her dower in real property only by some "act or consent." A year later, legislators clarified this point by referring to a written renunciation "under her hand, and acknowledged before some magistrate." This "volentary and free act," attested to and certified by a magistrate, forever barred her interest in such property, but theoretically, at least, the wife had agreed to the terms of the sale.[70] Presumably, the General Court envisioned not only a written consent whereby a wife would relinquish her dower interests, but a confirmation of that act by a magistrate as well. And even if this device was instituted to facilitate the transfer of property with a clear title, a woman could avail herself of it to protect her rights. Thus, if Marylynn Salmon is correct and in the latter half of the eighteenth century a wife in Massachusetts could not demand a private examination to protect the voluntary nature of her agreement to sell marital property, the earlier practice must have been abandoned somewhere along the line, to the detriment of the wife/widow.[71]

Each piece of legislation that committed Rhode Island and Massachusetts to the English laws governing femes covert and dower was nothing less than a building block of patriarchy. Each judicial decision that reinforced the idea of women as supplicants, dependent on the permission or assistance of a male authority figure, stripped women of what little independence they had possessed in the 1630s and 1640s. Although each individual change in the law and its application was something less than dramatic, cumulatively these changes had considerable impact on women's lives. And once assembled, seemingly unrelated facts, like scrambled puzzle pieces, create a picture. With fewer female conveyances, smaller property grants, greater male oversight, abandonment of joint ownership rights, and a focus on creditors' rights, the outline of a social structure begins to emerge.[72]

THE MARRIAGE PENALTY

The Puritans who emigrated from England in the 1630s based their perception of the ideal marriage on the social role played by that institution and on a cultural construction of male and female. The early body of laws relating to marriage conformed to their worldview but was effective only to the extent that the body of colonists shared that vision and willingly embraced its tenets. Thus, although femes covert laws governed seventeenth-century New England, their emphasis varied from place to place, and there is reason to believe that they were often observed in a manner unintended by their original framers.

Husbands and wives made arrangements that may not have been enforceable in law and depended solely on the mutual acquiescence of the parties involved. Henry Bull left his wife Ann one hundred pounds, noting that "the twenty pounds she borrowed of me to pay George Hatho for land she bought of him shall be part of said hundred." In such dry language Bull indicated that husbands and wives made contracts with each other (the legality of which was litigated to no certain end in Massachusetts in 1671) and that even as a married woman Ann contracted to purchase real property by herself.[73]

Although there is little evidence that married women took advantage of separate estates, it is likely that a variety of informal arrangements supplanted the need for such property formally set apart for their use. In his will, Boston brasier Henry Shrimpton noted that he had "freely allowed" his wife "all the Estate she had before she was my wife, the which she have had the Disposall of untill this Day." True, her separate use of the property rested on his consent, and we have no way of knowing how widespread this practice was, but even formally recognized separate estates required the cooperation and assent of various individuals. Moreover, there is no reason to believe that Massachusetts lawmakers discouraged the use of separate estates. When they surface in litigation, it is not because they are contested as a matter of law, but rather because of the bad faith of one of the parties. Such was the case when John Menzies placed twenty-five pounds in trust "for the Separate use" of his wife, Katharine, only to be deceived by the people on whom the Menzieses relied.[74]

Winking at the law could have benign—even positive—effects on women's lives, and there is abundant evidence that New Englanders ignored legal constraints on marriage when it suited them. Such evasion frequently worked to women's advantage by enlarging their sphere of economic opportunity. Theoretically, husbands controlled the personal property within the household, but it is likely that they only rarely interfered with their wives' attempts to enhance the family income, even though both partners were well aware of their rights (or lack thereof). In a conversation with Thomas Dorman, Ensign Houlet mentioned that he (Houlet) had borrowed money from Mrs. Houlet, who had obtained it by selling some of her geese and turkeys. Dorman reminded Houlet that his wife's fowl were hers only when he (Houlet) pleased. Houlet's response was very telling: "no I medle not with the geese nor turke's for they are hurs for she hath bene and is a good wife to me."[75] Both men knew the law, and although Goodwife Houlet's activities depended on her husband's goodwill, her husband clearly respected her economic enterprise and independence. Besides, her contribution to the family economy benefited them both.

According to law, married women were proscribed from entering into contracts; evidence that they did so permeates the records. Even the Town Selectmen contracted with married women to keep and maintain indigent people—although husbands generally collected the compensation for such services. And in Boston, the obligations contracted by a married woman were used to bolster a legal point: "the three shillings adistionall money payed by Dansons wife make plaine the confirmation of the bargaine"—the assumption being that Mrs. Danson's actions had solidified the deal.[76]

Nevertheless, a married woman's ability to contract could not be assumed, and where it served a litigant's purpose, such a right might be contested—although in the following Rhode Island case, to no avail. Elizabeth Scott, wife of John, asked Thomas Peckham to seek out and return a runaway slave, and in return Mrs. Scott agreed with Peckham to pay "all his expences . . . and allso to sattisfie [him] for his time and trouble." When the time came to pay Peckham, John Scott refused to honor his wife's agreement, and Peckham sued. John, in jail for his intransigence, defended himself on the grounds that "the plaintiff hath not sett forth any matter or cause sufficient in Law if [true] to oblige Defdt to pay the money demanded" because a wife's contract "cannot in law bind and oblige her husband without his assenting to it; unless for victuals drinke and necessary cloaths." And to seal his argument with a final flourish, Scott added: "many a man might be ruined by his wife if such contracts are allowed."

Despite Scott's eloquence (not to mention common law precedent), the court found for Peckham. Scott appealed, but the judgment was affirmed. Certain of his legal position, Scott took his grievance to the General Assembly of Rhode Island, where once again Peckham's argument was sustained, although his award was reduced. In Rhode Island a married woman could indeed contract and obligate her husband.[77]

Furthermore, seventeenth-century court records hint that married women in Rhode Island initiated civil actions by themselves. In 1658 the Rhode Island Court of Trials records that "Honorah Saull, the wife of Thomas Saull," commenced and won an action of debt against John Cowdall. The language of the complaint suggests that she was not seen as independent of her husband, but the rules of litigation did not appear to require joint proceedings, at least in the first half of the seventeenth century. Similarly, in New Hampshire in 1647 Darby Fields's wife brought a complaint against Thomas Laton "for annoyance dun by cattle."[78]

It is difficult to say whether the same flexibility existed in Massachusetts in the founding decades, but by the end of the century married women were not likely to sue or be sued in the absence of their husbands. In 1677 James Loyd sued Phillip Bullis for money "due for goods sold and delivered the wife of sd Bullis as shall appear by booke and bill under her hand." And although Sarah Fowler, an unmarried Boston wine retailer, could take Thomas Clarke to court for money damages in 1690, a year later it was "William Hall who marryed Sarah Fowler of Boston wine retailer" who was the recorded plaintiff in another action involving Sarah's transactions.[79]

Moreover, by the second decade of the eighteenth century the Rhode Island court records indicate that married women were no longer acting in their own behalf. Even widows who remarried in the middle of a lawsuit could expect technical difficulties, especially if they took on husbands seriatim. In response to Bathsheba Hart's suit against Stephen Mumford, Mumford argued that the plaintiff was "not rightly sett forth in the Declaration for she cannot be Bathsheba Hart and the widdow of Peter Bourse." To compound the legal tangle, Bathsheba had married Franklin Morton, who requested to have his name added as coplaintiff.[80] Mumford had, apparently, taken advantage of common law restrictions on femes covert to delay his own day of reckoning, making Bathsheba's role as widow and administratrix of Peter Bourse's estate more difficult.

When Magdalen Fromoget sued John Hardovin Le Touch in 1714, the latter defended himself by arguing that "the plaintiff cannot bring an action in her own name she being under Covert of her husband and all writts must be brought in his name or in both their names," an astounding plea, since he had recently sued her in her name alone.[81]

Throughout the 1730s Bethia Hedges was in and out of court in Newport, Rhode Island, both as plaintiff and defendant. And depending on one's perspective, she was either a conniving fraud or a splendid example of a woman who manipulated femes covert laws to her own advantage. Part of the reason Bethia prevailed in a 1735 suit initiated by Thomas Hicks was because he sued her as a widow and she claimed that, since her husband was alive, she could not be sued as such. As it turned out, John Hedges was, in fact, dead—and Bethia knew it—according to a 1735 deposition from John Osborn, who was present when Mrs. Hedges received news of her husband's demise in 1731.[82]

Moreover, the reason that John's death came to light at all was because it served Bethia's interest to reveal that information. In June 1735, one month after she agreed to arbitration in the Hicks matter, Bethia sued John Hunt for a debt of ninety-five pounds. Hunt requested an abatement because Bethia's husband was living (this was, after all, what she had just maintained) and, therefore, argued Hunt, Bethia could not bring suit in her own name. This is the context in which John and Mary Osborn described the circumstances of John Hedges's death, presumably at Bethia's request. By this time, however, the court appears to have had enough; for whatever combination of reasons, Bethia lost the case.[83]

Two years later, Bethia Hedges was in court again, this time defending herself against Job Caswell's claim of twenty-four pounds. In her response she asked the court to abate the action because "she at the Time the Note sued upon is said to be dated and made was under Covert and therefore could not make a Note worth anything." The court agreed, abated the suit, and awarded Bethia costs. If the court, in this case, was either following recent precedent or setting its own, the decision reversed the Peckham case of 1715, where an earlier court had upheld a wife's right to contract. On this occasion Bethia seems to have been concerned less about her civil rights than about the assets of the estate. In short, if the law allowed her to obligate her husband without his consent (as it had in 1715), Job could have come after the estate. In 1738/9 Bethia, once again a feme covert, was sued directly, nonetheless.[84]

Cases that confront gender rules were rare, and it is difficult to assess their meaning. The last group all took place in Rhode Island, where legal codes and legal conduct often went their separate ways, and it would be a mistake to generalize from Rhode Island's example. Yet it is fascinating to note how a system, disadvantageous to married women on the surface, could be improved by various strategies. Bethia's ploy probably worked as well as it did because she lived in Newport, where mariner husbands were away for months (even years) at a time without confirmation of their health or safety. The report of John Hedges's death came from Jamaica and was verified by someone who had seen his grave, but unless his widow chose to disseminate that information, other Newporters might simply assume he was still some-where in the Caribbean. John and Mary Osborn knew of Hedges's death, and Thomas Hicks must have suspected as much, but the Osborns confirmed the news only when Bethia had a purpose in revealing it.

In Rhode Island a dead husband was probably more advantageous to a woman—at least financially speaking—than one who was absent or whose fate was uncertain. In 1711 the General Assembly stipulated that wives of hus-bands who had been absent for three years could recover debts, rents, and profits from the estate of such husbands, and in 1717 it expanded the law to allow a wife to "demand, sue for, recover, possess, and improve" all real and personal property belonging to her spouse. Under neither law could she sell all or part of the estate, which probably thwarted her efforts to provide for herself and her children. Widows, especially those named in a will as legatees, were better positioned to alienate property, and by the 1770s the few female petitions to the Rhode Island General Assembly to sell real property were from women whose husbands were thought to be lost at sea but not yet presumed dead.[85]

The common law rule making a husband liable for debts contracted by his wife before marriage also left room for legal maneuvering. We will never know if (or how many) women married to relieve themselves of an onerous financial burden, but some, like Mary Mackree, must have taken that route: "I marryed Joseph Mackree Justly Expecting that he would help me in my dificulties . . . but . . . he took no care to pay any Debts for me." Nor can we prove that creditors instituted suits to recover from a husband what could not be recovered from his wife before the marriage. Did a married woman have better standing in court and were her chances of recovering a debt incurred when sole measurably increased if she sued jointly with her new husband? On the other hand, why would a potential suitor take such a risk? A new husband could be jailed for failing to pay his wife's old debts. Although historians may not be able to resolve these questions with certainty, existing cases leave no doubt of the legitimacy of the questions.[86]

— ⚡ —

The irony, of course, is that New England civil law protected the interests of women at the same time that it discriminated against them. Most important, it provided a framework within which personal or estate debt could be collected, no small matter to the people who depended on such income. Shopkeeper, landlady, executrix, nurse, and legatee could all bring grievances to legal forums where they would be fairly adjudicated. In these civil controversies there is simply no evidence that women (married or not) were treated unfairly within the perimeters of the judicial system. And the recording of wills and deeds served to protect her property rights as well as his.

To focus the discussion on the equity of gender-related laws is to miss the point, however, since the legal system itself had been weighted in favor of males—making it inequitable to begin with. Women were protected only as long as they conformed to established rules, and authorities were ready to pounce on women who, singly or collectively, threatened the social order that had been so carefully fabricated. Yet, notwithstanding the risks, many women refused to abide by legislation that restricted their lives, and their resistance is evidence of a social paradox: by establishing legal boundaries that were detrimental to the economic well-being of so many women, lawmakers encouraged lawbreakers. Some women were clever enough to manipulate the system without actually violating a particular statute; others evaded the law with greater abandon. All hoped to do so with impunity.

Dower, for example, provided great opportunity for mischief even as it offered a small measure of security. Massachusetts required a wife's written consent to any sale of property that would extinguish her dower rights. Her signature on the deed protected both buyer and potential widow, but from her perspective that may have been a drawback: once she certified to the voluntary nature of the act, she could not renege; the deed of sale barred dower. Thus, if she was slightly ambivalent, wanted to avoid a confrontation at home, or even chose to submit to her husband's wishes as a dutiful wife, she put herself in a difficult position by signing. A better tack for her was to avoid signing the deed if her husband and the buyer did not pressure her to do so—or perhaps even if they did. Then, if she changed her mind, she could claim her thirds after her spouse's death and enhance her own estate, at least during her lifetime.

Although the multiparty transaction involving Goodwife Shoare was convoluted, perhaps this is what she had in mind when she allowed herself to be "persuaded . . . not to give any Consent" to the sale of a house by her husband in 1659.[87] And this is exactly what the former widow Elisabeth Vicars did in 1676, when she petitioned the court to grant "her thirds" in a "house and land in Boston" that had been "alienated by her said husband Price in his lifetime unto Mr. John Joyliffe Shee not having given up her thirds." The court required Joyliffe to "set out" Elisabeth's thirds. Eunice Porter used the same ploy in 1660 when she demanded a one-third interest in houses and lands previously sold by her husband, Jonathan Porter. The buyer resisted, but the Essex County Court's verdict went to Eunice, even though four witnesses (three men, one woman) maintained that Eunice "manifested more willingness to sell than did her husband," and that she furthered the sale and "not a word or syllable passed her mouth concerning her thirds." Did Elisabeth or Eunice engage in subtle subterfuge? Maybe, maybe not, but they played their legal cards with skill and trumped their adversaries handsomely.[88]

Other women circumvented the rules out of desperation. Deserted by her husband and left with five small children, Mary Fordice was under such "great Difficulty to maintain her selfe and children" that she "bought several Pieces of land upon Credit in her own name." As a result, she had "got in debt" and needed to sell that property in order to pay "her just debts." Because she was a married woman, such transactions were technically invalid, and only a successful petition to the Rhode Island General Assembly could clear title to such a sale.[89]

Court records hint that as society became more structured and codified, as lawmakers took the rules of common law dower more seriously, as widows became more subject to male authority, women consistently sought ways to bypass the gender-based inequities that threatened their autonomy and economic status. Required to present estate inventories, an administratrix might render a fraudulent account—or none at all. For neglecting to report her husband's death or bring in an inventory of his estate, the court denounced Elizabeth Smith as an embezzler and made her liable for the debts of that estate in accordance with the penalties prescribed by the 1649 act. Mary Usher received only a fine for omitting to present an inventory of her husband's estate in a timely fashion, but she was nonetheless held accountable for the delay. Despite Smith's protestations, in both cases the widows had apparently decided that evasion was worth the risk, and hoped that the law would not catch up with them. When William Coddington, Newport town clerk, examined the Town Council records, he noted that as sole executrix, Mehitable Chace never "rendered any account of her executorship." Mehitable's actions—or lack thereof—might explain why, as the eighteenth century advanced, widows were less likely to be granted sole custody of an estate. Men were either more punctual or they were not held to the same standards: rarely, if ever, were they penalized for such dereliction.[90]

Allowed only one-third of the goods and chattels, a widow who delayed submission of an estate inventory could use up or secrete a considerable portion in the meantime. Indeed, even if she was left the entire movable estate, she could deplete it so that creditors would be frustrated. She might even "compound" with the creditors themselves.[91] That all of the above happened from time to time is clear from the language of the legislation designed to prevent such abuses. Rhode Island authorities barely concealed their frustration with widows who were "negligent" in submitting estate inventories or who were slothful in "proving the wills of the deceased" in the legislative language that demanded submission of such inventories and wills within a month of death. In Massachusetts any person suspected "to have concealed, imbezeled or conveyed away" any personal property of the deceased could be hauled into probate court, where she or he would be forced to take an oath of innocence. "Just suspicion of . . . Concealments" had, unfortunately, led to "great wrong and Injury."[92]

Legislators had creditors in mind when they drafted that language, but it is more likely that the Bostonian Henrietta Overing was thinking of her own wrongs and injuries when she refused to show Sheriff Polland any of the "goods chattels or Lands" formerly belonging to her deceased husband, John, after the sheriff complained he could not "find any." And despite a 1724 Rhode Island law requiring anyone in possession of a decedent's estate to swear that he or she would present all of it for inventory purposes, court testimony implicated Ruth Waterman in a scheme to remove property in order to deceive the creditors. Question: "Did Mrs Waterman tell you that the things you saw there [at Capt Andrew Waterman's house] were the widow Ruth Waterman's and you must not say any thing about it?" Answer: "Yes."[93] Were these widows being greedy, or did the law and changing economic conditions force them to protect themselves in whatever way they could? Did application of the law make enjoyment of one's property a criminal offense? Presumably it did: Rhode Island widows, like other debtors, went to jail if they did not pay their husbands' debts.[94]

Surely husbands knew in advance that their widows-to-be might end up in prison if the estate did not contain sufficient funds to satisfy debts. And just as surely, this would have been reason enough for a husband not to make his wife executrix of his estate. Indeed, perhaps this is the reason that in the second half of the eighteenth century the proportion of husbands excluding wives from executorships began to rise precipitously.[95] Conversely, a widow might refuse to administer the estate of a deceased spouse not because she felt incompetent to do so but, as Mary Mowry explained, "because the estate left would not discharge just debts, and pay legacies."[96]

Presumably historians, like the short arm of seventeenth-century law, will be unable to trace those who successfully evaded the rules and enjoyed more real and personal property than the law allowed. Moreover, this evidentiary gap probably distorts the historical record, since the status of such law evaders may be more reflective of society than the status of those for whom probate records survive. Laws denying women tavern or brewing licenses encouraged an illegal, underground trade, but what was the nature of that traffic and how great was it? Laws prohibiting the boarding of vagrant transients were routinely ignored, but did this human traffic measurably enhance female income?[97] Legal violations contained risk, but even the risk was gender based: women had more to lose than men if they chose conformity with the law.

~ CHAPTER 5 ~

Dependence, Disorder, and the Law

Rachel Webster's Story

*J*ohn and Rachel Webster were not an ideal couple any more than they were ideal citizens in mid-seventeenth-century Portsmouth, New Hampshire.[1] "She complained to the constabl" that he was "misusing" her. He drank too much and was in and out of court for debt. In 1656 John received a license "to keep the ordinary at strawbery bank" and to sell wine, strong water, and beer there, but when he applied for a renewal of that license in 1661, the court denied a permit for the sale of alcoholic beverages. He and his wife barely made ends meet, but they did manage to support themselves. John died in 1661 or 1662, leaving Rachel with debts she could not pay. As a result, she refused a role as administratrix and "oppenly decliared" her unwillingness "to have anything to doe with the said Estate." Rachel gave John's clothes away, a move that apparently offended his creditors.

To support herself, Webster applied "to have her license renewed," not only for "a house of com'on entertainment" but to sell wine as well. That she—and the court—considered it a renewal suggests an implicit understanding of her part in this family enterprise while John was alive. Nevertheless, her status as a widow prevented her from obtaining an independent license. Only if she took "an honest man into her house to govern the same" could she continue her business. Rachel appears to have entered into partnership with Richard Allison, and the two of them bought wine from Richard Cutt (presumably for her establishment), promising to pay him in cash and codfish.

For the next several years Rachel Webster was the only woman granted a license by the court, even though she was fined "for keeping bad order in her house" and was sued by Cutt in 1663 for failure to pay what she owed him. In 1666, however, after submitting what she probably thought was a routine renewal application, the court denied her request and granted her liberty "to sell beare and bread only." Two years later the county court ordered the Widow Webster to "take downe her signe and in case she refuse that then the Constable doe it."

Rachel Webster's difficulties with the law continued. In 1670 she and George Jones were caught "being naught and unseemly" together, and a year later she was penalized "for keeping Ill orders in her home by Letting persons have soe much drinke whereby they abuse themselves." By midsummer 1671 the court resolved to deal with Rachel Webster once and for all. "Being Informed," they said, that the Widow Webster lived alone, sold unlicensed rum and wine, and was suspected of "uncleanness," they ordered the Portsmouth Selectmen to "dispose of her into some good house of Government to Serviss and to worke and Labor." Furthermore, they were to "lett out her house" to pay for her maintenance elsewhere. Rachel's last confrontation with the law—so far as extant records permit a glimpse of her life—took place in June 1673, when she was presented "for being drunk."

— ≠ —

Heavily influenced by English precedent, Puritans believed that written laws reflecting consensual standards and sanctions acted as a framework within which disorder gave way to order. Theoretically, a society so structured provided stability for the women and men within its governance, and as officials enacted legislation they did so with the understanding that societal values were best protected through the legal system. Whether or not they were right is a moot point; more important, their values and the laws that conformed to them incorporated certain gendered premises. First, they believed that male supremacy required female dependence in most circumstances. Second, they maintained that women were responsible for social disorder, a notion that was consistent with their sometimes futile (but always creative) attempts to contain them through the legal system.

LAW AND A GENDERED ECONOMY

Female self-sufficiency was antithetical to a worldview predicated on dependence. If circumstances permitted women to acquire real property (and some measure of autonomy) during the first generation of settlement, it was an unintended by-product of frontier conditions. Eventually, the law caught up with women whose grandmothers had exercised independence in the absence of a legal code, and by the eighteenth century women's access to and control of property had been severely circumscribed.

The attempt to constrain female economic mobility may have been more systemic than systematic, but the end result was the same. A local ordinance in Boston, a resolution in Salem, a regulation in Newport, a court ruling in Portsmouth, and an attitude common to English colonists were enough to obstruct female economic viability. As each legal brick was added to the pyramid and women were shut out of various economic enterprises, they became increasingly dependent on men in both the public and private arenas. In turn, economic dependence accentuated male authority over women, a trend that accelerated in the eighteenth century. It backfired, of course, when a low urban sex ratio forced an increasing number of poor women to make excessive claims on the town purse, but such tensions only emphasize the price that a patriarchal society pays for keeping women in economic subjection.

It was not that seventeenth-century women were expected to be unproductive. To the contrary, only fornication, blasphemy, and perhaps a few other minor infractions surpassed idleness as sins. The Reverend Hugh Peter admonished his Boston congregation to make sure that people, "especially women and children in the winter time," were employed, since "idleness" led to "the ruin of both church and commonwealth." Idleness was a criminal misdemeanor and punished accordingly. Salemites sent Margarett Page to jail in Boston for being "a lazy idle and loytering person." Once there, she was "sett to work for her living" in various households. The court admonished Mary Boutwell for not working, living idly, and stealing. That theft took third place suggests the relative importance of each violation. Even a single mother with children would be supplied with necessaries only to supplement the income from "such worke, as shee is able to doe."[2]

Husbands and wives were economic partners whose joint efforts contributed to the well-being of the family. Ann Seten expected that "by their mutual Industry" she and her husband, Asa, would "support their Family with decency." The General Court of Massachusetts admonished not only John Stone but John Stone and his wife to make bigger bread.[3] Few documents record the specific tasks urban wives performed alongside their husbands to further the household economy, but their participation in and knowledge of the various trades and occupations common to seaport communities is not to be doubted.

At the same time that female productivity was ostensibly encouraged, however, competing cultural attitudes ensured that women would never be productive enough to be self-sustaining. And although economic regulations were rarely directed at women specifically, women suffered disproportionate hardships from their application. The cumulative effect of such legislation exacerbated female poverty, especially in seaport communities where the sex ratios showed numerical imbalances in favor of women before the end of the seventeenth century.

The food and beverage industries were carefully controlled by local officials, which meant that the tasks with which women were most closely affiliated could be used to enhance their income only with permission of the authorities. As early as 1635 the General Court licensed victualing houses, while a decade later innkeepers, keepers of cooks' shops, vintners, taverners, and public sellers of wine, ale, beer, and strong water were prohibited from marketing their wares without a license.[4]

Such procedures were not without transatlantic precedent, however. Sporadic licensing of brewers began in England in the fourteenth century and steadily increased through the Tudor and Stuart periods. In the 1630s English Puritans were particularly vociferous in their call for regulation and vigorous in their prosecution of unlicensed tipplers. They associated ale-houses with disorder and considered them stepping stones to poverty. And even if Puritan protests stopped short of calls for outright suppression, there was considerable support for control of the ever-increasing drink trade.[5]

The gendered nature of the business had also undergone change in the centuries prior to the Great Migration. In the early Middle Ages the majority of brewers (and probably sellers) of beer were female. During the fifteenth century, however, the proportion of women declined, and by the early seventeenth century the vast majority of tipplers were male, leaving only a small number of English widows in the trade.[6]

The general hostility toward female license holders traveled well and took American roots when Massachusetts lawmakers announced the terms by which licenses would be issued: "Every towne shall have liberty from time to time to choose a fitt man to sell wine, the same to be alowed by license from this Court." As a result, Goody Armitage received permission to keep her ordinary, "but not to drawe wine." In the latter part of the century, legis-lators refrained from singling out women for special restrictions, but urged the Selectmen of Boston to approve only "meet and fit" persons for public house permits.[7]

The records do not tell us whether fewer women applied for licenses, whether those that were granted included husband-and-wife teams (even if the license named only the husband), or whether the Selectmen of Boston and Salem simply found men more "meet and fitt" than women. Whatever the reasons, Massachusetts, Rhode Island, and New Hampshire authorities vigorously observed the law of the spirit and until the 1660s permitted only a few women to sell alcoholic beverages. Between 1660 and 1690 Massachusetts courts only reluctantly issued licenses to women (almost all of whom lived in Boston), although their hesitation may have had as much to do with the proliferation of watering holes as with the sex of the purveyor. At the same time, it is strange that female names are conspicuously absent altogether from the list of Salem licensees. Officials in Boston seem to have been far more willing than those in Salem, Newport, or Portsmouth to issue retailing licenses to women.[8] Indeed, as a general rule Rhode Island authorities showed an even stronger reluctance than their Massachusetts or New Hampshire counterparts to dispense licenses to women.

The number of female licensees increased dramatically in the 1690s. Most were issued in Boston, only a few in Salem and other towns in Essex County, and several in Portsmouth, New Hampshire. Surprisingly, the percentage of female retailers and innholders in Salem continued to lag behind similarly occupied women in Boston in the eighteenth century.[9] The numbers were not very large to begin with—in 1720 there were only sixteen licensed female retailers in Boston (and one in Salem in 1717)—but it is striking that in a community such as Salem, where there had been such aggressive women throughout the seventeenth century, they were routinely excluded from these occupations. One can only wonder if it was precisely because Salem women showed such spirit that they were subjected to such intense regulation.

Anglo-American cultural attitudes held women responsible for social unrest, and it may have been the association of alcohol and disorder that encouraged public officials to withhold licenses from women. Certainly seventeenth-century Salem was a disorderly society by New England standards, which may account for the reluctance of officials to grant licenses to women in general and to unmarried women in particular. In their quest for order, jurists and Selectmen were no less eager to regulate sex, and it may have been the unholy combination of fornication and flip that made the authorities hesitate to allow women to run taverns and sell alcoholic beverages. This bias did not go unnoticed, and when Margett More petitioned for a tavern license in 1765, she did so "notwithstanding" her status as a "singel woman."

Throughout the colonial period, more men than women received licenses for taverns, alehouses, and inns in Massachusetts.[10]

Indeed, male license holders always outnumbered females by a considerable margin, even as the sex ratio shifted in favor of women. In Boston in 1720 there were thirty-four male retailers, and in Salem in 1718 all twenty retailers were male. What seems to happen over time, however, is that women were less likely than men to be counted among the licensed innkeepers and tavernkeepers, while their relative proportion among the retailing population grew. Thus, in 1720, 31 percent of Boston's forty-two licensed innholders were female, as were 32 percent of the fifty retailers, while in 1765, 23.6 percent of the innkeepers in Boston were women, but 40 percent of the ninety-five retailers were female.[11] Since innkeeping was more lucrative than shopkeeping, these numbers show how law and cultural values worked in tandem to drive women into less profitable enterprises—as they had in Europe.

A similar pattern prevailed in Rhode Island, where by 1647 taverns, alehouses, and victualing houses were prohibited from operating without licenses (as were brewers), and males were the usual beneficiaries of such licenses in the latter half of the seventeenth century. The Town Council of eighteenth-century Newport was only slightly more generous with its liquor licenses, bestowing a handful on women during the first half of the century, and having second thoughts thereafter.[12]

In Portsmouth in 1686, seven men and no women held public house licenses, whereas four of the twenty New Hampshire retailers were female. Portsmouth women were not separately listed in 1686, but in the 1690s at least six female retailers were licensed in Portsmouth alone. On the eve of Revolution (1770) there were still no female tavernkeepers in Portsmouth, and perhaps only four of the nearly two hundred retailers in New Hampshire were women.[13]

Richard Wybird, a mariner, had married the widow Elizabeth Redford, who was one of the few licensed women in Portsmouth at the turn of the eighteenth century. Seeking to take advantage of her license without renewing it "in his own name," Wybird was sorely disappointed to learn that he was barred from selling alcoholic beverages by himself. Fearing "to be utterly ruined," Wybird petitioned to sell his stock of cider, beer, wine, and rum. The lieutenant governor and council rejected his request, which suggests that the authorities recognized separate economic activities on the part of husbands and wives, as well as joint family enterprises.[14]

Brewers, as distinct from innkeepers and retailers, were also forced to obtain licenses in Massachusetts in 1637 and were subject to regulation there-after. Although efforts to contain production and distribution met with some resistance in the 1630s, by the end of 1651 commercial brewing had been re-stricted to those who had "sufficient skill and knowledge in the arte or mis-tery of a brewer," language faintly reminiscent of European guilds and their penchant for exclusivity. As in Europe, American women were eased out of the lucrative large-scale commercial trade and were relegated to small retail establishments.[15]

When local authorities granted women retail licenses, restrictive provi-sions frequently accompanied the permits. Goody Upshall received permis-sion to draw beer "provided shee do committ the trust and care thearof to some able honest man." And the General Court granted Mrs. Clarke's peti-tion on the condition that "she is to continue or desist from keeping the ordinary as [the] Salem Court shall order," thus linking her livelihood to the whim of the court. Sometimes applicants were disallowed altogether: "the petition of Elizabeth Carter for aprobation of the Selectmen to bee a Retailer is answered in the Negative."[16]

The evidence suggests, however, that women seemed reluctant to accept a negative answer as the final word, and their evasion of the law parallels the same widespread circumvention practiced by their English cousins. Throughout the Puritan colonies unlicensed, underground merchandising of alcoholic beverages resisted regulation and surfaced only when the law caught up with an indiscreet seller. Anne Holliday was prosecuted "for selling beer by retail contrary to law," and Hope Dickson, Alice Clarke, and Eliza-beth Cunnigrave were convicted of selling strong beer without a license. Each of these malefactors received five-pound fines. Joanna Harris sold ale "at 3p. per quart" without a license, and it cost her five pounds as well.[17] By punish-ing these women, Boston jurists could be confident that they had contributed to a more orderly, stable society.

Alice Thomas, however, was every magistrate's worst nightmare. The County Court refused her request for a public house license, and she subse-quently appealed to the General Court to no avail. Thomas, however, was determined to sell alcoholic beverages with or without permission, and when the law finally pinned her down, she was convicted not only of "selling wine and Strong waters" without license but also of "giving frequent secret and unseasonable Entertainment in her house to Lewd Lascivious and notorious persons of both Sexes, giving them oppertunity to commit Carnall wick-edness."[18] In short, Alice Thomas had been running a whorehouse under the collective noses of the Boston authorities. Sex and alcohol: an unsaintly combination certain to stimulate the ultimate disorder.

Records for the middle and late 1670s show that more women than men were prosecuted for selling alcohol without a license, which could mean either that they were more willing to risk punishment or that the authorities averted their eyes when men engaged in illegal trafficking. In any case, when brought before the court, both men and women received the same fine. And in perspective it appears that the authorities took this black market trade seriously: in the 1670s both fornication before marriage and speech crimes rated only a two-pound penalty.

Whether it was because the court denied them a license or whether the license fee was beyond their means, women as well as men ran a risk not only of a hefty fine but also of incarceration until that fine was paid. A woman might also find herself behind bars until she found sureties for her good behavior, an effort that may have been more difficult for her than for her male counterparts. Sureties were always male.[19]

In 1727 Dorothy Stone, the wife of an Essex County fisherman, found herself on the wrong side of the law for retailing small "parcells" of strong drink without a license. "She did not deny the fact but pleaded her poverty," an excuse that softened the judge to the extent that he offered Mrs. Stone an option: to pay a ten-pound fine or to "stand closely and strictly committed in any of the common gaols of this county for forty days, and not to have the liberty of the Gaolers house or yard and pay costs of prosecution." A man similarly convicted at the same session received the same ten-pound fine, but without the alternative sentence.[20]

Illegal purveyors took an added risk by selling alcohol to Indians, a transaction that was prohibited with or without a license. Although the Suffolk County Court fined George Badcocke eighteen pounds for selling "strong waters" to the Indians—a sum indicative of the seriousness of the offense—the defendant petitioned for an abatement, arguing that the sale "was donne by his wife without his consent." In this instance the judges exhibited sympathy as well as empathy and abated two-thirds of his fine.[21] John Langsbury was merely admonished and forced to pay court fees after he told the court that his beer sale to some Indians "was small beere of a penny a quart." Jabez Eaton's wife, Elizabeth, was accused of selling an Indian three quarts of strong beer. Told to purge herself "by her oath" or subject herself to ten stripes or a twelve-pound fine, she took the oath.[22]

In Essex County two men testified that Goodwife Farefield sold strong drink to an Indian, to which she replied, "And why not we are all one mans children." Her egalitarianism notwithstanding, Mrs. Farefield's actions may suggest a social phenomenon that worked to the advantage of both women and Indians. Women had difficulty obtaining licenses to sell alcoholic beverages; Indians were prohibited from buying such drink. Their mutual interest was served, therefore, by this trade. It may also be less than coincidental that the witnesses against Mrs. Farefield were white males, a phenomenon that was repeated in Rhode Island.[23]

Many of the women who were accused of illicitly selling strong drink were actually licensed to do so, and the flurry of accusations, particularly in the 1720s, may have been deliberate harassment to discourage them from engaging in the trade. Supported by their licenses, a few pleaded not guilty and were either acquitted or dismissed. Others found that the court did not accept a license as prima facie refutation of the charge and fined them anyway. Still others, despite their licenses, pleaded guilty and were fined the usual ten pounds. Given the uncertainty of the outcome, such women had good reason to enter a guilty plea despite their innocence: courts were more lenient toward those who pleaded guilty than toward those who maintained their innocence but were convicted nonetheless.[24]

Denial of licenses became a cause célèbre on the eve of Revolution in Salem when a group of inhabitants petitioned the Court of General Sessions to protest the Selectmen's arbitrary refusal to grant new retailing permits. The petitioners admitted the "intemperate use of strong Drink" in Salem but demanded impartiality in the dispensing of licenses. "One sober [Man] or poor industrious widow," they argued, "has as equitable a Right to it as another." What is striking about the language of this petition is the implicit assumption that men and widows were equal in status, a point emphasized by the notation appended to the list of aggrieved citizens. Each of the six widows and three men named had "as equitable a Right to retail as fifty others of their Neighbours."[25] In such a way, perhaps, Salemites imbibed the spirit of the Revolution.

Alcoholic licenses could be expensive, even arbitrarily so. The Newport Town Council was empowered to raise the price of licenses "to such greater sums as they shall think needful," over and above the forty shillings established by the Rhode Island General Assembly. Coffee, tea, and chocolate sellers had also been licensed since the seventeenth century, but the Massachusetts legislature imposed additional burdens on these purveyors in the mid-eighteenth century by forcing them to pay excise taxes on both coffee and tea. In protest, Bostonians argued that "the Business of retailing Tea, Coffee etc. is mainly carried on by Widows and persons in low Circumstances ... and sho'd this Act continue ... there will be danger of their becoming a charge and burthen to the Town." Note the emphasis: not that these people would suffer economic deprivation, but that the town purse would be unduly strained.[26] If, in fact, women marketed coffee and tea in greater numbers than men, the licensing and excise fees fell more heavily on them as well, which may explain why sellers of these beverages were no more reluctant to evade the law than their neighbors who traded spirits (even at the risk of a fine).

During the seventeenth and eighteenth centuries the Massachusetts and Rhode Island legislatures, in company with more local governing bodies, passed other laws and ordinances that hampered the ability of women to sustain themselves, since many regulations affected clothing and food production. Within a few years of settlement, the Boston magistrates attempted to curb extravagance by prohibiting anyone from making or buying any woolen, silk, or linen apparel "with any lace on it, silver, gold, silke or thread." Two years later this legislation was reinforced by forbidding the sale of lace altogether, and tailors were enjoined from setting lace on any garment. And finally, in 1639: "no person hereafter shall be imployed in the making of any manner of lace," unless for export.[27]

Euro-Americans emigrated from a society where lacemakers were female, and in banning such activities, the Massachusetts authorities foreclosed another avenue of income for women. A modification of the law in 1651 that permitted colonists with estates of two hundred pounds to adorn themselves with gold and silver lace only partially addressed this issue.[28] Most lace would be imported from Europe.

The early establishment of public markets could also have impinged on women's ability to produce income. In 1633 Boston began to hold regular markets on Thursdays, and a year later, Wednesday was proclaimed Salem's official market day. Many people found a public market a more efficient way of trading goods, and from the very beginning, women as well as men had stalls in the market or shops in the marketplace.[29] Nevertheless, women and men do not necessarily adhere to the same schedules, and women as the primary nurturers and caretakers of young children may have found it difficult to buy and sell goods at a prearranged time at a central market. Furthermore, other restrictions, promulgated over time, hampered women more than men.

By the end of the first third of the eighteenth century Boston had established three town markets for country people to bring produce into town, all of which were open every day but Sunday. Market regulations prohibited the sale of "flesh, poultry, eggs, butter, meat, chees, Frute, Hearbes, [and] Rootes" (all of which were staples of the female economy) anywhere else in town, and promised a fine for each infraction. Bread and milk were excluded from these regulations, but the town officials clearly meant to prevent the sale of the proscribed items at private houses, warehouses, inns, alehouses, lanes, alleys, or streets. Hucksters were effectively discouraged from buying elsewhere in town and selling at the market.[30]

What may have inhibited women even more directly was the later imposition of rents on market stalls. At least as early as 1757 Boston Selectmen apportioned the size of stalls in Faneuil Market and "let them out to such Persons, and on such terms as they shall agree." Surely this extra expense must have precluded more women than men. Only Boston's desperate situation in 1776 forced the town fathers to offer stalls in Faneuil Hall gratis. Newport followed suit, and in 1760, when they raised money for a market at Long Wharf, the legislation stipulated that the upper part was to be made into stores for dry goods and rented out to best advantage.[31]

No individual piece of legislation was responsible for the feminization of poverty. Collectively, however, a combination of laws, ordinances, and regulations, acting in concert with cultural values, served to sideline women. By dividing people on the basis of the work skills they possessed, for example, legislators laid the groundwork for discrimination based on gender. In the 1630s "the beste sort of laborers" were differentiated from "inferior workmen," and even without guilds, workers received wages based on an assessment of their skills. Wage and price controls designed to prevent inflation probably minimized gender differences to some extent, but the resistance to and collapse of such regulations before the end of the seventeenth century permitted a modified free market to determine the value of labor.[32] And if economic reward reflected the degree to which such labor was evaluated, the records leave little doubt as to who was considered the best sort of worker. Not surprisingly, compensation rates often depended on the sex of the laborer, particularly as division of labor based on sex became more firmly entrenched over time.

In legal controversies over the value of work performed, the outcome usually depended on the opinion of male committees appointed to assess the worth of contested labor. Such a procedure left considerable room for bias if any of the committee members were conditioned to favor male efforts. Every so often a civil litigant would ask the courts to determine what he or she "reasonably deserved." Once again, it is likely that different standards were applied to men and women in reaching what the court thought were equitable decisions.[33] Spinners could not expect to be compensated at the same rate as carpenters; seamstresses did not reasonably deserve as much as blacksmiths. Katherine West thought that she was entitled to fifty-five pounds for nursing Joseph Shearman. Benjamin Shearman, who had promised to pay her what "she should reasonably deserve," thought otherwise.[34] Through such controversies the law offered ample opportunity for implementing discriminatory cultural values, which in turn had a negative effect on female earning power.

Institutional regulations also exacerbated female poverty by reinforcing work skills that provided only minimal income in the world beyond the workhouse walls. In 1740 the Boston workhouse claimed thirty-eight women, ten men, and seven children. At that time, although the "picking of oakum" (i.e., recycling old rope) was the common work of the house, tradesmen such as tailors, shoemakers, mopmakers, and nailers could perform their "business" in the workhouse. Women who were "capable" of work, however, were "employ'd in Carding and Spinning Wooll, Flax, Yarn for Mops, and Cotton Yarn for Candlewick, Knitting, Sewing etc"—work that rarely provided enough income for the necessities of life outside the workhouse.[35] Salem's workhouse rules, promulgated a decade later, emulated those of Boston down to the last spinning wheel, a decision that could hardly mitigate female poverty, since any effort to produce large quantities of woolen cloth was sure to meet with resistance from the British, who looked upon their own wool production as "their most favorite manufactory."[36]

Yet if authorities in Boston and Salem continued to expect productivity from the women they incarcerated, surviving records hint that in the outside world female idleness might be tolerated as it never would have been decades earlier. By the early 1670s it was usually males, not females, who were presented for being idle, which suggests either that women never acquired this habit or that officials were now reluctant to prosecute women who were less industrious than others. Although there were many single women who made every effort to support themselves, idleness was beginning to take on a gendered appearance.[37]

In eighteenth-century Rhode Island expectations about female productivity became even more minimal. At the same time that Boston was carefully framing its workhouse rules, the town fathers of Newport dispensed public money without any expectation of a quid pro quo. Perhaps the officials in Newport were simply more realistic and recognized the truth of Dinah Cahoon's assertion when she complained that she had "nothing but [her] hands to work for the support" of herself and her children. In essence, she was arguing that those hands could not provide adequate relief for her family, for which reason she turned to the town for assistance.

As a result, the town provided for her—and others like her. On a motion to redress Barbara Hills's poverty, the Newport Town Council ordered Samuel Dyre to supply her with whatever she needed until the next council meeting. When Susannah Lyons petitioned to be allowed "something," the council delegated Samuel Collins to address her needs. And Ann Hill, who was very poor and had three children, was allowed five pounds per week "till further orders."[38]

By the early 1770s the Salem Overseers of the Poor had followed Newport's example and consistently wrote out six-shilling money orders for needy women at various intervals: "April 1773 Mary Webb have order for 6/ being in low circumstances." Men almost never received money in this manner; they were far more likely to be paid by the Overseers for services rendered.[39] By Independence, therefore, a social pattern had been established whereby poor women (and particularly those with children) received government assistance in the form of stipends, but without any simultaneous effort to increase productive skills that would have made them self-supporting in the future.

Similarly, scattered evidence hints that regulations for houses of correction may have followed a pattern that corresponded to those for workhouses, even if the former initially employed gender-neutral work requirements for men and women who might be incarcerated. In 1656 the master of such a house supplied both men and women with "hempe, flax, or other materials," and these "delinquents" received their "bread and water, or other meane food," out of the proceeds "earned by his or her labour." The master was to "imploy him or her by dayly stint and if he or shee be stoborne, disorderly, or idle," the master could withhold food or employ "meet correction."[40] Given such discretion, it was within the director's power to treat men and women differently, but the intent of the legislators shows no such bias. In 1725, however, when Hannah Whitamore was committed to the Salem House of Corrections for "strolling about the streets vagabond like" and deserting "her last service," the Selectmen ordered a spinning wheel and wool "in order to her being Employed and set to work as the Law Directs."[41] Thus gender dictated the response to poor and disorderly women, which in turn reinforced the economic dependence of women on men and enhanced patriarchal authority.

REGULATING RELATIONS: MARRIAGE AND DIVORCE

To further social values through a gendered economy was one thing; to suppress disorder through control of sexuality quite another—even though both goals emanated from a single, integrated worldview. The most serious problem for scholars in unraveling these tangled issues is that successful fornicators and adulterers have left no paper trails to follow (which distinguishes them from people whose economic path is well marked). Thus, although legal documents suggest the boundaries of proper sexual behavior and tell something about those who are caught with their pants down, surviving records only hint at the degree to which such laws were observed by the people they were designed to govern.

The problem of illegal sexual relations was compounded by the laws governing the legal union of two people. Émigrés to Massachusetts Bay had good reason to be bewildered, given the inconsistent and evolving requirements for a bona fide marriage in seventeenth-century England. Theoretically, marriage there was a series of steps that included a written contract between parents, spousals (a formal exchange of oral promises, usually before witnesses), a public proclamation of banns, a church wedding, and consummation of the marriage. According to English ecclesiastical law, the spousals were as contractually binding as a church wedding, and indeed, any kind of exchange of promises before witnesses fulfilled the requirements for a valid marriage. The Catholic Church required a priest after 1563, an innovation eschewed by the Anglicans and one that made life for Catholics slightly more complicated but not impossible. During the sixteenth and seventeenth centuries people placed an ever greater emphasis on church weddings, although lawyers continued to recognize the spousals as definitive—and religious leaders increasingly denounced the practice.[42]

Puritan marriage followed English tradition except that Puritans did not recognize the role of the clergy, insisting instead on a civil ceremony to establish marital validity. Given the covert manner in which dissenters were forced to worship, however, it is unclear whether dissenting magistrates (under cover of conformity) performed English rites or whether some other tradition evolved. According to Patricia Crawford, the Anglican marriage ceremony (with a cleric presiding) remained popular even during the Interregnum, when civil magistrates became responsible for the union. Evidence suggests that civil ceremonies took place in Massachusetts for the first decade of its existence, although no law requiring written registration of a marriage appeared until 1639. Seven years later, Massachusetts Bay denied the legitimacy of alternative marriage rites by prohibiting any person but a civil magistrate from performing the ceremony.[43]

Thus, even though the world non-Puritans left behind included a variety of ways to tie the knot, no such legal options awaited them in Massachusetts. Confronted with lingering memories of countless celebrations in the parish churches, or the acceptance of binding vows in front of several friends, many inhabitants of the Bay Colony must have been uncertain about which nuptial path to follow. The few Catholics who invaded Massachusetts in disguise were at the greatest disadvantage, but those who were neither Catholic nor committed Puritans must have paused as well. Conscience or convenience might have taken over at this point, which would account for the surprising number of colonists who decided to shortcut the prescribed route to a legally sanctioned marriage by taking up residence together. Indeed, a memorandum attached to a 1689 abstract of New England laws hinted that "many thousands" considered the 1646 act unreasonable and showed their disdain by living together "unmarried." Such clandestine matches were rarely penalized as such but were rather treated as fornication cases.[44] Yet no matter how the authorities might have perceived such unions, it is likely that many, perhaps even a majority, of these couples considered themselves formally, if not legally, united.

It was the intention of the Puritan authorities that husbands and wives live together, preferably in harmony but even if the relationship was discordant. If the marriage fell into the latter category, town officials took it upon themselves to intervene. The Court of Assistants summoned James Davies "for his unquietness with his wife," and John and Elnor Peirce were admonished to see that better order be kept in their house.[45] Wives who sought to distance themselves from their husbands were ordered back; husbands were admonished to live with and support their wives. Sometimes the courts reunited a couple; sometimes they were unable to effect a reconciliation. Indeed, in many instances a refusal on the part of one party or the other led to a standoff that was beyond the court's ability to redress. The Grand Jury presented Sarah Pickering for living apart from her husband, but when the court received a letter from her husband declaring he would never come to her or take her back, the judge excused Sarah.

· Courts also censured married men for cavorting with other women, although such husbands rarely explained the reasons for their "wanton dalliance." Indeed, Robert Spurr was admonished for entertaining married men "to the greife of their wives." And in Essex County in the early 1640s more than two dozen men were presented for living apart from their wives.[46] Marital expectations also included proper maintenance of a wife by a husband. Should she lack "victuals clothing or fireing" because of his neglect or cruelty, the court would require him to mend his ways. The records are replete with evidence that Puritan families were often unloving and inconsiderate, and that protective strategies for wives and widows were far more necessary than one might expect.[47]

To adjudicate marital problems and protect the sanctity of marriage, the court heard testimony on the most intimate matters and refereed the most delicate issues. They agreed that Walter Hickson and Mary Bedwell (wife of Samuel) were keeping company and "being too familiar." Each had the option of fifteen stripes or a forty-shilling fine, and they were prohibited from seeing each other.[48] But if the law penalized both men and women for stretching the bonds of matrimony, the government assumed that wives needed greater regulation than husbands. Whether it was because women were disorderly to begin with, or whether they could not be trusted to contain their sexuality, no matter: female behavior was more carefully monitored than that of males.

For several decades after settlement, Boston's magistrates were content to single out individual women for occasional reprimands. Kathrine Cornish, wife of Richard, was one of many women who were "found suspicious of incontinency and . . . seriously admonished to take heede." In a similar vein, the Grand Jury presented Weybro Lovell (wife of Captain Lovell) for "light and whoarish behavior," and she too "was seriously admonished to repent, and walke humbly, chastly, and holily," in language that was restricted to female miscreants. More specifically, Elizabeth Wheeler and Joanna Peirce were presented for disorderly carriage in the house of Thomas Watts, "being married women and founde sitting in other mens laps with theire arms about theire necks."[49]

By 1674, however, the Massachusetts General Court apparently felt it had not done enough "to prevent [the] appearance of sinn and wickedness in any kind," and subsequently passed a resolution whereby it would no longer be lawful "for any single woman or wife in the absence of hir husband to entertaine or lodge any inmate or sojourner" unless the Selectmen of the town waived the rule. Punishment was a fine or ten stripes, and both single and married women were prosecuted under this regulation.[50]

Puritans also subscribed to the common seventeenth-century view that held a husband responsible for his wife's conduct. Whether it was to ensure a court appearance or simply to guarantee that whatever "crime" she committed would not be repeated, husbands were required to post hefty bonds "for their wives good behavior."[51] The reverse never appears in the records: no wife posted bond to ensure her husband's appropriate conduct. Under common law, married women could not make enforceable promises, but one suspects that common law notwithstanding, women would not have been found publicly guaranteeing spousal behavior. In such fashion the law reached into the household and subtly reinforced the patriarchal relationship between husband and wife, a process that showed no sign of reversal in the eighteenth century, despite the rhetoric of sentimentality.

Although marriage was the normal relationship between adult men and women, not every couple lived happily ever after, despite the best efforts of colonial officialdom. Unlike old England, New England permitted divorce in certain circumstances, and although such dissolutions were rare throughout the colonial era, divorce petitions provide a glimpse not only of marital expectations and disappointments but also of the relationship between women, economic dependence, and sexual promiscuity.[52]

Expectations clashed with reality when husbands failed to support their wives. Such situations, not as uncommon as once thought, left women with few alternatives. A husband who deserted his wife left her in a financially precarious situation. Usually unable to earn a living on her own, she could take up with another man—something many women did—but this left her open to adultery (or fornication) charges, even though her economic viability rather than her libido was at issue. She could also petition for divorce, although this did not necessarily improve her financial position and in the long run could worsen it, since absolute divorce erased dower rights.

Each scenario required state intervention, even if local officials were no better at resolving these ticklish situations than the individuals themselves. Should the state seek out an errant husband and force him to pay his wife's maintenance? Should the state act in the husband's stead and provide abandoned or divorced women with the necessities of life? The former course was often unrealistic, the latter a potentially expensive proposition, and one that again illustrates the tension between the desire to suppress female independence and the state's eagerness to be exonerated from an onerous financial burden. Eventually, the government would resolve some of these problems by formally linking divorce to maintenance or alimony, a fusion that at least theoretically reduced the appeal of extramarital liaisons based on financial need but still left women economically dependent on a male provider.

From the perspective of women themselves, however, the number and content of two centuries' worth of divorce petitions and related papers suggest that historians have too hastily concluded that it took a revolutionary movement to stimulate female individualism and activism in the area of divorce. Instead, the evidence reflects a strong sense of female self-awareness from the earliest decades of the seventeenth century as well as a willingness to resist an oppressive marriage. What they often lacked was the ability to extricate themselves from situations over which they had no control.

There was, as Nancy Cott demonstrates, a surge of divorce petitions submitted by women during the Revolutionary era, but the swell of applications alone does not necessarily demonstrate "a causal link" to the War for Independence. Similarly, the "emergent female individualism" and "new feminist sensitivity" that Sheldon Cohen attributes to "liberative Revolutionary ideology" emerged considerably earlier than Cohen indicates.[53] Indeed, it is somewhat patronizing—even demeaning—to suggest that New England women needed revolutonary rhetoric to stimulate a desire for freedom from an abusive or nonsupportive husband or to prod them to act on that desire.

A century before Americans sought political independence, Ann Tollman, a Rhode Islander, confessed to adultery after her husband, Peter, sought a divorce on those grounds. Despite the threat of a severe whipping, she refused to humble herself by returning to her husband and insisted that "she would rather cast herselfe on the mercy of God if he take away her life, than to returne"—which I take to mean that she would rather be dead. The Salem resident Katheren Ellenwood was even more explicit on this point in her petition for divorce in 1682. She was very young, she said, "and would rather die than live with this man" any longer.[54]

Horod Long Gardner insisted she would not return to George "whatever became of her." And according to court records, Abigail Snell not only obstinately refused to live with her husband but openly admitted that "Every time she saw him . . . she could kill him."[55] Whatever happened to submission and deference? Quite apart from the liberating experience that adultery appears to have been for some of these women, their collective attitude is every bit as antiauthoritarian as it would be at the end of the eighteenth century.

The words "freedom" and "liberty" were not added to the female vocabulary in 1776 either. In her 1716 divorce petition Meribah Edmonds asked "to be declared as free as when sole." And in 1739 Mercy Austin requested a divorce and the "Liberty of acting with the same Freedom with regard to herself as she had before her intermarriage." Nine years later, Marcy Olney's eloquence reminds us that women had already made the "causal link" between their personal happiness and independence several decades before the emerging nation became energized enough to act on the same principles.[56] Marcy's first husband left her in 1745. She remarried, only to find herself deserted once again—this time with six children to support. She petitioned for a divorce with the understanding that "liberty is the Darling of Every free Mind," and that she needed "her" liberty ("the" liberty is crossed out!) "to take Care of her Children."

Although some women assumed the right to an expansive personal liberty for themselves early on, it appears that male officials interpreted female liberty somewhat more narrowly. Throughout the seventeenth century divorce-granting authorities in Rhode Island and Massachusetts consistently severed the marital contract with the expectation that the female divorcée was "at liberty to marry with another man." That the same injunction did not apply to men is evident from the language used to grant Samuel Holton's divorce petition. The Court of Assistants "set him free and at liberty"—period.[57]

If the language of seventeenth- and eighteenth-century divorce petitions illustrates a sense of female awareness that predated the Independence movement, a numerical overview of extant applications indicates that the Revolutionary era had little quantitative impact as well. As Lyle Koehler demonstrates, the Massachusetts authorities entertained fifty-four divorce applications between 1620 and 1699. Thirty-nine wives and ten husbands sought release from their marital contract. Two applications were brought by mothers on behalf of their daughters, and the sponsors of three others are indeterminable.[58] Of the fifty-four petitions, the disposition of all but four were recorded. Only six of the remaining fifty were denied: three wives, two husbands, one daughter. In short, almost four times as many wives as husbands sought divorce and over 90 percent of these women met with success. Eighty percent of the men won divorces. In the eighteenth century this pattern alters dramatically.

According to Nancy Cott's figures, fifty husbands but only forty-seven wives petitioned for divorce in Massachusetts between 1692 and 1764, with the number of male petitions beginning to exceed those of women in 1725. Fifty-one percent of women and 68 percent of men received favorable decrees. The number of female petitions rose perceptibly in the years between 1765 and 1786 (eighty-two petitions), but of that number only fifty were granted (61 percent), a greater percentage than during the first half of the eighteenth century but nowhere near the seventeenth-century success rate. Of the fifty-one males who sought divorce between 1765 and 1786, thirty-five received favorable action—the same percentage as earlier in the century. The application ratio of wives to husbands was also considerably lower at the end of the eighteenth century than it had been during the seventeenth century.[59]

In Rhode Island the story bears some similarities, although the numbers are considerably smaller. During the seventeenth century eight women, six men, and three "others" petitioned for divorce. The authorities denied only one petition, although it is unclear whether it was from a wife or husband. Although several couples did not receive absolute divorce decrees but rather permission to separate, officials did not force incompatible couples to live together. During the first half of the eighteenth century in Rhode Island, ten women and five men sought divorces. Almost all of the complainants were awarded either an absolute divorce or separation.[60] Thus, in both colonies more women than men initially petitioned for divorce.

What also seems to parallel the Massachusetts experience is the shifting ratio of male to female petitions in the mid-eighteenth century. Between 1758 and 1775 thirteen men and seven women pressed for divorce in Newport, Rhode Island, while between 1735 and 1764 in Massachusetts, thirty-eight men and thirty-two women petitioned for the same end.[61] In both cases it is a striking turnabout, although the grounds on which husbands in both Rhode Island and Massachusetts were likely to sue—adultery—may suggest that dissatisfied wives were assertively taking the one path that would eventually terminate their marriage. Adultery gave women economic leverage in those circumstances where husbands were financially unsupportive, and the fact that such extramarital liaisons were often presented as cohabitation or desertion (as opposed to one-night stands) suggests that women may have considered them a substitute for divorce. In any case, women admitted adultery charges far more often than they denied them.

Finally, it should be noted that when the wheel turned full circle at the end of the eighteenth century, divorce petitions in Rhode Island followed the same pattern that they did in Massachusetts. Between 1780 and 1786 in New-port alone, twelve women but only five men petitioned for divorce, and dur-ing the following decade this trend became even more apparent.

Although the escalation of female divorce petitions in the Revolutionary era suggests a correlation between the two, there are equally likely reasons, in Rhode Island at least, why such petitions proliferated at that time. Although absolute divorces had been granted in that colony since the mid-seventeenth century, the 1749 statute investing justices of the Superior Court with power to grant divorces in all cases where persons had been injured by a "Breach of the Marriage-Covenant" created some anxiety among local officials.[62] Four years after its passage, the Town Council of Newport voiced its concerns about the implications of that law in a petition to the Rhode Island General Assembly. "There is," the councillors noted, "no Provision made for the maintenance of any woman who shall or may be Divorced from Her Hus-band . . . By Means whereof . . . if she be incapable of getting a Living may become a Town Charge." Assuming that this liberal law might open the floodgates of divorce actions, and eager to distance government from any financial responsibility for a large pool of unattached women, the General Assembly swiftly amended the 1749 law to provide maintenance "in every case" of divorce. Such financial support would be assigned from the "Estate of her late Husband, as the Circumstances . . . may reasonably admit," or as an annual sum for life or while she refrained from remarrying.[63]

How quickly women became generally aware of this amendment is not known, but in 1762, when Sarah McWilliams sued her husband, John, for divorce, Robert Campbell deposed that he had told John McWilliams that Sarah "could oblige him to support her in a Separate Estate." Thus it was during this period that women, conscious of their economic dependence, received some assurance that their ex-husbands would continue to be re-sponsible for their support. In effect, this modified the common law rule that precluded dower in cases of absolute divorce.[64]

Changing economic conditions in the port cities may also have encour-aged women to consider divorce as a means of advancing their self-interest. The common law rule that denied women dower rights in absolute divorce cases was meaningful only when an estate contained a reasonable amount of real property. But by the mid-eighteenth century fewer men owned real property in Boston, Salem, Portsmouth, and Newport, and thus fewer women could look forward to a future share of such property. Moreover, widows were only second in line (behind creditors) to receive personal property, which meant that there was no real economic advantage to remaining in a disagreeable marriage—especially if a husband did not meet his personal obligations to support his wife.

The seaport economy was also undergoing another transition in the second half of the eighteenth century: wages and cash were replacing the barter system. In a hostile marriage earlier in the century, an errant husband might not claim a plum cake, pair of shoes, or appliquéd quilt, but in the later decades he might well demand his estranged wife's cash earnings—and by law he was entitled to them. The only way she could protect her income was through an absolute divorce, and it is clear from the petitions that this was a matter of some concern. Ann Seten is a case in point.

Ann married Asa Seten in 1768 "in hopes of enjoying with Satisfaction an agreeable Companion for life." Although Ann had been a good wife, Asa deserted her after two years, leaving her with a young child and no support. As a result, Ann "was obliged to apply herself to daily Labour for the maintenance of herself and child." Nine months later, Asa returned, sought out Ann's employers, "insisted" on "the pay for her weaving," and then added gratuitously that he "would be Damd before she should have any of it." He then absconded for a second time. Fearful that he would make good on his promise to return and "distress her," Ann petitioned for divorce. She requested the divorce "to keep what trifle she [could] earn for the support of herself and child." The court granted her an absolute divorce.[65]

George Bliss abandoned his wife, Sarah, one month after their marriage in 1789, leaving her without any means of support. By 1795 she had given up hope of his return, especially since rumor had it that George was about to take a second wife in Maryland. The issue of bigamy notwithstanding, Sarah was left with lingering doubts about the security of her income. She petitioned for divorce so she might "convert the fruits of her industry to her own use." The court granted her request and awarded her alimony in the form of George's personal property "now in her hands"—property that would have fallen into the hands of his creditors had she waited (as his wife) for his demise.[66]

Alice Brayton was also deserted by a husband who refused to contribute to her support. In her divorce petition in 1795, Brayton further stipulated that she was "under great apprehension that she may be subjected to further inconvenience from the controul which the said John may have and exercise as well over her person as the fruits of her industry." Realistically, the judges could not prevent "inconvenience" to her person, but they could preserve her earnings, and the court granted her a divorce from her mariner husband.[67]

It is not likely that justices in either Massachusetts or Rhode Island were enthusiastic about the burgeoning number of divorce petitions from women. The low sex ratio had not escaped anyone's notice, and by granting divorces, the courts were adding (however minimally) to a pool of unattached women who would escape the control, guidance, or suasion of a male head of household. Nevertheless, economic reality prevailed over patriarchal pretensions in this one round as budget-conscious governments came to see divorce as a means of protecting their official pocketbooks from the supplications of financially strained women whose husbands had repudiated their obligations.

It hardly matters whether women had internalized the idea that men were responsible for their economic well-being or whether they latched on to the ideology to ensure for themselves a portion of marital property to which they felt entitled. What matters is that a patriarchal society had created a pool of dependent women and by the mid-eighteenth century had to contend with the consequences of that achievement. And although governmental decisions resolved the problem by holding estranged husbands accountable, individual men resisted this aspect of patriarchal structure. In her petition, Ann Little asked to be "provided for" from the estate of her husband. Her husband, Robert, protested on the grounds that she was "a well hearty Woman and able to work and maintain herself" without his help.[68] This dialogue, with all the inherent tensions it implies about male responsibility and female capability, would be repeated over the next two centuries.

PREVENTING PROMISCUITY

In their pursuit of sexual order, the founders made superhuman efforts to contain sexual intercourse to marriage, an effort doomed to failure because a surprisingly large number of settlers did not cooperate in the quest for sexual sainthood. The court records suggest that fornication reached epidemic proportions from time to time, and whether these documents accurately reflect social patterns or not, prosecutions for that offense died down only after the middle of the eighteenth century. Perhaps Laurel Ulrich is right and informal mechanisms of control monitored communal norms as court intervention waned, but the spiraling illegitimacy rate suggests that the community was no more successful than the courts in reducing the number of out-of-wedlock births.[69]

The documents also indicate that while men and women were both brought to trial, convicted, and sentenced for out-of-wedlock sex in the seventeenth century, women were held more responsible for what appeared to be a spiraling fornication rate.[70] In Newport in 1671 Martha Hicks pleaded guilty to fornication with Nicholas Browne and was fined forty shillings. Nicholas, however, pleaded not guilty and was acquitted. In a more complex case, Shadrach Manton was indicted for having "carnall Copulation" with Mary Pray, wife of Richard Pray. Shadrach pleaded not guilty and was acquitted; Mary pleaded guilty and was offered the choice of a whipping or a ten-pound fine. One might argue that Mary's punishment was minimal, since she could have been charged with adultery, but the existence of a double standard is painfully obvious nonetheless. Moreover, at least some Newporters questioned the inconsistency of such verdicts, because when Howlong Harris appeared in court to answer carnal copulation charges in 1682, the indictment left the matter "to the Judgment of the bench, alleadging that the man being cleered, she could not be guilty."[71]

Not only could a woman be found guilty, but she could also be found guilty by the court after being acquitted by the jury. In 1671 Grace Lawton was accused of adultery but exculpated by the jury. Nevertheless, the court declared itself "wholy dissatisfyed with that verdict" and refused to "cleere her" after the prosecution argued that "there was a failer in the Testimony he depended on or otherwise he had produced other Testimony." Whatever this says about due process in seventeenth-century Rhode Island, Lawton must have been released eventually, because she was tried again for adultery in 1673 and once again acquitted.[72]

The vast majority of colonial women were never hauled before the court on fornication charges, nor were more than a handful indicted for adultery. Men were condemned for fornication and punished for adulterous activities as well. Yet the biased treatment that many women experienced as their cases were adjudicated reflects an attitude that permeated the larger community and had lasting ramifications. Since the crimes for which women were prosecuted and punished in the seventeenth century were overwhelmingly sexual in nature, and since women rather than men often bore the brunt of the punishment, it is evident (and not surprising, given their cultural baggage) that the leaders of the community held women responsible for the sexual

mores of that society and tried to govern their behavior—and the social order—through the control of female sexual conduct. Thus Margery Rugs was
sentenced to a whipping in 1640 "for intiseing and allureing George Palmer,"
and although George admitted his part, he was merely set in the stocks.[73]

Young unmarried women were considered the most likely candidates for
unseemly sexual behavior, which was why the Salem authorities were disin-
clined to distribute parcels of land to them in the early 1630s. A few widows
were the recipients of such largesse, and only with the greatest reluctance on
the part of Governor Endicott, who exhibited concern about "presedents and
evil events of graunting lotts unto single maidens." In the most becoming
manner, "Debora Holmes refused Land being a maid," presumably in recognition of the fact that it "would be a bad president to keep hous alone."[74]

Throughout the colonial period, courts held women to a higher standard
than men for sexual disorder, and as a result of this rationale women were
more severely chastised for lapses from prescribed norms. Thus, Katherine
Gray was whipped for "filthy and unchast" behavior with Thomas Elkyn,
but Elkyn received no punishment. Unsure of the exact components of an
adulterous act, the Massachusetts Bay Court of Assistants punished Bethiah
Bulloine and Elizabeth Hudson for "suspicion of adultery" upon testimony
of their lying in bed with Peter Turpin. Turpin went unreprimanded. Testimony placed Mary Plumm, "naked to her shift," in Timothy Connell's chamber late at night "in a suspitious manner" because in that same room "were
two men in Bed." For being caught in this compromising position, Mary was
sentenced to twenty stripes and committed to the house of correction "till a
Service be provided for her" by the Selectmen of Dorchester. For her disorderly conduct (as defined by the court) she was, therefore, contained.[75]

The policy of integrating lesser crimes within greater ones also had a
disproportionate effect on women who were perceived as having engaged in
sexually inappropriate behavior. Even if convictions for adultery or fornication seemed remote, the authorities were not without recourse or imagination. As a result, far more women than men were convicted of "behavior"
that was alternately filthy, unchaste, light, ill, or scandalous. "Miscarriage,"
punishable by law, could be unchaste, gross, or very filthy, and women were
condemned on all counts.[76]

Efforts to control sexuality through female conduct persisted in the eighteenth century. When the watchmen of Boston found Margaret Knight and
Abigail Knap shut up with two men in a barn, the women were brought
before the court as "lewd disorderly persons." As punishment for their be-

havior they were ordered to the House of Correction, "there to receive the Discipline of the House and be kept to labour there until they shall be discharged by order of this Court or of two Justices of the Peace." The male partners in crime were not punished, and the women were incarcerated for an indeterminate period of time. Similarly, when Priscilla Hall was convicted of "being found in Bed undressed with Samuel Butler," she was sentenced to a whipping. Yet when the same court found Robert Fellows guilty of being in bed with Anne Chapman, he was merely ordered not to leave the jurisdiction and "to be of good Behaviour."[77] Although such cases do not appear with great frequency, these particular incidents depict how society held women accountable for deviant conduct and the lengths to which male authorities would go to preserve sexual order.

Women were aware of the discriminatory treatment they faced if brought up on charges of sexual misconduct. Acquittal was unlikely, and as N. E. H. Hull points out, a posttrial conviction usually resulted in a harsher sentence than one dispensed as a result of a guilty plea. By the 1720s, Massachusetts women almost always pleaded guilty to fornication or bastardy charges and were ordinarily given the choice of a fine or a whipping. In an unusual instance where a woman entered a not-guilty plea to a fornication charge, she was convicted and sentenced to a whipping, with no monetary alternative.[78]

Efforts to contain sexuality might require the removal of certain women altogether. In eighteenth-century Rhode Island women made up the majority of those warned out of various communities. Half of those handed their walking papers were women without husbands, of whom 40 percent were never married, 34 percent were abandoned, divorced, or separated, and 20 percent were widowed. Their average age (between twenty-seven and twenty-eight), was considerably lower than that of males similarly warned out of town, and although economic issues played a role in the decision to export these transients, it was also likely that officials were satisfied that they rid themselves of potentially disorderly females.[79] Shunned by one town, shunted to another, the self-esteem of such unwanted women could only have been adversely affected.

Society's belief in female culpability extended to cases of rape. In 1638 the Boston magistrates meted out a whipping for a man convicted of fornication; his partner was whipped for "yielding . . . without crying out and concealing it 9 or 10 dayes." When two men "ravished" two young girls, they were whipped—and so were the girls. And when Christopher Portingall was accused of raping Abigail Crane, both were held until they gave bond for their appearance.[80] Rapes were probably rare in early New England—at least, they rarely appear in the court records—but the manner in which they were resolved leaves little doubt that the authorities believed that female complicity was involved in some undefined manner.

Moreover, discriminatory attitudes toward women reveal themselves through the punishments assigned to various crimes as well as to the alleged criminals themselves. In meting out penalties for various infractions, male authorities made decisions influenced by a gendered outlook on life. In Salem in 1647, the court fined Richard Pray forty shillings for contempt of court and twenty shillings for beating his wife. Bastardy was a female crime that fetched a five-pound or ten-stripe penalty in 1723; in the same court, same session, a man who was convicted of shooting another in the leg received a two-pound fine.[81] Do such inequities appear regularly in the records? No, but they appear often enough to make a compelling argument for a social vision in which physical abuse of women was not of great concern, and a social construction that held women accountable for disorder.

One last irony: even if a man and woman were both convicted of sexual deviancy and received an equal number of lashes, the fact that they were required to strip "from the girdle upwards" for this public spectacle suggests that her punishment included a greater degree of humiliation.[82] Surely the court must have recognized that the same sentence would have a different effect on a woman for whom, paradoxically, the punishment as well as the crime contained a sexual component.

Although minority women endured the usual disadvantages of a system bent on regulating female sexual behavior, their alleged sexual promiscuity added another dimension to slander cases involving white females. A woman who brought slander charges was usually the object of sexual slurs.[83] The case became racially charged and the insult compounded, however, when a white woman was maligned as "a Negro Whore."[84] Calling white women "Negro whores" simultaneously degraded black females and reinforced racial stereotypes. The use of such labels also acted to control the behavior of white females by implying that although such conduct might be expected of black women, white women should show their superiority by conforming to prescribed sexual codes. Accusations of miscegenation projected the racial slight to yet another level.

In Rhode Island Rebecca Baily sued Elizabeth Greenman (through her husband) for saying that Rebecca was "a Negroes whore and Caesar Fry hath beine with her In the Little Stable . . . as often as he hath fingers and Toes."[85]

In Rebecca's mind the charge was injurious enough to demand five hundred pounds in damages. The jury thought otherwise and allowed her only five shillings, a determination that could mean either that the testimony was suspect or that the matter did not warrant such excessive compensation. Either way, race and sex were integral to the case.

Race and sex collided in the Massachusetts courts in other ways. Since the English were more restrictive about divorce than the Indians, they prosecuted Indians for adultery and bigamy in cases where the Indians may have considered themselves divorced by their own rules and therefore free to cohabit with someone else.[86] The court did not inflict the death penalty on Sarah Ahaton, "an Indian squa," for "committing adultery with Joseph an Indian," but sentenced her to a severe whipping nonetheless. Because the marital status of the woman alone determined the nature of an adulterous act, Joseph received no sentence, making it eminently clear to Indian women that in matters of sex, as well as property, they were better off under Indian law.[87]

The declining legal status of Indian women as they came under English control is revealed in less overt ways as well. Take, for example, the Grand Jury indictment against Samuel Judkins for his "great incivillity" toward Sarah. The jury was ready to indict only "iff Indian Testymony be valid."[88] On the one hand, an Indian woman had her cause adjudicated; on the other, the court had reservations about doing so on the basis of her testimony. This attitude reflects a not so subtle shift from the way in which a comparable case was handled four decades earlier.

— ≠ —

The amazing growth and prosperity of the New England colonies was a mixed blessing for women. On the one hand, many shared in that prosperity; on the other, many were marginalized as state building intensified and they were excluded from the public sphere—as well as public space. In some circles this was all to the good, since public women were potentially disruptive and any reduction in the number of women engaged in public activities diminished the likelihood of disorder.

Originally, the line between public and private was only vaguely defined, which meant that women could glide from one to the other nearly as easily as Alice slipped through the looking glass. Houses and churches were, after all, scenes of political as well as religious activity. In the early 1630s the Massachusetts Court of Assistants met at the governor's house, allowing the governor's wife, and presumably other women, access to information as the deputies discussed affairs of state. Through the early decades of the eighteenth century, Salem's Selectmen were meeting at private homes, where thin walls were no match for loud voices. A number of women must have attended to conversation as well as business as they took "care and paines" to lodge deputies and provide hungry lawmakers with a "dyet."[89]

As buildings were constructed for official use, however, public and private became disengaged, and women found themselves increasingly distanced from centers of power. But it was not just the imposing presence of physical structures in urban New England that closed off avenues of information and inhibited informal participation in the communal deliberation process. In communities that relied on unofficial means of social control and where neighbors admonished neighbors, women played an important public role. But once that control was transferred from neighborly rebuke to a formal judicial system, women became further removed from recognized positions of authority.

As the number of male officials multiplied, public authority increased commensurately, particularly over women. Female behavior was more closely monitored in Newport, Boston, Portsmouth, and Salem because the low sex ratio ensured an excessive number of potentially disorderly women who could threaten the stability of the towns. It was not just young, unmarried women who were the objects of watchful eyes, however, but married women whose husbands were away at sea, a factor that exaggerated public patriarchy in the seaports as town officials substituted for absent husbands. Sailors from American and foreign ports mingled with female residents in the New England coastal towns. Strangers became friends and friends occasionally became lovers, which in some undefined way confirmed the worst fears of the concerned mates who sailed from port to port themselves.

According to sociologists, men are less able to control women from a distance, and to compensate for this abandonment of responsibility in the New England seaports, where many men were abroad for months at a time, heavy patriarchal obligations fell upon town officials. In Boston, Overseers of the Poor ruled on all relief applications and administered town charity funds. By a provincial law of 1735, their number was increased from eight to twelve, and each overseer supervised a ward where he exercised the power to warn out, apprentice children, and issue warrants for poor relief.[90] In Salem, the Selectmen carried out much the same duties, and in Newport those burdens were shared by the Town Council and Overseers (whose members were, not surprisingly, often one and the same).

Poor widows with children were subject to the greatest scrutiny, since Selectmen and Overseers could indenture the children of mothers suspected of being unable to support them. Esther Harrison petitioned the court in 1722 for the return of two of her children who had been placed in the almshouse by the Overseers of the Poor. She had the opportunity, she explained, to indenture her son, and prayed that "she may have the disposal of her own Child to a good master to her Satisfaction." She also requested the return of her daughter "to tend her Young child whereby the sd Petitioner maybe enabled to carry on her work of a Tayler and maintain herself and children at home."[91] The court dismissed Harrison's petition.

Three years later, Esther Rowd complained that shortly after she had placed her son Humphrey Harrison as apprentice to a tailor, the Overseers of the Poor "under Colour of Law" had removed him and bound him to a farmer instead. Whether or not this was the same Esther Harrison, now remarried, no matter. Once again, the court dismissed the petition—a reminder that some women were denied responsibility for the lives of their children. Rowd's phrase, "under Colour of Law," tells us exactly what she thought of such proceedings.[92]

Yet, over the course of two centuries, urban women in colonial New England were increasingly prevented from acquiring the means to sustain themselves and their children. No one could have predicted that the infant villages of the 1630s would become the thriving cities of the eighteenth century, nor could they have foreseen the preponderance of women in those port towns. Nevertheless, the legal system, with layer upon layer of rules, regulations, ordinances, and codes, prevented most women from maximizing their opportunities and achieving anything more than a minimal standard of living in the absence of husbands, father, brothers, and sons. Given the Anglo-American cultural heritage, however, these developments were neither surprising nor, from a patriarchal standpoint, necessarily undesirable, since they also addressed another problem that had peculiarly American roots.

Anglo-Americans emigrated from a society where property holding was the basis of political power, and where property was more concentrated in male hands than in New England, making it relatively easy to exclude Englishwomen from political participation on those grounds alone. Thus, if independent landholding was to be the basis of political rights in New England, and the extent of available property permitted American women to accumulate enough to qualify as bona fide political participants, such opportunities might translate into dangerous precedents. If these ideas were even subliminally present, all the more reason to prevent women from acquiring property, since property not only encouraged autonomy and control of self but might also tempt women to claim political rights as well.[93] There can be little doubt that power follows property, and widespread property ownership among men might have even strengthened patriarchy on this side of the Atlantic in proportion to the number of men and amount of property owned. In contrast, exclusion of women from possession of property deprived them of power. Thus, female dependence had advantages from a number of different perspectives, not the least of which was that by controlling property, the law controlled women.

~ CHAPTER 6 ~

Patriarchy Preserved

Eunice Greenman's Story

*E*unice Greenman's parents raised their daughter properly.[1] By her own account Eunice had "always from her childhood behaved herself soberly and
virtuously and thereby gained the good esteem and favour of her neighbours."
Such an upbringing created great expectations: Eunice anticipated "a reasonable
preferment in marriage," and "a comfortable fortune in the world." It probably
came as no surprise to her, therefore, when she caught the eye of Christopher
Almy Jr., scion of one of Newport's oldest and most distinguished families. In
early May 1715 Almy began to "make suit" to Eunice and, as she later related,
"pretended a marriage courtship." The relationship began innocently enough,
but in March 1719 Christopher "with many repeated protestations of love and
promises to marry . . . inticed and deceived her and begot her with child."

Christopher stalled for several months but in late September 1719 finally
published banns "in order to be married to Eunice Greenman." Eunice must
have become increasingly uneasy, however, as Christopher continued to drag his
feet on the way to the altar. Her suspicions were confirmed when she learned that
her betrothed had "deserted her" and was making "suit" to Elizabeth Almy—
probably a distant relative. The banns between Christopher Almy and Elizabeth
Almy were signed in late March 1720, the publication of which "brought . . . great
shame and dishonour" to Eunice. She tried to stop the marriage, and on 28 April
1720 two judges signed an order forbidding the union between Christopher and
Elizabeth until the matter was sorted out in court. Two days later, despite the
injunction, a justice married the Almys in Tiverton. Elizabeth was sixteen,
Christopher five days short of twenty-two.[2]

At the trial in the fall of 1721, Eunice's friends rallied around her in the hope
of forestalling charges of promiscuity. Ruth Wanton testified that she "knew Eu-

nice Greenman for four years preceding the time of her having a child by Christopher Almy" and that "she had behaved herself very discreetly and soberly and kept [her]self reserved from company of any other man except . . . Christopher." Elizabeth Scott added that she often saw Christopher call on Eunice, and that Eunice lived "a sober, retired life."

Eunice and her friends need not have worried. Christopher Almy never denied his paternity. He admitted that he was the father of Eunice's child to both of Eunice's sisters, and to celebrate the birth or as a token of affection "he gave the infant a pair of gold Buttons." Christopher indicated that he intended to marry Eunice "but his father hindered him." The records do not reveal the reasons for Captain Job Almy's alleged resistance, but the fact that the Greenmans lacked the same class status as the Almys (Eunice earned her living as a spinster) might have been reason enough. Nevertheless, Christopher declared himself ready to marry Eunice, "notwithstanding his father being against itt."

It was all talk. Moreover, by the fall of 1721 Eunice was suffering from such depression that her mother feared "Unis would make away with herself." Called to the Greenman home, Susanah Bayley recalled that "in the chamber of [the] house she saw . . . Unis sit upon the bed crying" and heard her mother ask where her penknife was, whereupon Eunice "pulled it out and gave it to her mother."

Whether the participants in this drama of seduction, betrayal, and abandonment exaggerated the story for the court's benefit or not, the judges were sympathetic to Eunice's plight. They awarded her two hundred pounds in damages, which was fifty pounds less than she had requested but sent a clear message to Almy nonetheless. Christopher's sympathy and love for Eunice was not commensurate with this sum, however, and he appealed to the General Assembly for reversal on the grounds that he had never promised marriage in writing. He lost. A decade later, Eunice, now a schoolteacher, was still without a husband.

— ≠ —

Gordon Wood maintains that the extraordinary changes wrought by the radicalism of the American Revolution affected women as well as men. "With the Revolution," he argues briefly, "men lost some of their earlier patriarchal control over their wives and property." Relying on one secondary source, Wood tries to reconcile the irreconcilable: "Although wives continued to remain dependent on their husbands, they did gain greater autonomy." I have argued elsewhere that any efforts to improve the status of women in the postwar years were overwhelmed by the legacy of historical forces that created and nurtured female dependence.[3] The preceding chapters on religion, the economy, and law elaborate on this earlier theme and reinforce the conclusion that because of the ways in which American society evolved during the colonial period, the Revolution could not have been a liberating experience for American women.

Such a betrayal of revolutionary potential was not triggered only by social forces, however. Deeply instilled ideas about the family and the state, the nature of womanhood, and the roles that men and women should play in life's theater continually influenced decisions made in houses of worship, market halls, and courts of law. Moreover, the American collective memory was of mixed parentage, and as the colonies came of age, Americans showed an ever greater respect for their European ancestry—especially for an intellectual tradition that discouraged equality between women and men. This chapter superimposes several centuries of hotly contested European ideology on the two centuries of American religious, economic, and legal experience discussed above. The widespread acceptance of Old World attitudes suggests that such an intellectual tradition, no less than indigenous social factors, would have deflated any revolutionary trial balloon that attempted to float feminist principles.

Furthermore, the language of revolution was gendered in such a way as to preserve the status quo. Dependence debilitated men but refined women; independence strengthened men but corrupted women. These ideological contradictions required some interpretive adroitness, but such was the creativity of the American intellect in that turbulent epoch that eventually the discordant elements were orchestrated into a gendered body of thought that harmonized with revolutionary rhetoric. That integrated set of beliefs, filtered through a European heritage that exalted various feminine attributes, was eventually reduced to what we call Republican Motherhood.

Republican Motherhood has received a generally favorable press. Despite Linda Kerber's cautious analysis and occasionally negative assessment of this phenomenon, most scholars have responded positively to the concept on the assumption that it was a creative attempt by the Revolutionary generation to fashion a political role for white middle- and upper-class women.[4] Given its job description, many historians have also accepted Republican Motherhood as an avenue of advancement for women, at least to the extent that Americans of the early republic advocated female education, which in turn led to greater literacy among women, proliferation of female academies, and finally a subversion of the highly touted political motive behind female learning (to produce the virtuous sons of a republican citizenry).[5]

More importantly, the majority of historians have maintained that Republican Motherhood flourished in the context of a relatively new relationship: the companionate marriage, a union based on friendship and equality rather than on patriarchy and hierarchy. According to Jan Lewis, "Revolutionary-era writers held up the loving partnership of man and wife in opposition to patriarchal dominion as the republican model for social and political relationships." Indeed, scholars such as Melvin Yazawa have eagerly celebrated the demise of patriarchy as a triumph of the Revolutionary era: "the erosion of patriarchal authority in the eighteenth-century family dovetailed nicely with the dissolution of the imperial family."[6]

Although a number of historians have some ambivalence about the influence of Republican Motherhood, only a few have directly challenged the suppositions upon which it rests as an American innovation, an educational springboard, and an egalitarian alternative to the patriarchal model.[7] A closer and more sustained look at the evidence, however, suggests that the genesis of Republican Motherhood was European rather than American, that the ideology predated the American Revolution by at least 150 years, and that its main tenets were vigorously advocated whenever European women attempted to transgress their culturally imposed boundaries. Furthermore, the extent to which women could or should be educated and the justification for that education had been an inherent part of the *querelle des femmes,* or "woman question," for several centuries. The American Revolution stimulated another debate on this subject but added nothing substantive to the arguments on either side.

Companionate marriage was indeed a theoretical coordinate of Republican Motherhood. Yet friendship between husband and wife was no more innovative than the supposedly new role for mothers; by the eighteenth century it had been incorporated into prescriptive literature for at least three hundred years. Moreover, historians who have argued that the companionate marriage was based on a more egalitarian relationship between husband and wife have made an anachronistic leap of faith. In the seventeenth and eighteenth centuries, friendship between husband and wife did not presume equality. The most prevalent and popular literature recognized a hierarchal relationship among married couples, and even the most radical European feminists accepted the necessity of a submissive, yielding wife.

There is scant evidence that Americans, either male or female, challenged these basic assumptions even as the Revolution stimulated leveling tendencies among men. Given the political, economic, ideological, legal, and religious constraints that for two centuries had combined to make women increasingly dependent and invisible, it was hardly likely that Americans would quickly reverse gear. Instead, the challenge of the Revolutionary years may be more accurately understood as an effort to devise a political theory that effectively dismantled the paternalistic, patriarchal, hierarchal, and dependent relationship between Great Britain and the colonies without disturbing the paternalistic, patriarchal, hierarchal, and dependent relationship between husband and wife. Republican Motherhood, an old ideology resurrected for the occasion, was eminently successful in meeting that challenge.

THE FAMILY AND THE STATE

The process of constructing such a seemingly paradoxical theory was made easier for Americans by their British brethren, who had wrestled with the same problem well over a century earlier in the context of monarchal absolutism. An analogy between the family and the state had formed the basis of their heated discussion, and although the parallel had long historical roots, it was left to Civil War absolutists to fully explore the relationship between the two patriarchal institutions. Thus, in order to justify the doctrine of unlimited submission to the monarch, mid-seventeenth-century royalists likened the role of the king to the role of the husband and father. Just as the marriage contract was hierarchal and unalterable they argued, so was the contract between subject and sovereign. Just as the wife, by entering into the marriage contract had agreed to unlimited submission to her husband, so did subjects agree to submit to the crown. In both cases, consent once given could not be retracted: women could not divorce their husbands; subjects could not divorce their king.[8] The supporters of Charles I maintained that neither contract contained the right of resistance, much less the right of rebellion.

In their haste to refute such arguments, Parliamentarians—without adequate consideration of the implications—agreed that marriage and the state were appropriate comparisons, but that there were limitations to the authority of the monarch, just as there were to the father and husband. Extending the argument to its logical conclusion (logical for Parliamentarians, that is), the more radical writers asserted that if a husband transcended certain boundaries, his wife had the right not only to oppose him but, in extreme cases, to separate from him. In a dangerous expansion of this thesis, John

Milton's treatise on divorce argued unequivocally for separation of husband and wife on the most modest of grounds.[9]

The notion of male superiority and marital hierarchy was so ingrained that it may not have occurred to most of these spokesmen that they had unwittingly paved the way for a challenge to their authority within the family unit. Robert Filmer, however, a staunch supporter of a royal absolutism that originated from a divinely sanctioned family order, immediately recognized the potential for familial disaster in his opponents' line of reasoning and lost no time in pointing out the obvious: in an egalitarian state of nature, servants, children, and women ("especially virgins") would have status equal to masters, fathers, and husbands. Surely, Filmer posited, that could not have been his adversaries' position.[10]

John Locke joined the literary fracas several decades later when he penned his first treatise on government to support the Glorious Revolution and to refute Filmer's theory of monarchal absolutism. In so doing, however, he came even closer than his predecessors to undermining the basis for marital patriarchy. Locke's mission was to prove that monarchal government did not originate from family government, as Filmer claimed, but rather from consent and contract. By extending his argument to the institution of marriage—and elaborating on it—he laid the groundwork for what would eventually become a feminist challenge.

Because women as well as men were equal in the state of nature, Locke maintained, the marital contract required the consent of both parties, and by the act of marrying, women freely accepted the terms of an agreement that was, in fact, an inegalitarian bargain. But, according to Locke (and more specifically to Samuel von Pufendorf, upon whose writings Locke so freely drew), the terms of that contract were negotiable and alterable—a potential threat to the benefits husbands derived from a preordained patriarchal pact. Yet even in the absence of negotiation, husbands did not have absolute sovereignty or natural authority over wives any more than monarchs had absolute sovereignty or natural authority over subjects. Certainly God had never given Adam such a grant of government in either the civil or familial context. Husband and wife shared power.[11]

Locke modified the potential ramifications of his argument in his second treatise, but continued to muddy the waters by adding to the arguments in favor of the right to divorce. Once the ends of marriage were secured (procreation, education, inheritance), the marriage might even be dissolved, he hinted—a position from which even Pufendorf would have distanced himself.[12]

Despite their validation of consent and contract in both family and state, Pufendorf and Locke were required by the patriarchal tradition to repudiate the implications of their theory so far as it gave wives an advantage over subjects. Thus with a blatant disregard for consistency they both concluded that husbands, after all, were more equal than wives. Notwithstanding the "charms of love" and "ties of friendship" that bound husband and wife, "this Contract (the Husband having the better Part in the Terms and Conditions, and the additional Advantage of his Sex) seems to be form'd in the manner of those Leagues and Covenants which we call Unequal; so that the wife is bound to Obedience, and the Husband rather to Protection." In sum, the contract was not quite negotiable after all.[13]

According to Pufendorf, God ordained and Parliament ratified this arrangement, assertions that legitimized divine sovereignty in family government just after Pufendorf had taken great pains to repudiate it in civil government. Moreover, Locke realized (albeit somewhat belatedly) that husbands and wives might not always agree "and therefore being necessary, that the last Determination, i.e. the Rule, should be placed somewhere, it naturally falls to the Man's Share, as the abler and stronger."[14] Exactly why this was so was left unsaid.

By the time Locke published the two treatises, the question of whether women had souls was long settled; even the controversy over the rationality of female intellect was about to be resolved favorably to women. Therefore, the only justification left to fall back upon was God and biological determinism, and both Pufendorf and Locke did so with the expectation, no doubt, that they had rescued patriarchal marriage from its precarious position within the contractual theory of government.

Despite Locke's potentially useful pointers, only a few seventeenth-century feminists had anything to say about the marriage contract. It is unlikely they missed the implications of Locke's theory, yet only a handful on either side of the English Channel made any attempt to confront him or to question his inconsistencies. The English feminist Mary Astell did so with great fervor but little effectiveness: "If absolute Sovereignty be not necessary in a State, how comes it to be so in a Family? Or if in a Family why not in a State. . . . If the Authority of the Husband, so far as it extends is sacred and inalienable, why not that of the Prince?" In short, why were men "abler and stronger"? The question was also raised on the British stage: "The argument's good between king and people, why not between husband and wife?"[15] Why not, indeed?

Female submissiveness was so ingrained, however, that even Astell stopped short of linking the right of resistance in civil society to the right of resistance in conjugal society. She did not support Milton's position on divorce, and despite the acuity of her questions, she was unable to come to grips with the obvious answers. Instead, she propounded prescribed doctrines and reminded women not to exert their own will in anything once they "made Choice of a Lord and Master." It was a French author, writing at the same time, who was willing to confront the issue directly, and in so doing carry Locke's contract theory much further along the road than Locke, or even Astell, would have been willing to travel. "When a husband turns extravagant, unjust, or inhumane," maintained the Seigneur de Saint-Evremond, "he turns tyrant, he breaks society, which he contracted for with his wife. The right of separation is already made; the judges make it not, they only publish its validity by a solemn declaration."[16]

If the American Revolution had really been a watershed for women, as some historians claim, early republicans would have seized the moment to debate the relationship between the family and the state—and women's place in both—as an offshoot of the contract theory they espoused with such enthusiasm. Since the arguments on both sides had been formed a century earlier, Americans of the Revolutionary generation did not even need to construct new theory. Instead, they ignored those passages from classical writers, commonwealth's-men, and Whigs that linked gender to contract. Such selectivity raises questions about the motive and intent of the Revolutionary generation. Indeed, given the long-standing European precedents, the absence of any feminist dialogue is rather striking.

SEVENTEENTH-CENTURY REPUBLICAN MOTHERHOOD

John Locke and his coterie of contractual theorists need not have worried about the threat to patriarchal authority within the family. By 1700 women were being buffeted on all sides with prescriptive literature that reinforced female submissiveness, obedience, and virtue at the same time that it exalted the institution of marriage and motherhood. This literary assault had been under way for several decades, ever since the English Civil War had stimulated women to consider their own status in light of the great issues of the day: power, allegiance, liberty, and slavery. During that heady period, Englishwomen seized upon opportunities to enlarge their spheres of activity by routinely petitioning Parliament. They also rioted against enclosures and demonstrated for political ends. They litigated, wrote pamphlets, preached, and prophesied. They showed increasing interest in sexual freedom. After Charles II was restored to the throne, women were forced back into their prescribed roles by a renewed advocacy of traditional patriarchal values. As Bridget Hill notes, the English Civil War was a threat to husbands as well as kings.[17]

It was women's growing affiliation with left-wing Civil War religious sects that most disturbed the traditionalists. Brownists, Independents, Baptists, Millenarians, Ranters, and most particularly the Levellers had a great influence on women who were attracted to the idea of spiritual equality and individual conscience. Women listened carefully to the Levellers, who elaborated upon an argument whereby men and women, born free and equal, could be governed only by their own consent. These powerful doctrines resonated within the family, where critics insisted that such radical notions undermined unity and male rule, a fear that was exacerbated by continental feminists, whose works deploring domestic tyranny began to appear in English translation.[18]

The Restoration temporarily stifled these echoing challenges to male supremacy, a by-product of which was a deliberate attempt to reestablish the family model along traditional lines. Radical views were suppressed, and women were exhorted to concentrate on their roles as wives and mothers. And although Englishwomen became more accomplished as their education improved, according to one eighteenth-century writer, they were both debased and poorly respected after their short period of empowerment.[19]

Furthermore, the increased emphasis on breast-feeding toward the end of the seventeenth century not only sentimentalized motherhood but also served to exclude women from competing activities, and late-century playwrights implied that husbands could maintain control over their wives by urging them to nurse their infants.[20] Public women were a disorderly threat; homebound women could not develop group consciousness.

Enforced domesticity served another purpose in late seventeenth- and early eighteenth-century England. These transitional years set the stage for England's emergence from a precapitalist society into one marked by industrial revolution. In the privacy of the domestic sphere women acted as consumers, thus serving the economic as well as the political needs of the state. Consequently, when the winds of war finally abated at the end of the eighteenth century and Americans sought new economic opportunities, they were already keenly aware that women, in their role as homemakers, would be uniquely positioned to feed the economy as well as their families.[21]

The latter half of the seventeenth century saw parallel developments in France. Women overstepped their boundaries and championed political factions in the civil and religious unrest known as the Fronde, only to retreat as the reign of the Sun King dampened their enthusiasm. Even worse, the French *précieuses*, wielding power in salons and at court, had taken on public roles. Many were feminists who equated marriage with slavery and insisted that their domination by men was contrary to natural rights and natural law. The *précieuses* thought that female virtues (tenderness, politeness, sentimentality), combined with public influence, could help to restructure society. Their antagonists agreed but were threatened by both method and potential result. The argument formulated by the antifeminists was a desperate attempt to return women to the home. As in England, they extolled marriage and the place of virtuous women in it. Women's role was to be exclusively domestic, limited to household management and the education of children. A properly submissive wife and mother would be rewarded by a loving relationship with her husband. In her study of the French *précieuses*, Carolyn Lougee maintains that women's very salvation was linked to marriage and a properly attentive motherhood.[22] Women could reform society, but only through the virtuous education of children.

François de Salignac de La Mothe-Fénelon (1651–1715) was France's most articulate spokesperson for this point of view. Women's duties kept them "quietly occupied in their homes," wrote Fénelon. By "every detail of domestic life" they "decide what touches the human race most nearly. . . . They affect most closely the good or bad habits of practically all mankind." In short, "the world . . . is the sum total of families; and who can civilize it more effectively than women. . . . Such then are the duties of women, and they are scarcely less important to the public than those of men, since women have a household to rule, a husband to make happy, and children to bring up well."[23] By 1687 Fénelon had already refined the concept of Republican Motherhood—a century before Americans had need of such a doctrine.

During the eighteenth century the exaggerated regard for domesticity increased in the context of a general agreement that the best interest of a nation was served by women in their roles as wives and mothers. Writers in

France as well as England took up their quills on this subject, emphasizing as they did so, the public nature of marriage and motherhood. And if Fénelon's succinct writing set the tone, Rousseau's flowery elaboration augmented the argument nearly six decades later: "The destiny of your sex will always be to govern ours. Happy are we so long as your chaste power, exerted solely within the marriage bond, makes itself felt only for the glory of the state and the well-being of the public. . . . It is for you, by your kindly and innocent dominion and by your subtle influence, to perpetuate love of the laws within the state and concord among citizens."[24]

The sanctity of domesticity was brought home nowhere more clearly than in the *Moral Tales* of Jean-François Marmontel (1723–99). In one of his more popular stories, "The Good Husband," a newly remarried widow, Hortensia, felt restrained by her husband's attempt to suppress her "love of liberty," and prevent her from seeing her friends. She rebels, and he is reduced to tears by the thought that she preferred "a frivolous world" to the company of her husband. Filled with remorse, Hortensia repents: "I had forgot that I was a mother; I was going to forget that I was a wife. You recal [*sic*] me to those duties; and those two bands united bind me for all my life."[25] The moral of the story: liberty and willfulness were the attributes of a bad wife. The rest of Marmontel's tales harp on the same theme. Combined with other French and English sources, the entire package provided a literary synthesis for the American version of Republican Motherhood.

THE EDUCATION OF WOMEN

The post-Revolutionary years saw Americans emphasize the importance of education to the citizens of the new republic. Their discussion of female education, however, was unrevolutionary and must be understood in the context of a long-standing debate on the nature of women, the so-called *querelle des femmes*. Authors as far back as Plato and Plutarch had contemplated a broad range of issues relating to gender, but this particular phrase, and the paper war it sparked, took on added meaning during and after the Renaissance. With regard to education, the debate revolved around three essential questions: Were women capable of being educated? Why should women be educated? What should be the components of a female education?

By the late seventeenth century the first question was no longer a subject of heated controversy, given the development of a consensus that women possessed the capability for intellectual improvement. But why bother? The answer to this question was fully compatible with the values of the patriarchal, hierarchal society in which the question arose in the first place. Women should be educated to make them more agreeable and pleasing to men, especially in their roles as wives and mothers. Education made women better companions and helpmeets, and better equipped to educate their children. They would become more virtuous by reading the Bible and other religious tracts. In turn, by providing a "vertuous Education" for their daughters and by exhibiting such learning as to "stir up" their sons, women would be "beneficial to the Nation."[26]

Acceptance of this line of reasoning translated into broader educational opportunities in both England and France by the end of the seventeenth century, a trend that accelerated throughout the eighteenth century, particularly in France. Female illiteracy declined, and educational accomplishments became positive attributes. Women were less likely to be ridiculed for their achievements, although some writers still disparaged female wits. The content of female education at that time requires deeper analysis, however, because widespread acceptance of a curriculum appropriate to women would have a profound impact on the way Americans approached the same issue at the end of the eighteenth century, when literacy itself was less of a problem than the nature of education.

Seventeenth-century proponents of education for women understood that patriarchal values required a patriarchal education. To disregard such a curriculum could only result in a fulfillment of Erasmus's prediction that educated women would resist their subjection. More than 150 years after Erasmus, the English feminist Mary Astell slyly agreed. In the absence of a proper course of study, she noted amiably, women might make "unworthy and mischievous choices," choices that might even propel them toward rebellion.[27] A selective education was the safest way to reinforce and perpetuate social values.

It is unlikely that anyone systematically thought all this through, and far more likely that, in proposing the content of female education, people acted on assumptions about women's place in society that stemmed from a common world outlook. Both women and men were acculturated to share such perceptions, and even women who held educational deprivation partly responsible for their subservient status accepted as a truth their own intellectual inferiority and limited potential. One might argue that these women paid lip service to their allotted roles in the hope of placating those who were all too suspicious of the implications of female education. Yet the cacophony of voices in support of a God-ordained male superiority lends credence to the argument that many women had internalized ideas about their inherent mental weakness.

It is disappointing that Locke, who maintained that girls should be educated as readily as boys, said almost nothing about the components of female education in his long treatise on that subject. But the French theologian Fénelon most assuredly did, and he was widely read, admired, and quoted in France, England, and eventually America. Fénelon based his plan of learning on the assumption that "women's intellect" was "feeble." Since "women should not govern the state or make war or enter the sacred ministry . . . they can dispense with some of the more difficult branches of knowledge which deal with politics, the military art, jurisprudence, philosophy, and theology. Even the majority of the mechanical arts are not suitable for them." Fénelon disapproved of novels, plays, or adventure stories with a "romantic love interest." There was no need for girls to study the classics or modern languages. It was important for them to be able to read and write in their own language, and arithmetic would be of value to them as housewives. Above all, they should exercise reason and judgment.[28]

With minor variations, Fénelon's guidelines became the mainstay of female education in the eighteenth century for middle- and upper-class families in both England and France. To be sure, radical thinkers were critical of such a limited education. A decade earlier, François Poulain de La Barre sought to incorporate math, science, history, and philosophy into a female curriculum, but his ideas did not gain general acceptance. He argued, however, that women were capable of logic, rhetoric, law, and politics. The Encyclopedists were also supportive of a more enriched course of study for women, going so far as to advocate the same education for both sexes. During the late eighteenth century some French women were even exposed to math, physics, and algebra, but these were exceptions.[29]

Influential, mainstream authors such as Jean-Jacques Rousseau (1712–78) propounded an education that corresponded with women's place in society. Although he recognized the importance of education for women, Rousseau mocked "learned" ladies and took the position that "a female wit is a scourge to her husband"—a notion that John Adams would later admit he shared. Rousseau's ideal partner for Emile, Sophie, was not an avid reader, although her education had not been neglected. "Her mind knows little, but is trained to learn." Her husband was best suited to be her teacher. *Emile* was enormously popular in America from 1763 onward.[30]

Other French authors influenced educational philosophy as their works traveled to England and then crossed the Atlantic. Pierre-Joseph Boudier de Villemert designed a female education appropriate to a society where "all that regards the inside of the house is the business of the wife, as the business without is that of the husband." According to Boudier de Villemert, women should be educated to enhance their conversation, but "they ought to avoid abstruse sciences and thorny researches, the particulars of which oppress their minds." History, the Bible, and physics (a succession of observations and experiments) were permissible, theology and romances were not. The latter "hurt the mind."[31]

Rousseau notwithstanding, the English tradition of female education was even more conservative than the French to the extent that even feminists rarely called for equal education. English Protestant reformers, who emphasized the Bible rather than the classics, were also more willing, as time went on, to exclude the Greek and Latin languages and classical authors than were Catholic humanists such as Juan Luis Vives (active 1540–1600).[32] Male schooling might include Latin and Greek texts if the goal was to improve rhetorical skills that would be advantageous in the business or political world. Because women were not expected to seek public life, such subjects could be eliminated from their program altogether.

When English authors espoused the inclusion of moral philosophers (Plato, Cicero, Seneca, Plutarch, and Aristotle) in a female curriculum, it was usually in whatever English-language editions were available. As one Englishwoman explained to Samuel Richardson: "I hate to hear Latin out of a woman's mouth. There is something in it, to me masculine." Texts translated from Latin into the vernacular for the use of women could also be edited to serve contemporary needs. Contraceptive information was routinely deleted from every medieval Latin gynecological text translated into English.[33]

An extremely progressive English education for women at the end of the seventeenth century might have included half-time studies of singing, writing, and accounting, with half-time studies in Latin, French, Greek, or Hebrew, as well as natural history ("the Names, Natures, Values Use of Herbs, Shrubs, Trees, Mineral-Juices, Metals and stones"). An even more advanced program would add astronomy, geography, arithmetic, and history.[34] This, however, was an exceptional program. More representative of English thinking at the turn of the eighteenth century was Daniel Defoe, who strongly supported education for women in the belief that women had "souls capable of the same accomplishments with men." Nevertheless, his proposed program included only history, music, dancing, languages, and grammar, since he concurrently assumed that female education should be designed toward making women fit companions for men.[35]

Of all the English prescriptive literature on female education, the works of James Fordyce appear to have been among the most widely read by the American Revolutionary generation. Fordyce's *Sermons to Young Women,* an instant success when it was published in London in 1766, could claim five American printings between 1767 and 1796 (in addition to at least eleven British editions). The sermons even had the imprimatur of Abigail Adams: "I cannot say how much I admire them," she wrote to her sister, Mary Smith Cranch.[36]

Coming from a woman who criticized male tyranny and female subjugation, and who strongly encouraged female education, Adams's admiration of Fordyce is rather surprising. He preached meekness, submission, reticence, domesticity, and obedience. He assured his readers that "women's minds are less vigorous than men's," and that "war, commerce, politics . . . abstract philosophy, and all the abstruser sciences, are most properly the province of men." His recommendations for female education included history (along with biography and memoirs), travel literature, geography, astronomy, fables, visions, allegories, dramatic writings, poetry, certain novels, and natural and moral philosophy. He strongly disapproved of a learned woman who exhibited her knowledge or disputed with men.[37] One would like to think that Abigail was being facetious and that she could not say "how much" she admired Fordyce's *Sermons* because such admiration was, in fact, totally absent. A double entendre of this nature would have been consistent with eighteenth-century literature and within Adams's competence, but such an interpretation must remain, alas, within the realm of speculation.

Having been inundated for decades (indeed, centuries) by an endless barrage of advice literature on education, the contents of which reflected the standards of a patriarchal society, it is not surprising that Revolutionary era proponents of female education were unable to envision alternatives. Even Judith Sargent Murray, who recognized that a more complete education set men "far above" equally competent women, did not call for revolutionary reform but for an education that included astronomy, where women "might catch a glimpse of the immensity of the Deity," geography, wherein "she would admire Jehova in the midst of his benevolence," and natural philosophy, where "she could adore the infinite majesty of heaven ... and as she traversed the reptile world, she would hail the goodness of a creating God." Murray linked female education with marital happiness and domestic tranquillity. Indeed, she emphasized the virtues of motherhood and the happiness women could expect from it.[38]

In the *Gleaner Papers* Murray's call for independent women who could, if necessary, circumvent the marriage market or survive the economic burdens of widowhood showed limited vision as well. The specific "accomplishments" she would have offered a daughter appear to encompass music, drawing, arithmetic, writing, astronomy, geography, French, and needle skills—none of which would have ensured financial viability, much less well-being. She specifically rejected female entry into politics, commerce, the military, or professions, and thus her narrow expectations produced a narrow educational philosophy. Murray's proposal for self-reliant women did not include the means to make them so.

In truth, Murray had not advanced from the position taken by Bathsua Makin over a hundred years earlier, when Makin pointed out that skilled tradeswomen, "if they happen to be widows, will be able to understand and manage their own Affairs." And Murray's condemnation of a society that unhesitatingly propelled women toward marriage merely paraphrased the English writer John Hill, who wrote under the pseudonym of Juliana Seymour several decades earlier. To recognize the problem was hardly revolutionary; to suggest the means to overcome it would have been. Nevertheless, Murray's public conservatism may be more revealing of the possible limits of reform in the 1790s than of her personal convictions. Murray's private correspondence advocated Latin study for women; the absence of any such proposal in her published works suggests a fear of jeopardizing publication altogether if she openly espoused such a radical scheme.[39]

Benjamin Rush, sometimes thought of as an equal opportunity educator, was no less a product of his time than Murray. Linda Kerber puts his curriculum in proper perspective, although she does not emphasize the assumptions that spawned such a course of study or its debt to John Fordyce, whose sentiments were more reactionary than revolutionary.[40] To Rush, as to others before him, a "peculiar and suitable education" made a woman "an agreeable companion for a sensible man." As mothers, women needed to be qualified to instruct their sons "in the principles of liberty and government." Essential knowledge included the English language, spelling, grammar, and penmanship.

Rush advocated some understanding of figures and bookkeeping so a wife might assist her husband, just as Makin promoted education as a tool to make women "useful to their Husbands in their Trades." Geography, chronology, history, biography, and travels were part of a proper female education, and "in some instances" so were the first principles of astronomy, natural philosophy and chemistry, "particularly . . . as are calculated to prevent superstition . . . and such as are capable of being applied to domestic, and culinary purposes." Religious matter, poetry, and moral essays were suitable reading material; novels were not. Truly, Rush's "thoughts upon female education" were "accomodated [*sic*] to the present state of society, manners, and government in the United States of America."[41]

Rush's program for young men emphasized a different course of study. Although he did not ignore religion or history, Rush stressed political instruction (republican principles), languages, eloquence, the origin and present state of commerce, as well as the nature and principles of money. Rush advocated chemistry for males in order to further agricultural and manufacturing improvements. In addition, males were to be educated in the general principles of legislation by attending the courts of justice.[42] Clearly, the instruction of men and women was intended to reinforce the values of a society in which public and domestic spheres were becoming increasingly polarized and gendered.

If Americans selected strands of thought from the great seventeenth- and eighteenth-century theorists to weave a political doctrine suited to revolutionary needs, they were no less discriminating when they sought to devise an educational strategy appropriate to the new republic. The former was radical, the latter conservative. Had they wanted to apply revolutionary principles to education for women, they need not even have concerned themselves with a theory of education. Had they wished to move forward, they could have culled from the writings of earlier thinkers such as Poulain de La Barre and d'Alembert, or more contemporary ones such as Catherine Macaulay and Mary Wollstonecraft, who called for equal education for women and men. Charles Brockden Brown's paradise may have included equal education for women, but his placement of that equality in a fantasy world only underscores his reluctance to demand redress of the problem in the real world.[43] A truly egalitarian rhetoric in the American Revolutionary era would have included such a demand.

This is not to argue that such demands would have been addressed, but rather to emphasize the absence of any radical dialogue when, if Gordon Wood is correct, radicalism was a pervasive part of American consciousness. The Englishwoman Wollstonecraft, not the American woman Murray, understood the path to female independence and self-reliance when she proposed that women be permitted to study medicine, business, and politics. Science, math, and debate were the keys to advancement, not languages, geography, and sewing. But even if Wollstonecraft's tracts were available in 30 percent of American libraries, her influence was marginal in America, as was Catherine Macaulay's, even though the latter was highly regarded by both John and Abigail Adams.[44]

An education to make women self-reliant and independent was not on the American agenda because it was antithetical to the needs and "genius" of the new nation. Some writers may have insisted that an independent, single life was preferable to an unhappy marriage, but marriage was still the norm, expectation, and hope on both sides of the Atlantic both before and after the Revolution.[45]

The irreconcilable viewpoints expressed by Abigail Adams demonstrate most clearly the conflicts faced by progressive American women. On the one hand, Adams was a staunch advocate of "learned women." On the other hand, she may actually have favored John Fordyce, who preached meekness, domesticity, and obedience. Americans at the end of the eighteenth century refused to confront the incompatibility of educational equality and submissiveness, and even those who spoke in favor of female advancement were all too willing to accept what had already been acceptable for a century. Women might engage in debate on a theoretical level, but to argue or dispute with men was still unacceptable. Separate and unequal education based on alleged female attributes precluded personal achievement in mathematics or the sciences and eliminated the ability to advance technology in the incipient industrial society. In the decades to follow, some women would earn a living by teaching and writing, but those professions were the only ones open to them. The Revolution may have encouraged the spread of female academies, but they were few nonetheless, and their curriculum ensured conformity to the status quo.

THE COMPANIONATE MARRIAGE

Seventeen hundred years before the American Revolution, Plutarch (46?–120?) advocated a marital arrangement based on affection, companionship, and friendship—with more than a touch of patriarchal authority to cement the union. Although women were to honor and submit to their husbands, "it behooves a husband to control his wife, not as a master does his vassal, but as the soul governs the body, with the gentle hand of mutual friendship and reciprocal affection. For as the soul commands the body, without being subject to its pleasures and inordinate desires, in like manner a man should so exercise his authority over his wife, as to soften it with complaisance, and kind requital for her affectionate submission." Plutarch's message, with minor variations, would be repeated for nearly two millennia.[46]

Before the end of the century in which the printing press opened the written word to a wider audience, authors were paying tribute to marriage. In 1472 the Bamberg humanist Albrecht Von Eyb sketched a family portrait that looked not only back to Plutarch but also forward to the more romantic vision of eighteenth-century Europe. "What could be happier and sweeter than the name of father, mother, and children . . . where the children hang on their parents' arms and exchange many sweet kisses with them, and where husband and wife are so drawn to one another by love and choice, and experience such friendship between themselves that what one wants, the other also chooses." Venetians as well as Germans exhibited affection between husbands and wives in fifteenth-century documents, a tribute, as one historian interprets the phenomenon, to a woman's economic importance.[47]

Nearly a half century after Von Eyb, the great Dutch theologian Erasmus (1466?–1536) took up his pen on this subject and wrote a treatise on marriage, in which he maintained that women should be considered the companion of men in both mind and body: "for with our other friends we be conjoined only with the benevolence of minds. With our wife we be coupled with most high love." A wife was her husband's best friend, "a sweet companion of youth, a kind solace of age."[48]

Although the idea of a companionate marriage long preceded the Reformation, that religious upheaval may have resulted in even greater emphasis on compatibility, friendship, and love within the marital union, as Protestant theologians attempted to glorify marriage at the expense of celibacy. By the end of the sixteenth century English Puritans had expressed these ideas forcefully and with grace: "the husband is not to command his wife in manner, as the Master his servant, but as the soul doth the body, as being conjoined in like affection and good will; just as the soul in governing the body tendeth to the benefit and commodity of the same, so ought the dominion and commandment of the husband over the wife ... tend to rejoice and content her."[49] Robert Cleaver, the author of this tract, had read Plutarch with care. For the next two hundred years and more, the idea of a loving, patriarchal marriage would be described in various ways, but no one would evoke sharper images than Cleaver.

From the middle of the seventeenth century onward, the most prominent and not-so-prominent European authors contributed sentences, paragraphs, and treatises to the body of prescriptive literature on marriage and the family. Each paid homage to the affection between husband and wife. Pufendorf saw the union as one assisted by "the Engagements of Friendship and the Charms of Love." George Savile, marquis of Halifax, spoke of a husband's "kindness" and "tenderness." Madame de Maintenon (1635–1719) advised the duchess of Burgundy to let the duke of Burgundy be her "best Friend" and "only confident."[50]

Although it is difficult to gauge the relationship of rhetoric to reality, many historians agree that during the seventeenth century Englishwomen in particular had come to expect affection in marriage.[51] The turn of the eighteenth century, therefore, represented no new pattern of thinking on the ideal relationship between husband and wife. What seems to have happened is that an increasing number of authors turned their attention to this topic, whether in the form of satire, advice literature, correspondence, or a new literary genre, the novel.

The English novel gained prominence in the 1740s thanks to the craftmanship of Samuel Richardson (1689–1761), whose heroines Pamela and Clarissa became household icons on both sides of the Atlantic. Henry Fielding (1707–54) and Laurence Sterne (1713–68) competed with Richardson for a portion of the novel-reading public, and the trio shared an unrivaled popularity in America during the years preceding the Revolution. Yet despite the eminence of those authors, it is nonetheless true that women wrote the majority of English novels published between 1692 and 1800. Readership paralleled authorship, and by midcentury in England, sentimental fiction was produced with a predominantly middle-class female audience in mind. After the Revolution, when Americans entered the novel-writing business, such fiction appeared to be directed toward a youthful and particularly female audience as well.[52]

Novels advocated, validated, and extolled the marital state. They encouraged mutuality of affection and romanticized the tender relationship between husband and wife. They warned of uncontrolled sexuality outside marriage and the unbridled lust of seducing suitors. In short, they set standards and reinforced guidelines for appropriate middle-class heterosexual behavior. Through the novels women also learned that selection of a suitable mate was empowering and that careful consideration of a spouse's attributes in advance could maximize the potential for happiness. Furthermore, *Pamela* was more than a novel of character, seduction, and virtue; it was a novel of upward mobility. Pamela was a servant, as were many of her devoted English and American admirers, and it could hardly have escaped their notice that their heroine married her boss, even if that marriage lacked the happiness to which Pamela—and most women—aspired.

Despite their alleged subversiveness, however, despite the coded yet implicit warnings against subjecting oneself to a tyrannical master-for-life, despite their lesson plan for a happy life, fictional works remained just that— fantasy—an escape from an all too real world where few viable alternatives awaited even the most discerning maiden. Novels extolling marriage may even have been a source of frustration to young, female urban readers who were undoubtedly aware of the all too real demographics of Boston, Salem, Newport, and Portsmouth.

One might interpret the emphasis on affectionate relationships as a reflection of a society that accepted tenderness as a norm and as an indication of respect for women, whose expectations of a happy marriage would be enhanced in such circumstances. But if the exaggerated importance of the family coincided with the attempt to suppress vociferous and assertive women in the English post–Civil War decades, if the stress on love within marriage corresponded with the anti-*précieuses* movement in France, if the accolades bestowed upon reproductive women coexisted with a disparagement of productive women, then perhaps the rhetoric represented a posturing that did not redound to the benefit of women after all. Perhaps the excessively loud prescriptive message in the eighteenth century was less a source of romantic inspiration and more an early version of subliminal advertising—in this case to restrict female activity in order to meet specific social, economic, or political needs. As Anthony Fletcher concludes in his recent study, "romantic love proved to be patriarchy's strongest bulwark."[53]

It is not so much that eighteenth-century authors from Chapone to Defoe, Eugenia to Franklin, Gregory to Hume, Montesquieu to Pompadour,

Pope to Richardson, and Rousseau to Swift elevated marital affection to a new plateau, but rather that the companionate unions they exalted (and which were created by female "choice" and "consent") were also unambivalently based on a hierarchal relationship in which male authority could not be challenged. Female submission was the key to conjugal happiness, and publishers disseminated this message through multiple printings of popular works in England and America.

Left unspoken, but implied nonetheless, was the understanding that affection was a reward. Only a virtuous wife, one who proved herself submissive, obedient, selfless, and pious, deserved a husband's love. As numerous studies have shown, women internalized this message, and as literacy spread (in part because of the novel), so did transmission of this idea and its negative effect on the female psyche. Dana Jack maintains that romantic love obscured the problem of inequality while prescribed relations between husband and wife left a husband in control of his wife's self-esteem. Her role was to please him, and this imperative acted to reinforce gender inequality. Her self-worth depended on his approval.[54]

LINGUISTIC GYMNASTICS

Yet although the essence of the message remained the same over the centuries, the meaning of certain words within that message changed over time, a result, perhaps, of changing human relationships. Friendship, originally presumed to be a relationship among equals, needed redefinition to accommodate new class divisions and gender roles. If, for example, wives were friends to their husbands, did this imply equality as well? Under the rules and expectations of a patriarchal society this was unacceptable, and friendship, therefore, became compatible with hierarchy. To confuse the matter, however, marital hierarchy acquired an eighteenth-century definition that reconciled it with equality.

Despite the accomplishments of his feminist disciple Marie de Gournay, the essayist Montaigne (1533–92) maintained that women (including wives) could not be true friends. Decades later, Francis Bacon (1561–1626) agreed, and in an early seventeenth-century essay he alluded to a problem that later writers would stumble over in their haste to reconcile what was essentially unreconcilable. True friendship, he pointed out, presupposed equality, and thus certain relationships precluded friendship: "A man cannot speak . . . to his wife but as a husband." Bacon's argument rested on the assumption that certain hierarchal relationships could not be leveled. In a treatise on the subject some years later, however, Jeremy Taylor (1613–37) argued otherwise, although he did so without elaboration: "marriage is the Queen of Friendship . . . made sacred by vows and love."[55]

At the end of the seventeenth century George Savile, marquis of Halifax, published a pamphlet on the perils of marriage and how to overcome them. Less concerned with friendship than with the denial of equality, Savile emphasized the "inequality" he perceived "in the sexes." Threatened by the anti-authoritarian implications of the Glorious Revolution, Savile hastened to reinforce a God-ordained marital orthodoxy. It was, he said, "for the better Oeconomy of the world" that men, "who were to be the Law-givers, had the larger share of *Reason* bestow'd upon them." Women were "better prepar'd for Compliance." Husbands and wives could be friends, but only within a hierarchal relationship—a somewhat peculiar modification of Bacon.[56]

For the eighteenth century to create a ménage à trois out of husband, wife, and friendship without disturbing the hierarchal nature of the relationship, it was necessary for writers to resort to a literary sleight of hand. Admitting that "friendship amongst equals is the most lasting," Dr. Johnson then proceeded to define equality in terms of education and religion.[57] Similar tastes and habits of life translated into marital equality, as did a parity in economic standing. Thus, by applying a limited and specific definition to equality, husbands and wives could be both friends and equals as well as friends and unequals.

In *The New Whole Duty of Man*, a best-selling piece of English prescriptive literature that had seen twenty-one editions by 1766, the anonymous author acknowledged what everyone already knew: equality had to "yield" in the interest of "unity." Although husbands and wives should be "friends and companions," that same "unity" implied the "necessity of government," which presumed female "subjection" and male "superiority," a condition "necessary to the support of rule and order, and . . . rightly placed in husbands rather than in wives."[58]

By the mid-eighteenth century equality and hierarchy were reconciled to the point where their dichotomy no longer needed an elaborate explanation. Thus, although affection, tenderness, companionship, and happiness were all integral to marriage, so too were female submissiveness and male domination. The most widely reprinted and presumably popular works in the American Revolutionary era accepted these matrimonial conditions and contradictions.

Had John Gregory lived long enough, he would have seen *A Father's Legacy to His Daughters* sail through twenty-two American editions between 1775 and 1799. In that work he admitted that husbands could be tyrants, advocated "a single life" in preference to an unhappy marriage, and maintained that women were meant to be the "companions and equals" of men. But how did this equality work in practice? Not in strength, courage, or understanding, to be sure, and in a companion piece Gregory resorted to what can only be called an early version of the separate but equal doctrine. "Our business is without doors. All the rougher and more laborious parts in the great scene of human affairs fall to our share. . . . The greatest glory of woman lies in private and domestic life, as friends, wives, and mothers." At the same time, Gregory left no doubt about who was in charge of both arenas: "the form of power and authority, to direct the affairs of public societies and private families, remains indeed with us."[59] Some spouses were more equal than others.

John Hill, or Juliana Seymour, as he liked to be known, assured his readers of the great friendship between husband and wife. And although affection and love were the basis of marriage, a good wife retained a sense of her husband's "superiority" because "he has a Right to expect it." And in David Hume's flawless world, all aspects of male-female relations would be carried on "with perfect equality." But alas, nature had "given *man* the superiority above woman, by endowing him with greater strength both of mind and body," and although members of "the male sex, among a polite people," were civil, generous, and respectful to women, they still retained authority over them.[60]

Unlike Hume, Benjamin Franklin refused to blame nature when he added his voice at midcentury to the chorus of writers on marriage. The end of marriage was happiness, he agreed, but "whatever tyrannic and arbitrary power the laws of a country may give a man over his wife, or should they do the reverse, there is no such kind of dominion derived from reason or nature." Having established the absurdity of parties voluntarily binding themselves "to an imperious or tyrannical sway," Franklin pursued his argument further. Only "reason and prudence" dictated the "standard of obedience" within marriage. Yet Franklin was clearly uneasy with the egalitarian implications that might be drawn from his argument, and he hastened to clarify his position. Since men's reasoning power was stronger and their experience greater, it was only reasonable that women should be submissive and deferential to them. "This," Franklin concluded, "certainly is to put the affair on a right footing."[61] Nature, it appears, did have something to do with it, after all.

One of the most important mid-eighteenth-century tracts was Robert Dodsley's *Economy of Human Life,* which was first published in 1750 and maintained an enthusiastic audience well into the beginning of the twentieth century. English, Italian, French, and German editions permeated the marketplace, and by 1769 it had already been translated into Russian. At various times it was bound with similar works such as Gregory's *A Father's Legacy* or Kenrick's *Whole Duty of Women,* which reinforced the message by process of duplication. The essence of Dodsley's message was compatible with that of his countrymen: woman was made to be the "reasonable companion" of man, but "submission and obedience" were "the lessons of her life."[62]

Hester Chapone's "letters" carried the same message and reached a wide audience as well. On the eve of the American Revolution the book was already in its fourth edition, and it reiterated what readers had come to expect. Since "the highest kind of friendship" was found in the conjugal relationship, modest, virtuous, and meek women were advised to seek "the best blessings this world can afford": "a faithful union with a worthy man" who would direct his wife's steps "in safety and honor."[63]

In a sense, the same message that reconciled equality with hierarchy by deftly manipulating the definition of equality and by establishing the guidelines for authority and obedience also sought to reconcile another pair of irreconcilables: submission and empowerment. And the implications of that message were multilayered. Not only were women to be empowered through submissive behavior—thus making it unnecessary (and unreasonable) for them to assert themselves—but such behavior was the key to a successful marriage as well. The Age of Enlightenment constantly spoke to what was reasonable for men and women; thus, should women fail to exhibit behavior appropriate to the desired end of marriage, it was only reasonable that the resulting unhappiness was their fault.

The marquis of Halifax explained it all very well. In his prescriptive treatise, Savile maintained that since women were the weaker sex it was "reasonable" for men to rule over them. But, added Savile, through compliance and obedience "you have it in your power not only to free your selves, but to subdue your Masters; and without violence throw both their Natural and Legal Authority at your feet."[64]

Abigail Adams reminded her husband of this (without attribution) in May 1776, and to be certain he understood the message, she added a couplet from one of her favorite poets: "charm by accepting, by submitting sway / yet have our Humour most when we obey." There is less banter in this letter of Abigail's than there was in the one of 31 March when she asked John to "Remember the Ladies." It was his response to that letter on 14 April that provoked Abigail's further comments, and if nothing else, her words serve as a reminder that she was an intellectual product of her time.[65]

"Men are sooner persuaded by silence, when it shews submission without sullenness, than by angry arguments," insisted the twenty-first edition of *The New Whole Duty of Man* in 1766, although one is left to wonder why acquiescent silence might be taken as dissent.[66] In any case, most literature advised that men would sooner yield to cheerful persuasion than to a combative display of temper. Since husbands could be counted on to succumb to "mildness," it was "always the fault of the woman if the husband does not enter into her views. . . . She is not born to command, but she is in a state to govern him who commands." It was a short step from this position to one where, according to Hester Chapone, the happiness of a woman's husband, children, and servants depended on her temper, and an even shorter one to the assertion that "there is only one Path by which a married woman can arrive at Happiness, and this is by conforming herself to the sentiments of her Husband."[67]

For women, acceptance of these rules of conduct meant internalization of empowerment on specious and contradictory grounds—grounds that may have limited rather than enhanced the expectation of a happy marriage. It was incongruous that female resistance and rebellion continued to be unreasonable and unnecessary at precisely the time when resistance and rebellion against Great Britain were becoming both reasonable and, as it turned out, necessary. Yet this paradox resolves another: its acceptance (or internalization) explains why American women were reluctant to take up their own cause in those tumultuous years. To them, submission was strength—a belief that made oppression less oppressive.[68]

The Revolutionary generation made no attempt to apply egalitarian theories to marriage. Indeed, for at least two centuries they had attempted to reconcile equality with inequality in order to preserve conjugal patriarchy. Since that doctrine was firmly established and supported by public opinion, there was no stimulus for change. A husband's rule was limited, but it existed nonetheless. Americans were reassured by the Baron von Pufendorf that it was not "repugnant to the Law of Nature, for a Wife to be subjected to her Husband. . . . For the Fear of Supreme Authority, and the Endearments of

Conjugal Affection are really no more destructive of each other than the Sovereignty of the Prince extinguisheth the Love of the Subject."[69]

In the end, the Baron Montesquieu (1689–1755) resolved any lingering doubts about the reconciliation of equality and inequality by circumventing natural law and natural rights altogether. Democracy itself would be "corrupted," he insisted, not only in the absence of equality, but when society degenerates "into a spirit of extreme equality, and when every citizen wants to be upon a level with those he has chosen to command him." When the people refuse to let a duly appointed government perform its assigned functions, "virtue can no longer subsist in the republic." Respect ceases not only for "senators" but also, by extension, for "old age." The result is social chaos: "If respect ceases for old age, it will cease also for parents; deference to husbands will be likewise thrown off, and submission to masters. . . . Wives, children, slaves, will shake off all subjection. No longer will there be any such thing as manners, order, or virtue." Accordingly, a truly democratic society must avoid both extremes—"the spirit of inequality," which leads to aristocracy or monarchy, and "the spirit of extreme equality," which leads to "despotism and conquest."[70]

It only remains to return to Plutarch, as did the editor of the *Matrimonial Preceptor* in the late eighteenth century when he compiled a collection of sixty-five pieces, described as "instructive hints to those who are like to be married." The "classic authors" who were represented in this book agreed on most aspects of married life and emphasized the importance of friendship and affection between husband and wife. Each piece focused on the achievement and preservation of a loving relationship. Some digressed long enough to offer admonitions to the occasionally brutal husband, but none challenged the hierarchal nature of marriage or the characteristics of a good wife. Most of the authors had originally published their pieces during the 1700s, but the inclusion of Plutarch and Pliny was testimony to an intellectual tradition that had remained essentially unchanged for at least eighteen hundred years.

THE THREAT; OR, WHAT MIGHT HAVE BEEN

In a familial rather than a political context, the theories from which Americans carefully constructed their evolving position papers were more a threat than a source of inspiration. Indeed, it was the fear that Locke's brilliant analysis could be applied to the family as well as to the state that must have caused the greatest uneasiness among those who had a stake in conjugal patriarchy.

On its most elementary level, Lockean doctrine required mutual consent to marriage. Since the terms of this "voluntary Compact between Man and Woman" were negotiable, women were not automatically relegated to a subservient position "if the Circumstances either of her Condition or Contract with her Husband should exempt her from it." The Bible did not grant Adam unlimited authority over Eve, nor by extension, did it grant such power to other husbands. All Genesis implied, argued Locke, is that if God "would order it so, that she should be subject to her husband," and that "the Laws of Mankind and customs of Nations have ordered it so." The latter statement appeared to require some explanation, and thus Locke added—somewhat gratuitously—that there was "a Foundation in Nature" for such laws.[71] Carried over the threshold of mere insinuation, such assertions (at least all but the last) could have jeopardized male domination, and it is hardly surprising that rebellious pamphleteers marginalized that portion of Locke's argument.

They had chosen to forget that marriages had been forged by civil contracts until 1691 in Massachusetts, and it was only after that date that ministers officiated at such occasions. The shift away from a contractual union to one based on biblical prescriptions reinforced the patriarchal nature of marriage by emphasizing its inegalitarian underpinnings. Whether anyone had ever considered the relationship in this context is a moot point: revolutionary New Englanders would not have been willing to reopen this chapter of their Puritan legacy.

David Hume also created potential problems for American revolutionaries (who were otherwise taken by his arguments) by insisting that overbearing male sovereignty was "a real usurpation, and destroys that nearness of rank, not to say equality, which nature has established between the sexes." Hume, like Locke, addressed the marriage contract (albeit in a different context), and he added a touch of rationality to what otherwise would have been merely a paraphrase of Locke's thesis. "Nature, having endowed man with reason, has not so exactly regulated every article of his marriage contract, but has left him to adjust them, by his own prudence, according to his particular circumstances and situation."[72]

Equality? Regulation of contract? Particular circumstances? The implications of these ideas could have turned the world upside down. Might these passages be interpreted to mean that women had some say over property and self after marriage? Even worse, Hume envisioned a situation where women might resist male authority altogether, in response to overbearing domination. "Tyrants . . . produce rebels," he noted, "and all history informs us, that rebels when they prevail, are apt to become tyrants in their turn." This was not good news for men with patriarchal aspirations, and as a result, Hume "could wish" for a society where neither marriage partner had "pretensions to authority," and where all decisions were made on the basis of "perfect equality."[73] That his solution was framed as a "wish" indicates his perception of reality as well as the utopian nature of any attempt to redress marital inequality. Yet there it was in ink on paper in the context of marriage: "Tyrants produce rebels." And although the radical feminist Mary Astell had said much the same thing—"Tyranny . . . provokes the oppress'd to throw off even a Lawful Yoke that sits too heavy"—Hume had a legitimacy that Astell lacked.[74]

Throughout history, rebels had overthrown governments. If a government, originally based on consent, could be overthrown when a tyrannical monarch abused his trust, why was it that the same rules did not apply to a marriage based on consent where a husband betrayed his duty? But what were a husband's duties? Was it affection and kindness? Protection? Security? What were the boundaries of his authority? At what point did resistance become an appropriate response to alleged grievances? Americans avoided these issues not because they were unaware of them but precisely because they were the same questions being asked about the relationship between the colonies and King George. It was crucial to the preservation of a patriarchal social order that everyone pretend no link existed between the state and the family when (as a matter of history and literature) everyone knew that it did.

The idea that women were born into a state of freedom and equality carried even more threatening baggage, as Jean-Jacques Rousseau would have been the first to admit. As he traced the evolution of the human family, Rousseau noted that in archaic times, "mutual affection and liberty" were the sole bonds of this "little society," and it was "at this stage" that "the first differences were established in the ways of life of the two sexes which had hitherto been identical."[75] It mattered little whether Rousseau was right or wrong. What mattered was that by taking this position, Rousseau was also suggesting that gender roles were culturally determined rather than ordained by God, an argument that undermined the last refuge of patriarchal domination. His contemporary Voltaire (1694–1778) was in substantial agreeement, maintaining as he did that women's inferiority was a product of circumstance rather than nature.[76] Circumstance, as opposed to divine mandate, could be altered, although neither Rousseau nor Voltaire would have been enthusiastic about this prospect.

Moreover, these literary giants coupled with James Otis—"are not women born as free as men?"—meant more than double trouble, since Otis had put the American imprimatur on a very awkward component of revolutionary doctrine.[77] Otis did not pursue the matter, but his pamphlet was widely disseminated and applauded, giving support to the whole, if not the part. Even the most superficial acceptance of female equality would have made women's exclusion from civil participation difficult. Better to juggle equality with inequality, add inferiority and weakness, and keep all the balls in the air at once.

That some people were indeed conscious of the social tightrope on which these arguments were balanced is evident from the seemingly lighthearted exchange of letters between Abigail and John Adams, in which they applied the words "tyrant" and "rebellion" to the marital relationship. Yet John's response to his wife's initial foray indicates that on some level he really did feel threatened. Neither they nor any other American, it seems, was prepared for a serious dialogue on the subject, but the Adamses' epistolary conversation is evidence that they, at least, understood full well the connection between the family and the state, even as they recognized that any debate on the subject would be perpetually tabled. It is not so much that the Revolutionary generation refused to act on egalitarian impulses as they related to women— realistically speaking, that would have been too much to ask at that time and place. But that they did not even entertain the subject on any sustained level suggests that equality was constructed, contained, and dispensed with care. It is not too much to hypothesize that as American men came closer to renouncing the patriarchal authority of George III, they became proportionately more fearful of a similar loss of authority vis-à-vis their own subjects. If this is true, the renunciation of imperial patriarchy may have exacerbated rather than mitigated domestic patriarchy.

It was bad enough that women might want to control their own lives through a negotiated marriage contract, bad enough that women might take it into their heads that the relationship between bodily health and the health of the body politic might mean that women should have control over their bodies, but what if David Hume were right and married women really had a "love of dominion"? Did this mean they would want to control their husbands? A woman who challenged her traditional role in society was a disorderly woman, and disorderly women were threatening in terms of the damage they could inflict on society. They were, after all, responsible for the English Civil War, and historians have noted how fear of such disorder acted to stimulate the anxiety level of those in authority, which in turn prompted an assertion of even greater authority.[78]

The English attempted to reduce disorderly female activism in the post–Civil War years and again at the end of the first decade of the eighteenth century, when women engaged in political demonstrations on behalf of either Whigs or Tories. The *Spectator* tried to dissuade women from such disorderly conduct, urging them to abandon partisan politics in favor of a united gender-based opposition to a common enemy. "English women . . . should . . . distinguish themselves as tender mothers, and faithful wives, rather than as furious partizans," since "the family is the proper province for private women to shine in."[79]

During the reign of George III Englishwomen were once again charged with disorder, but this time their unseemly behavior was said to contribute to social malaise (marked by corruption, joyless homes, and conjugal infidelity) rather than to political unrest, as it had a century earlier. "Impudence, levity, and incontinence" were responsible for the unhealthy atmosphere (especially at court and in the cities), and unless manners took a turn for the better, according to one writer, the English would soon rival the French for dissipation, "unmanly pleasures . . . and emasculating luxuries." By returning to the "domestic virtues" that Englishwomen formerly practiced with such skill, the problem of disorder would be resolved. Those women who gave family values first priority were asked to set examples for others. If under the reign of Queen Anne women were "friends and companions, without ceasing to be wives and mothers," surely they could be so again.[80]

Clearly, by the 1770s the Anglo-American world was already swept up in a renewed emphasis on motherhood, the duties of wives, and the sanctity of the family. Although Antoine Thomas, the author of the above-quoted tract, did not invest motherhood with political importance, other writers had already done so. By implication, as well as overt expression, a nation was best served by orderly women. A patriarchal society that restricted women to their domestic sphere ensured that order.

What is mildly puzzling about the resurgence of domestic rhetoric in the American Revolutionary era is that American women had not shown any conspicuous tendency toward disorder. They had, of course, participated in various riots, particularly those associated with food products such as tea, coffee, and sugar, but their collective activism was limited to imperial and colonial issues.[81] Their public participation in the form of boycott was supported, indeed encouraged, by those in authority; their more spontaneous presence during food riots was met by indulgence rather than criticism. Moreover, these female activists were noticeably reticent about pressing issues that related to them as women. American women, who had one of the highest literacy rates of women anywhere in the eighteenth-century world, women who, like Cato, knew that "all men would be tyrants," and who quoted Halifax's maxims of state, refrained from extending the debate to their own frame of reference.[82]

Only as individuals did women petition for redress of particular grievances, and only as supplicants did they couch petitions in revolutionary language. There was no sustained discourse, no visible manifestation of group consciousness, no attempt to apply the artful new theories of state government to family government in a serious manner. Although the women who engaged in political satire in Philadelphia in the 1790s clearly recognized the inequities of American gender relations, they resorted to a literary device that, like the novel, was less confrontational than a head-on attack and could be dismissed as parody. Women did not employ group protest on their own behalf, but they might have, and that potential for disorder was apparently danger enough. Americans may not have quoted Mary Astell, but it was unlikely they were ignorant of her existence.

Had they not been programmed by the literature of submission, women might have pursued the literature of sedition to assist them in formulating an ideology relevant to their aspirations. If Pufendorf and Locke could be selectively applied to a negotiated marriage contract, if Hume and Otis could be quoted with authority on the equality of the sexes, one can easily speculate on the uses to which other theorists might have been put without their consent.

In a celebrated treatise Jonathan Mayhew spoke to the issue of submission, and although his followers would have denied the implications of his argument, the good minister did, in fact, maintain that the Apostle Paul never intended "to teach that children, servants, and wives should, in all cases whatever, obey their parents, masters, and husbands respectively, never making any opposition to their will." Moreover, Mayhew continued, even when submission to "the higher powers" was appropriate, it was not to those who merely held the "*title*" of rulers, "but only to those who *actually* perform[ed] the duty of rulers by exercising a reasonable and just authority for the good of human society." To oppose a reasonable and just authority "agreeable to the will of God" was equivalent to resisting God himself, but people were under no obligation to submit to rulers who acted "in contradiction to the public good."[83] Why was there no American to substitute "women" for "people," "husbands" for "rulers," and "well-being of family" for "public good"?

Locke, of course, had also argued resistance. But it was one thing to appropriate a secular philosopher in support of one's position, quite another to borrow from a respected man of the cloth. Here was an American minister who could have been quoted or paraphrased to put God and the female sex on better footing. In short, Mayhew stood for the proposition that God did not always demand submission from women who were subject to overbearing husbands.

The duel over Parliamentary omnipotence that resulted in the creative and startling American improvisation, dual sovereignty, was another area particularly relevant to marital relations. Locke had hinted at the possibility of mutual economic responsibility when he insisted that husbands had authority only over "the things of their common Interest and Property." Indeed, Locke would have had the first couple share power as lord and lady of the world with joint dominion "over the Creatures, or *Property* in them." Moreover, "a mistress of a Family" had as much authority over the "several Persons" in that family as did her husband. Locke's advancement of parental power as a literal translation of the Fifth Commandment was, in fact, a familial construction of dual sovereignty.[84]

Hume, who was already too dangerously egalitarian for comfort, would have divided marital authority between husband and wife "as between 2 equal members of the same body," a solution that sounds for all the world comparable to the plan American radicals were trying to effect between Great Britain and the colonies.[85] If the dividing line between the absolute sovereignty of Parliament and the absolute dependence of the colonies could be rewritten by John Dickinson and James Wilson to arrogate more power to the colonies, why couldn't the same kind of redrafting improve the position of wives within the family commonwealth? Would such a theory have been rejected? Of course. But it was never even formulated. Why was there no one to edit the major seventeenth- and eighteenth-century writers and create for women what revolutionaries had so skillfully crafted for the American cause? After all, wrote Mary Wollstonecraft, "the *divine right* of husbands, like the divine right of kings, may, it is hoped, in this enlightened age, be contested without danger."[86]

Divorce was the only private matter that came even close to approximating the discourse on the public level, but even here the discussion appears to have revolved around economics and affection rather than individual rights. A few people recognized that the pursuit of happiness may have implied a right to dissolve an unhappy marriage, and a Philadelphia pamphleteer even drew on John Milton's polemical tract, but Americans did not even come close to developing an argument to which some of their favorite theorists could have subscribed.[87]

Locke was far more radical than Pufendorf on this issue, and where the latter would permit divorce only with "very weighty cause" such as refusal of sex, adultery, or desertion, the former insisted that there was no inherent reason why all marriage contracts should be perpetual. Once procreation, education, and inheritance were provided for, the reasons for marriage were satisfied. Thus, husbands and wives had liberty to separate "where natural Right, or their Contract allows it."[88] Revolutionary ideology had repudiated the idea of consent as a one-shot deal, and James Wilson would be only one of many Americans to insist that continuous consent was a prerequisite of political legitimacy. Applied to marriage and linked to Locke, this interpretation would have added weight to the arguments in favor of divorce. Not surprisingly, it worked in reverse when applied to women: once a woman "consented" to marriage, she agreed to be ruled in perpetuity by the sovereign she had chosen.[89]

In the end, what-was prevailed over what-might-have-been, and American women (at least white women), who never asked for anything, gained nothing from the heady revolutionary rhetoric. Nevertheless, even if there was virtually no likelihood of female protest (much less resistance), the very prospect of such disorder was threatening enough to evoke the usual response, and once the guns were lowered, voices were raised to refuse demands that had never been made.

A century earlier, Englishwomen had demanded rights because of their contributions during the English Civil War. They had spied, built fortifications, and raised money, just as American women did in their own eighteenth-century civil war. But seventeenth-century Englishwomen argued on their own behalf as well, by demanding the right to petition equally with men: "Have we not an equal interest with the men of this Nation in those liberties and securities contained in the Petition of Right, and other good Laws of the Land? Are any of our lives, limbs, liberties or goods to be taken from us more than from men?" And as Patricia Higgins has noted, Englishwomen took the Leveller position that their equality in religious matters should extend to civil matters as well.[90] Despite their efforts, however, Englishwomen achieved no new liberties for themselves, and perhaps the collective Anglo-American memory was at work in the 1780s reminding American women of the futility of any assault on the inequities that governed their lives, even as the same collective memory readied those who anticipated such an assault.

— ≠ —

The French also sought to impose order and prevent women from assuming public roles in the late seventeenth century by glorifying marriage. Virtue, submission, and domesticity were linked to a role that gave women responsibility for household management, childhood education, and spousal affection. During the eighteenth century the combination of a growing bourgeoisie, expanding trade, and a revolution in behavior heightened the feeling of disorder with which women were identified and for which they were excoriated. The story of disorderly women in France culminates in the French Revolution, after which the French equivalent of Republican Motherhood reached its apogee.[91]

The excesses of the French Revolution and the role of French women in that upheaval exacerbated the fears of Americans as well, which in turn accelerated the calls for female domesticity. It did not help the immediate cause of American women for French women to have demanded both political and marital rights in written documents, in addresses to the National Assembly, and as militant demonstrators. They demanded the right to bear arms, a liberal divorce law, and a more egalitarian system of inheritance. The grounds upon which they made these claims indicate that French feminists, male and female, took equality and universal rights seriously. Indeed, the egalitarian Cercle Social (which included Condorcet among its members) maintained that a democratic nation was the sum of voluntary, consensual, egalitarian families.[92]

For one dazzling moment it looked as though French women might achieve at least some of their goals, but after a short experiment with a divorce law, a more repressive mood set in. Not surprisingly, antifeminists trotted out the equivalent of Republican Motherhood as a solution for the problem of disorderly women and the chaos such women caused. Physical differences between men and women were emphasized to neutralize egalitarian claims.[93] Republican Motherhood provided a controlled setting for female "political activity" and became the alternative of choice for French legislators, who saw it as an opportunity to deny women a more public presence.[94] Although some would argue to the contrary, the preponderance of evidence suggests that the status of French women had actually worsened in relative terms by the end of the eighteenth century. Nevertheless, it was their collective action during the Revolution, not in the alleged benefits of a political domesticity, that provided the basis for future feminist action.[95]

Like American women, French women subscribed to Republican Motherhood because they believed it reconciled domesticity with a form of political citizenship, however marginal and indirect. Where French and American Republican Motherhood appear to part company, however, involves the father's role in the family unit. The new French patriarchy rehabilitated fatherhood, exalted a father's affection for his family, and restored him as head of a family that he was to nurture and guide rather than tyrannize. Although much of that rhetoric would have been familiar to eighteenth-century Americans, who had, for a long time past, immersed themselves in the literature of the affectionate family and nonpatriarchal father, there appears to have been less emphasis on republican fatherhood in the new nation, and more attention paid to the metaphorical father in the personification of George Washington.[96]

The glorification of motherhood at the end of the eighteenth century in both France and the United States is strikingly reminiscent of a similar sequence of events a century earlier in Europe, and it may have gained impetus from the desire to repair war losses and stimulate repopulation. At the end of the War of the Austrian Succession (1740–48), Montesquieu hinted at such a policy in *L'esprit des loix,* where he spoke of remedying a "depopulation" that resulted from accidents, wars, and pestilence. And in the aftermath of devastating World War II losses, Americans once again relegated women to the home with what were, by this time, eerily familiar justifications. Adlai Stevenson reminded the politically astute members of the Smith commencement class of 1955 that their participation in politics was through their roles as wife and mother. "Women, especially educated women, have a unique opportunity to influence us, man and boy."[97] Jean-Jacques Rousseau had cast a long shadow.

How the ideology of Republican Motherhood affected urban societies with low sex ratios (where the fantasies, expectations, or aspirations of many single women would be dashed) is hard to gauge. Judith Sargent Murray tried to raise the self-esteem of women who by choice or chance would remain single, but in fact, she gave them few realistic alternatives. The economic instability of women propelled them toward marriage, even if the ideology had not been persuasive in and of itself. And the combination of these two factors may have made Republican Motherhood yet more attractive to the least affluent women—as a means of upward mobility. For African American women the paradox was even more evident: as blacks they aspired to independence; as women, they may have become acculturated to the rhetoric of dependence. The few Indians who lived in white, urban households were not likely to have escaped the cult of domesticity either.

One might even argue that the widespread literacy of American urban women, which would be further augmented in the new nation, made it all the easier for that ideology to gain such a tenacious grip on their collective minds. A high literacy rate was one product of a large middle-class population—an American population that during the seventeenth and eighteenth centuries, thanks to European antecendents and precedents, had developed moral principles and guidelines for itself, among which were the trappings of Republican Motherhood.

Epilogue

A backward glance from our perch beyond the post-Revolutionary decades brings to mind the forest/tree metaphor. As individuals, women often negotiated life's contract quite successfully, but collectively they suffered a deterioration in economic standing, a growing public invisibility, and a heightened reliance on male decision making in the New England seaports during the seventeenth and eighteenth centuries. The decline was gradual, the result of interconnected forces that worked effectively (if not always deliberately) to thwart female advancement.

This sequence of associated events confirms Judith Bennett's hypothesis about the reinforcement value of interlocking patriarchal institutions. If, for example, female dependence was related to the tendency of women, willingly or unwillingly, to come under the sway of male oversight, then the simultaneous assault by religious, economic, and legal institutions exacerbated that process at the same time that intellectual backup stimulated and intensified it. Thus, ministers and church elders, merchants and Overseers of the Poor, Selectmen and judges acted in harmony to restrain women who, by their very nature (not to mention numbers), threatened an orderly society.

The urban setting and sex ratio also conspired to defeat female improvement along the lines postulated by a liberal, progressive interpretation of American history even though that environment offered multiple opportunities for women. As informal urban institutions evolved into a coherent framework of government, such organizational structure facilitated control of the disproportionately female population in these seaboard communities. Codification of indigenous laws, conformity with common law, and the establishment of tiers of governmental apparatus made containment of women a more efficient process—a testament to Gerda Lerner's theory about the effects of state building.

Given such coordination, it is hardly surprising that women's voices grew weaker and their presence dimmer in each of the urban arenas discussed above. If, during the eighteenth century, lay-clerical quarrels were aired for all the world to see, women were relegated to the sidelines in this public spectacle.[1] Women became second-string players in the economic contests of the eighteenth century as well, a development that acted as both cause and effect of the legal disabilities that influenced their lives. Debt loads increased, women had difficulty obtaining credit, creditors were favored over widows. And by having a higher literacy rate than their country cousins, urban women were all the more able to reaffirm their conduct through the prescriptive—and popular—literature of the day.

In various ways, of course, New England women rocked the boat by circumventing some of the worst aspects of patriarchal control. They capitalized on their supposed piety and held religious meetings to discuss God knows what, they bargained and traded and contracted in defiance of common law, they withheld and wasted estate assets, and they manipulated female stereotypes to further their own ends. When Abizag Taperill was indicted for absenting herself from meeting for several months, she "pleaded she knew noe Law against it." As a weak female, ignorant of the laws, she would be pitied rather than penalized for her delinquency, and all the judge could do was admonish her to attend in the future. Alas, poor Abizag; she knew full well.[2]

Urban New England women—and by extension American women—did not demand rights in the Revolutionary era because, unlike European women, they had no militant tradition to call upon. English and French women had such a legacy, but by the 1760s that past was too remote from the American collective memory to stimulate activism. Furthermore, there were no female groups on this side of the Atlantic, as there were in England and France, through which women could identify on the basis of gender. Nearly two centuries of conditioning ensured that the way in which the American Revolutionary generation conceived of its world would affect the way its constituents acted in it.[3]

From this perspective, the revolutionary moment was neither radical nor a watershed for American women. Those who disregard America's commitment to patriarchal rule and plead for a historical interpretation that favors enlightened exceptionalism have overlooked the conditions that made large-scale change all but impossible at that time and place. Indeed, a discourse that emphasizes female achievement in the Revolutionary era not only ignores the dynamics that shaped the relationship between American women and men at the end of the eighteenth century, but also obscures the historical differences between Europeans and Americans that would continue to influence the lives of women in the Atlantic world for the next two hundred years.

Notes

PROLOGUE

1. Gerda Lerner, *The Creation of Patriarchy* (New York: Oxford University Press, 1986), 54–55, 167, 217.

2. Judith Bennett, "Patriarchy in the Secular Sphere," paper presented at the Tenth Berkshire Conference on the History of Women, Chapel Hill, N.C., 8 June 1996.

INTRODUCTION

1. Hamilton meandered through New England in the summer of 1744. See Alexander Hamilton, *Gentleman's Progress: The Itinerarium of Dr. Alexander Hamilton, 1744*, ed. Carl Bridenbaugh (Chapel Hill: University of North Carolina Press, 1948), xv, 144–46, 111.

2. Joseph Bennett, "History of New England" (1740), in *Massachusetts Historical Society Proceedings* 5 (1861): 110.

3. Hamilton, *Gentleman's Progress*, 134, 116, 141, 112, 146.

4. Ibid., 157, 156, 150, 151.

5. Ibid., 125, 127; James Birket, *Some Cursory Remarks Made by James Birket in His Voyage to North America* (1750–51) (New Haven: Yale University Press, 1916), 8.

6. Hamilton, *Gentleman's Progress*, 119; Birket, *Some Cursory Remarks*, 15–16.

7. Herbert Moller, "Sex Composition and Correlated Culture Patterns of Colonial America," *William and Mary Quarterly* 2 (April 1945): 117–18, 120–21; Roger Thompson, "Seventeenth-Century English and Colonial Sex Ratios: A Postscript," *Population Studies* 28 (March 1974): 153–65; Lois Green Carr and Lorena Walsh, "The Planter's Wife: The Experience of White Women in Seventeenth-Century Maryland," *William and Mary Quarterly* 34 (1977): 545.

8. SPG Records, Rev. Mr. John Weeks to Sec. [of SPG], Marblehead, Mass., 2 April 1770, letterbook B, vol. 22, p. 253, United SPG Archives, London.

9. Newport Town Records, Vault B, Newport Historical Society, Newport, R.I. (hereafter abbreviated as NHS), book 3, Land Evidences, p. 294.

10. Gov. Francis Bernard to the Board of Trade, 5 September 1763, in Josiah H.

Benton, *Early Census Making in Massachusetts, 1643–1765* (Boston: Charles E. Goodspeed, 1905), 55.

11. Ezra Stiles, *Extracts from the Itineraries and Other Miscellanies of Ezra Stiles, D.D., LL.D., 1755–1794,* ed. Franklin B. Dexter (New Haven: Yale University Press, 1916), 13, 213.

12. In New York City in 1749 white females also outnumbered white males, but the ratio was not as pronounced as in New England. What makes New York distinctive is that there were more black females than black males. The surprising lack of a pre-Revolutionary census for Pennsylvania makes any estimate of Philadelphia's sex ratio difficult. Nevertheless, the 1790 federal census shows that Philadelphia's population was fairly well-balanced, with only a very slight female majority. On the basis of that information, it is unlikely that an earlier census would have shown a severe imbalance. Robert V. Wells, *The Population of the British Colonies in America before 1776: A Survey of Census Data* (Princeton: Princeton University Press, 1975), 121–23, 143; Bureau of the Census, *Heads of Families at the First Census of the United States Taken in the Year 1790* (Penn.) (Washington: Government Printing Office, 1908), 10.

13. Roger Thompson, *Women in Stuart England and America* (London: Routledge, 1974, 1978), 31; Cotton Mather, *Ornaments for the Daughters of Zion* (1692), a facs. ed. (Delmar, N.Y.: Scholars' Facsimile and Reprints, 1978), 110.

14. Extract from the *Boston Gazette,* 12 August 1734, reprinted in *William and Mary Quarterly* 9 (1952): 394.

15. *Records Relating to the Early History of Boston* (Boston: Rockwell and Churchill, 1876–1909), 15:369. Vols. 1–22 of this series were issued as *Report of the Records Commissioners.*

16. Evarts B. Greene and Virginia D. Harrington, *American Population before the Federal Census of 1790* (New York, 1932; Gloucester, Mass.: P. Smith, 1966), 22.

17. Bureau of the Census, *Heads of Families at the First Census of the United States Taken in the Year 1790* (Mass.) (Washington: Government Printing Office, 1908), 183–95.

18. Joseph B. Felt, *Annals of Salem,* 2d ed. (Salem, Mass.: W. and S. B. Ives, 1845–49), 2:410–11; Benton, *Early Census Making in Massachusetts;* Bureau of the Census, *Heads of Families* (Mass.), 93–98; William Bentley, *Diary of William Bentley, D.D.* (Salem, Mass., 1905; Gloucester, Mass.: P. Smith, 1962), 1:7.

19. "Account of the People in the Colony of Rhode Island, Whites and Blacks" (1755), NHS; "An Account of the Number of Families and Inhabitants of the Town of Newport, 1774," R. I. State Archives, Providence; Manuscript Census, Newport, R.I., 1782, Rhode Island Historical Society, Providence, R.I. (hereafter abbreviated as RIHS); Bureau of the Census, *Heads of Families at the First Census of the United States Taken in the Year 1790,* (R.I.)(Washington: Government Printing Office, 1908), 9, 19–23.

20. "A General Account of the Number of Inhabitants of the Several Towns in the Province of New Hampshire as Appears by the Returns of the Selectmen from Each Place in the Year 1767," Sec. of State Records, Census and Inventory Records,

box 1, Dept. of State, Division of Records Management and Archives, Concord, N.H.; Bureau of the Census, *A Century of Population Growth* (Washington: Government Printing Office, 1909), 150, 152; the figures for 1773 and 1775 may be found in box 27, Dept. of State Records, Division of Records Management and Archives, Concord, N.H.

21. Bureau of the Census, *Heads of Families at the First Census of the United States Taken in the Year 1790* (N.H.) (Washington: Government Printing Office, 1908), 78–82.

22. For data and an examination of the implications of a low sex ratio on Bermuda, see Elaine Forman Crane, "The Socioeconomics of a Female Majority in Eighteenth-Century Bermuda," *Signs: Journal of Women in Culture and Society* 15 (1990): 231–58.

23. Robert V. Wells, *The Population of the British Colonies,* 76.

24. Felt, *Annals of Salem,* 2:410–11.

25. Gary Nash, *The Urban Crucible: Social Change, Political Consciousness, and the Origins of the American Revolution* (Cambridge: Harvard University Press, 1979), 172, 465.

26. Alexander Keyssar, "Widowhood in Eighteenth-Century Massachusetts," *Perspectives in American History* 8 (1974): 51, 53–54, 90–94.

27. Wells, *Population of the British Colonies,* 76–77; Marcia Guttentag and Paul F. Secord, *Too Many Women? The Sex Ratio Question* (Beverly Hills, Calif.: Sage, 1983), 69, 77, 164.

28. *Early History of Boston,* 1:158–70; Bureau of the Census, *Heads of Families* (Mass.), 183–95.

29. Daniel Scott Smith, "Female Householding in Late Eighteenth-Century America and the Problem of Poverty," *Journal of Social History* 28 (1994): 83.

30. Wells, *Population of the British Colonies,* 58, 108, 128–29, 190–91, 248, 317–19; "Inhabitants of the Town of Newport, 1774," R.I. Archives.

31. "Inhabitants of the Town of Newport, 1774," R.I. Archives; Bureau of the Census, *Heads of Families* (R.I.).

32. The 1687 tax list may be found in *Early History of Boston,* 1:91–133.

33. Bettye H. Pruitt, ed., *The Massachusetts Tax Valuation List of 1771* (Boston: G. K. Hall, 1978). For comparisons with Philadelphia see Billy G. Smith, *The "Lower Sort": Philadelphia's Laboring People, 1750–1800* (Ithaca: Cornell University Press, 1990).

34. Bureau of the Census, *Heads of Families* (N.H.), 78–82. The same phenomenon seems to have existed in Philadelphia in the postwar years, when "women appear to have created occupational residential clusters, often choosing to live next-door to or near other female-headed laboring class households" (Jeanne Boydston, "The Woman Who Wasn't There: Women's Market Labor and the Transition to Capitalism in the United States," *Journal of the Early Republic* 16 [summer 1996]: 193–94).

35. Mary Beth Norton, "'My Resting Reaping Time': Sarah Osborn's Defense of Her 'Unfeminine' Activities, 1767," *Signs: Journal of Women in Culture and Society* 2

(1976): 528. See also Carroll Smith-Rosenberg, "The Female World of Love and Ritual: Relations between Women in Nineteenth-Century America," *Signs: Journal of Women in Culture and Society* 1 (1975): 1–30.

36. Wells, *Population of the British Colonies,* 86.

37. Ibid.; Benton, *Early Census Making in Massachusetts.*

38. "Inhabitants of New Hampshire" (1767, 1773), Dept. of State, Concord; Bureau of the Census, *A Century of Population Growth,* 156.

39. "Account of People in Rhode Island" (1755), NHS; "Inhabitants of the Town of Newport, 1774," R.I. Archives; MS Census, Newport (1782), RIHS.

40. Benton, *Early Census Making in Massachusetts;* "Inhabitants of the Town of Newport, 1774," R.I. Archives; MS Census, Newport (1782), RIHS.

41. "Inhabitants of the Town of Newport, 1774," R.I. Archives; MS Census, Newport (1782), RIHS.

CHAPTER 1

1. Christine Alice Young, *From "Good Order" to Glorious Revolution: Salem, Massachusetts, 1628–1689* (Ann Arbor: UMI Research Press, 1978, 1980), 35–36; Robert G. Pope, ed., *The Notebook of The Reverend John Fiske, 1644–1675* (Salem, Mass.: Essex Institute [hereafter abbreviated as EI], 1974), 244–45.

2. Young, *From "Good Order" to Glorious Revolution,* 35; James Duncan Phillips, *Salem in the Seventeenth Century* (Boston: Houghton Mifflin, 1933), 114.

3. George F. Dow, ed., *Records and Files of the Quarterly Courts of Essex County, Massachusetts, 1638–1683* (Salem, Mass.: EI, 1911–21), 1:7 (1637); Phillips, *Salem in the Seventeenth Century,* 349, 361, 345.

4. Pope, ed., *Notebook of the Reverend John Fiske,* 241–42.

5. John Russell Bartlett, *Records of the Colony of Rhode Island and Providence Plantations in New England* (Providence, R.I.: A. Crawford Greene and Brother, 1856), 1:20 (1638).

6. For a thoughtful dialogue about these issues see Judith M. Bennett, "Medieval Women, Modern Women: Across the Great Divide," in *Culture and History, 1350–1600: Essays on English Communities, Identities, and Writing,* ed. David Aers (London: Harvester Wheatsheaf, 1992), 147–75. Bennett sees more continuity than change and cautions against interpreting change as disadvantageous to women. Bridget Hill has responded to Bennett in an essay in which she confirms a downward spiral and grounds female dislocation in economic change ("Women's History: A Study in Change, Continuity, or Standing Still?" *Women's History Review* 2, no. 1 [1993]: 5–22). Bennett has stood by her position and maintains that patriarchal domination throughout the centuries overshadows any other factors that have affected women's condition ("Women's History: A Study in Continuity and Change," *Women's History Review* 2, no. 2 [1993]: 173–84).

7. Jo Ann McNamara and Suzanne Wemple, "The Power of Women through the Family in Medieval Europe, 500–1100," in *Women and Power in the Middle Ages,*

ed. Mary Erler and Maryanne Kowaleski (Athens: University of Georgia Press, 1988), 90–92, 95; Suzanne Wemple, "Sanctity and Power: The Dual Pursuit of Early Medieval Women," in *Becoming Visible: Women in European History,* ed. Renate Bridenthal, Claudia Koonz, and Susan Stuard (Boston: Houghton Mifflin, 1987), 147, 138.

8. McNamara and Wemple, "Power of Women," 96; Michelle Zimbalist Rosaldo, "Women, Culture, and Society: A Theoretical Overview," in *Women, Culture, and Society,* ed. Michelle Zimbalist Rosaldo and Louise Lamphere (Stanford: Stanford University Press, 1974), 36; Kathryn L. Reyerson, "Women in Business in Medieval Montpellier," in *Women and Work in Preindustrial Europe,* ed. Barbara Hanawalt (Bloomington: Indiana University Press, 1986), 117; Martha C. Howell, "Citizenship and Gender: Women's Political Status in Northern Medieval Cities," in *Women and Power in the Middle Ages,* ed. Erler and Kowaleski, 47, 51, 53.

9. Susan Amussen, *An Ordered Society: Gender and Class in Early Modern England* (New York: Blackwell, 1988), 187; Susan Cahn, *Industry of Devotion: The Transformation of Women's Work in England, 1500–1660* (New York: Columbia University Press, 1987), 118; Samia I. Spencer, ed., *French Women and the Age of Enlightenment* (Bloomington: Indiana University Press, 1984), 7; Mary Elizabeth Perry, *Gender and Disorder in Early Modern Seville* (Princeton: Princeton University Press, 1990), 177; William Monter, "Protestant Wives, Catholic Saints, and the Devil's Handmaid: Women in the Age of the Reformation," in *Becoming Visible,* ed. Bridenthal et al., 204; Lawrence Stone, *The Family, Sex, and Marriage in England 1500–1800,* abridged ed. (New York: Harper and Row, 1979), 110–11.

10. Joan B. Landes, *Women and the Public Sphere in the Age of the French Revolution* (Ithaca: Cornell University Press, 1988), 22.

11. Martha C. Howell, "Women, the Family Economy, and the Structure of Market Production in Cities of Northern Europe during the Late Middle Ages," in *Women and Power,* ed. Erler and Kowaleski, 214. Gerda Lerner's analysis of archaic times is suggestive of this same interpretation; see Gerda Lerner, *The Creation of Patriarchy* (New York: Oxford University Press, 1986), esp. 167.

12. Jane Tibbetts Schulenburg, "Female Sanctity: Public and Private Roles, ca. 500–1100," in *Women and Power,* ed. Erler and Kowaleski, 105–6; Wemple, "Sanctity and Power," 131, 136; Jane T. Schulenburg, "Women's Monastic Communities, 500–1100: Patterns of Expansion and Decline," in *Sisters and Workers in the Middle Ages,* ed. Judith M. Bennett, Elizabeth A. Clark, Jean F. O'Barr, B. Anne Vilen, and Sarah Westphal-Wihl (Chicago: University of Chicago Press, 1989), 214.

13. Margaret L. King, *Women of the Renaissance* (Chicago: University of Chicago Press, 1991), 82.

14. David Hall, "The Love of God and the Desire for Learning: Libraries and Literacy in Medieval English Nunneries," and Monica H. Green, "Women as Owners of Medical Books in Medieval Europe," papers presented at the conference "Learning, Literacy, and Gender in the Middle Ages," Fordham University, 30 March 1996.

15. King, *Women of the Renaissance,* 94–95; Merry E. Wiesner, *Women and Gender in Early Modern Europe* (Cambridge: Cambridge University Press, 1993), 61.

16. Carol Neel, "The Origins of the Beguines," in *Sisters and Workers,* ed. Bennett et al., 240–260; King, *Women of the Renaissance,* 104.

17. Wiesner, *Women and Gender,* 181; King, *Women of the Renaissance,* 101–2; Schulenburg, "Women's Monastic Communities," 225–26, 234; Gerda Lerner, *The Creation of Feminist Consciousness: From the Middle Ages to 1870* (New York: Oxford University Press, 1993), 73; Susan M. Stuard, "The Dominion of Gender: Women's Fortunes in the High Middle Ages," in *Becoming Visible,* ed. Bridenthal et al., 158.

18. Brenda M. Bolton, "Mulieres Sanctae," in *Women in Medieval Society,* ed. Susan M. Stuard (Philadelphia: University of Pennsylvania Press, 1976), 143, 149.

19. King, *Women of the Renaissance,* 104, 111; Stuard, "The Dominion of Gender," 168; Penelope Johnson, "The Cloistering of Medieval Nuns: Release or Repression, Reality or Fantasy?" in *Gendered Domains: Rethinking Public and Private in Women's History,* ed. Dorothy O. Helly and Susan M. Reverby (Ithaca: Cornell University Press, 1992), 39; Monter, "Protestant Wives," 209; Wiesner, *Women and Gender,* 194.

20. Roger Thompson, *Women in Stuart England and America* (London: Routledge and Kegan Paul, 1974), 84; Natalie Z. Davis, *Society and Culture in Early Modern France* (Stanford: Stanford University Press, 1975), 78, 89; Lerner, *Creation of Feminist Consciousness,* 129–30; Linda Woodbridge, *Women and the English Renaissance: Literature and the Nature of Womankind, 1540–1620* (Urbana: University of Illinois Press, 1984), 130; Monter, "Protestant Wives," 208.

21. Wiesner, *Women and Gender,* 69.

22. Davis, *Society and Culture,* 88–89; Monter, "Protestant Wives," 206; Wiesner, *Women and Gender,* 192; King, *Women of the Renaissance,* 138; Lyndal Roper, *The Holy Household: Women and Morals in Reformation Augsburg* (Oxford: Clarendon Press, 1989), 264; Patricia Crawford, *Women and Religion in England, 1500–1720* (London: Routledge, 1993), 40.

23. Davis, *Society and Culture,* 85.

24. Monter, "Protestant Wives," 207; Davis, *Society and Culture,* 80, 81.

25. Thompson, *Women in Stuart England,* 85–86; Roper, *Holy Household,* 54.

26. Thompson, *Women in Stuart England,* 122–23; Herbert Moller, "Sex Composition and Correlated Culture Patterns of Colonial America," *William and Mary Quarterly* 2 (April 1945): 141.

27. Thompson, *Women in Stuart England,* 91; Wiesner, *Women and Gender,* 181.

28. Wiesner, *Women and Gender,* 232; Natalie Z. Davis and Arlette Farge, eds., *History of Women in the West,* vol. 3, *Renaissance and Enlightenment Paradoxes* (Cambridge: Harvard University Press, 1993), 445.

29. Hanawalt, ed., *Women and Work,* 115; Maryanne Kowaleski, "Women's Work in a Market Town: Exeter in the Late Fourteenth Century," in *Women and Work,* ed. Hanawalt, 147–48, 151; Eileen Power, *Medieval Women* (Cambridge: Cambridge University Press, 1975), 60–61, 66; King, *Women of the Renaissance,* 62–67.

30. Reyerson, "Women in Business," 119, 120–23.

31. Natalie Zemon Davis, "Women in the Crafts in Sixteenth-Century Lyon," in *Women and Work,* ed. Hanawalt, 174–75, 180.

32. David Herlihy, *Opera Muliebria: Women and Work in Medieval Europe* (New York: McGraw-Hill, 1990), 148, 150.

33. Wiesner, *Women and Gender*, 92, 94, 95, 96; Diane Willen, "Women in the Public Sphere in Early Modern England: The Case of the Urban Working Poor," in *Gendered Domains*, ed. Helly and Reverby, 188–89.

34. Herlihy, *Opera Muliebria*, 149; Barbara A. Hanawalt, "Peasant Women's Contribution to the Home Economy in Late Medieval England," in *Women and Work*, ed. Hanawalt, 2; Wiesner, *Women and Gender*, 92.

35. Power, *Medieval Women*, 60–61; Mary Prior, "Women and the Urban Economy: Oxford, 1500–1800," in *Women in English Society, 1500–1800*, ed. Mary Prior (London: Methuen, 1985), 93–117; Elizabeth Fox-Genovese, "Women and Work," in *French Women and the Age of Enlightenment*, ed. Spencer, 117; Howell, "Women, the Family Economy," 201–14; Maryanne Kowaleski and Judith Bennett, "Crafts, Gilds, and Women in the Middle Ages: Fifty Years after Marian K. Dale," in *Sisters and Workers*, ed. Bennett et al., 12–13, 18, 20; Olwen Hufton, "Women, Work, and Family," in *A History of Women in the West*, vol. 3, *Renaissance and Enlightenment Paradoxes*, ed. Davis and Farge, 25.

36. Herlihy, *Opera Muliebria*, 176–77; Stuard, ed., *Women in Medieval Society*, 4–5; Hanawalt, ed., *Women and Work*, vx; Reyerson, "Women in Business," 117; Landes, *Women and the Public Sphere*, 22; Howell, "Citizenship and Gender," 37; Howell, "Women, the Family Economy," 199.

37. Cahn, *Industry of Devotion*, 3–4; Hufton, "Women, Work, and Family," 25; Hanawalt, ed., *Women and Work*, xv; Stuard, "The Dominion of Gender," 153.

38. Davis, *Society and Culture*, 126; Amussen, *Ordered Society*, 120; Stuard, "The Dominion of Gender," 170; Bridget Hill, ed., *The First English Feminist: Reflections on Marriage and Other Writings by Mary Astell* (New York: St. Martin's Press, 1986), 21; King, *Women of the Renaissance*, 67–68; Herlihy, *Opera Muliebria*, 176; Fox-Genovese, "Women and Work," 120.

39. Howell, "Women, the Family Economy," 207; Wiesner, *Women and Gender*, 92, 102–3; M. E. Perry, *Gender and Disorder*, 13.

40. Power, *Medieval Women*, 60–62; Kowaleski "Crafts, Gilds, and Women," 13, 23; King, *Women of the Renaissance*, 67; Herlihy, *Opera Muliebria*, 178; Bennett, "Medieval Women," 159; Howell, "Women, the Family Economy," 213–14; Davis, *Society and Culture*, 94; Davis, "Women in the Crafts," 185; Wiesner, *Women and Gender*, 95.

41. Howell, "Women, the Family Economy," 200–201.

42. G. J. Barker-Benfield, *The Culture of Sensibility: Sex and Society in Eighteenth-Century Britain* (Chicago: University of Chicago Press, 1992), 93ff.

43. Howell, "Women, the Family Economy," 199; Stuard, "Dominion of Gender," 153, 170; Cahn, *Industry of Devotion*, 45ff., 122; Fox-Genovese, "Women and Work," 124; Wiesner, *Women and Gender*, 97; Barker-Benfield, *Culture of Sensibility*, xxv; Bennett, "Medieval Women," 158–59, argues that because women achieved neither substantial income nor status from brewing, their retreat from this trade cannot be considered a major decline. Perhaps not, but considered with other evidence, it

suggests a pattern and a sequence of events that robbed women of what little auton-omy they possessed. See also Judith Bennett, "Patriarchy in the Secular Sphere," pa-per presented at the Tenth Berkshire Conference on the History of Women, 8 June 1996, and Judith M. Bennett, *Ale, Beer, and Brewsters in England: Women's Work in a Changing World, 1300–1600* (New York: Oxford University Press, 1996).

44. Hanawalt, ed., *Women and Work,* 11.

45. Davis, *Society and Culture,* 94; Wiesner, *Women and Gender,* 88, 92, 97, 107–8; King, *Women of the Renaissance,* 71–73; Herlihy, *Opera Muliebria,* 149–50; Hanawalt, ed., *Women and Work,* xii, 11; Christine Klapisch-Zuber, "Women Servants in Florence during the Fourteenth and Fifteenth Centuries," in *Women and Work,* ed. Hanawalt, 65; Davis, "Women in the Crafts," 178; Cahn, *Industry of Devotion,* 36.

46. Cahn, *Industry of Devotion,* 45ff; Howell, "Women, the Family Economy," 207, 215; Cahn, *Industry of Devotion,* 48; Davis, "Women in the Crafts," 188; Howell, "Women, the Family Economy," 215; Barker-Benfield, *Culture of Sensibility,* 93; Roper, *Holy Household,* 49.

47. Howell, "Women, the Family Economy," 206, 215; Howell, "Citizenship and Gender," 47; Cahn, *Industry of Devotion,* 45; Wiesner, *Women and Gender,* 103; Davis, "Women in the Crafts," 188; Davis, *Society and Culture,* 126.

48. Fox-Genovese, "Women and Work," 123; Wiesner, *Women and Gender,* 95–96; Erler and Kowaleski, eds., *Women and Power,* 5; M. E. Perry, *Gender and Dis-order,* 32; Roper, *Holy Household,* 47.

49. Virginia DeJohn Anderson, "The Origins of New England Culture," *William and Mary Quarterly* 48 (1991): 234–35.

50. Gary M. Walton and James F. Shepherd, *The Economic Rise of Early America* (Cambridge: Cambridge University Press, 1979), 69, 71, 83, 85.

51. Carl Bridenbaugh, *Fat Mutton and Liberty of Conscience: Society in Rhode Island, 1636–1690* (Providence: Brown University Press, 1974), 56–57, 77–78.

52. Walton and Shepherd, *Economic Rise,* 159.

53. W. H. Crawford, "Women in the Domestic Linen Industry," in *Women in Early Modern Ireland,* ed. Margaret MacCurtain and Mary O'Dowd (Edinburgh: Ed-inburgh University Press, 1991), 255.

54. Walton and Shepherd, *Economic Rise,* 49.

55. Alice Clark, *Working Life of Women in the Seventeenth Century* (1919; reprint, London: Routledge and Kegan Paul, 1982), 221, 223; Judith Bennett, "The Village Ale Wife: Women and Brewing in Fourteenth-Century England," in *Women and Work,* ed. Hanawalt, 22.

56. Richard B. Morris, *Government and Labor in Early America* (1946; reprint, Boston: Northeastern University Press, 1981), 139–42, 387.

57. Roper, *Holy Household,* 49.

58. Howell, "Women, the Family Economy," 201, 204; Walter Newbury Shipping Book, NHS; Aaron Lopez Account Book, no. 767, "Taylor's and Spinners Book," NHS.

59. For evidence of decline in female political participation as societies matured, see Heath Dillard, "Women in Reconquest Castile," in *Women in Medieval Society,*

ed. Stuard, 84; Adrienne Rogers, "Women and Law," in Spencer, ed., *French Women and the Age of Enlightenment*, 7.

60. Stuard, *Women in Medieval Society*, 5; Prior, "Women and the Urban Economy," 110.

61. Fox-Genovese, "Women and Work," 120.

62. Gloria L. Main, "Gender, Work, and Wages in Colonial New England," *William and Mary Quarterly* 51 (1994): 64; Wiesner, *Women and Gender*, 87.

63. Erler and Kowaleski, eds., *Women and Power*, 4; Wemple, "Sanctity and Power," 141.

64. McNamara and Wemple, "Power of Women," 96; Stuard, "The Dominion of Gender," 161, 163, 164.

65. Wiesner, *Women and Gender*, 108; Davis, *Society and Culture*, 306; Davis, "Women in the Crafts," 185.

66. Philippe Ariès, *Centuries of Childhood: A Social History of Family Life* (Paris, 1960; New York: Random House, 1962), 354, 356. See also George Duby, *La société aux XI et XII siècles dans la région maconnaise* (Paris: SEVPEN, 1971), and P. Petiot, "La famille en France sous l'Ancien Régime," in *Sociologie comparée de la famille contemporaine, colloques du CNRS*, 1955.

67. Wiesner, *Women and Gender*, 33; Amussen, *Ordered Society*, 84–85.

68. Susan Staves, *Married Women's Separate Property in England, 1660–1833* (Cambridge: Harvard University Press, 1990), 4, 28, 30, 132, 135, 158–59.

69. Davis, *Society and Culture*, 126; A. Rogers, "Women and Law," 36, 43; Kowaleski, "Women's Work in a Market Town," 146; Marian K. Dale, "The London Silk Women of the Fifteenth Century," in *Sisters and Workers*, ed. Bennett et al., 31; Prior, "Women and the Urban Economy," 103.

70. A. Rogers, "Women and Law," 35; Wiesner, *Women and Gender*, 62, 99, 110.

71. Otis G. Hammond, ed., *New Hampshire Court Records, 1640–1692*, State Papers Series ([Concord]: State of New Hampshire, 1943), 40:226–27.

72. Wemple, "Sanctity and Power," 139.

73. Power, *Medieval Women*, 96.

74. King, *Women of the Renaissance*, 219–22.

75. Katherine Usher Henderson and Barbara F. McManus, *Half Humankind: Contexts and Texts about Women in England, 1540–1640* (Urbana: University of Illinois Press, 1985), 11.

76. King, *Women of the Renaissance*, 170–71.

77. Lerner, *Creation of Feminist Consciousness*, 199.

78. Martine Sonnet, "A Daughter to Educate," in Davis and Farge, eds. *History of Women* 3:116.

79. King, *Women of the Renaissance*, 168–69, 171; Barker-Benfield, *Culture of Sensibility*, xviii; Wiesner, *Women and Gender*, 119; Davis, *Society and Culture*, 73.

80. King, *Women of the Renaissance*, 174.

81. Lerner, *Feminist Consciousness*, 198–99; King, *Women of the Renaissance*, 112–13; Sonnet, "Daughter," 120.

82. Mary Astell, "A Serious Proposal to the Ladies . . . by a Lover of Her Sex"

(1694, 1697), in *First Feminists: British Women Writers, 1578–1799*, ed. Moira Ferguson (Bloomington: Indiana University Press; Old Westbury, N.Y.: Feminist Press, 1985), 181–90; King, *Women of the Renaissance*, 232–33.

83. Wiesner, *Women and Gender*, 86, 92; King, *Women of the Renaissance*, 72.

84. Fox-Genovese, "Women and Work," 118–19; Wiesner, *Women and Gender*, 94–96; Davis and Farge, eds., *History of Women* 3:120, 129.

85. Wiesner, *Women and Gender*, 95; Willen, "Women in the Public Sphere," 185–86; Fox-Genovese, "Women and Work," 121–22.

86. Merry E. Wiesner, "Spinning Out Capital: Women's Work in the Early Modern Economy," in *Becoming Visible*, ed. Bridenthal et al., 236; Wiesner, *Women and Gender*, 62.

87. Stuard, "The Dominion of Gender," 170; Hanawalt, ed., *Women and Work*, xv; Davis, "Women in the Crafts," 188.

88. Bolton, "Mulieres Sanctae," 144–45. For an interesting discussion of the effects of the depletion of Seville's male population in the sixteenth century, see M. E. Perry, *Gender and Disorder*, 97.

89. Wiesner, "Spinning Out Capital," 226. King, *Women of the Renaissance*, 114; Bridget Hill, *Women, Work, and Sexual Politics in Eighteenth-Century England* (Oxford: Blackwell, 1989), 225.

90. Stuard, "The Dominion of Gender," 167.

91. Hufton, "Women, Work, and Family," 26; Steven Ozment, *When Fathers Ruled: Family Life in Reformation Europe* (Cambridge: Harvard University Press, 1983), 1; J. A. Goldstone, "The Demographic Revolution in England: A Reexamination," *Population Studies* 49 (1986): 5–33; Hill, *Women, Work, and Sexual Politics*, 225.

92. Wiesner, *Women and Gender*, 62. Lyndal Roper maintains that this figure was 20 percent in Reformation Germany (*Holy Household*, 32).

93. Herlihy, *Opera Muliebria*, 134; King, *Women of the Renaissance*, 29; Roper, *Holy Household*, 50.

94. Wiesner, *Women and Gender*, 62.

95. Ibid., 189, 192.

96. Gary Nash, *The Urban Crucible: The Northern Seaports and the Origins of the American Revolution*, abridged ed. (Cambridge: Harvard University Press, 1986), 68, 117–22.

CHAPTER 2

1. Sarah Haggar Wheaten Osborn left memoirs that were edited and published by the Reverend Samuel Hopkins. See Samuel Hopkins, *Memoirs of the Life of Mrs. Sarah Osborn* (Catskill, N.Y.: N. Elliot, 1814), esp. 19, 50–53, 70–73, 76–77, 80–83. See also Mary Beth Norton, "'My Resting Reaping Times': Sarah Osborn's Defense of Her 'Unfeminine' Activities, 1767," *Signs: Journal of Women in Culture and Society* 2 (winter 1976): 515–29; Sheryl A. Kujawa, "The Great Awakening of Sarah Osborn and

the Female Society of the First Congregational Church in Newport," *Newport History* 65 (spring 1994): 133–53.

2. Sarah Osborn to Joseph Fish, undated, Sarah Osborn Papers, American Antiquarian Society, Worcester, Mass. (hereafter abbreviated as AAS).

3. Sarah Osborn to Joseph Fish, 3 June 1751, Osborn Papers, AAS.

4. Sarah Osborn to Joseph Fish, 28 February–7 March 1767, in Norton, "Resting, Reaping Times," 523, 527, 528.

5. Sarah Osborn to Joseph Fish, undated, Osborn Papers, AAS.

6. Retha M. Warnicke, *Women of the English Renaissance and Reformation* (Westport, Conn: Greenwood Press, 1983), 167, 194.

7. Ibid., 171; Jacqueline Eales, "Samuel Clarke and the 'Lives' of Godly Women," in *Women in the Church,* ed. W. J. Sheils and Diana Wood (Oxford: Blackwell, 1990), 374; Marie B. Rowlands, "Recusant Women, 1560–1640," in *Women in English Society, 1500–1800,* ed. Mary Prior (London: Methuen, 1985), 150–51; Keith Thomas, "Women and the Civil War Sects," *Past and Present* 13 (April 1958): 45.

8. Charmarie Jenkins Blaisdell, "Women in the Lutheran and Calvinist Movements," in *Triumph over Silence: Women in Protestant History,* ed. Richard Greaves (Westport, Conn.: Greenwood Press, 1985), 20, 17; Phyllis Mack, "Women as Prophets during the English Civil War," *Feminist Studies* 8 (spring 1982): 22.

9. Susan Wabuda, "Shunamites and Nurses of the English Reformation: The Activities of Mary Glover, Niece of Hugh Latimer," in *Women in the Church,* ed. Sheils and Wood, 343; Eales, "Samuel Clarke," 374; Mack, "Women as Prophets," 28.

10. Thomas, "Women and the Civil War Sects," 46; Francis J. Bremer, *The Puritan Experiment* (New York: St. Martin's Press, 1976), 47–49; T. J. Wertenbaker, *The Puritan Oligarchy: The Founding of American Civilization* (New York: Grosset and Dunlap, 1947), 29.

11. Mack, "Women as Prophets," 24–25; Anne Laurence, "A Priesthood of She-Believers: Women and Congregations in Mid-Seventeenth-Century England," in *Women in the Church,* ed. Sheils and Wood, 363.

12. Clare Cross, "The Religious Life of Women in Sixteenth-Century Yorkshire," in *Women in the Church,* ed. Sheils and Wood, 313–15, 320; Rowlands, "Recusant Women," 167–72.

13. Gloria Main, "Naming Children in Early New England, 1620–1795," paper presented to the Philadelphia Center for Early American Studies, 7 April 1995, p. 19 and table 8; Mary was the most popular New England name for daughters long before William and Mary ascended the throne. English naming patterns for girls were remarkably similar. See Scott Smith-Bannister, *Names and Naming Patterns in England 1538–1700* (New York: Oxford University Press, 1997), chap. 8. See also Eamon Duffy, "Holy Maydens, Holy Wyfes: the Cult of Women Saints in Fifteenth and Sixteenth Century England," in *Women in the Church,* ed. Sheils and Wood, 178, 180, 186–87, 189–90, 192, 196.

14. "A View of Popishe Abuses Yet Remaining in the English Church for the Which Godly Ministers Have Refused to Subscribe," in *Puritan Manifestoes: A Study of the Origin of the Puritan Revolt,* ed. W. H. Frere and C. E. Douglas (New York:

Burt Franklin, 1907, 1972), 21, 26; Greaves, *Triumph over Silence*, 5. Evidence suggests that Puritan parents felt a strong need to baptize their children; see David D. Hall, *Worlds of Wonder, Days of Judgment: Popular Religious Belief in Early New England* (New York: Knopf, 1989), 153–54. Benjamin Colman to Robert Wodrow, 9 December 1717, in Neil Caplan, ed., "Some Unpublished Letters of Benjamin Colman, 1717–1725," *Massachusetts Historical Society Proceedings* 77 (1965): 107.

15. William Coster, "Purity, Profanity, and Puritanism: The Churching of Women, 1500–1700," in *Women in the Church*, ed. Sheils and Wood, 377; Patricia Crawford, *Women and Religion in England, 1500–1720* (London: Routledge, 1993), 55.

16. New England clergymen might also draw on European tradition in ways that were antithetical to Puritanism. The Reverend Samuel Skelton, first minister of the First Church of Salem, forced women to wear veils after 1630 "under penalty of non-communion, urging the same as a matter of duty and absolute necessity." This practice was eschewed by English dissenters as demeaning to women. William Hubbard, *A General History of New England from the Discovery to 1680*, 2d ed. (Boston: Little and Brown, 1848), in *Massachusetts Historical Society Collections*, 2d series (Boston, 1848), 5:117; Christine Alice Young, *From 'Good Order' to Glorious Revolution in Salem, Massachusetts, 1628–1689* (Ann Arbor: UMI Research Press, 1978, 1980), 56; Frere, ed., *Puritan Manifestoes*, 21.

17. John Winthrop, *Winthrop's Journal: History of New England, 1630–1649*, ed. James K. Hosmer (New York: Scribners, 1908), 1:168 (1635/1636); Kenneth Silverman, *The Life and Times of Cotton Mather* (New York: Harper and Row, 1984), 379.

18. Marian C. Donnelly, *The New England Meetinghouses of the Seventeenth Century* (Middletown, Conn.: Wesleyan University Press, 1968), 10, 14, 39; John F. Martin, *Profits in the Wilderness: Entrepreneurship and the Founding of New England Towns in the Seventeenth Century* (Chapel Hill: University of North Carolina Press, 1991), appendix 2, pp. 311–15.

19. Donnelly, *New England Meetinghouses*, 16, 101; Edmund W. Sinnott, *Meetinghouse and Church in Early New England* (New York: McGraw-Hill, 1963), 5.

20. Perry Miller, *Errand into the Wilderness* (Cambridge: Harvard University Press, 1956, 1984), 142.

21. Roger G. Kennedy, *American Churches* (New York: Crossroad, 1982), 156–57, 188, 190; Donnelly, *New England Meetinghouses*, 106.

22. Margaret Aston, "Segregation in Church," in *Women in the Church*, ed. Sheils and Wood, 242, 263, 290, 281.

23. Peter Mallary and Tim Imrie, *New England Churches and Meetinghouses, 1680–1830* (New York: Vendôme Press, 1985), 30; Donnelly, *New England Meetinghouses*, 69; Kennedy, *American Churches*, 192; Sinnott, *Meetinghouse and Church*, 33; Records of the Town of Portsmouth, 1645–1713, vol. 1, part 2, pp. 305–8 (1693–94), Portsmouth Public Library, Portsmouth, N.H.

24. For seating shifts in Gloucester's First Parish, see Christine Leigh Heyrman, *Commerce and Culture: The Maritime Communities of Colonial Massachusetts, 1690–1750* (New York: Norton, 1984), 147–49. M. Halsey Thomas, ed., *The Diary of Samuel*

Sewall (New York: Farrar, Straus and Giroux, 1973), 2:993; Richard D. Pierce, ed., *Records of the First Church of Boston, 1630–1868* (Boston: Colonial Society of Massachusetts, 1961), 1:153, 163, 258; Hamilton A. Hill, *History of the Old South Church, Boston, 1669–1884* (Boston: Houghton Mifflin, 1890), 1:348; Second and Seventh Church Records (Boston), vol. 5A, Massachusetts Historical Society, Boston, Mass. (hereafter abbreviated as MHS); Mallary and Imrie, *New England Churches,* 50; First Congregational Church Records (Newport, 1743–1831), vol. 333 (1753), NHS; George C. Mason, *Annals of Trinity Church, Newport, Rhode Island, 1698–1821* (Newport, R.I.: Evans Printing House, 1890), 1:126–27; William Bentley, *The Diary of William Bentley, D.D.* (Salem, Mass.: EI, 1905; reprint, Gloucester, Mass.: Peter Smith, 1962), 1:4; "Plat of the Pews below Stairs in the Second Congregational Church [Newport], and Names of Owners" (1803), Second Congregational Church Records (Newport), box 205, NHS; Trinity Church (Newport) Record Book (1731–1805), p. 121 (1772); East Church (Salem) Record Book, vol. 2 (1757–93), esp. 1769, EI; Records of the Town of Portsmouth, 1645–1713, vol. 1, part 2, pp. 305–8 (1693–94), Portsmouth Public Library, Portsmouth, N.H.

25. Salem's First Congregational Church was founded in 1629; Boston's in 1630. John Clarke founded the First Baptist Church in Newport in or about 1644 according to William McLoughlin, and in 1648 according to Ezra Stiles; see William G. McLoughlin, *New England Dissent, 1630–1833: The Baptists and the Separation of Church and State* (Cambridge: Harvard University Press, 1971), 1:11, and Elaine Forman Crane, *A Dependent People: Newport, Rhode Island, in the Revolutionary Era* (New York: Fordham University Press, 1985), 131, table 6, for a list of Newport churches and dates of founding as reported by Ezra Stiles. See also Richard Gildrie, *Salem, Massachusetts, 1626–1683: A Covenant Community* (Charlottesville: University Press of Virginia, 1975), 14; Nathaniel Bouton, ed., *Documents and Records Relating to the Province of New-Hampshire from the Earliest Period of Its Settlement,* vol. 1 (1623–86) (Concord, N.H.: George E. Jenks, 1867), 108–13.

26. Gildrie, *Salem, Massachusetts,* 53; Pierce, ed., *First Church of Boston,* 1:xix; William H. Upham, ed., "Beverly First Church Records," *Essex Institute Historical Collections* 35 (1899): 178, 183; Second Congregational Church (Newport), 1728, vol. 838B, p. 54, NHS.

27. For examples of exceptions see Mary Maples Dunn, "Saints and Sisters: Congregational and Quaker Women in the Early Colonial Period," *American Quarterly* 30 (1978): 582–601; Gerald Moran, "'Sisters' in Christ: Women and the Church in Seventeenth-Century New England," in *Women in American Religion,* ed. Janet Wilson James (Philadelphia: University of Pennsylvania Press, 1980), 47–67; Richard D. Shiels, "The Feminization of American Congregationalism, 1730–1835," *American Quarterly* 33 (1981): 46–62; Susan Juster, *Disorderly Women: Sexual Politics and Evangelicalism in Revolutionary New England* (Ithaca: Cornell University Press, 1994); Rosemary Skinner Keller, "New England Women: Ideology and Experience in First Generation Puritanism," in *Women and Religion in America,* vol. 2, *The Colonial and Revolutionary Periods,* ed. Rosemary Radford Ruether and Rosemary Skinner Keller (San Francisco: Harper and Row, 1983), 132–92.

28. See Dunn, "Saints and Sisters," Moran, "'Sisters' in Christ," and Shiels, "Feminization of American Congregationalism," passim.

29. Patricia Crawford, *Women and Religion in England,* 143, notes that in most of the English separatist congregations women outnumbered men by the mid-seventeenth century, sometimes by a ratio of 2:1.

30. Moran, "'Sisters' in Christ," 50; Dunn, "Saints and Sisters," 35–36; Edmund S. Morgan, *The Gentle Puritan: A Life of Ezra Stiles* (Chapel Hill: University of North Carolina Press, 1962), 188; Second and Seventh Church Records (Boston), 1:63–82, MHS; First Baptist Church (Newport, 1644–1864), Roll of Members, vol. 1169, NHS; Seventh Day Baptist Records (Newport), 1708–1817, vol. 1400, p. 7, NHS; First Congregational Church (Newport), 1721, box 40, folder 1, NHS; Second Baptist Church Records (Newport), vol. 1656, NHS; Franklin B. Dexter, ed., *The Literary Diary of Ezra Stiles* (New York: Scribners, 1901), 1:145. There were curious exceptions. The First Baptist Church of Boston admitted more men than women in nearly every year between 1665 and 1758. Between the latter year and the Revolution, more women than men were admitted (78/55), but the males probably retained their overall numerical superiority. First Baptist Church Records (Boston), MHS; East Church (Salem) MS I, Misc. 1707–1804 (esp. 1718), EI.

31. "Scituate and Barnstable Church Records," in *New England Historical and Genealogical Register* 10 (1856), 40; Pierce, ed., *First Church of Boston,* 22, 26; James F. Hunnewell, ed., *Records of the First Church in Charlestown, Massachusetts, 1632–1789* (Boston, 1880), v; Upham, ed., "Beverly First Church Records," *Essex Institute Historical Collections* 36 (1900): 303. Communicants were recognized as "visible saints"—men and women who had achieved salvation and had been accepted as church members.

32. Crawford, *Women and Religion in England,* 144–47.

33. "Records of the Congregational Church in Topsfield," copied by George F. Dow, *Topsfield Historical Society Collections* 14 (1909): 12. Benjamin Colman to Robert Wodrow, 23 January 1719, in Niel Caplan, ed., "Some Unpublished Letters of Benjamin Colman, 1717–1725," *Massachusetts Historical Society Proceedings* 77 (1965): 110–11. Pierce, ed., *First Church of Boston,* 1:160, 191, 192.

34. First Congregational Church Records (Essex, Mass.), 1752–1878, EI; "Byfield Parish Records, 1706–1762," *Essex Institute Historical Collections* 89 (1953): 165–66; Martin, *Profits in the Wilderness,* 218–19, 277–80, 283–84.

35. Robert G. Pope, ed., *The Notebook of the Reverend John Fiske, 1644–1675* (Salem, Mass.: EI, 1974), 57, 64–65; Hill, *Old South Church,* 1:28.

36. Hill, *Old South Church,* 1:83–84, 163.

37. Trinity Church (Newport) Record Book (1731–1805), NHS; First Baptist Church (Newport) Record Book, p. 51, NHS; Stiles, *Literary Diary,* 1:145; Juster, *Disorderly Women,* 7, 11, 124ff.

38. Winthrop, *Journal,* 1:107; Thomas Lechford, *Plain Dealing, or News from New England* (1641; New York: Johnson Reprint Corp., 1969), 18–19, 22.

39. Gildrie, *Salem, Massachusetts,* 53; Lechford, *Plain Dealing,* 23; R. Pope, ed., *Notebook of John Fiske,* 4, 106; Dunn, "Saints and Sisters," 34.

40. Charles H. Pope, transcriber, *Records of the First Church at Dorchester in New England, 1636–1734* (Boston: G. H. Ellis, 1891), 67; *Plymouth Church Records, 1620–1859* (Boston: Colonial Society of Massachusetts, 1920), 22:201.

41. C. Pope, trans., *First Church at Dorchester,* 55; R. Pope, ed., *Notebook of John Fiske,* 86.

42. Gildrie, *Salem, Massachusetts,* 53; Pierce, ed., *First Church of Boston,* 1:46.

43. "Danvers Church Records," *New England Historical and Genealogical Register* 11 (1857): 133–34; *Plymouth Church Records,* 22:164.

44. "Proceedings of Excommunication against Mistress Ann Hibbens of Boston (1640)," in *Remarkable Providences,* ed. John Demos (New York: Braziller, 1972), 224.

45. The records go on to say that the congregation concurred unanimously with the church in calling the Reverend Mather Byles to be their pastor; Eighth Church Records (Boston), MHS.

46. Laurence, "Priesthood of She-Believers," 363; Crawford, *Women and Religion in England,* 143; Winthrop, *Journal,* 1:110.

47. *The Manifesto Church: Records of the Church in Brattle Square, Boston, 1699–1872* (Boston: Benevolent Fraternity of Churches, 1902), vii–viii.

48. Ibid., 67.

49. Ibid., 71.

50. Benjamin Colman, *Gospel Order Revived, Being an Answer to a Book Lately set forth by the Reverend Increase Mather by Sundry Ministers of the Gospel in New-England* ([New York]: William Bradford, 1700), 19, 20.

51. John Higginson and Nicholas Noyes to the "Undertakers" of the Brattle Street Church, 19 November 1699, reprinted in Samuel K. Lothrop, *A History of the Church in Brattle Street, Boston* (Boston, 1851), 34.

52. Benjamin Colman to Robert Wodrow, 23 January 1719, in Caplan, ed., "Letters of Benjamin Colman," 110–11.

53. *Plymouth Church Records,* 22:160, 174; Eighth Church Records (Boston), MHS.

54. Andrew Oliver and James Bishop Peabody, eds., *The Records of Trinity Church, Boston,* 2 vols. (Boston: Colonial Society of Massachusetts, 1980), 1:55–60, 80, 81, 86, 104–5.

55. Richard D. Pierce, ed., *The Records of the First Church in Salem, Massachusetts, 1629–1736* (Salem, Mass.: EI, 1974), xiii–xiv; East Congregational Church Records, 29 May 1783, EI.

56. Trinity Church (Newport) Record Book, NHS; Stiles, *Literary Diary,* 1:147.

57. Seventh Day Baptist Church (Newport) Records, vol. 1400, p. 4, NHS; Second Baptist Church (Newport) Records, vol. 1657, p. 25, NHS.

58. Stiles, *Literary Diary,* 1:146.

59. Ibid., 146–47; Second Baptist Church (Newport) Records, vol. 1657, NHS.

60. Friends Monthly Meeting (Newport) Records, 1676–1707, vol. 1936, NHS.

61. Friends Women's Monthly Meeting (Newport) Records, vol. 814 (1759–84), pp. 77, 93, 106–7, NHS. See also vol. 813 (1690–1759).

62. Benjamin Colman to Robert Wodrow, 9 December 1717, in Caplan, ed.,

"Letters of Benjamin Colman," 107; "Records of the Fifth Parish of Gloucester, Now Rockport," *Essex Institute Historical Collections* 21 (1884): 158, 226, 234.

63. R. Pope, ed., *Notebook of John Fiske,* 107.

64. First Congregational Church of Essex, formerly Second Congregation of Ipswich, Miscellaneous Records, 1705–1927, folder marked 1705–1815, EI. This admission policy seems to have been in effect in 1763/64.

65. Pierce, ed., *First Church in Salem,* 146 (1687); R. Pope, ed., *Notebook of John Fiske,* 186; Second and Seventh Church (Boston) Records, vol. 3, MHS; Seventh Day Baptist (Newport) Records, vol. 1400, p. 37, NHS.

66. C. Pope, trans., *First Church at Dorchester,* 72–73.

67. *Plymouth Church Records,* 22:150.

68. First Congregational Church (Essex, Mass.) Records, 1725–1869, pp. 9, 52–53, EI. Seventeen women signed by their mark, as did three men.

69. Hopkins, *Memoirs of the Life of Mrs. Sarah Osborn,* 50, 52, 70–73.

70. Sheryl A. Kujawa, "The Great Awakening of Sarah Osborn and the Female Society of the First Congregational Church in Newport," *Newport History* 65 (spring 1994): 146; Stiles, *Literary Diary,* 1:44 (1770).

71. "Danvers Church Records," *New England Historical and Genealogical Register* 11 (1857): 319.

72. Ibid.

73. See Pierce, ed., *First Church of Boston,* 1:32–33, for reference to a committee composed of brethren and sisters (1640); Friends Monthly Meeting (Newport) Records, vol. 1936, passim.

74. Ibid., vol. 814, p. 119.

75. Seventh Day Baptist Church (Newport) Records, vol. 1400 (1721/2), p. 52, vol. 2052 (1692–1836), p. 71 (1699), NHS.

76. Ibid., vol. 1400 (1718, 1772), pp. 4, 136; Friends Women's Monthly Meeting (Newport) Records, vol. 813 (1721), NHS.

77. Gerda Lerner quite rightly maintains that the hegemony of patriarchal thought is due not to its superiority but rather to the systematic silencing of other voices. Gerda Lerner, *The Creation of Feminist Consciousness: From the Middle Ages to 1870* (New York: Oxford University Press, 1993), 281–82.

78. Pierce, ed., *First Church of Boston,* 1:32–33, 37.

79. Ibid., 1:22, 25, 62, 70.

80. "Scituate and Barnstable Church Records," *New England Historical and Genealogical Register* 10 (1856): 41; Daniel Appleton White, *New England Congregationalism in Its Origin and Purity: Illustrated by the Foundation and Early Records of the First Church in Salem and Various Discussions Pertaining to the Subject* (Salem, Mass., 1861), 28–29; Pierce, ed., *First Church of Boston,* 1:55; C. Pope, ed., *First Church at Dorchester,* 51.

81. George Francis Dow, ed., *Records and Files of the Quarterly Courts of Essex County, Massachusetts, 1638–1683* (Salem, Mass.: EI, 1911–21), 1:68, 99.

82. Dow, ed., *Essex County Quarterly Courts,* 2:314, 190, 221, 8:367.

83. Ibid., 1:99, 58.

84. Laurence, "Priesthood of She-Believers," 352–57.

85. Winthrop, *Journal*, 1:234.

86. Friends Monthly Meeting Records (Newport), 1739–73, vol. 809, passim, NHS; Pierce, ed., *First Church of Boston*, passim; Pierce, ed., *First Church in Salem*, 153 (1681).

87. Nathaniel B. Shurtleff, ed., *Records of the Governor and Company of the Massachusetts Bay in New England* (Boston: William White, 1853–54), vol. 4 (part 1), p. 52 (1651).

88. File "Containing matters relating to church affairs in Ipswich" (1729–33), AAS; Pierce, ed., *First Congregational Church in Salem*, 153.

89. In 1644 the Reverends Norris and Sharp from Salem opposed separate dismissals. A controversy erupted over this issue when it was noted that the sisters had not requested their dismissal. See R. Pope, ed., *Notebook of John Fiske*, 6, 14–15, 17, 19; see also Pierce, ed., *First Church of Boston*, 1:23; R. Pope, ed., *Notebook of John Fiske*, 14–15, 19; White, *New England Congregationalism*, 33 [1637?]; Pierce, ed., *First Church in Salem*, 228.

90. "Danvers Church Records," *New England Historical and Genealogical Register* 11:321; C. Pope, ed., *First Church at Dorchester*, 61–62.

91. Upham, ed., "Beverly First Church Records," *Essex Institute Historical Collections* 35 (1899): 178; Pierce, ed., *First Church in Salem*, 158, 225, 262, 264, 228.

92. Laurel Ulrich, *Good Wives: Image and Reality in the Lives of Women in Northern New England, 1650–1750* (New York: Knopf, 1982), 218–19; Hill, *Old South Church*, 1:164–65.

93. "Petition to the Brethren of the North Church Meeting at the Old House," Misc. Bound Petitions (Church), 22 January 1741/2; Second and Seventh Church (Boston) Records, vol. 6, MHS.

94. Dow, ed., *Essex County Quarterly Courts*, 2:218, 220, 225, 264, 314–15.

95. Juster, *Disorderly Women*, 99.

96. Winthrop, *Journal*, 1:286–87.

97. Shurtleff, *Records*, 3:413 (1656); vol. 4 (part 1), p. 272 (1656).

98. First Baptist Church (Newport) Records, vol. 1167, p. 23, NHS.

99. Hill, *Old South Church*, 1:51; Seventh Day Baptist Church (Newport) Records, vol. 1400, pp. 87, 104, (1734, 1738), NHS; First Congregational Church (Newport), vol. 832, p. 108 (1773), NHS. Second Baptist Church (Newport) Records, vol. 1657, p. 30, NHS; Stephen P. Sharples, *Records of the Church of Christ at Cambridge in New England, 1632–1830* (Boston: E. Putnam, 1906), 252.

100. Dow, ed., *Essex County Quarterly Courts*, 2:108, 193, 216, 220, 225, 264, 314–15, 155. To put the fine in perspective, it is notable that each absence brought a fifty-shilling penalty, while assault and attempted rape resulted in a forty-shilling punishment.

101. "A Short Story of the Rise, Reign and Ruin of the Antinomians," in Winthrop, *Journal*, 1:250 (n.d.)

102. Upham, ed., "Beverly First Church Records," *Essex Institute Historical Collections* 35 (1899): 192; Pierce, ed., *First Church of Boston*, 1:208, 210.

103. King's Chapel (Boston) Records: Wardens and Vestry Records, 1686–1919, box 1, vol. 16 (1724), MHS; Second Baptist Church (Newport) Records, vol. 1657, p. 35, NHS; Second and Seventh Church (Boston) Records, vol. 12A, MHS.

104. "Byfield Parish Records, 1706–1762," *Essex Institute Historical Collections* 89 (1953): 163–94; First Congregational Church (Newport) Records, vol. 333 (1753), NHS; "Truro Church Records," *Mayflower Descendant* 30 (1932): 156.

105. King's Chapel (Boston) Records, box 1, vol. 16, MHS; Oliver, ed., *Trinity Church*, 188.

106. Seventh Church (Boston) Records, vol. 12, p. 17, MHS; *Manifesto Church*, 24.

107. Sharples, *Church of Christ at Cambridge*, 180.

108. Hill, *Old South Church*, 1:418.

109. Friends Women's Monthly Meeting (Newport), vol. 814, p. 170; *Plymouth Church Records*, 22:360, 361.

110. Hill, *Old South Church*, 1:382; Friends Women's Monthly Meeting (Newport), vol. 814, p. 62; Bentley, *Diary*, 1:48.

111. Pierce, ed., *First Church of Boston*, 1:120; Upham, ed., "Beverly First Church Records," *Essex Institute Historical Collections* 36 (1900): 305 [1732/3]; Records "Containing matters relating to church affairs in Ipswich" (1734), AAS; Pierce, ed., *First Church in Salem*, 190; "First Church: Handwritten copies of Church Records, 1629–1772" (Salem), by Thomas Barnard, pastor, 1755–72, p. 45 (1703), EI.

112. Pierce, ed., *First Church of Boston*, 1:155; Hill, *Old South Church*, 1:133; C. Pope, ed., *First Church at Dorchester*, 67.

113. *Watertown Records Comprising East Congregational and Precinct Affairs, 1697–1737* (Boston: Watertown Historical Society, 1906), 111; Second Congregational Church (Newport), vol. 836F, p. 45 (1766), NHS.

114. Second Baptist Church (Newport) Records, vol. 1657, p. 21.

115. Stiles, *Literary Diary*, 1:147.

116. Gerald F. Moran, "'The Hidden Ones': Women and Religion in Puritan New England," in *Triumph over Silence*, ed. Greaves, 138.

117. Friends Women's Monthly Meeting (Newport), vol. 814, pp. 124, 131 (1775) NHS.

118. Ibid., pp. 165, 224–25, 72, 106–7, 211, NHS.

119. Ibid., p. 127, NHS.

120. Pierce, ed., *First Church of Boston*, 1:32–33 and passim. Although Baptist women were not named to committees, there may have been informal meetings of men and women considerably later in time: "a privat meeting of Several of the Brethren and Sisters" reconciled differences between members (Seventh Day Baptist [Newport] Records, vol. 1400, p. 37 [1700], NHS). Ibid., vol. 2052, pp. 91, 155–57.

121. Pierce, ed., *First Church of Boston*, 1:57ff; Hill, *Old South Church*, passim; Second and Seventh Church (Boston) Records, vol. 12, MHS; "Danvers Church Records," *New England Historical and Genealogical Register* 12:248 (1729).

122. Pierce, ed., *First Church of Boston* 1:13; Hunnewell, ed., *First Church in Charlestown*, 8, 9, 134, 135; Sharples, *Church of Christ at Cambridge*, 36.

123. Upham, ed., "Beverly First Church Records," *Essex Institute Historical Collections* 41 (1905): 219 (1772); "Records of the First Church in Marshfield, Massachusetts," *Mayflower Descendant* 11 (1909): 37.

124. Carole Shammas, "Anglo-American Household Government in Historical Perspective," *William and Mary Quarterly* 52 (1995): 120.

125. David Konig, *Law and Authority in Puritan Massachusetts: Essex County, 1629–1692* (Chapel Hill: University of North Carolina Press, 1979), 126.

126. Patricia Bonomi, *Under the Cope of Heaven: Religion, Society, and Politics in Colonial America* (New York: Oxford University Press, 1986), 8, 9.

127. William McLoughlin, *Revivals, Awakenings, and Reform* (Chicago: University of Chicago Press, 1978), 57, 54, 51.

128. Second Congregational Church (Newport) Records, vol. 836F, p. 47 (1771), NHS.

129. For the ways in which religion fueled female activism in the Revolutionary era, see Laurel Thatcher Ulrich, "'Daughters of Liberty': Religious Women in Revolutionary New England," in *Women in the Age of the American Revolution*, ed. Ronald Hoffman and Peter J. Albert (Charlottesville: University Press of Virginia, 1989), 211–43, and Elaine Forman Crane, "Religion and Rebellion: Women of Faith in the American War for Independence," in *Religion in a Revolutionary Age*, ed. Ronald Hoffman and Peter J. Albert (Charlottesville: University Press of Virginia, 1994), 52–86.

CHAPTER 3

1. For records relating to Horod Long, see John R. Bartlett, ed., *Records of the Colony of Rhode Island and Providence Plantations in New England (1636–1792)* (Providence: A. Crawford Greene and Brother, 1856), 2:99–105, 119–20, 126.

2. *Rhode Island Court Records: Records of the Court of Trials of the Colony of Providence Plantations* (Providence: RIHS, 1922), 1:13 (1655).

3. *R.I. Court Records,* 2:65, 70 (1668).

4. *Newport Mercury,* 3 August 1772.

5. William H. Whitmore, ed., *The Colonial Laws of Massachusetts Reprinted from the Edition of 1672, with the Supplements through 1686* (Boston: S. Greene, 1887), 141.

6. Stephen Innes notes that in seventeenth-century England gender lines were blurred to the extent that men would spin. He says there is no evidence of this task being performed by men in the North American colonies (Innes, paper delivered at Columbia University Seminar in Early American History, 13 December 1983).

7. For a starting place in the literature of separate spheres see Linda K. Kerber, "Separate Spheres, Female Worlds, Woman's Place: The Rhetoric of Women's History," *Journal of American History* 75 (1988–89): 9–39. Carole Shammas convincingly demonstrates that Americans—particularly urban Americans—spent a considerable part of their income on textiles (Carole Shammas, *The Pre-industrial Consumer in England and America* [Oxford: Clarendon Press, 1990], 64–65. Charles Brockden

Brown, *Alcuin: A Dialogue* (New York, 1798; Northampton, Mass.: Gehenna Press, 1970), 29.

8. Some historians will go so far as to argue the importance of the domestic economy in preindustrial North America, but fall short of recognizing the role of women as a feature of that economy. See Peter D. Hall, "Family Structure and Economic Organization: Massachusetts Merchants, 1700–1850," in *Family and Kin in Urban Communities, 1700–1930,* ed. Tamara K. Hareven (New York: New Viewpoints, 1977), 39 and passim. John McCusker, while recognizing that "the household was the predominant unit of production," includes very little about female participation in that production (John McCusker and Russell R. Menard, *The Economy of British America, 1607–1789* [Chapel Hill: University of North Carolina Press, 1985], 246, 53n.

9. Timothy Burbank/Hannah Collins diaries, EI. Collins was no match for midwife Patience Turner of Newport, however, who delivered 2,782 infants between 1746 and 1762; see Sylvia Frey and Marian Norton, eds., *New World, New Roles: A Documentary History of Women in Pre-Industrial America* (Westport, Conn.: Greenwood Press, 1986), 166–67.

10. Lists of people holding licenses in Boston; see James Otis Sr. Collection, Hancock Collection, and Miscellaneous Bound, MHS. Henry Channing was seventy-five when he recorded this information in 1835. His parents were John Channing (1714–71) and Mary Chaloner Robinson Channing (1721–90). "Particulars furnished by Henry Channing respecting his father and mother in 1835," in *Notes Concerning the Channing Family,* collected by Edward Tyrrel Channing (Boston, 1895), 4, 5; Gibbs-Channing Family Records, box 2048, NHS.

11. Assessment List of £3110 Lawful Money . . . by Order of the General Assembly . . . of Rhode Island . . . 1760, Rhode Island State Archives, Providence; Tax assessment for the town of Newport, 1772, NHS; *James Coggeshall v. Walter Cranston, John Smith and Temperance Grant* (1747), in Jane Fiske, comp., "Gleanings from the Newport Court Files," unpublished manuscript, New England Historic Genealogical Society, Boston, 301. See also Patricia A. Cleary, "'She Merchants' of Colonial America: Women and Commerce on the Eve of Revolution," Ph.D. diss., Northwestern University, 1989.

12. William Waine receipt book, 1728–44, AAS; Aaron Lopez "Tailors and Spinners Book," nos. 767 and 715 (passim), NHS.

13. Samuel Grant account book, 1737–60, AAS; Sarah Osborn to Joseph Fish, 3 June 1751, Osborn Papers, AAS.

14. Thomas Robinson, account book, spermaceti, 1762–70, box 1 (new acquisition); Thomas Robinson, account book of whale oil business, 5 October 1770–1772, box 3 (new acquisition); Thomas Robinson, account book, 1753–94, NHS. For many years Robinson had been a member of an intercolonial group of merchants who described themselves as manufacturers of spermaceti candles and who monopolized the trade in headmatter. Robinson's operation may have been similar to that of the Brown family of Providence. The Browns ran a spermaceti candle works that employed over two-hundred spinners in the early 1770s, the vast majority of whom were female. *Commerce of Rhode Island,* 2 vols., MHS Collections, 7th series, vol. 9 (Bos-

ton: MHS, 1914), 1:97–98, 137–38; Brown Family Business Records, Accounts, Spermaceti Candle Works, 1771–83, B.1 F.2, John Carter Brown Library, Brown University. I am indebted to Catherine Osborne DeCesare, a doctoral candidate at Providence College, for drawing my attention to the Browns' candle manufactory.

15. Isaac Stelle Ledger Book, 1741–64, p. 47, NHS; "An Account of the Number of Families and Inhabitants of the Town of Newport, 1774," Rhode Island State Archives.

16. The heading is a quotation from the *Newport Mercury,* 18 December 1767. Claudia Goldin has estimated the ratio of female to male full-time earnings at 0.288 for agriculture in 1815 and at 0.371–0.303 for manufacturing in 1820, a ratio that improves in the early years of industrialization (at least for young, unmarried women). Claudia Goldin, *Understanding the Gender Gap: An Economic History of American Women* (New York: Oxford University Press, 1990), 60. See also Gloria L. Main, "Gender, Work, and Wages in Colonial New England," *William and Mary Quarterly* 51 (1994): 48 (table 3). In general, Main's figures are congruent with Goldin's, although Main suggests the income gap may have started to close in the decade before the Revolution.

17. According to Jackson T. Main, the daily wage in New England before the Revolution averaged about 2s currency or 1s 8d stg. per day without food or lodging (Jackson T. Main, *The Social Structure of Revolutionary America* [Princeton: Princeton University Press, 1965], 70). This study has not converted currency to a common denominator. Rhode Island, for example, used old and new tenor to calculate wages and prices. The ratio of old tenor to new tenor was approximately 25:1. For additional information on wages see McCusker and Menard, *Economy of British America,* and Nash, *Urban Crucible.* Engs Family Papers, box 198, folder 5, NHS; Dow, ed., *Essex County Quarterly Courts,* 8 (1680–83), p. 279; Aaron Lopez "Stitchers Book," 1769, NHS; Nathaniel Rogers notebook, 1746–76, MHS. All comparisons are in local currency.

18. Stevens Family account book, pp. 28, 16, AAS; Thomas Richardson petty account book, 1722–54, pp. 38, 43, NHS; John Banister cash book, 1747–51, NHS; Jonathan Easton ledger, 1749–66, pp. 90, 88, NHS; James Taylor account book no. 498, p. 19, NHS; William Engs, ledger B, NHS.

19. James Taylor account book no. 498, pp. 19, 59, NHS.

20. Jonathan Easton ledger, 1749–66, p. 153, NHS; Isaac Stelle daybook, no. 1496, 1755–61, p. 183, NHS; Thomas Richardson, petty account book, 1722–54, pp. 61, 70 (Richardson's entries continue until 1770); Aaron Lopez papers, box 177, folder 1, NHS. Widespread slave ownership by white women in Bermuda was a means of economic security; see Elaine Forman Crane, "The Socioeconomics of a Female Majority in Eighteenth-Century Bermuda," *Signs: Journal of Women in Culture and Society* 15 (winter 1990): 243, 245–47.

21. Robert Gibbs ledger, 1660–1708, AAS; Selectmen's Records, Salem, Mass., pp. 85–93, 712, 717, 743–50, box 4, folder 6, EI.

22. Jabez Carpenter ledger, 1755–72, pp. 94, 115.

23. Main, "Gender, Work, and Wages," 48 (table 3); Congregational Church Records (Newport), box 40, folder 3, NHS; Jonathan Easton ledger, 1749–66. NHS.

24. Elaine Forman Crane, *A Dependent People: Newport, Rhode Island, in the Revolutionary Era* (New York: Fordham University Press, 1985), 69 and n. 80; Merry E. Wiesner, *Women and Gender in Early Modern Europe* (Cambridge: Cambridge University Press, 1993), 87.

25. Isaac W. Hammond, ed., *Miscellaneous Provincial and State Papers, 1725–1800* (Manchester, N.H.: John B. Clarke, 1890), 18:225. Eight of the fifteen women signed with their "mark" rather than a signature.

26. Abner Goodell, *Acts and Resolves, Public and Private, of the Province of Massachusetts Bay* (Boston: Wright and Potter, 1869–1922), 1:213, 258; the clause about women was deleted in the following legislative session. Folder marked "Census and Inventory 1742," New Hampshire Department of State, Division of Records Management and Archives, Concord; for ways in which towns sought to mitigate the impact of taxation on women see Elaine Forman Crane, "Dealing with Dependence: Paternalism and Tax Evasion in Eighteenth-Century Rhode Island," in *Women and the Law: The Social Historical Perspective*, ed. D. Kelly Weisberg (Cambridge: Schenkman, 1982), 1:28.

27. The 1687 tax list may be found in *Records Relating to the Early History of Boston* (Boston: Rockwell and Churchill, 1876–1909), 1:91–133. Volumes 1–22 of this series were issued as *Report of the Records Commissioners.*

28. Bettye H. Pruitt, ed., *The Massachusetts Tax Valuation List of 1771* (Boston: G. K. Hall, 1978).

29. *Acts and Laws of His Majesty's Colony of Rhode-Island and Providence Plantations, Made and Passed since the Revision in June 1767* (Newport, R.I.: Solomon Southwick, 1772), 90–91. The act was passed in February 1769 and amended in May 1769. See also *Acts of the [Rhode Island] General Assembly* 9 (1766–70), NHS.

30. Assessment List (1760), R. I. State Archives; Tax Assessment for the town of Newport, 1772, NHS; "List of Inhabitants of the Town of Salem about 1754," EI.

31. Alice Hanson Jones, *Wealth of a Nation to Be: The American Colonies on the Eve of Revolution* (New York: Columbia University Press, 1980), 323, 198, 224–25, 214, 199n; Alice Hanson Jones, *American Colonial Wealth: Documents and Methods* (New York: Arno Press, 1978), 2:607–800 [Essex County], 887–1022 [Suffolk County].

32. *Probate Records of Essex County, Massachusetts, 1635–1681* (Salem, Mass.: EI, 1916–20), vol. 1 (1635–63), vol. 2 (1665–74), vol. 3 (1675–81).

33. Nash, *Urban Crucible*, 64–65.

34. Overseers of the Poor Records (Boston), Almshouse Admissions, box 9, folders 1 and 2, MHS; an edition of these records prepared by Eric G. Nellis is forthcoming from the Colonial Society of Massachusetts. See also David Rothman, *Discovery of the Asylum: Social Order and Disorder in the New Republic* (Boston: Little, Brown, 1971), 39–42.

35. *Salem Town Records* (Salem, Mass.: EI, 1913, 1934), 2:323ff; Overseers Records (oversize), box 1, folder 2, MHS; Carl Bridenbaugh, *Cities in Revolt: Urban Life in America, 1743–76* (New York: Knopf, 1955; Oxford University Press, 1971), 125.

36. "Account of Payments to the Poor by Samuel Whitwell, an Overseer from

April 4, 1769 to March 22, 1792," MHS; *Early History of Boston*, 15:369; *Boston Gazette*, 27 August 1751.

37. "An Account of the Number of Families and Inhabitants of the Town of Newport, 1774," R.I. Archives, Providence.

38. Second Church Records (Boston), 1:91–93 (1674–75), MHS; Old North Church Records, vol. 5B, "Second Church," MHS; King's Chapel Records (Boston), Financial Records, 1724–1899, box 1, folder 26, MHS.

39. Court Records, Essex County, Mass., vols. marked "Sessions Dec. 1709 to July 1726," "Sessions April 1740 to Dec. 1743," "Sessions July 1744 to Sept. 1761," EI; Douglas Lamar Jones, "The Strolling Poor: Transiency in Eighteenth-Century Massachusetts," in *Interpreting Colonial America*, ed. James K. Martin (New York: Harper and Row, 1978), 691. Between March 1766 and June 1767, 112 single males, 138 single females, 7 females and children, 22 couples, and 55 couples with children were warned out of Essex County (Essex County Court Records, "Sessions, Dec. 1761 to Oct. 1778," EI). See also Ruth Wallis Herndon, "Warned Out in New England: Eighteenth-Century Tales of Trouble," paper presented to the Philadelphia Center for Early American Studies, 22 September 1995, pp. 13, 16.

40. James K. Somerville, "The Salem (Mass.) Woman in the Home, 1660–1770," *Eighteenth-Century Life* 1 (1974): 11–14.

41. Crane, *A Dependent People*, 83; "An Account of the Number of Families and Inhabitants of the Town of Newport, 1774," R.I. Archives, Providence; Pruitt, *Massachusetts Tax Valuation List*, 1771; Overseers of the Poor Records (Boston), Almshouse Admissions, box 9, folders 1 and 2, MHS.

42. Jonathan Easton ledger, 1749–66, p. 90, NHS; Isaac Stelle daybook no. 1496, 1755–61, p. 166, NHS; Court records, 26 December 1752, vol. marked "Sessions July 1744 to Sept. 1761"; 18 January 1726, "Sessions Sept. 1726 to March 1744," EI; Selectmen's Records, Salem, Mass., EI; Court Records, vol. marked "Sessions, Dec. 1761 to Oct. 1778," EI.

43. Slavery Papers, box 7, New-York Historical Society; Gracy [Walch] to Mr. Lotrop, 25 March 1776, Martha Mackloud to Aaron Lopez, 25 May 1776, Lopez Papers, NHS.

44. Town of Portsmouth (N.H.) Records, vol. 2, part 1, 1695–1779, FO28-FA, 8 October 1710, Portsmouth, N.H., Public Library.

45. Town of Portsmouth Records, vol. 2, part 1, 1695–1779, FO59-FA, 28 May 1722; Selectmen's Records, Salem, Mass., 17 November 1749, EI; Newport, R.I., Town Meeting Records, 1679–1776 (copied), book 2007, p. 674, 30 April 1760. For Boston's attempt to contain its soaring welfare costs in the 1740s and 1750s by confining women to the workhouse and almshouse or by enticing them to private manufactories, see Nash, *Urban Crucible*, 116–22.

46. "An Act Empowering Overseers of the Poor of Newport to commit persons to work house" and "An Act empowering Overseers of the Workhouse to Secure the Town from Costs Arising from idle and disorderly persons" (1753, 1767), *Acts and Laws of the English Colony of Rhode Island and Providence Plantations in New England in America* (Newport, R.I.: Samuel Hall, 1767), 197–99.

47. Records of the Superior Court (N.H.), 1750–54, p. 527, 1755–57, p. 113, State Records and Archives, Concord, N.H.; Selectmen's Records, Salem, Mass., 3 August 1724, 11 January 1724/5, EI.

48. Mary Forrester to Aaron Lopez, 22 October 1776, Lydia Bissell to Aaron Lopez, 18 March 1776, Lopez Papers, NHS.

49. Charter of the Marine Society, NHS. The Fellowship Club evolved into the Marine Society; see also Fellowship Club Minutes, 1772–99, pp. 7, 10, 12 (1772, 1773), NHS.

50. "Rules and Orders for the Management of the Work House lately Erected in the Town of Salem for the Employing and maintaining the Idle and Poor belonging to sd Town (Labor improbus omnia vincit) [1749]," Public Welfare Department, vol. 14 (1749–98), EI; "Rules and Orders for the Management of Work House in Boston" [c. 1740?] Overseers of the Poor Records, box 13, folder 1, MHS; Salem Town Records (passim), EI; Town Meeting Records, Newport, R.I., 1679–1779 (copied), book 2007, pp. 890–92, 137, NHS.

51. Selectmen's Records, Salem, Mass. (passim), EI. Susan Boyle argues the reverse: "The prolonged absences of their menfolk gave wives additional power and ample opportunity to function as deputy husbands, protecting their own interests and those of their families" (Susan C. Boyle, "Did She Generally Decide? Women in Ste. Genevieve, 1750–1805," *William and Mary Quarterly* 44 [1987]: 775–89).

52. John Banister account book no. 65A, 1739–46, p. 304, NHS; Thomas Richardson petty account book no. 487, 1722–54, pp. 478, 516, 540, 546 (1722–26), NHS. Elizabeth Carpenter's ledger is one of the few surviving female account books. Carpenter was a Newport shopkeeper, and her detailed records during 1743 show more transactions with women than do those of any other similarly occupied tradesperson. Carpenter listed her female customers by their first and last names, with an occasional notation to indicate widowhood. If Carpenter was systematic about this designation, the absence of such a notation in the vast majority of cases suggests that most of the women listed were either currently married or never married. Newport's sex ratio was still fairly balanced in 1743. Carpenter's ledger may be found at the Newport Historical Society.

53. John Banister account book no. 65A, 1739–46, NHS; Thomas Richardson petty account book no. 487, 1722–54, passim (esp. 1737–49) and pp. 38, 43; Isaac Stelle, "calf skin book" 1741–64, p. 47.

54. Jonathan Easton ledger, 1749–66, p. 153, NHS.

55. Dow, ed., *Essex County Quarterly Courts*, 1:54 (1643); Second Baptist Church Records (Newport), no. 1657, p. 33 (1741).

56. Bureau of the Census, *Historical Statistics of the United States: Colonial Times to 1970* (Washington: Government Printing Office, 1975), 1:215.

57. Charles Brewster, *Rambles about Portsmouth*, 1st ser. (Portsmouth, N.H., 1873, 1971), 159; Salem town records (MS), 1694–99, 1701–2, 1768–75, pp. 98, 239, 805, 806, EI; "Town Records of Salem" (1634–59), 1:1–242; vols. 2–3 (1659–91), passim (Salem, Mass., 1913, 1934). Moreover, even some contemporary historians have omitted women from records or studies for various reasons or no reason at all. David Konig

excluded women from his sample because they had a different relationship to law (David T. Konig, *Law and Society in Puritan Massachusetts: Essex County, 1629–1692* [Chapel Hill: University of North Carolina Press, 1979], 155). Harold Worthley "deliberately" omitted women's religious society proceedings from his extensive church inventory (Harold T. Worthley, *An Inventory of the Records of the Particular [Congregational] Churches of Massachusetts Gathered 1620–1805* [Cambridge: Harvard University Press, 1970], xi). In his "snapshot" of Fairfield, Connecticut, Jackson T. Main stated, "I omit women and nonresidents here and hereafter" (Jackson T. Main, *Society and Economy in Colonial Connecticut* [Princeton: Princeton University Press, 1985], 63, n. 2). Because Maryland records mention very few women, Gloria Main decided that their wills and inventories deserved a separate study; in her book, "women's estates have been excluded" (Gloria L. Main, *Tobacco Colony: Life in Maryland, 1650–1720* [Princeton: Princeton University Press, 1982], 48, n.1.

58. Records of the Inferior Court of Common Pleas, Salem, Mass., vols. marked "Sessions, July 1744 to Sept. 1761," p. 50, "Sessions, July 1692 to Sept. 1709," p. 36, "Sessions, Sept. 1726 to March 1744," p. 17, "Sessions, Dec. 1709 to July 1726," p. 2, "Sessions, July 1744 to Sept. 1761," p. 50; Jonathan Easton ledger, 1749–66, p. 90.

59. Thomas Richardson petty account book, 1722–54, pp. 516, 540, 546, NHS; John Banister ledger, 1739–46, p. 304, NHS.

60. John Briggs account book, 1710–21, MHS.

61. Mary Cranch accounts, English/Touzel/Hathorne Papers, 1661–1851, EI; Dr. John Clarke and his son William Clark, account book, 1732–71, pp. 20, 38, MHS.

62. Samuel Ingersoll's book, 1685–95, EI; John Chaloner account book, 1746–63, AAS.

63. Thomas Robinson's account book, 1753–94, p. 28, NHS; Jabez Carpenter's ledger, 1755–72, p. 74, NHS; Mary Prior, "Women and the Urban Economy: Oxford, 1500–1800," in *Women in English Society, 1500–1800,* ed. Mary Prior (London: Methuen, 1985), 94.

64. Salem Town Records, Selectmen's Records Copied, 1709–11, box 2, folder 2, pp. 14, 18, 20, 27, 30, 71; folder 7, pp. 662, 668, 671, EI.

65. Isaac Stelle ledger book, 1741–64, NHS.

66. Dow, ed., *Essex County Quarterly Courts,* 8:194–95 (1681); Isaac Stelle ledger book, 1741–64; *Newport Mercury,* 26 November 1764, 6 December 1773; Peter Verstilles account book, 1754–60, p. 68, MHS; "Petition of Ebenezer Frost, July 19, 1773," *New England Historical and Genealogical Register* 11 (1857): 322; Overseers of the Poor Records, box 1, folder 2, MHS.

67. John Farnam account book, entries for 1725, 1726, 1732, 1733, EI; Otis G. Hammond, ed., *New Hampshire Court Records, 1640–1692,* State Papers Series ([Concord]: State of New Hampshire, 1943), 40:472–73.

68. *Newport Mercury,* 20 October 1769; Rhode Island Petitions, vol. 11 (part 1), p. 90 (1763), R. I. State Archives, Providence; Fiske, comp., "Gleanings," 134 (1725).

69. Cotton Mather, *Ornaments for the Daughters of Zion* (1692; Delman, N.Y.: Scholars' Facsimiles and Reprints, 1978), 112. For an explanation of the role of "deputy husband" see Laurel T. Ulrich, *Good Wives: Image and Reality in the Lives of*

Women in Northern New England, 1650–1750 (New York: Knopf, 1980), 35–50. Historians generally subscribe to Ulrich's position. According to Julie Matthaei, even though examples of women doing men's work have been found for every trade, women entered these areas of work "only as stand-ins for male family members" (Julie A. Matthaei, *An Economic History of Women in America: Women's Work, the Sexual Division of Labor, and the Development of Capitalism* [New York: Schocken Books, 1982], 67ff).

70. See C. Dallett Hemphill, "Women in Court: Sex-Role Differentiation in Salem, Massachusetts, 1636–1683," *William and Mary Quarterly* 39 (January 1982): 169, 170, for marital partnerships that modified patriarchal relationships; *Robert Robinson v. Benjamin Church* (1733), in Fiske, comp., "Gleanings," 232. Most feminist historians argue otherwise and would agree with Heidi Hartmann that before the introduction of capitalism, a patriarchal system was established in which men controlled the labor of women and children in the family (Heidi Hartmann, "Capitalism, Patriarchy, and Job Segregation by Sex," *Signs: Journal of Women in Culture and Society* 1 [1976]: 138). See also Christine Stansell, *City of Women: Sex and Class in New York, 1784–1860* (New York: Knopf, 1986), 217.

71. James Taylor account book no. 498, p. 27, NHS. The "wife" is almost always referred to without mention of her name. This is in striking contrast to the ledger of Elizabeth Carpenter, who carefully recorded the full names of her many female customers (NHS); John Touzel account book, 1721–40, EI.

72. John Hovey account book, 1696–1721, EI; see especially 1708–15, and p. 31. Joshua Buffum account book, 1672–1704, p. 101, EI.

73. *Early History of Boston,* 7:58; Thomas Richardson petty account book, 1722–54, pp. 516, 540, 546, NHS; John Banister ledger, 1739–46, p. 304, NHS; English/Touzel/Hathorne Papers, 1661–1851, box 5, folders 6–8, EI.

74. Aaron Lopez, "Tailors and Spinners Book" no. 767 (1769, 1774), NHS; John Briggs account book, 1710–21, p. 18, MHS; Thomas Amory account book, 1720–28, MHS. See, for example, Abigail Adams to John Adams, 17 June 1782, in *Adams Family Correspondence,* ed. L. H. Butterfield and Marc Friedlaender (Cambridge: Harvard University Press, 1973), 4:326–29.

75. Thomas Richardson petty account book no. 487, 1722–54, pp. 38, 43, 25, NHS; Thomas Dean account book, 1723–1802, memo book, 1728–1812; see receipts, 1760–70, EI.

76. William Waine receipt book, 1728–44, and papers, esp. 1752, 1753; John Touzel account book, 1721–40, p. 54; Thomas Maule receipt book, 1681–1701, pp. 37, 93, EI; Isaac Stelle daybook, 1755–61, p. 153, NHS; John Banister receipt and waste book, pp. 69, 526, NHS.

77. Moses Little account book, 1743–71, esp. 1760, EI. The degree to which women were literate is a subject of controversy. Kenneth Lockridge maintains that by the middle of the eighteenth century (1758–62) approximately 68 percent of the women in Boston were literate, and that the rate declined to 60 percent by 1787. More recently, Joel Perlmann and Dennis Shirley have argued that New England women may have achieved near universal literacy by 1780. Mary Beth Norton, how-

ever, asserts that the Revolution was the turning point in female literacy and that the rate rose afterward as a result of the emphasis placed on female education and the new female academies. Kenneth A. Lockridge, *Literacy in Colonial New England: An Enquiry into the Social Context of Literacy in the Early Modern West* (New York: Norton, 1974), 24, 41; Joel Perlmann and Dennis Shirley, "When Did New England Women Acquire Literacy?" *William and Mary Quarterly* 48 (1991): 50–67; Mary Beth Norton, letter to the editor, *William and Mary Quarterly* 48 (1991): 639–45.

78. *Samuel Holmes v. William May* (1715), in Fiske, comp., "Gleanings," 61; *John Chapman v. Nicholas Migood* (1723), in Fiske, comp., "Gleanings," 113; see also bill signed by Joanna Chapman for services rendered, among file papers in *John Chapman v. John Fling* (1725), in Fiske, comp., "Gleanings," 139.

79. *Rebecca May v. Peter Treby* (1729), in Fiske, comp., "Gleanings," 203.

80. *Othniel Tripp v. Jahleel Brenton* (1719), in Fiske, comp., "Gleanings," 84. See *Sarah Cutlove v. James May* (1720/1), in Fiske, comp., "Gleanings," 90; Cutlove signed the bill for strong water delivered to May from the distillery she and her husband William ran. See also *Christopher Almy v. Benjamin L'homedieu* (1726), in Fiske, comp., "Gleanings," 158, where Almy's wife, Mary, testified about a bill.

81. Christine Heyrman has commented on the "receding of women from public view" in Marblehead, Massachusetts, during the mid-eighteenth century (Christine Leigh Heyrman, *Commerce and Culture: The Maritime Communities of Colonial Massachusetts, 1690–1750* [New York: Norton, 1984], 381–83).

82. Joshua Buffum account book, 1672–1704, passim, EI.

83. Robert Gibbs account book, 1660–1708, AAS.

84. Peter Burr account book, 1695–99, MHS; Aaron Lopez papers, new acquisition, NHS.

85. Walter Newbury shipping book, 1673–88, NHS; Thomas Richardson petty account book, 1722–54, pp. 501, 519, NHS; Samuel Ingersoll's book, 1685–95, EI.

86. William Waine receipt book, 1728–44, AAS; Jabez Carpenter ledger book, 1755–72, NHS; William Redwood ledger book, Historical Society of Pennsylvania.

87. Benjamin Greene account book, 1734–58, and waste book, 1764–82, MHS; Peter Verstilles account book, 1754–60, MHS.

88. Goldin, *Understanding the Gender Gap*, 47, 55.

89. Alice Clark was one of the earliest historians to connect female loss of status with industrialism; see Alice Clark, *Working Life of Women in the Seventeenth Century* (London, 1919; London: Routledge and Kegan Paul, 1982). In the 1970s Joan Hoff Wilson alludes to this issue in "The Illusion of Change: Women and the American Revolution," in *The American Revolution: Explorations in the History of American Radicalism*, ed. Alfred A. Young (DeKalb: Northern Illinois University Press, 1976), 383–445. In the same year, Ann Gordon and Mari Jo Buhle described the role of women in the preindustrial economy and the negative changes wrought by the move toward market capitalism. See Ann D. Gordon and Mari Jo Buhle, "Sex and Class in Colonial and Nineteenth-Century America," in *Liberating Women's History: Theoretical and Critical Essays*, ed. Berenice A. Carroll (Urbana: University of Illinois Press, [c. 1976]), 278–300. See also Maxine Berg, *The Age of Manufactures, 1700–1820: Indus-*

try, Innovation, and Work in Britain, 1700–1820 (New York: Oxford University Press, 1986), and Cornelia Hughes Dayton, *Women before the Bar: Gender, Law, and Society in Connecticut, 1639–1789* (Chapel Hill: University of North Carolina Press, 1995), for further and more detailed discussions of women and changing economic trends. Most recently, Jeanne Boydston has tackled the connection between women's status and capitalism in her thoughtful essay "The Woman Who Wasn't There: Women's Market Labor and the Transition to Capitalism in the United States," *Journal of the Early Republic* 16 (summer 1996): 183–206. Boydston's frame of reference is Philadelphia, and while some of what she says may apply to women in the New England seaports, her assumption that the power women achieved in the postwar dairying industry "probably occurred in women's participation in family urban businesses" as well (195) cannot be substantiated. Furthermore, while I agree that women were visibly present in the cities of the early republic, I would suggest that their presence had changed both qualitatively and quantitatively from what it had been in the earlier period.

90. Prior, "Women and the Urban Economy," 93ff; Hall, "Family Structure and Economic Organization," 39, 46–48, 50.

91. Hemphill, "Women in Court," 172; Carol F. Karlsen, *The Devil in the Shape of a Woman: Witchcraft in Colonial New England* (New York: Norton, 1987), 145–46.

92. Stephen Innes, paper delivered to Columbia University Seminar in Early American History, 13 December 1983; see Joan Hoff Wilson's comments on women and credit in "The Illusion of Change," 396–97. Bruce Mann, "Neighbors and Strangers: Legal Change and the Nature of Community in Connecticut, 1690–1760," paper delivered at the Organization of American Historians conference, 13 April 1986, and *Neighbors and Strangers: Law and Community in Early Connecticut* (Chapel Hill: University of North Carolina Press, 1987), 29–30.

93. See, for example, the story of Peter January's manufactory in James Henretta, "The Transition to Capitalism in America," paper presented to the Philadelphia Center for Early American Studies, 13 May 1988 (unpaginated); Goldin, *Understanding the Gender Gap*, 49.

94. The economic position of women was negatively affected by a declining land supply, the decreasing likelihood that they would manage estates or control property, and the increasing propensity of children to acquire a larger portion of the husband's estate, as well as women's acquisition of personal rather than real property. Poorhouse records show an increase in the number of women unable to provide for themselves, and tax records indicate a decline in economic standing. See Elaine Forman Crane, "Dependence in the Era of Independence: The Role of Women in a Republican Society," in *The American Revolution: Its Character and Limits*, ed. Jack P. Greene (New York: New York University Press, 1987), 253–75.

95. Christine Delphy, *Close to Home: A Materialist Analysis of Women's Oppression* (Amherst: University of Massachusetts Press, 1984), 60, 38, 67; Gregory H. Nobles, "Wages for Women in Seventeenth-Century Massachusetts: A Case Study of John Pynchon's Household Servants," paper presented to the Fifth Berkshire Conference on the History of Women, 16–18 June 1981, 7.

96. Richard B. Morris, *Government and Labor in Early America* (1946; Boston: Northeastern University Press, 1981).

97. Shammas, *Pre-industrial Consumer,* 54 (table 3.1); "The Answer of Francis Bernard Esq. Governor of his Majesty's Province of Massachusetts Bay to the Queries proposed by the Right Honorable The Lords Commissioners for Trade and Plantations," 5 September 1763, reprinted in Josiah H. Benton, *Early Census-Making in Massachusetts, 1643–1765* (Boston: Charles E. Goodspeed, 1905), 51.

98. Edward Chappell, "Housing a Nation: The Transformation of Living Standards in Early America," in *Of Consuming Interests: The Style of Life in the Eighteenth Century,* ed. Cary Carson, Ronald Hoffman, and Peter J. Albert (Charlottesville: University Press of Virginia, 1994), 188–89, 214, 216, 218–19.

99. T. H. Breen, "'Baubles of Britain': The American and Consumer Revolutions of the Eighteenth Century," in *Of Consuming Interests,* ed. Carson et al., 454, 456–57; Thomas Richardson ledger book, p. 61, NHS. In 1763 legal money and old tenor were exchanged at a ratio of 23½:1.

100. Job Townsend ledger book, 1750–93, NHS.

101. Richard Bushman, *The Refinement of America: Persons, Houses, Cities* (New York: Knopf, 1992), 440–42; Jeanne Boydston, *Home and Work: Housework, Wages, and the Ideology of Labor in the Early Republic* (New York: Oxford University Press, 1990), 7–11.

102. Jacques-Pierre Brissot de Warville, *New Travels in the United States of America, 1788* (Cambridge: Harvard University Press, 1960), 93.

103. Marcus Rediker, *Between the Devil and the Deep Blue Sea: Merchant Seamen, Pirates, and the Anglo-American Maritime World, 1700–1750* (New York: Cambridge University Press, 1987), 73.

CHAPTER 4

1. Petition of Samuel Hinks to the Governor and General Assembly (1719), Dept. of State, Division of Records Management and Archives, Concord, N.H. See also Nathaniel Bouton, comp., *Documents and Records Relating to the Province of New Hampshire* (1692–1722) (Manchester, N.H.: John B. Clarke, State Printer, 1869), 3:297, 319, 756, 766, 773, 775, 776; Henry Harrison Metcalf, ed., *Probate Records of the Province of New Hampshire* [State Papers Series] (Bristol, N.H.: R. W. Musgrove, 1914), 31:641; 32:126.

2. Marylynn Salmon, *Women and the Law of Property in Early America* (Chapel Hill: University of North Carolina Press, 1986), 13.

3. Nathaniel B. Shurtleff, ed., *Records of the Governor and Company of the Massachusetts Bay in New England* (Boston: William White, 1853–54), 2:273 (1649); John Noble, ed., *Massachusetts Colony Court of Assistants Records, 1630–1690* (Boston: Rockwell and Churchill Press, 1901–28), 1:153 (1679), 1:193 (1681), 1:273 (1684), 1:275, 294 (1685); *Records of the Suffolk County Court, 1671–1680,* Publications of the Colonial Society of Massachusetts Collections, vols. 29 and 30 (Boston: Colonial Society

of Massachusetts, 1933), 30:825 (1677), 30:1141 (1679/80); Petition of Mary Hawse (1730), R.I. Petitions, 2:28 (October 1730), R.I. State Archives.

4. Shurtleff, *Records,* 2:54 (1643), 4 (part 2): 11 (1661), 2:273 (1649), 3:67 (1646).

5. Noble, *Court of Assistants* 1:189 (1681). See the petition from a woman on behalf of her brother, as well as the petition he submitted himself. The court granted the request, although it is impossible to say whether they were swayed by his or her request (Shurtleff, *Records,* 5:7 [1674]).

6. See the petitions in behalf of Alice Tilly in the box marked "Photostats 1647–1650," MHS.

7. Shurtleff, *Records,* 3:197, 209 (1650).

8. Petition of Deborah Johnson (1743), R.I. Petitions, 5:47.

9. Petition of Grizel Cotton (1731), R.I. Petitions, 2:51; Petition of Experience Briggs (1744), R.I. Petitions 5:95.

10. It is interesting to note differences among the colonies with respect to petitions. Deborah Rosen has found that in New York petitioning "was a form of justice used more often by women than by men," and that economic impoverishment compelled them to petition for permission to beg—a request that would have been most unusual in New England (Deborah Rosen, "Women and Justice in Colonial New York: Examining the Practical Reality of Common Law Restraints," paper presented to the Columbia University Seminar on Early American History and Culture, 13 May 1997, 10, 14).

11. See also Noble, *Court of Assistants,* 1:295 (1685); Suffolk County, Superior Court of Judicature (December 1718), 257. In October 1772 Rhode Island resident Elizabeth Arnold objected to certain jurors (R.I. Petitions, 15:21). Noble, *Court of Assistants,* 1:29 (1674).

12. See Bruce Mann, "The Formalization of Informal Law: Arbitration before the American Revolution," *New York University Law Review* 59 (1984): 443–81; David T. Konig, *Law and Society in Puritan Massachusetts: Essex County, 1629–1692* (Chapel Hill: University of North Carolina Press, 1979), 109; Jane Fiske, ed., [R.I.] General Court of Trials (1671), 2. Fiske, editor of the *New England Historical and Genealogical Register* at the New England Historic Genealogical Society in Boston, is in the process of transcribing these records. This citation is from "Book A," the manuscript of which is located at the Rhode Island Judicial Archives, Pawtucket, R.I.

13. Meecum (March 1715), Dyre (March 1719), records of the Rhode Island Court of Trials, Rhode Island Judicial Archives, Pawtucket. Both cases have surviving file papers.

14. Suffolk County, Court of Common Pleas (January 1752), 131, Mass. Archives, Boston; Suffolk County, Superior Court of Judicature (November 1752), 147, Mass. Archives.

15. Shurtleff, *Records,* 2:219 (1647).

16. Mary Beth Norton, "Women as Witnesses in Maryland Criminal Prosecutions, 1636–1683," paper presented at the Seventh Berkshire Conference on the History of Women, 19 June 1987.

17. John Winthrop, *Winthrop's Journal: History of New England, 1630–1649,*

ed. James Kendall Hosmer (New York: Scribners, 1908), 2:15 (1640); Fiske, comp., "Gleanings", 332 (1763).

18. See the case of Joseph, an Indian accused of murdering his wife, in Noble, *Court of Assistants* 1:295–96 (1685), 1:29 (1674); Winthrop, *Journal,* 1:67 (1631); see the claims and counterclaims in *Christopher Champlin gentleman v. Betty Thompson (Indian woman) spinster,* in Fiske, comp., "Gleanings," 235 (1733).

19. Suffolk County, Superior Court of Judicature (November 1720), 328; (August 1728), 177; Suffolk County, Court of General Sessions (October 1727), 116–17, Mass. Archives. See similar instances in Rhode Island where two women sued to confirm their freedom in the aftermath of the Revolution; R.I. Petitions (1784), 21:65; (1785) 22:72, R.I. State Archives.

20. Shurtleff, *Records,* 1:201 (1637), 292 (1640), 317 (1641). It is possible that the coats may have been invested with political significance. In a 1667 letter addressed to the chief sachem of the Mohawks, the Massachusetts magistrates reminded the Indians that "your people would not medle with any Indians that woare English cloakes" (Shurtleff, *Records,* 4 [part 2]: 361 [1667]).

21. Winthrop, *Journal,* 2:160 (1644); Shurtleff, *Records,* 2:55 (1643/4).

22. Shurtleff, *Records,* 4 (part 2): 357–60 (1667), 378 (1668).

23. Hugo Grotius, *De jure belli ac pacis libritres* (1625), as discussed in Richard S. Hartigan, *The Forgotten Victim: A History of the Civilian* (Chicago: Precedent, 1982), 99–100.

24. Winthrop, *Journal,* 1:218–20 (1637).

25. Ibid., 1:225, 227 (1637), 2:172 (1644). See also Shurtleff, *Records,* 5:97 (1776), where documents describe a battle in which loyal Indians killed twenty of the enemy, "of which were four squaws."

26. Dow, ed., *Essex County Quarterly Courts,* EI, 1:vi. Some women could read even if they had never learned to write, but the regulation must have caused some inconvenience in a litigious society.

27. Fiske, comp., "Gleanings," 203 (1729).

28. Shurtleff, *Records,* 2:261 (1648); Petition of Patience Hall (1733), R.I. Petitions, 2:98.

29. Suffolk County, Court of Common Pleas (January 1752), 131; Essex County, Superior Court of Judicature (June 1750), 4, Mass. Archives; file papers in *Christopher Almy v. Eunice Greenman,* September 1721, March 1722, R.I. Judicial Archives; Suffolk County, Court of General Sessions (1727/8), 137, (1728), 151.

30. Carole Shammas, Marylynn Salmon, and Michel Dahlin, *Inheritance in America from Colonial Times to the Present* (New Brunswick, N.J.: Rutgers University Press, 1987), 59.

31. For similar trends in Connecticut see Cornelia Hughes Dayton, *Women before the Bar: Gender, Law, and Society in Connecticut, 1639–1789* (Chapel Hill: University of North Carolina Press, 1995).

32. There were approximately 1,107 petitions to the Rhode Island General Assembly between 1725 and 1750, of which 118 were from women. During the next twenty-five years, 93 women submitted petitions of a total of 1,570 petitions. The

number of female petitions rose again in the last quarter of the eighteenth century (139 of 1,492, or 9.3 percent), but many of these appeals were war related. See R.I. Petitions, passim. On court-appointed arbitrators see, for example, Suffolk County, Court of Common Pleas (January 1752), 111, 112, 164.

33. Suffolk County, Superior Court of Judicature (November 1752), 160, 161; (February 1753), 244; (February 1773), 8, 10; Essex County, Superior Court of Judicature (October 1752), 199.

34. Newport Town Council records, passim, NHS.

35. "Body of Liberties," in *The Laws and Liberties of Massachusetts, 1641–1691,* facs. ed., John D. Cushing, comp. (Wilmington, Del.: Scholarly Resources, 1976), no. 79, 3:699. In this sense *competent* meant "suitable to a person's rank or position; suitable or sufficient for a comfortable living" (OED).

36. *The Book of the General Lawes and Libertyes Concerning the Inhabitants of Massachusets Collected Out of the Records of the General Court for the Several Years wherin They Were Made and Established* (Cambridge, Mass., 1648), 17; William H. Whitmore, ed., *The Colonial Laws of Massachusetts: Reprinted from the Edition of 1672, with the Supplements through 1686* (Boston: S. Greene, 1887), 42.

37. Shurtleff, *Records,* 1:201 (1637), 2:287 (1649). For similar problems in Rhode Island, see John Russell Bartlett, ed., *Records of the Colony of Rhode Island and Providence Plantations in New England, 1636–1792* (Providence, R.I.: A. Crawford Greene and Brother, 1856–65), 1:127–28 (1644).

38. Shurtleff, *Records,* 2:281 (1649); *Suffolk County Court,* 29:79 (1671/2), 29:225 (1672/3), 29:434 (1674), 30:641 (1675), 30:1098 (1679). Massachusetts was not the first New England colony to institute such vague guidelines. The 1647 Rhode Island code allowed the Town Council to make "an equal and just" distribution of intestates' estates (Bartlett, *Records,* 1:188).

39. "For Avoyding all fraudulent conveyances," in Shurtleff, *Records,* 1:306 (1640), 2:287 (1649).

40. Shurtleff, *Records,* 3:80 (1646), 3:140 (1648), 3:197 (1650), 3:271 (1652), 3:347 (1654), 4 (part 1): 65 and passim (1651 ff.), 4 (part 2): 47 (1662), 3:280 (1652).

41. Dow, ed., *Essex County Quarterly Courts,* 2:207 (1660). The authorities were responding to situations such as the following: "Mary, wife of William Chichester, deposed that her husband at one time owned a house at Marblehead, said to have belonged some time before to Edward Bartol. She had heard her husband and others say that her husband bought it of Mr. Heale of Boston . . . and her husband enjoyed it for about 2 years and then sold it; this was about 14 years since." William had abandoned his wife and several children, and Mary had "no means to bring them up."

42. Shurtleff, *Records,* 3:422–423 (1657), 5:301 (1680).

43. Ibid., 3:271 (1652), 3:389 (1655), 4 (part 2): 524 (1672), 5:146 (1677), 5:174 (1677).

44. Cushing, comp., *Laws and Liberties,* no. 14, 3:691.

45. Salmon, *Women and the Law of Property,* 144; Shurtleff, *Records,* 1:43 (1629).

46. *Suffolk County Court* 30:843 (1677).

47. Abner Goodell, *Acts and Resolves, Public and Private, of the Province of Massachusetts Bay* (Boston: Wright and Potter, 1869–1922), 8:641, 126, 156, 203, 492–93 (1705–6).

48. *Suffolk County Court*, 30:1029–37 (1679), quotes on 1032, 1033, 1035.

49. Shurtleff, *Records,* 2:165 (1646), 3:177 (1649), 3:216–17 (1650), 3:384 (1655). Stephen Botein makes this point from a different perspective: "Throughout the seventeenth century, most colonial judges had been inattentive to particular 'common law' rules and so in practice had dispensed 'equity' without caring or often even realizing what it was" (Stephen Botein, *Early American Law and Society* [New York: Knopf, 1983], 57).

50. Shurtleff, *Records,* 4 (part 2): 382 (1668), 5:326 (1681); *Suffolk County Court,* 29:492 (1674); Shurtleff, *Records,* 5:459 (1684), 5:479, (1685), 5:483 (1685), 5:298 (1680), 5:316 (1681), 5:358 (1682), 5:487 (1685), 5:490 (1685).

51. Ibid., 3:389 (1655), 3:84 (1646), 3:116 (1647).

52. *Suffolk County Court,* 29:225 (1672/3), 29:434, 438, (1674), 30:595, 598, 601, 630 (1675), 30:780, 781, 786 (1676/7); Goodell, *Acts and Resolves,* 10:619 (1725/6), 11:250 (1727/8), 13:33, 63 (1741/2), 14:325 (1749/50), 18:55–56 (1765/6).

53. Shurtleff, *Records,* 4 (part 2): 439 (1669), 466–67 (1670), 5:459 (1684); *Suffolk County Court,* 29:492 (1674).

54. "An Act for the Settlement and Distribution of the Estates of Intestates" (1692), in *Acts and Laws of His Majesty's Province of the Massachusetts-Bay in New England* (Boston: S. Kneeland, 1759), 3; *Book of Laws* (1648), 17; Whitmore, *Colonial Laws,* 42.

55. "An Act for Equal Distribution of Insolvent Estates" (1696), *Acts and Laws* (1759), 66; *Suffolk County Court,* 29:345 (1673); "An Act in Addition to and Explanation of Distribution of Intestate Estates" (1710), *Acts and Laws* (1759), 163–64; Shammas et al., *Inheritance in America,* 35.

56. "Supplement to Act Entitled An Act for Making Lands and Tenements Liable for Payment of Debt 1696" (1719), *Acts and Laws* (1759), 204. Cornelia Dayton maintains that the enormous debt expansion of the 1720s transformed civil litigation in Connecticut, which in combination with other factors led to a dramatic decline of women's presence in court (Dayton, *Women before the Bar,* 8).

57. Bartlett, *Records,* 1:127–28 (1644).

58. Horatio Rogers et al., eds., *Early Records of the Town of Providence* (Providence, R.I.: Snow and Farnham, 1892), 1:30–34 (1657ff); "An Act for the Probate of Wills and Granting of Administrations" (1663), in *Acts and Laws of His Majesty's Colony of Rhode Island and Providence Plantations In America* (Newport, R.I.: James Franklin, 1730), 5; "An Act for Quieting Possessions, and Avoiding Suits at Law" (1711), *Acts and Laws* (1730), 68.

59. Bartlett, *Records,* 1:188; *Acts and Laws* (1730), 6. Rhode Island's reference to just and equal allotments in 1647 anticipated Massachusetts's action by two years. "An Act for Distribution and Settling of Intestate Estates" (1718), in *Acts and Laws of*

His Majesty's Colony of Rhode Island and Providence Plantations in America (Boston: John Allen for Nicholas Boone, 1719), 95; "An Act for Distribution and Settling of Intestate Estates, (repealed 1728)," *Acts and Laws* (1730), 163.

60. "An Act for Putting in Force the Laws of England in This Colony Where No Provision Be Made by the Acts of This Colony" (1700), *Acts and Laws* (1730), 42; *Acts and Laws . . . from Anno 1745, to Anno 1752* (Newport, R.I.: J. Franklin, 1752), 71; *Acts and Laws . . . of the English Colony of Rhode Island and Providence Plantations in New England in America,* revised codification (Newport, R.I.: Samuel Hall, 1767), 55.

61. "An Act for the Registering Deeds and Conveyances" (1714), *Acts and Laws* (1730), 73.

62. Bartlett, *Records,* 3:105 (1681).

63. *Acts and Laws* (1730), 3, 6, (1767), 216, (1719), 4; (R.I.) *General Assembly Acts* (May 1766–February 1770), NHS, 92–93. For an exception, see the Newport Town Council records for 16 May 1769 (16:45), NHS.

64. "An Act for Distribution and Settling of Intestate Estates" (1718), *Acts and Laws* (1719), 95; "An Act for the Distribution of Insolvent Estates" (1758), *Acts and Laws* (1767), 154–57. "An Act for Making the Real Estate of Deceased Persons Liable to Satisfy Their Debts" (1769), in *Acts and Laws of His Majesty's Colony of R.I. and Providence Plantations, Made and Passed since the Revision in June, 1767* (Newport, R.I.: S. Southwick, 1772), 11.

65. Petition of Dinah Cahoon (1737), R.I. Petitions, 3:124; Petition of Ann Tyler (1773), R.I. Petitions, 3:56. See also the successful attempts by Dr. Norbert Wigneron to obtain the property of Mary Elsworth DeGrove that had been set aside for her children by Clement Elsworth in a prenuptial agreement with Deric DeGrove (*Norbert Wigneron v. Mary Degrove* [1729] in Fiske, comp., "Gleanings," 206). Mary De-Grove won in the lower court, Wigneron appealed, and the Superior Court reversed judgment. General Court of Trials/Superior Court of Judicature, book B, p. 256 (1729); p. 373 (1730), Rhode Island Judicial Archives.

66. *Suffolk County Court,* 30:598 (1675); Shurtleff, *Records,* 5:216–17 (1679).

67. Shurtleff, *Records,* 5:315 (1681). For interesting insight into how Indian women (in this case, Cherokees) lost power as a result of tribal interaction with Anglo-Americans, see Theda Perdue, "Cherokee Women and the Trail of Tears," in *Unequal Sisters: A Multicultural Reader in U.S. Women's History,* ed. Vicki L. Ruiz and Ellen C. DuBois, 2d ed. (New York: Routledge, 1994), 32–43.

68. Shurtleff, *Records,* 5:533–35 (n.d.); See also Perdue, "Cherokee Women," 33.

69. Goodell, *Acts and Resolves* 13:96 (1741/2), and passim, esp. vol. 14.

70. Shurtleff, *Records,* 2:281. The 1660 and 1672 law codes required a wife's consent in writing. *Book of the General Lawes and Libertyes* (Cambridge, Mass., 1660), 26; "General Laws and Liberties" (Cambridge, Mass., 1672), 42, in Cushing, comp., *Laws and Liberties,* 2:268.

71. See the deed of land from Christ[r] Lattamore and his wife, Mary. The deed is dated 1 February 1663 and the acknowledgment bears the date 10:8:64, whereby Mary released her thirds (Dow, ed., *Essex County Quarterly Courts,* 8:28–29 [1680]). Salmon, *Women and the Law of Property,* xiv, 6, 186.

72. Goodell, *Acts and Resolves,* vols. 17–18 (1761–74) passim. Widows were more frequently joined by new husbands or adult sons in court actions than they had been in the past; Suffolk County, Superior Court of Judicature, November 1723 and August 1728, passim; Petition of Ann Tyler to sell real estate "seized in her own right" to pay her husband's debts, R.I. Petitions (1773), 15:56; Kim Lacy Rogers, "Relicts of the New World: Conditions of Widowhood in Seventeenth-Century New England," in *Woman's Being, Woman's Place: Female Identity and Vocation in American History,* ed. Mary Kelley (Boston: G. K. Hall, 1979), 40–41, 43; Fiske, comp., "Gleanings," 170, 204, 206.

73. In *Clarke v. Nicholls* (1671) an unsure jury brought in the following special verdict: "If man and wife have power to make bargains with another that will stand good in Law then wee finde for the plantiffe . . . if not we finde for the Defendent" (*Suffolk County Court,* 29:5 [1671]; Will of Henry Bull, 11 December 1693, in Fiske, comp., "Gleanings," 22.

74. Will of Henry Shrimpton, 17 May 1666, *Suffolk County Wills: Abstracts of the Earliest Wills upon Record in the County of Suffolk, Massachusetts, from the New England Historical and Genealogical Register* (Baltimore: Genealogical Publishing Co., 1984), 261. Suffolk County, Superior Court of Judicature (February 1725/6), 53; Salmon, *Women and the Law of Property,* 8, 132.

75. Dow, ed., *Essex County Quarterly Courts,* 8:10 (1680).

76. See the agreement between the Selectmen of Salem and Mrs. Sarah Bishop, wife of Edward Bishop (Salem Town Records, Selectmen's Records, box 2 [15 November 1710], 71); *Suffolk County Court,* 30:1091 (1679/80).

77. Fiske, comp., "Gleanings," 58; R.I. General Court of Trials, "Book A" (March 1714/5), 218, (September 1715), 226; file papers, *Thomas Peckham v. John Scott* (September 1715), Rhode Island Judicial Archives.

78. *Rhode Island Court Records: Records of the Court of Trials of the Colony of Providence Plantations* (1647–70) (Providence: RIHS, 1922), 1:49; Otis G. Hammond, ed., *New Hampshire Court Records, 1640–1692,* in State Papers, New Hampshire ([Concord]: State of New Hampshire, 1943), 40:29.

79. *Suffolk County Court* 30:82 8 (31 July 1677); Noble, *Court of Assistants,* 1:322 (1690), 350 (1691).

80. *Bathsheba Hart v. Stephen Mumford,* file papers September 1717, R.I. Judicial Archives; Fiske, comp., "Gleanings," 58, 59. See also *Nicholas Carr . . . and Mary his wife v. Joseph Scott* (1754), in Fiske, comp., "Gleanings," 306. This is a suit to force Scott to pay Mary Carr a stipulated sum yearly according to an agreement. Scott responded that at the time of the agreement, Mary Carr was Mary Gould (widow), and therefore the current suit was invalid.

81. *Magdalen Fromoget v. John Hardovin Le Touch,* file papers September 1714, R.I. Judicial Archives; *John Hardovin Le Touch v. Magdalen Fromoget* September 1714, Docket Book, R.I. Judicial Archives.

82. *Thomas Hicks v. Bethia Hedges,* Newport County, Court of Common Pleas, "Book A," p. 335 (1735), R.I. Judicial Archives; Fiske, comp., "Gleanings," 257, (1736).

83. *Bethia Hedges v. John Hunt,* R.I. Superior Court of Judicature, "Book B," p. 515 (1736), R.I. Judicial Archives.

84. *Job Caswell v. Bethia Hunt widow,* Newport County, Court of Common Pleas, "Book A," p. 483 (1737), and file papers, R.I. Judicial Archives; Petition of Bethia Hedges (1738/9), R.I. Petitions 3:136.

85. "An Act for Granting Administration to the Wives of Persons Three Years Absent and Unheard Of," *Acts and Laws* (1730), 69, 86–87; *Acts and Laws* (1767), 217–18. R.I. Petitions (1772–75), vol. 15, passim; see also Petition of Elizabeth Barker (October 1763), 11:95, and Petition of Marcy Dexter (October 1770), 14:70, R.I. Petitions.

86. *The Laws Respecting Women,* reprinted from the J. Johnson edition [London, 1777] (Dobbs Ferry, N.Y.: Oceana, 1974), 152. Petition of Mary Mackree to the Governor and Council (1739/40), New Hampshire Petitions, Dept. of State, Division of Records Management and Archives, Concord, N.H. Fiske, comp., "Gleanings," 68–69 (1716), 177 (1728), 180 (1728), 205 (1729), 213 (1730); Essex County, Court of Common Pleas (26 September 1752), 391, EI; Suffolk County, Superior Court of Judicature (December 1718), 253, (August 1725), 27; see also the Boston Town Meeting report where it was resolved that the tax collector could bring an action against a husband for his wife's arrears when sole (*Records Relating to the Early History of Boston* [Boston: Rockwell and Churchill, 1876–1909], 16:101–2 [1763]).

87. Noble, *Court of Assistants,* 3:73–74 (1659).

88. *Suffolk County Court,* 30:755 (1676); Dow, ed., *Essex County Quarterly Courts,* 2:251 (1660). See also *Katherine West of Newport, Widow of Henry West . . . v. Job Almy of Tiverton,* in an action of dower (1764); this dispute concerns the widow's dower rights in property allegedly sold by Henry West in 1753 (Fiske, comp., "Gleanings," 341).

89. Rhode Island Colony Records (ms), 4:421 (26 November 1723), R.I. State Archives. Fordice received permission to sell.

90. *Suffolk County Court,* 30:592 (1675), 781 (1676–77); Fiske, comp., "Gleanings," 376 [1771].

91. Essex County, Court of General Sessions (25 June 1695) [unpaginated], EI; Suffolk County, Superior Court of Judicature (December 1718), 259–60; *Suffolk County Court,* 29:27 (1671).

92. Newport Town Council records (January 1713), 2:567; "An Act in Addition to the Act for the Equal Distribution of Insolvent Estates" (1700), *Acts and Laws* (1759), 114; see also Suffolk County, Superior Court of Judicature (December 1718), 259.

93. Suffolk County, Court of Common Pleas (July 1751), 63; "An Act for Empowering the Town Council to Secure the Personal Estate of Deceased Persons" (1724), *Acts and Laws* (1730), 134; R.I. Petitions (1795), 29:82, 85.

94. Fiske, comp., "Gleanings," 170 (1727), 204, 206 (1729); R.I. Petitions, 28:145 (1794), 29:82 (1795).

95. Shammas et al., *Inheritance in America,* 59.

96. Bartlett, *Records,* 2:244–45 (1669).

97. Salem Town Records, Selectmen's Records, p. 72, (15 November 1710), EI.

CHAPTER 5

1. For information on the Websters see Otis G. Hammond, ed., *New Hampshire Court Records, 1640–1692,* in State Papers, vol. 40 ([Concord]: State of New Hampshire, 1943), 87, 88, 121, 160–61, 166, 167–68, 171, 176, 499–500, 177, 184, 185, 225, 240, 253, 259, 512, 513, 517, 269, 289.

2. Winthrop, *Journal,* 1:179 (1636); Noble, *Court of Assistants,* 2:37 (1633), 119 (1642/3); Essex Institute, *Historical Collections* (Salem, Mass.: Essex Institute Press, 1859–   ), 9:124, 140, 147 (1643/4); Dow, ed., *Essex County Quarterly Courts,* 1:20 (1640).

3. *Ann Seten v. Asa Seten* (1774), Newport County Superior Court of Judicature, book F, p. 91; Shurtleff, *Records,* 1:278 (1639).

4. Shurtleff, *Records,* 1:140 (1634/5), 2:100 (1645), 2:253 (1648).

5. Peter Clark, *The English Alehouse: A Social History, 1200–1830* (London: Longman, 1983), 28, 166–67.

6. Ibid., 21, 30, 78–79.

7. Shurtleff, *Records,* 1:279 (1639), 2:46 (1643), 5:450 (1684). Eventually the sale of tea, coffee, and chocolate was licensed as well. *Suffolk County Court,* 29:85 (1671/2); Essex County, Court of General Sessions, 31 March 1752, EI.

8. *Suffolk County Court,* 29:122 (1672); 29:259–63 (1673); 29:445 (1674); 30:812 (1677); Dow, ed., *Essex County Quarterly Courts,* passim; Lyle Koehler, "Female Innkeepers and Liquor-Sellers in New England, 1620–99," in *A Search for Power: The "Weaker Sex" in Seventeenth-Century New England* (Chicago: University of Illinois Press, 1980), 460–63.

9. Compare Suffolk County, Court of General Sessions (1720), 41–42, (1723), 223–24, (1731), 351–53, Massachusetts Archives; Essex County, Court of General Sessions, June 1717, July 1718, EI.

10. Petition of Margett More to the Selectmen of Boston, 22 August 1765, Misc. Bound Petitions, MHS; the eight Selectmen granted More's petition. For examples of seventeenth-century license distribution see *Early History of Boston,* 7:87, 203, 207, 215.

11. Suffolk County, Court of General Sessions (1720), 41–42, (1723), 223–24, (1731), 351–53, Massachusetts Archives; July 1737, James Otis Sr. Collection, MHS; 14 June 1765, Misc. Bound, MHS.

12. Stanley Baron, *Brewed in America: A History of Beer and Ale in the United States* (Boston: Little, Brown, [1962]), 40–41; Bartlett, *Records,* 1:185; Newport Town Council records, passim, NHS.

13. *New Hampshire Court Records,* 40:404 (1686); "Minutes of General Sessions, 1770," box 1 (Inferior Court of Common Pleas, Court of Quarter Sessions Minutes), State Archives, Concord, N.H.

14. Petition of Richard Wybird (1701), Division of Records Management and Archives, Dept. of State, Concord, N.H.

15. Shurtleff, *Records,* 1:214 (1637), 4 (part 1): 59 (1651); *Early History of Boston,* 7:203 (1690), 207 (1691), 215 (1693). See Judith M. Bennett, *Ale, Beer, and Brewsters in*

England: Women's Work in a Changing World, 1300–1600 (New York: Oxford University Press, 1996).

16. *Early History of Boston*, 7:15 [1663]; Shurtleff, *Records*, 2:193 (1647); Dow, ed., *Essex County Quarterly Courts*, 1:123 (1647); Salem Town Records, Selectmen's Records, box 2, p. 61 (12 June 1710), p. 65 (14 July 1710), EI.

17. Clark, *English Alehouse*, 170; *Suffolk County Court*, 29:221 (1662/3), 524 (1674), 491–92 (1674).

18. Shurtleff, *Records*, 4 (part 2): 378 (1668); *Suffolk County Court*, 29:82–83 (1671/2).

19. *Suffolk County Court*, 29:114 (1672), 189 (1672).

20. Essex County, Court of General Sessions, 1 August 1727, p. 23.

21. It may also have been a matter of law. In Rhode Island, at least, a husband was legally responsible for the penalties his wife incurred by selling alcohol in small quantities without a license (*Acts and Laws* [1730], 179); Shurtleff, *Records*, 4 (part 1): 342 (1658).

22. *Suffolk County Court*, 29:484, 491 (1674).

23. Dow, ed., *Essex County Quarterly Courts*, 8:436 (1682); Newport Town Council records 1:208–9 (1706), 2:405 (1711), 2:372 (1712/3), NHS.

24. Mass., Court of General Sessions (Essex and Suffolk Counties) 3 April 1722 (p. 129), 30 April 1722 (p. 130), 29 July 1723 (p. 221); 31 March 1725 (p. 319); 4 April 1727 (p. 70); 2 January 1727/8 (p. 137); 29 July 1728 (pp. 173–74); 2 April 1728 (p. 148), 26 April 1731 (p. 336). See the lists of licenses for tavernholders, innkeepers, and retailers: Mass., Court of General Sessions (Essex and Suffolk Counties), 25 July 1720 (pp. 41–42), 18 July 1722 (pp. 146–48), 31 July 1723 (pp. 223–24); 21 July 1724 (pp. 278–81), 16 July 1725 (pp. 343–46); 22 July 1726 (pp. 39–43); 25 July 1727 (pp. 95–99); 23 July 1728 (pp. 166–170). N. E. H. Hull, *Female Felons: Women and Serious Crime in Colonial Massachusetts* (Urbana: University of Illinois Press, 1987), 120–21.

25. Selectmen's Records, Salem, Mass., 14 July 1773, box 4, folder 10, EI.

26. Bartlett, *Records*, 4:64 (1709); *Suffolk County Court*, 29:85 (1671/2); Essex County, Court of General Sessions, 31 March 1752 [unpaginated]; *Early History of Boston* (1750), 14:180.

27. Shurtleff, *Records*, 1:126 (1634), 183 (1636), 274 (1639).

28. Ibid., 4 (part 1): 60–61 (1651).

29. Noble, *Court of Assistants*, 2:40 (1633); Shurtleff, *Records*, 1:127 (1634); *Early History of Boston*, 2:83 (1644).

30. *Early History of Boston*, 12:46–48, 80–82 (1733).

31. Ibid., 14:317 (1757), 18:265 (1776); Bartlett, *Records*, 6:238 (1760).

32. Shurtleff, *Records*, 1:109 (1633); Noble, *Court of Assistants*, 2:5, 6, 12, 36 (1630–33); Shurtleff, *Records*, 1:111 (1633), 127 (1634), 159 (1635), 183 (1636).

33. Fiske, ed., [R.I.] *General Court of Trials* (1676), 52. This entry is from "Book A," the manuscript of which is at the Rhode Island Judicial Archives, Pawtucket. Suffolk County, Court of General Sessions, 30 January 1726/7, 59; Suffolk County, Superior Court of Judicature, February 1726/7, p. 77, October 1728, 180.

34. *Katherine West v. Benjamin Shearman*, in an action of assumpsit (1757), in Fiske, comp., "Gleanings," 326.

35. *Early History of Boston*, 12:273 (1740/1), 235–38, "Rules and Orders for the Management of the Work House in Boston."

36. "Rules and Orders for the Management of the Work House Lately Erected in the Town of Salem for the Employing and Maintaining the Idle and Poor" [1749], Public Welfare Dept. Records, vol. 14 (1749–98), p. 3, EI. In March 1751 the Rhode Island legislature passed an act for promoting the raising of flax and wool "and for the manufactory of the same into cloth." In June portions of the act were repealed because the bounty on woolen manufactured goods might displease Great Britain (Bartlett, *Records*, 5:318).

37. *Suffolk County Court*, passim. There appears to have been ongoing ambivalence about the lengths to which women should go to support themselves, a particular problem in communities with low sex ratios. See Fiske, comp., "Gleanings," 106, 213; Petition of Ann Franklin (1736), R.I. Petitions, 3:82.

38. R.I. Petitions, 3:124 (1737); Newport Town Council records, 8:139 (1740/1), 13:1 (n.d. but vol. marked 1760–63).

39. "Rules for the Workhouse in Salem" [1749], 1772ff (unpaginated).

40. Shurtleff, *Records*, 3:399 (1656).

41. Salem Town Records, Selectmen's Records, box 2, pp. 725, 769 (21 April 1724, 13 August 1725), EI.

42. Lawrence Stone, *The Family, Sex, and Marriage* (New York: Harper and Row, 1979), 30–32.

43. Patricia Crawford, *Women and Religion in England, 1500–1720* (London: Routledge, 1993), 55; Edmund S. Morgan, *The Puritan Family: Religion and Domestic Relations in Seventeenth-Century New England* (New York: Harper and Row, 1944, 1966), 30–33; Chilton L. Powell, "Marriage in Early New England," *New England Quarterly* 1 (1928): 329.

44. Powell, "Marriage in Early New England," 330–33.

45. Shurtleff, *Records*, 1:296 (1640); Noble, *Court of Assistants*, 2:107 (1641).

46. *Suffolk County Court*, 29:232 (1672/3), 29:517 (1674), 30:676 (1675/6); Dow, ed., *Essex County Quarterly Courts*, 1:50, 51 (1642/3), 83 (1645).

47. *Suffolk County Court*, 30:1063 (1679); Dow, ed., *Essex County Quarterly Courts*, 8:17 (September 1680). See Salmon, *Women and the Law of Property*, 8, 9, 13, 123.

48. *Suffolk County Court*, 29:442–43 (1674).

49. Noble, *Court of Assistants*, 2:74 (1637/8), 65 (1636/7); *Suffolk County Court*, 29:443 (28 April 1774).

50. Shurtleff, *Records*, 5:4 (1674); *Suffolk County Court*, 30:781 (1676/7); 868 (1677); 943 (1678).

51. Dow, ed., *Essex County Quarterly Courts*, 1:13 (1639); Shurtleff, *Records*, 1:123 (1634), 219 (1637/8), 317 (1641); Noble, *Court of Assistants*, 2:90 (1639).

52. For an overview and analysis of divorce in seventeenth- and eighteenth-

century Massachusetts, Rhode Island, and New Hampshire, see George Elliott Howard, *A History of Matrimonial Institutions, Chiefly in the United States and England* (Chicago: University of Chicago Press, 1904), 2:328–66; Nancy F. Cott, "Divorce and the Changing Status of Women in Eighteenth-Century Massachusetts," *William and Mary Quarterly* 33 (1976): 586–614; D. Kelly Weisberg, "Under Great Temptations Here: Women and Divorce in Puritan Massachusetts," in *Women and the Law: The Social Historical Perspective*, ed. D. Kelly Weisberg (Cambridge: Schenkman, 1982), 2:117–131; Sheldon S. Cohen, "The Broken Bond: Divorce in Providence County, 1749–1809," *Rhode Island History* 44 (1985): 67–79; Sheldon S. Cohen, "What Man Hath Put Asunder: Divorce in New Hampshire, 1681–1784," *Historical New Hampshire* 41 (1986): 118–41.

53. Cott, "Divorce," 592; Cohen, "Broken Bond," 78.

54. Bartlett, *Records,* 2:122–24 (1665); Dow, ed., *Essex County Quarterly Courts,* 8:356 (1682).

55. Bartlett, *Records,* 2:99 (1665); Newport County Superior Court of Judicature, book E, p. 376 (1768), R.I. Judicial Archives.

56. Meribah Edmond's divorce petition (1716) in R.I. Colony Records (MS), 4:153, R.I. State Archives; *Mercy Austin v. Benoni Austin* divorce petition, R.I. Petitions, vol. 5, p. "D" (1739/40), R.I. State Archives ; Marcy Olney's divorce petition, R.I. Petitions, 7:139 (1748), R.I. State Archives.

57. Noble, *Court of Assistants,* 1:227 (1682), 168 (1680), 197 (1681); Shurtleff, *Records,* 3:350 (1654), 5:248–49 (1679).

58. Koehler, *Search for Power,* appendix 1, "Petitions for Divorce in New England, 1620–1699."

59. Cott, "Divorce," table 1, p. 592.

60. Koehler, *Search for Power,* appendix 1; Bartlett, *Records,* 3:11; Petition Collection, passim, R.I. State Archives.

61. Plaintiffs Index and Defendants Index, Newport County Superior Court of Judicature, books E and F, as well as file papers, R.I. Judicial Archives.

62. "An Act against Adultery, Polygamy, and Unlawfully Marrying Persons; and for the Relief of Such Persons as Are Injured by the Breach of Marriage Covenants" (1749), (R.I.) *General Assembly Acts* (1747–50), 53–54, NHS; R.I. Petitions, 8:109 (1753).

63. "An Act in Addition to an Act, Entitled An Act against Adultery, Polygamy, and Unlawfully Marrying Persons; and for the Relief of Such Persons as Are Injured by the Breach of Marriage Covenants" (1754), (R.I.) *General Assembly Acts* (1754–56), 23.

64. Newport County, Superior Court of Judicature (1762), book E, p. 199, R.I. Judicial Archives.

65. *Ann Seten [Setin] v. Asa Seten* (1774), Newport County Superior Court of Judicature, book F, p. 91, R.I. Judicial Archives.

66. *Sarah Bliss v. George Bliss* (1795), Newport County Superior Court of Judicature, book F, p. 389, R.I. Judicial Archives.

67. *Alice Brayton v. John Brayton* (1795), Newport County Superior Court of Judicature, book F, p. 396.

68. Petition of Ann Little, R.I. Petitions, 2:74 (1732); Petition of Robert Little, R.I. Petitions, 2:130 (1733).

69. Carole Shammas, "Anglo-American Household Government in Comparative Perspective," *William and Mary Quarterly* 52 (January 1995): 121; Laurel T. Ulrich, *A Midwife's Tale: The Life of Martha Ballard, Based on Her Diary, 1785–1812* (New York: Knopf, 1990), 148–49.

70. For a discussion of fornication prosecutions and the double standard, see Ulrich, *A Midwife's Tale*, 148, and William Nelson, *Americanization of the Common Law: The Impact of Legal Change on Massachusetts Society, 1760–1830* (Cambridge: Harvard University Press, 1975), 110–11. Although N. E. H. Hull maintains that the criminal justice system treated women fairly in the seventeenth and eighteenth centuries, her own statistics argue otherwise: "Between 1673 and 1774 there were 38 indictments for adultery heard in the highest courts, 30 of which were against women" (Hull, *Female Felons*, 101–2, 141, 13, 31–32).

71. Fiske, ed., R.I. General Court of Trials (1671), 9–10; (1672), 15–16; (1682), 114.

72. Ibid., (1671, 1673), 10, 36.

73. Noble, *Court of Assistants*, 2:93 (1640).

74. Essex Institute, *Historical Collections*, 9:26, 28, 32 (1636).

75. Noble, *Court of Assistants*, 2:48 (1634), 3:191 [1667]; *Suffolk County Court*, 29:125 (1672).

76. Noble, *Court of Assistants*, 2:48 (1634), 2:74 (1638), 2:89, 90, (1639), 2:94, 95 (1640), 2:108 (1641); 1:56 (1675), 1:197 (1681).

77. Suffolk County, Court of General Sessions, 25 September 1723, p. 238, 27 July 1724, pp. 282, 284.

78. Hull, *Female Felons*, 120–21; Suffolk County, Court of General Sessions, 2 April 1728, p. 147.

79. Ruth Wallis Herndon, "Warned Out in New England: Eighteenth-Century Tales of Trouble," paper presented to the Philadelphia Center for Early American Studies, 22 September 1995, 13, 16.

80. Noble, *Court of Assistants*, 2:79 (1638), 2:121 (1642), 1:230 (1683).

81. Dow, ed., *Essex County Quarterly Courts*, 1:136 (1647); Suffolk County, Court of General Sessions, 25 September 1723, 233, 236.

82. Noble, *Court of Assistants*, 1:114 (1677), 138 (1678).

83. Mary Beth Norton, "Gender and Defamation in Seventeenth-Century Maryland," *William and Mary Quarterly* 44 (January 1987): 3–39.

84. *Welch v. Tufts*, Middlesex County, Mass., Superior Court of Judicature (January 1760), 3.

85. *Rebecca Baily v. John Greenman*, September 1724, file papers, R.I. Judicial Archives.

86. Shammas, "Anglo-American Household Government," 112.

87. Shurtleff, *Records*, 4 (part 2): 408 (1668). For rules governing adultery in

Massachusetts see Edgar J. McManus, *Law and Liberty in Early New England: Criminal Justice and Due Process, 1620–1692* (Amherst: University of Massachusetts Press, 1993), 23. See also the bigamy charges against Joseph Indian in *Suffolk County Court,* 29:485 (1674).

88. Noble, *Court of Assistants,* 3:222 (1673); Bartlett, *Records,* 3:238 (1688).

89. Noble, *Court of Assistants,* 2:2 (1630); Shurtleff, *Records,* 1:75 (1630), 2:116 (1645), 2:117 (1645); Salem Town Records, Selectmen's Records, 14 (1709).

90. Deborah Gray White, "Female Slaves: Sex Roles and Status in the Antebellum Plantation South," in *Unequal Sisters,* ed. Ruiz and DuBois, 25–26. Carl Bridenbaugh, *Cities in the Wilderness: The First Century of Urban Life in America, 1625–1742* (New York: Oxford University Press, 1938, 1971), 392–93.

91. Suffolk County, Court of General Sessions (April 1722), 134.

92. Suffolk County, Court of General Sessions (March 1725), 314.

93. John Adams wrestled with this problem and ultimately argued that even the acquisition of property did not provide women with enough independent judgment to make political decisions; see John Adams to James Sullivan, 26 May 1776, in Robert J. Taylor et al., eds., *The Papers of John Adams* (Cambridge: Belknap Press of Harvard University Press, 1979), 4:211.

CHAPTER 6

1. Records relating to Eunice Greenman may be found in Jane Fiske, comp., "Gleanings from the Newport Court Files," 91–93, 225. See also John R. Bartlett, *Records of the Colony of Rhode Island and Providence Plantations in New England* (Providence, R.I.: A. Crawford Greene and Brother, 1856), 4:313 (1722), and the file papers accompanying *Christopher Almy v. Eunice Greenman* and *Eunice Greenman v. Christopher Almy,* September 1721 and March 1722, Docket 207, 214, R.I. Judicial Archives, Pawtucket.

2. James M. Arnold, *Vital Records of Rhode Island, 1636–1850* (Providence: Narragansett Historical Publishing Co., 1893), 4:4 (Newport); 4:51 (Portsmouth, R.I.).

3. Gordon S. Wood, *The Radicalism of the American Revolution* (New York: Vintage Books, 1993), 183–84; Elaine Forman Crane, "Dependence in the Era of Independence: The Role of Women in a Republican Society," in *The American Revolution: Its Character and Limits,* ed. Jack P. Greene (New York: New York University Press, 1987), 253–75.

4. Linda K. Kerber, *Women of the Republic: Intellect and Ideology in Revolutionary America* (Chapel Hill: University of North Carolina Press, 1980). As Mary Beth Norton concludes: "What truly distinguished the Revolutionary era from preceding decades was that Americans initiated a public dialogue on the subject of women and their proper roles. . . . During and after the Revolution that topic aroused considerable public comment for the first time. . . . The new interest in women flowed directly from a combination of wartime experiences and republican ideology" (Mary Beth Norton, "The Evolution of White Women's Experience in Early America,"

American Historical Review 89 [1984]: 616). Nancy Cott also asserts that the 'cult of true womanhood' and the 'cult of domesticity' . . . first became conspicuous in the early nineteenth century" (Nancy F. Cott, *The Bonds of Womanhood: "Woman's Sphere" in New England, 1780–1835* [New Haven: Yale University Press, 1977], 1).

5. See, for example, Kathryn Kish Sklar, "The Founding of Mount Holyoke College," in *Women of America: A History,* ed. Carol Berkin and Mary Beth Norton (New York: Houghton Mifflin, 1979), 180; Ann D. Gordon, "The Young Ladies Academy of Philadelphia," in *Women of America,* ed. Berkin and Norton, 86–87; Cathy Davidson, "The Novel as Subversive Activity: Women Reading, Women Writing," in *Beyond the American Revolution: Explorations in the History of American Radicalism,* ed. Alfred Young (DeKalb: Northern Illinois University Press, 1993), 283–316; Susan Stabile, "'I wou'd wish our Present Leaders Might Have a Three-Fold Dose, at the Dawn and close of every day': Philadelphia Women Political Satirists as Moral Physicians," paper presented to the Philadelphia Center for Early American Studies, 5 May 1995.

6. Jan Lewis, "The Republican Wife: Virtue and Seduction in the Early Republic," *William and Mary Quarterly* 44 (October 1987): 689; Melvin Yazawa, *From Colonies to Commonwealth: Familial Ideology and the Beginnings of the American Republic* (Baltimore: Johns Hopkins University Press, 1985), 3. See also Jay Fliegelman, *Prodigals and Pilgrims: The American Revolution against Patriarchal Authority, 1750–1800* (Cambridge: Cambridge University Press, 1982), esp. chap. 5; Gordon Schochet, *Patriarchalism in Political Thought* (Oxford: Blackwell, 1975), 273.

7. For an opposing viewpoint, see Edith B. Gelles, *Portia: The World of Abigail Adams* (Bloomington: Indiana University Press, 1992), 133–34. Gelles argues that the patriarchy uses motherhood to further its own goals. See also Margaret A. Nash, "Rethinking Republican Motherhood: Benjamin Rush and the Young Ladies' Academy of Philadelphia," *Journal of the Early Republic* 17 (1997): 188–89, and Chandos M. Brown, "Mary Wollstonecraft, or, The Female Illuminate: The Campaign against Women and 'Modern Philosophy' in the Early Republic," *Journal of the Early Republic* 15 (1995): 394. A few historians of Europe have also taken less positive positions. See, for example, Carole Pateman, *The Sexual Contract* (Stanford: Stanford University Press, 1988), 90; Marlene Legates, "The Cult of Womanhood in Eighteenth-Century Thought," *Eighteenth-Century Studies* 10 (1976): 26–31, 39; Gerda Lerner, *The Creation of Feminist Consciousness from the Middle Ages to 1870* (New York: Oxford University Press, 1993), 212–15.

8. Susan Amussen, *An Ordered Society: Gender and Class in Early Modern England* (New York: Blackwell, 1988), 61. For an excellent discussion of the subject, see M. L. Shanley, "Marriage Contract and Social Contract in Seventeenth-Century English Political Thought," *Western Political Quarterly* 32 (1979): 79–91.

9. William Bridge, *The Wounded Conscience Cured* (London, 1642), 44; Henry Parker, *Jus populi* (London, 1644), 4–5; Henry Palmer, *Scripture and Reason Pleaded for Defensive Armes* (London, 1643), 35–36; Shanley, "Marriage," 79, 81–84; John Milton, *The Doctrine and Discipline of Divorce, Restor'd to the Good of Both Sexes* (London: T.P. and M.S., 1643).

10. Schochet, *Patriarchalism,* 201–2; Robert Filmer, "The Anarchy of a Limited

or Mixed Monarchy" (1648), in *Patriarcha and Other Writings*, ed. Johann P. Sommerville (Cambridge: Cambridge University Press, 1991), 142. For a perceptive analysis of the Filmerian model, see Mary Beth Norton, *Founding Mothers and Fathers: Gendered Power and the Forming of American Society* (New York: Knopf, 1996).

11. John Locke, *Two Treatises of Government* (1690), ed. Peter Laslett (Cambridge: Cambridge University Press, 1960), 2d treatise, sec. 78, p. 337, sec. 82, 83, pp. 339–40, 1st treatise, sec. 29, p. 179, sec. 47, 48, pp. 191–92; Samuel von Pufendorf, *De jure naturae et gentium* (1672), *Of the Law of Nature and Nations* (1st English translation, 1703; London: Walthoe, Wilkins, et al., 1729), 567, 570.

12. Locke, *Two Treatises*, 2d treatise, sec. 81, p. 339; Pufendorf, *De jure*, 579.

13. Pufendorf, 570.

14. Ibid., 571; Locke, *Two Treatises*, 2d treatise, sec. 82, p. 339.

15. Mary Astell, "Some Reflections upon Marriage" (1700), in *The First English Feminist: Reflections upon Marriage and Other Writings by Mary Astell*, ed. Bridget Hill (New York: St. Martin's Press, 1986), 76; Sir John Vanbrugh, *The Provok'd Wife* (1697), quoted in Alice Browne, *The Eighteenth-Century Feminist Mind* (Detroit: Wayne State University Press, 1987), 93.

16. Astell, "Some Reflections upon Marriage," 70; Claude Erard and C. Marguetel de Saint-Denis, Seigneur de Saint-Evremond, *The Arguments of Monsieur Erard, for Monsieur the Duke of Mazarin . . . And the Factum for Madam the Dutchess of Mazarin . . .* (London, 1699), 148–49.

17. See Jerome Nadelhaft, "The Englishwoman's Sexual Civil War: Feminist Attitudes towards Men, Women, and Marriage, 1650–1740," *Journal of the History of Ideas* 43 (1982): 558; Bridget Hill, introduction, in Astell, *The First English Feminist*, 18–19, 39–43.

18. Keith Thomas, "Women in the Civil War Sects," *Past and Present* 13 (April 1958): 44–47, 52, 54–55; François Poulain de La Barre, *The Equality of the Sexes* (1673; English trans., 1677; Manchester: Manchester University Press, 1990); Jacques du Bosc, *The Complete Woman* (1632; English trans., London, 1639).

19. Hill, introduction, in Astell, *The First English Feminist*, 39–43, 18–19, 21–22; Keith Thomas, "Women and the Civil War Sects," 55; [Antoine Leonard] Thomas, *Essay on the Character, Manners, and Genius of Women in Different Ages* (Paris: Moutard, 1772; Philadelphia: Robert Aitken, 1774), 2:92, 95, 98.

20. Susan Cahn, *Industry of Devotion: The Transformation of Women's Work in England, 1500–1660* (New York: Columbia University Press, 1987), 178. See also Ruth Perry, "Colonizing the Breast: Sexuality and Maternity in Eighteenth-Century England," in *Forbidden History: The State, Society, and the Regulation of Sexuality in Modern Europe*, ed. John C. Fout (Chicago: University of Chicago Press, 1992), 107–37.

21. Cahn, *Industry of Devotion*, 2, 4; Moira Ferguson, ed., *First Feminists: British Women Writers, 1578–1799* (Bloomington: Indiana University Press; Old Westbury, N.Y.: Feminist Press, 1985), 16.

22. Carolyn Lougee, *The Paradis des Femmes: Women, Salons, and Social Strati-*

fication in Seventeenth-Century France (Princeton: Princeton University Press, 1976), 3–5, 17, 32–33, 59, 65.

23. François de Salignac de La Mothe-Fénelon, *Fénelon on Education: A Translation of the "Traité de l'éducation des filles" and Other Documents Illustrating Fénelon's Educational Theories and Practice, Together with an Introduction and Notes,* trans. H. C. Barnard (Cambridge: Cambridge University Press, 1966), 2, 3. Fénelon's treatise was first published in France in 1687 and in England in 1707.

24. Samia Spencer, ed., *French Women in the Age of Enlightenment* (Bloomington: Indiana University Press, 1984), 14 (introduction); Cissie Fairchild, "Women and Family," in ibid., 101; Jean-Jacques Rousseau, *A Discourse on Inequality* (1754; New York: Viking Penguin, 1984), 65.

25. Jean-François Marmontel, *Moral Tales* (London: F. C. and J. Rivington, 1821), 293–318; quotations are from 300, 316. The tales first appeared in *Mercure de France,* beginning in 1756. English translations were published in 1764.

26. Bathsua Pell Makin, "An Essay to Revive the Antient Education of Gentlewomen" (1673) in *First Feminists,* ed. Ferguson, 138–39; see Browne, *Eighteenth-Century Feminist Mind,* 6, 83.

27. Makin, "Essay," 135–36; Jacob Bouton, *Mary Wollstonecraft and the Beginnings of Female Emancipation in France and England* (Amsterdam: H. J. Paris, 1922; Philadelphia: Porcupine Press, 1975), 18; Darline Gay Levy and Harriet B. Applewhite, "Women and Political Revolution in Paris," in *Becoming Visible: Women in European History,* ed. Renate Bridenthal, Claudia Koonz, and Susan Stuard (Boston: Houghton Mifflin, 1987), 289; Mary Astell, "A Serious Proposal to the Ladies" (1694), in *First Feminists,* ed. Ferguson, 189.

28. Peter Gay, ed., *John Locke on Education* (New York: Bureau of Publications, Teachers College, Columbia University, [c. 1964]); *Fénelon on Education,* 2, 5, xxxiv.

29. *Fénelon on Education,* xxxiii; J. Bouton, *Mary Wollstonecraft,* 55; Samia I. Spencer, "Women and Education," in *French Women,* ed. Spencer, 93–94.

30. Jean-Jacques Rousseau, *Emile* (1762; London: Dent, 1911; Rutland, Vt.: Tuttle, 1992), 371, 373. In response to a letter from Abigail Adams, John replied that "your sentiments of the Importance of Education in Women, are exactly agreeable to my own. Yet the Femmes Scavans, are contemptible Characters" (John Adams to Abigail Adams, 25 August 1776, in *Adams Family Correspondence,* ed. L. H. Butterfield [Cambridge: Harvard University Press, 1963], 2:109). A *femme scavan* or *savante* was a *précieuse,* bluestocking, or scholar. Howard Mumford Jones, "The Importation of French Books in Philadelphia, 1750–1800," *Modern Philology* 32 (1934–35): 166.

31. Pierre-Joseph Boudier de Villemert, *The Friend of Women* (1758, English editions, 1766, 1768), published in Philadelphia as *The Ladies Friend: Being a Treatise on the Virtues and Qualifications Which Are the Brightest Ornaments of the Fair Sex and Render Them Most Agreeable to the Sensible Part of Mankind* (Philadelphia, 1771), 147, 26–29.

32. Katherine U. Henderson and Barbara F. McManus, *Half Humankind: Contexts and Texts of the Controversy about Women in England, 1540–1640* (Urbana: University of Illinois Press, 1985), 82.

33. Lady D. Bradshaigh to Samuel Richardson (n.d.), in *Correspondence of Samuel Richardson*, ed. A. L. Barbauld (London: Richard Phillips, 1804), 6:53. John Adams agreed with this as well; in a letter to his daughter he warned her not to "tell many people" of her studies, since "it is scarcely reputable for young ladies to understand Latin and Greek" (John Adams to Abigail Adams 2d, 18 April 1776, in *Adams Family Correspondence*, 1:388). *New York Times*, 8 March 1994, C10.

34. Makin, "Essay," 141.

35. Daniel Defoe, *Essays upon Several Projects; or, Effectual Ways for Advancing the Interests of the Nation* (London: Thomas Ballard, 1702), 292, 299, 302.

36. James Fordyce, *Sermons to Young Women*, 2 vols. (London: A. Millar and T. Cadell, 1766); Abigail Adams to Mary Smith Cranch, 31 January 1767, in *Adams Family Correspondence*, 1:61.

37. Fordyce, *Sermons*, 1:271–72, 278, 283–84.

38. Judith Sargent Murray, "On The Equality of the Sexes" (1790) in *The Feminist Papers*, ed. Alice S. Rossi (New York: Columbia University Press, 1973), 20–21; Judith Sargent Murray, *The Gleaner* (1792–94, 1798) (Schenectady, N.Y.: Union College Press, 1992), no. 91, p. 731.

39. Murray, *Gleaner*, xiv; no. 7, p. 58; no. 17, p. 139; no. 91, pp. 730–31; Makin, "Essay," 137; John Hill, *On the Management and Education of Children*, "by Juliana-Susannah Seymour" (1754; New York: Garland, 1985), 177–78. I am grateful to Prof. Sheila Skemp, author of a forthcoming biography of Judith Sargent Murray, for sharing the information about Murray's correspondence. Private correspondence also reveals that Mary Wollstonecraft was more widely read in late eighteenth-century America than historians formerly suspected, which again may reflect the conservatism of American attitudes toward gender. Mary Kelley, "Educating Women in Early America: Formal and Informal Systems," paper presented at a conference entitled "Benjamin Franklin and Women," at the Franklin Institute, Philadelphia, 9 April 1994.

40. Kerber, *Women of the Republic*, 210–13.

41. Makin, "Essay," 137; Benjamin Rush, "Thoughts upon Female Education, Accomodated [*sic*] to the Present State of Society, Manners, and Government in the United States of America" (1787), in *Essays Literary, Moral and Philosophical* (Philadelphia: Thomas and Samuel Bradford, 1798), 76, 77, 79, 80, 81, 82, 85.

42. Benjamin Rush, "Of the Mode of Education Proper in a Republic," in *Essays*, 17, 18, 19.

43. For d'Alembert see J. Bouton, *Mary Wollstonecraft*, 55; Clare G. Moses, "The Legacy of the Eighteenth Century: A Look at the Future," in *French Women*, ed. Spencer, 407; Catherine S. Macaulay, "Letters on Education," (1790), in *First Feminists*, ed. Ferguson, 401, 408; Mary Wollstonecraft, "A Vindication of the Rights of Woman" (1792), in *Feminist Papers*, ed. Rossi, 68–69; Charles Brockden Brown, *Alcuin: A Dialogue* (1798; Northampton, Mass.: Gehenna Press, 1970), 56, 60.

44. Wollstonecraft, "Vindication," 69; Macaulay, "Letters," 401, 408. Cathy N. Davidson, *Revolution and the Word: The Rise of the Novel in America* (New York: Oxford University Press, 1986), 131. John Adams was a correspondent of Catherine

Macaulay; see *Adams Family Correspondence*, 1:74, n. 4, and Abigail Adams to Isaac Smith Jr., 20 April 1771, in *Adams Family Correspondence*, 1:77.

45. Hester Chapone, *Letters on the Improvement of the Mind, Addressed to a Young Lady* (1773; London: H. Hughs, 1774), 122–23. John Gregory, *A Father's Legacy to His Daughters* (1765; London: W. Strahan and T. Cadell, 1784), 109, 110. In 1790 Enos Hitchcock explained "the necessity of educating females in a manner suited to the genius of the government" (Enos Hitchcock, *Memoirs of the Bloomsgrove Family: In a Series of Letters to a Respectable Citizen of Philadelphia* [Boston: I. Thomas and E. T. Adams, 1790], 2:29).

46. Plutarch, "Conjugal Precepts," no. 33, in *Plutarch's Essays and Miscellanies* (New York: Colonial, 1905), 2:498. For an in-depth examination of this subject see Alan Macfarlane, "Romantic Love," in *Marriage and Love in England: Modes of Reproduction, 1300–1840* (Oxford: Blackwell, 1986), 174–208.

47. Van Eyb quoted in Stephen Ozment, *When Fathers Ruled: Family Life in Reformation Europe* (Cambridge: Harvard University Press, 1983), 7; Stanley Chojnacki, "The Power of Love: Wives and Husbands in Late Medieval Venice," in *Women and Power in the Middle Ages*, ed. Mary Erler and Maryanne Kowaleski (Athens: University of Georgia Press, 1988), 128.

48. Erasmus, "A Right Fruitful Epistle . . . in Laud and Praise of Matrimony" (1518), trans. Richard Taverner (London, 1536), in Joan Larsen Klein, ed., *Daughters, Wives, and Widows: Writings by Men about Women and Marriage in England, 1500–1640* (Urbana: University of Illinois Press, 1992), 82, 83.

49. Robert Cleaver, "A Godly Form of Householde Government" (London, 1598), in *Womanhood in Radical Protestantism*, ed. Joyce L. Irwin (New York: Mellen, 1979), 80.

50. Pufendorf, *De jure*, 570; George Savile, Marquis of Halifax, "The Lady's New Year's Gift; or, Advice to a Daughter," in *Miscellanies* (1688; London: Matt. Gillyflower, 1700), 31; Françoise d'Aubigné, Marquise de Maintenon, "To the Dutchess of Burgundy" (1700), in *Letters of Madame de Maintenon and Other Eminent Persons in the Age of Lewis XIV* (Dublin: George Faulkner, 1753), 177.

51. Merry E. Wiesner, *Women and Gender in Early Modern Europe* (Cambridge: Cambridge University Press, 1993), 60.

52. G. J. Barker-Benfield, *The Culture of Sensibility: Sex and Society in Eighteenth-Century Britain* (Chicago: University of Chicago Press, 1992), 169, 12; Davidson, *Revolution and the Word*, 8, 112–13.

53. Cahn, *Industry of Devotion*, 152, 172–73; Lougee, *Paradis des Femmes*, 59; Ruth Perry, "Colonizing the Breast," 109; Anthony Fletcher, *Gender, Sex, and Subordination in England, 1500–1800* (New Haven: Yale University Press, 1995), 400.

54. Dana Crowley Jack, *Silencing the Self: Women and Depression* (Cambridge: Harvard University Press, 1991), 43, 44, 66, 76.

55. Montaigne, Michel Eyquem de, "Of Friendship," in *The Essays; or, Morall, Politike and Militarie Discourses of Col. Michel de Montaigne: The First Book* (1580; London, 1603); Francis Bacon, *The Essays; or, Counsels, Civil and Moral, of Francis Ld. Verulam, Viscount of St. Albans* (1625; Mt. Vernon, N.Y.: Peter Pauper Press,

n.d.), 104, 112; Jeremy Taylor, *The Measures and Offices of Friendship* (London, 1657, 1662).

56. Savile, "The Lady's New Year's Gift," 13–14. Fifteen editions of this treatise appeared between 1688 and 1765; it was extremely popular among American readers.

57. "On the Nature and End of Marriage, and the Means by which the End Is to Be Obtained," in *The Matrimonial Preceptor; or, Instructive Hints to Those Who Are Like to Be Married: Gathered from the Works of the Most Classic Authors* (1755; New Haven, Conn.: N. Whiting, 1829), 14–15.

58. *The New Whole Duty of Man* (1741; London: John Hinton, 1766), 219–21.

59. John Gregory, *A Father's Legacy to His Daughters*, 6–7, 110; and Gregory, *A Comparative View of the State and Faculties of Man, with Those of the Animal World* (London: J. Dodsley, 1765), 116–18.

60. John Hill, *The Conduct of a Married Life: Laid Down in a Series of Letters Written by the Honourable Juliana-Susannah Seymour to a Young Lady, Her Relation, Lately Married* (London: R. Baldwin, 1754), 130, 10, 198; David Hume, "Of Love and Marriage" (1741–42), in David Hume, *Essays, Moral, Political and Literary* (London: Oxford University Press, 1963), 554; and Hume, "Of the Rise and Progress of the Arts and Sciences," in *Essays*, 133.

61. Benjamin Franklin, *Reflections on Courtship and Marriage, in Two Letters to a Friend* (Philadelphia: Benjamin Franklin, 1746), 59–60. The most recent edition of the Franklin papers questions the attribution of this pamphlet; see *The Papers of Benjamin Franklin*, ed. Leonard W. Labaree et al. (New Haven: Yale University Press, 1961), 3:74.

62. Robert Dodsley, *The Economy of Human Life* (1750; Philadelphia, 1772), part 3, 27–28. William Kenrick, *The Whole Duty of Woman; or, A Guide to the Female Sex, Written by a Lady* (1753; London: Dean and Munday, n.d.). Kenrick copies paragraphs without attribution from Savile's "Lady's New Year's Gift."

63. Chapone, *Letters*, 96, 110, 122.

64. Savile, "Lady's New Year's Gift," 16, 13–14.

65. Abigail Adams to John Adams, 7 May 1776, in *Adams Family Correspondence*, 1:402; Alexander Pope, "Epistle II, To a Lady: Of the Character of Women" (1735), in Pope, *Poetical Works*, ed. Herbert Davis (London: Oxford University Press, 1966), 298. AA personalized both quotes. See also AA to JA, 31 March 1776, and JA to AA, 14 April 1776, in *Adams Family Correspondence*, 1:369–70, 381–83.

66. *New Whole Duty of Man*, 226–27.

67. Boudier de Villemert, *The Ladies Friend*, 149–50; Chapone, *Letters*, 129, 136–37; John Hill, *Conduct of Married Life*, 2.

68. Katharine M. Rogers, *Feminism in Eighteenth-Century England* (Urbana: University of Illinois Press, 1982), 245.

69. Pufendorf, *De jure*, 570.

70. Montesquieu, Charles-Louis de Secondat, baron de La Brède et de, *Spirit of the Laws* (*D'esprit des loix*, 1748; Berkeley: University of California Press, 1977), book 8, chap. 2, 171.

71. John Locke, *Two Treatises*, 2d treatise, sec. 78; 1st treatise, sec. 47, pp. 337, 190–92.

72. Hume, "Of Polygamy and Divorce," 233, 234.

73. Hume, "Of Love and Marriage," 553–54.

74. Astell, "Some Reflections upon Marriage," 131.

75. Rousseau, *A Discourse on Inequality*, 112.

76. Moses, "Legacy," 407.

77. James Otis, "The Rights of the British Colonies Asserted and Proved" (1764), in *Pamphlets of the American Revolution*, ed. Bernard Bailyn (Cambridge: Harvard University Press, 1965), 1:420.

78. Hume, "Of Love and Marriage," 553; Cahn, *Industry of Devotion*, 172–73; Amussen, *An Ordered Society*, 122; see also M. E. Perry, *Gender and Disorder in Early Modern Seville*, for an analysis of another society that responded to disorder by containment of women.

79. *Spectator*, no. 81 (2 June 1711; London: F. C. and J. Rivington, 1817), 2:101; G. J. Barker-Benfield, *The Culture of Sensibility*, 307–8.

80. [Antoine-Leonard] Thomas, *Essay*, 2:102–17.

81. See Alfred F. Young, "The Women of Boston: 'Persons of Consequence' in the Making of the American Revolution, 1765–76," in *Women and Politics in the Age of the Democratic Revolution*, ed. Harriet B. Applewhite and Darline G. Levy (Ann Arbor: University of Michigan Press, 1990), 181–226; Barbara Clark Smith, "Food Rioters and the American Revolution," *William and Mary Quarterly* 51 (1994): 3–38.

82. By the end of the eighteenth century, 40 percent of English women and 27 percent of French women could sign their names. By comparison, half of New England women could sign their names by 1795. Martine Sonnet, "A Daughter to Educate," in *A History of Women in the West*, vol. 3, *Renaissance and Enlightenment Paradoxes*, ed. Natalie Zemon Davis and Arlette Farge (Cambridge: Harvard University Press, 1993), 130; Kenneth A. Lockridge, *Literacy in Colonial New England* (New York: Norton, 1974), 38–43. Abigail Adams to John Adams, 31 March 1776, 7 May 1776, in *Adams Family Correspondence*, 1:370, 402. See also John Trenchard and Thomas Gordon, *Cato's Letters; or, Essays on Liberty, Civil and Religious, and Other Important Subjects* (London: Russell and Russell, 1733), 2:55.

83. Jonathan Mayhew, "A Discourse Concerning Unlimited Submission and Nonresistance to the Higher Powers" (Boston, 1750), in Bailyn, *Pamphlets*, 224, 226, 229, 231.

84. Locke, *Two Treatises*, 2d treatise, sec. 82, 86, pp. 339, 341, 1st treatise, sec. 29, p. 179.

85. Hume, "Of Love and Marriage," 554.

86. Wollstonecraft, "Vindication," 55.

87. Kerber, *Women of the Republic*, 159–84, esp. p. 180.

88. Pufendorf, *De jure*, 579; Locke, *Two Treatises*, 2d treatise, sec. 82, p. 339.

89. Bernard Bailyn, *The Ideological Origins of the American Revolution* (Cambridge: Harvard University Press, 1967), 174; see also Joan Hoff, *Law, Gender, and*

Injustice: A Legal History of U.S. Women (New York: New York University Press, 1991), 24–25.

90. Nadelhaft, "Englishwomen's Sexual Civil War," 558; Patricia Higgins, "The Reactions of Women, With Special Reference to Women Petitioners," in *Politics, Religion and the English Civil War,* ed. Brian Manning (London: Edward Arnold, 1973), 216–17.

91. Lougee, *Paradis des Femmes,* 65; Joan B. Landes, *Women and the Public Sphere in the Age of the French Revolution* (Ithaca: Cornell University Press, 1988), 129–51; Elizabeth Fox-Genovese, "Women and Work," in *French Women,* ed. Spencer, 113–14.

92. Gary Kates, "'The Powers of Husband and Wife must be Equal and Separate': The Cercle Social and the Rights of Women, 1790–91," in *Women and Politics,* ed. Applewhite and Levy, 163–80.

93. R. Perry, "Colonizing the Breast," 115. To explain their denial of civil rights to women in the 1778 Massachusetts Constitution, legislators argued that women did not possess sufficient discretion because of their "natural tenderness and delicacy of their minds," attributes that no doubt justified "their retired mode of life, and various domestic duties" (Robert J. Taylor, ed., *Massachusetts, Colony to Commonwealth: Documents on the Formation of Its Constitution, 1775–1780* [Chapel Hill: University of North Carolina Press, 1961], 81).

94. Lynn Hunt, *The Family Romance of the French Revolution* (Berkeley: University of California Press, 1992), 152.

95. Landes, *Women and the Public Sphere,* 129–51; presenters on a panel entitled "Women, Gender, and the French Revolution: From Representation to Practices" argued that some aspects of the lives of French women improved in the postrevolutionary years (Tenth Berkshire Conference on the History of Women, 9 June 1996, University of North Carolina, Chapel Hill).

96. Hunt, *Family Romance,* 152, 164, 190; Fliegelman, *Prodigals and Pilgrims,* 197–226.

97. Montesquieu, *Spirit of the Laws,* book 23, chap. 28, 315; Betty Friedan, *The Feminine Mystique* (New York: Dell, 1974), 53.

EPILOGUE

1. James Fenimore Cooper Jr., "A Participatory Theocracy: Church Government in Colonial Massachusetts, 1629–1769," Ph.D. diss., University of Connecticut, 1987.

2. Hammond, ed., *New Hampshire Court Records,* 40:187 (1663).

3. For consideration of this thesis see Sherry B. Ortner, *Making Gender: The Politics and Erotics of Culture* (Boston: Beacon Press, 1996).

Bibliography

A NOTE ON THE PRIMARY SOURCES

Compiling material for the introduction was made easier by the number of colonial census lists that have been published. In the end, however, the most helpful were those in manuscript, since they were also more detailed than the tallies that eventually made their way to the official records. Particularly useful were manuscript census lists from Newport and Portsmouth.

Primary materials for chapter 2 include all published seventeenth- and eighteenth-century church records for Boston, Salem, Newport, and Portsmouth, as well as for smaller coastal towns in Essex County, Massachusetts. In addition, church records in manuscript were consulted at the Massachusetts Historical Society, Essex Institute, Newport Historical Society, and American Antiquarian Society. New Hampshire repositories in Concord and Portsmouth yielded little substantive information on church affairs apart from genealogical data.

For the chapter on women and the economy, the most important manuscript sources include all extant colonial merchants' ledgers for Boston, Salem, Newport, and Portsmouth in the above archives. Also extremely useful were newspapers, official town records (such as town meeting minutes, tax assessments, land evidence documents, and records kept by Overseers of the Poor), as well as selected family papers. Stray documents in manuscript such as lists of people holding licenses or workhouse rules also assisted in filling out the economic picture.

All published legal records for seventeenth-century Boston and Salem have been consulted. These include laws, case records, and legislative proceedings. In addition, Salem's legal documents in manuscript (including Salem Selectmen's Records, etc.) were examined at the Essex Institute. Eighteenth-century civil and criminal court records (both trial and appellate) for Boston and Salem have been read in manuscript either at the Massachusetts Archives in Boston or on microfilm. Eighteenth-century laws were read in published compilations.

Newport's seventeenth- and eighteenth-century laws have also been consulted in published compilations. Some of Newport's seventeenth-century court records have been published; much is still in preparation for publication. All published material and documents undergoing editing have been analyzed. Newport's seventeenth- and eighteenth-century criminal and civil court records in manuscript (including file papers) may be found at the Rhode Island Judicial Archives in Pawtucket. The Rhode Island State Archives in Providence holds an interesting collection of eighteenth-century Equity Court records. All those documents have been read at the repositories or on microfilm. Rhode Island also has an extraordinary collection of petitions in manuscript at the Rhode Island State Archives. All Newport County petitions from 1725 onward have been examined.

Seventeenth- and eighteenth-century legal proceedings from Portsmouth have been published in the New Hampshire Provincial and State Papers series and have been read in that form. Eighteenth-century legal documents in manuscript, including petitions, were selectively analyzed in Portsmouth and Concord.

PUBLISHED PRIMARY AND SECONDARY SOURCES

Acts and Laws of His Majesty's Colony of Rhode Island and Providence Plantations in America. Newport, R.I.: James Franklin, 1730.

Acts and Laws of His Majesty's Colony of Rhode Island and Providence Plantations in America. Boston: John Allen for Nicholas Boone, 1719.

Acts and Laws of His Majesty's Colony of Rhode-Island and Providence Plantations, Made and Passed since the Revision in June 1767. Newport, R.I.: Solomon Southwick, 1772.

Acts and Laws of His Majesty's Province of the Massachusetts-Bay in New England. Boston: S. Kneeland, 1759.

Acts and Laws of the English Colony of Rhode Island and Providence Plantations in New England in America. Newport, R.I.: Samuel Hall, 1767.

Acts and Laws . . . from Anno 1745, to Anno 1752. Newport, R.I.: J. Franklin, 1752.

Acts of the [Rhode Island] General Assembly. Newport, R.I.: Newport Historical Society [dated by year].

Amussen, Susan. *An Ordered Society: Gender and Class in Early Modern England.* New York: Blackwell, 1988.

Anderson, Virgina D. "The Origins of New England Culture." *William and Mary Quarterly* 48 (1991): 231–37.

Applewhite, Harriet B., and Darline G. Levy, eds. *Women and Politics in the Age of the Democratic Revolution.* Ann Arbor: University of Michigan Press, 1990.

Archer, Richard. "New England Mosaic: A Demographic Analysis of the Seventeenth Century." *William and Mary Quarterly* 47 (1990): 477–502.

Ariès, Philippe. *Centuries of Childhood: A Social History of Family Life.* New York: Random House, 1962.

Arnold, James M., *Vital Records of Rhode Island, 1636–1850.* 19 vols. Providence, R.I.: Narragansett Historical Publishing Co., 1893.

Astell, Mary. "A Serious Proposal to the Ladies . . . by a Lover of Her Sex." In Moira Ferguson, ed., *First Feminists: British Women Writers, 1578–1799,* 181–90. Bloomington: Indiana University Press; Old Westbury, N.Y.: Feminist Press, 1985.

———. "Some Reflections upon Marriage." In Bridget Hill, ed., *The First English*

Feminist: Reflections upon Marriage and Other Writings by Mary Astell, 190–97. New York: St. Martin's Press, 1986.

Aston, Margaret. "Segregation in Church." In W. J. Shiels and Diana Wood, eds., *Women in the Church*, 237–94. Oxford: Blackwell, 1990.

Aubigné, Françoise d' [Marquise de Maintenon]. *Letters of Madame de Maintenon and Other Eminent Persons in the Age of Lewis XIV.* Dublin: George Faulkner, 1753.

Bacon, Francis. *The Essays; or, Counsels, Civil and Moral, of Francis Ld. Verulam, Viscount of St. Albans.* 1625. Reprint. Mt. Vernon, N.Y.: Peter Pauper Press, n.d.

Bailyn, Bernard. *The Ideological Origins of the American Revolution.* Cambridge: Harvard University Press, 1967.

Bailyn, Bernard, ed. *Pamphlets of the American Revolution.* Cambridge: Harvard University Press, 1965.

Barbauld, A. L., ed. *Correspondence of Samuel Richardson.* 6 vols. London: Richard Phillips, 1804.

Barker-Benfield, G. J. *The Culture of Sensibility: Sex and Society in Eighteenth-Century Britain.* Chicago: University of Chicago Press, 1992.

Baron, Stanley. *Brewed in America: A History of Beer and Ale in the United States.* Boston: Little Brown, [1962].

Bartlett, John R. *Records of the Colony of Rhode Island and Providence Plantations in New England.* 10 vols. Providence, R.I.: A. Crawford Greene and Brother, 1865.

Belknap, Jeremy. *The History of New Hampshire.* 3 vols. New York: Arno Press, 1972.

Bennett, Joseph. "History of New England." 1740. In *Massachusetts Historical Society Proceedings* 5 (1861).

Bennett, Judith M. *Ale, Beer, and Brewsters in England: Women's Work in a Changing World, 1300–1600.* New York: Oxford University Press, 1996.

———. "Medieval Women, Modern Women: Across the Great Divide." In David Aers, ed., *Culture and History, 1350–1600; Essays on English Communities, Identities and Writing*, 147–75. London: Harvester Wheatsheaf, 1992.

———. "Patriarchy in the Secular Sphere." Paper presented at the Tenth Berkshire Conference on the History of Women, Chapel Hill, N.C., 8 June 1996.

———. "The Village Ale Wife: Women and Brewing in Fourteenth-Century England." In Barbara Hanawalt, ed., *Women and Work in Preindustrial Europe*, 20–36. Bloomington: Indiana University Press, 1986.

———. "Women's History: a Study in Continuity and Change." *Women's History Review* 2 (1993): 173–84.

Bennett, Judith M., Elizabeth A. Clark, Jean F. O'Barr, B. Anne Vilen, and Sarah Westphal-Wihl, eds. *Sisters and Workers in the Middle Ages.* Chicago: University of Chicago Press, 1989.

Bentley, William. *The Diary of William Bentley, D.D.* 4 vols. Salem, Mass.: Essex Institute, 1905. Reprint. Gloucester, Mass.: Peter Smith, 1962.

Benton, Josiah H. *Early Census Making in Massachusetts, 1643–1765.* Boston: Charles E. Goodspeed, 1905.

Berg, Maxine. *The Age of Manufactures: Industry, Innovation, and Work in Britain, 1700–1820*. New York: Oxford University Press, 1986.

Birket, James. *Some Cursory Remarks Made by James Birket in His Voyage to North America, 1750–1751*. New Haven: Yale University Press, 1916.

Blaisdell, Charmarie J. "Women in the Lutheran and Calvinist Movements." Richard Greaves, ed., In *Triumph over Silence: Women in Protestant History*, 13–44. Westport, Conn.: Greenwood Press, 1985.

Bolton, Brenda M. "Mulieres Sanctae." In Susan M. Stuard, ed., *Women in Medieval Society*, 141–58. Philadelphia: University of Pennsylvania Press, 1976.

Bonomi, Patricia. *Under the Cope of Heaven: Religion, Society, and Politics in Colonial America*. New York: Oxford University Press, 1986.

Book of the General Lawes and Libertyes. Cambridge, Mass., 1660.

Book of the General Laws and Libertyes Concerning the Inhabitants of Massachusetts Collected Out of the Records of the General Court for the Several Years wherin They Were Made and Established. Cambridge, Mass., 1648.

Botein, Stephen. *Early American Law and Society*. New York: Knopf, 1983.

Boudier de Villemert, Pierre Joseph. *The Ladies Friend: Being a Treatise on the Virtue and Qualifications Which Are the Brightest Ornaments of the Fair Sex and Render Them Most Agreeable to the Sensible Part of Mankind*. Philadelphia, 1771.

Bouton, Jacob. *Mary Wollstonecraft and the Beginnings of Female Emancipation in France and England*. Amsterdam: H. J. Paris, 1922. Reprint. Philadelphia: Porcupine Press, 1975.

Bouton, Nathaniel, ed. *Documents and Records Relating to the Province of New-Hampshire*. vol. 1. Concord, N.H.: George E. Jenks, 1867.

―――. *Documents and Records Relating to the Province of New Hampshire*. vol. 3. Manchester, N.H.: John B. Clarke, State Printer, 1869.

Boydston, Jeanne. *Home and Work: Housework, Wages, and the Ideology of Labor in the Early Republic*. New York: Oxford University Press, 1990.

―――. "The Woman Who Wasn't There: Women's Market Labor and the Transition to Capitalism in the United States." *Journal of the Early Republic* 16 (1996): 183–206.

Boyle, Susan C. "Did She Generally Decide? Women in Ste. Genevieve, 1750–1805." *William and Mary Quarterly* 44 (1987): 775–89.

Breen, T. H. "'Baubles of Britain': The American and Consumer Revolutions of the Eighteenth Century." In Cary Carson, Ronald Hoffman, and Peter J. Albert, eds., *Of Consuming Interests: The Style of Life in the Eighteenth Century*, 444–82. Charlottesville: University Press of Virginia, 1994.

Bremer, Francis J. *The Puritan Experiment*. New York: St. Martin's Press, 1976.

Brewster, Charles. *Rambles about Portsmouth*. 1st series. Portsmouth, N.H., 1873, 1971.

Bridenbaugh, Carl. *Cities in Revolt: Urban Life in America, 1743–1776*. New York: Knopf, 1955. Reprint. New York: Oxford University Press, 1971.

―――. *Cities in the Wilderness: The First Century of Urban Life in America, 1625–1742*. 1938. Reprint. New York: Oxford University Press, 1971.

———. *Fat Mutton and Liberty of Conscience: Society in Rhode Island, 1636–1690.* Providence, R.I.: Brown University Press, 1974.

Bridge, William. *The Wounded Conscience Cured.* London, 1642.

Brissot de Warville, Jacques. *New Travels in the United States of America, 1788.* Cambridge: Harvard University Press, 1960.

Brown, Chandos M. "Mary Wollstonecraft, or, The Female Illuminate: The Campaign against Women and 'Modern Philosophy' in the Early Republic." *Journal of the Early Republic* 15 (1995): 389–424.

Brown, Charles B. *Alcuin: A Dialogue.* New York, 1798. Reprint. Northampton, Mass.: Gehenna Press, 1970.

Browne, Alice. *The Eighteenth-Century Feminist Mind.* Detroit: Wayne State University Press, 1987.

Bureau of the Census. *A Century of Population Growth.* Washington: Government Printing Office, 1909.

———. *Heads of Families at the First Census of the United States Taken in the Year 1790.* (Mass.) Washington: Government Printing Office, 1908.

———. *Heads of Families at the First Census of the United States Taken in the Year 1790.* (N.H.) Washington: Government Printing Office, 1908.

———. *Heads of Families at the First Census of the United States Taken in the Year 1790.* (Penn.) Washington: Government Printing Office, 1908.

———. *Heads of Families at the First Census of the United States Taken in the Year 1790.* (R.I.) Washington: Government Printing Office, 1908.

———. *Historical Statistics of the United States: Colonial Times to 1970.* 2 vols. Washington: Government Printing Office, 1975.

Bushman, Richard. *The Refinement of America: Persons, Houses, Cities.* New York: Knopf, 1992.

Butterfield, L. H., et al., eds. *Adams Family Correspondence.* 6 vols. Cambridge: Harvard University Press, 1973– .

"Byfield Parish Records, 1706–1762." *Essex Institute Historical Collections* 89 (1953): 163–94, 253–73, 376–92.

Cahn, Susan. *Industry of Devotion: The Transformation of Women's Work in England, 1500–1660.* New York: Columbia University Press, 1987.

Caplan, Niel, ed. "Some Unpublished Letters of Benjamin Colman, 1717–1725." *Massachusetts Historical Society Proceedings* 77 (1965): 101–42.

Carr, Lois G., and Lorena Walsh. "The Planter's Wife: The Experience of White Women in Seventeenth-Century Maryland." *William and Mary Quarterly* 34 (1977): 542–71.

Chapone, Hester. *Letters on the Improvement of the Mind, Addressed to a Young Lady.* London: H. Hughs, 1774.

Chappell, Edward. "Housing a Nation: The Transformation of Living Standards in Early America." In Cary Carson, Ronald Hoffman, and Peter J. Albert, eds., *Of Consuming Interests: The Style of Life in the Eighteenth Century,* 167–232. Charlottesville: University Press of Virginia, 1994.

Chojnacki, Stanley. "The Power of Love: Wives and Husbands in Late Medieval Venice." In Mary Erler and Maryanne Kowaleski, eds., *Women and Power in the Middle Ages*, 126–48. Athens: University of Georgia Press, 1988.

Clark, Alice. *Working Life of Women in the Seventeenth Century*. London: Routledge and Kegan Paul, 1982.

Clark, Peter. *The English Alehouse: A Social History, 1200–1830*. London: Longman, 1983.

Cleary, Patricia A. "'She Merchants' of Colonial America: Women and Commerce on the Eve of Revolution." Ph.D. diss., Northwestern University, 1989.

Cleaver, Rober. "A Godly Form of Householde Government." In Joyce L. Irwin, ed., *Womanhood in Radical Protestantism*, 70–86. New York: Mellen, 1979.

Cohen, Sheldon S. "The Broken Bond: Divorce in Providence County, 1749–1809." *Rhode Island History* 44 (1985): 67–79.

———. "What Man Hath Put Asunder: Divorce in New Hampshire, 1681–1784." *Historical New Hampshire* 41 (1986): 118–41.

Coleman, Benjamin. *Gospel Order Revived, Being an Answer to a Book Lately set forth by the Reverend Increase Mather by Sundry Ministers of the Gospel in New-England*. [New York]: William Bradford, 1700.

Commerce of Rhode Island. Massachusetts Historical Society Collections. 2 vols. [7th series, vol. 9.] Boston: Massachusetts Historical Society, 1914.

Cooper, James Fenimore, Jr. "A Participatory Theocracy: Church Government in Colonial Massachusetts, 1629–1769." Ph.D. diss. University of Connecticut, 1987.

Coster, William. "Purity, Profanity and Puritanism: The Churching of Women, 1500–1700." In W. J. Shiels and Diana Wood, eds., *Women in the Church*, 377–87. Oxford: Blackwell, 1990.

Cott, Nancy F. *The Bonds of Womanhood: "Woman's Sphere" in New England, 1780–1835*. New Haven: Yale University Press, 1977.

———. "Divorce and the Changing Status of Women in Eighteenth-Century Massachusetts." *William and Mary Quarterly* 33 (1976): 586–614.

Crane, Elaine F. "Dealing with Dependence: Paternalism and Tax Evasion in Eighteenth-Century Rhode Island." In D. Kelly Weisberg, ed., *Women and the Law: The Social Historical Perspective*, 1:27–44. 2 vols. Cambridge, Mass.: Schenkman, 1982.

———. "Dependence in the Era of Independence: The Role of Women in a Republican Society." In Jack P. Greene, ed., *The American Revolution: Its Character and Limits*, 253–75. New York: New York University Press, 1987.

———. *A Dependent People: Newport, Rhode Island, in the Revolutionary Era*. New York: Fordham University Press, 1985.

———. "Religion and Rebellion: Women of Faith in the American War for Independence." In Ronald Hoffman and Peter J. Albert, eds., *Religion in a Revolutionary Age*, 52–86. Charlottesville: University Press of Virginia, 1994.

———. "The Socioeconomics of a Female Majority in Eighteenth-Century Bermuda." *Signs: Journal of Women in Culture and Society* 15 (1990): 231–58.

Crawford, Patricia. *Women and Religion in England, 1500–1720*. London: Routledge, 1993.

Crawford, W. H. "Women in the Domestic Linen Industry." In Margaret MacCurtain and Mary O'Dowd, eds., *Women in Early Modern Ireland*, 255–264. Edinburgh: Edinburgh University Press, 1991.

Cross, Clare. "The Religious Life of Women in Sixteenth-Century Yorkshire." In W. J. Shiels and Diana Wood, eds., *Women in the Church*, 307–24. Oxford: Blackwell, 1990.

Cushing, John D., comp. *The Laws and Liberties of Massachusetts, 1641–1691*. Facsimile ed. 3 vols. Wilmington, Del.: Scholarly Resources, 1976.

Dale, Marian K. "The London Silk Women of the Fifteenth Century." In Judith M. Bennett, Elizabeth A. Clark, Jean F. O'Barr, B. Anne Vilen, and Sarah Westphal-Wihl, eds., *Sisters and Workers in the Middle Ages*, 26–38. Chicago: University of Chicago Press, 1989.

"Danvers Church Records." *New England Historical and Genealogical Register* 11 (1857): 131–35, 316–25.

Davidson, Cathy N. "The Novel as Subversive Activity: Women Reading, Women Writing." In Alfred Young, ed., *Beyond the American Revolution: Explorations in the History of American Radicalism*, 283–316. DeKalb: Northern Illinois University Press, 1993.

———. *Revolution and the Word: The Rise of the Novel in America*. New York: Oxford University Press, 1986.

Davis, Natalie Z. *Society and Culture in Early Modern France*. Stanford: Stanford University Press, 1975.

———. "Women in the Crafts in Sixteenth-Century Lyon." In Barbara Hanawalt, ed., *Women and Work in Preindustrial Europe*, 167–97. Bloomington: Indiana University Press, 1986.

Davis, Natalie Z., and Arlette Farge, eds. *Renaissance and Enlightenment Paradoxes*. Vol. 3 of *History of Women in the West*, George Duby and Michelle Perrot, general eds. Cambridge: Harvard University Press, 1993.

Dayton, Cornelia H. *Women before the Bar: Gender, Law, and Society in Connecticut, 1639–1789*. Chapel Hill: University of North Carolina Press, 1995.

Defoe, Daniel. *Essays upon Several Projects; or, Effectual Ways for Advancing the Interests of the Nation*. London: Thomas Ballard, 1702.

Delphy, Christine. *Close to Home: A Materialist Analysis of Women's Oppression*. Amherst: University of Massachusetts Press, 1984.

Dillard, Heath. "Women in Reconquest Castile." In Susan M. Stuard, ed., *Women in Medieval Society*, 71–94. Philadelphia: University of Pennsylvania Press, 1976.

Dodsley, Robert. *The Economy of Human Life*. Philadelphia, 1772.

Donnelly, Marian C. *The New England Meetinghouses of the Seventeenth Century*. Middletown, Conn.: Wesleyan University Press, 1968.

Dow, George, F., ed. *Records and Files of the Quarterly Courts of Essex County, Massachusetts, 1638–1683*. 8 vols. Salem, Mass.: Essex Institute, 1911–21.

————. "Records of the Congregational Church in Topsfield." *Topsfield Historical Society Collections* 14 (1909): 5–87.

Du Bosc, Jacques. *The Complete Woman* [1632]. London, 1639.

Duby, George. *La société aux XI et XII siècles dans la région maconnaise.* Paris: SEVPEN, 1971.

Duffy, Eamon. "Holy Maydens, Holy Wyfes: the Cult of Women Saints in Fifteenth- and Sixteenth-Century England." In W. J. Shiels and Diana Wood, eds., *Women in the Church,* 175–96. Oxford: Blackwell, 1990.

Dunn, Mary M. "Saints and Sisters: Congregational and Quaker Women in the Early Colonial Period." *American Quarterly* 30 (1978), 582–601.

Eales, Jacqueline. "Samuel Clarke and the 'Lives' of Godly Women." In W. J. Shiels and Diana Wood, eds., *Women in the Church,* 365–76. Oxford: Blackwell, 1990.

Erard, Claude, and C. Marguetel de Saint-Denis, Seigneur de Saint-Evremond. *The Arguments of Monsieur Erard, for Monsieur the Duke of Mazarin . . . and the Factum for Madam the Dutchess of Mazarin.* London, 1699.

Erasmus. "A Right Fruitful Epistle . . . in Laud and Praise of Matrimony." In Joan L. Klein, ed., *Daughters, Wives, and Widows: Writings by Men about Women and Marriage in England, 1500–1640,* 65–89. Urbana: University of Illinois Press, 1992.

Fairchild, Cissie. "Women and Family." In Samia I. Spencer, ed., *French Women in the Age of Enlightenment,* 97–110. Bloomington: Indiana University Press, 1984.

Felt, Joseph B. *Annals of Salem.* 2d ed. 2 vols. Salem, Mass.: W. and S. B. Ives, 1845–49.

Fénelon, François de Salignac de La Mothe-. *Fénelon on Education: A Translation of the "Traité de l'éducation des filles" and Other Documents Illustrating Fénelon's Educational Theories and Practice, Together with an Introduction and Notes.* Trans. H. C. Barnard. Cambridge: Cambridge University Press, 1966.

Ferguson, Moira, ed. *First Feminists: British Women Writers, 1578–1799.* Bloomington: Indiana University Press; Old Westbury, N.Y.: Feminist Press, 1985.

Filmer, Robert. "The Anarchy of a Limited or Mixed Monarchy." In Johann P. Sommerville, ed., *Patriarcha and Other Writings,* 131–71. Cambridge: Cambridge University Press, 1991.

Fiske, Jane, comp. "Gleanings from the Newport Court Files." Unpublished manuscript. New England Historic Genealogical Society, Boston.

————. "[R.I.] General Court of Trials, Book 'A.'" Unpublished manuscript. New England Historic Genealogical Society, Boston.

Fletcher, Anthony. *Gender, Sex, and Subordination in England, 1500–1800.* New Haven, Yale University Press, 1995.

Fliegelman, Jay. *Prodigals and Pilgrims: The American Revolution against Patriarchal Authority, 1750–1800.* Cambridge: Cambridge University Press, 1982.

Fordyce, James. *Sermons to Young Women.* 2 vols. London: A. Millar and T. Cadell, 1766.

Fox-Genovese, Elizabeth. "Women and Work." In Samia I. Spencer, ed., *French Women and the Age of Enlightenment,* 111–27. Bloomington: Indiana University Press, 1984.

Franklin, Benjamin. *Reflections on Courtship and Marriage, in Two Letters to a Friend.* Philadelphia: Benjamin Franklin, 1746.

Frere, W. H., and C. E. Douglas, eds. *Puritan Manifestoes: A Study of the Origin of the Puritan Revolt.* 1907. Reprint. New York: Burt Franklin, 1972.

Frey, Sylvia, and Marian Norton, eds. *New World, New Roles: A Documentary History of Women in Pre-Industrial America.* Westport, Conn: Greenwood Press, 1986.

Friedan, Betty. *The Feminine Mystique.* New York: Dell, 1974.

Gay, Peter, ed. *John Locke on Education.* New York: Bureau of Publications, Teachers College, Columbia University, [c. 1964].

Gelles, Edith B. *Portia: The World of Abigail Adams.* Bloomington: Indiana University Press, 1992.

Gildrie, Richard. *Salem, Massachusetts, 1626–1683: A Covenant Community.* Charlottesville: University Press of Virginia, 1975.

Goldin, Claudia. *Understanding the Gender Gap: An Economic History of American Women.* New York: Oxford University Press, 1990.

Goldstone, J. A. "The Demographic Revolution in England: A Re-examination." *Population Studies* 49 (1986): 5–33.

Goodell, Abner. *Acts and Resolves Public and Private of the Province of Massachusetts Bay.* 21 vols. Boston: Wright and Potter, 1869–1922.

Gordon, Ann D. "The Young Ladies Academy of Philadelphia." In Carol Berkin and Mary Beth Norton, eds., *Women of America: A History,* 68–91. New York: Houghton Mifflin, 1979.

Gordon, Ann D., and Mari Jo Buhle. "Sex and Class in Colonial and Nineteenth-Century America." In Berenice A. Carroll, ed., *Liberating Women's History: Theoretical and Critical Essays,* 278–300. Urbana: University of Illinois Press, c. 1976.

Gospel Order Revived, Being an Answer to a Book Lately Set Forth by the Reverend Increase Mather by Sundry Ministers of the Gospel in New-England. [New York]: William Bradford, 1700.

Greaves, Richard, ed. *Triumph over Silence: Women in Protestant History.* Westport, Conn.: Greenwood Press, 1985.

Greene, Evarts B., and Virginia D. Harrington. *American Population before the Federal Census of 1790.* New York, 1932. Reprint. Gloucester, Mass.: P. Smith, 1966.

Gregory, John. *A Comparative View of the State and Faculties of Man, with Those of the Animal World.* London: J. Dodsley, 1765.

———. *A Father's Legacy to His Daughters.* London: W. Strahan and T. Cadell, 1784.

Guttentag, Marcia, and Paul F. Secord. *Too Many Women? The Sex Ratio Question.* Beverly Hills, Calif.: Sage, 1983.

Hall, David D. *Worlds of Wonder, Days of Judgment: Popular Religious Belief in Early New England.* New York: Knopf, 1989.

Hall, Peter D. "Family Structure and Economic Organization: Massachusetts Merchants, 1700–1850." In Tamara K. Hareven, ed., *Family and Kin in Urban Communities, 1700–1930,* 38–61. New York: New Viewpoints, 1977.

Hamilton, Alexander. *Gentleman's Progress: The Itinerarium of Dr. Alexander Hamil-*

ton, 1744. Ed. Carl Bridenbaugh. Chapel Hill: University of North Carolina Press, 1948.

Hammond, Otis G., ed. *New Hampshire Court Records, 1640–1692.* Provincial and State Papers Series, vol. 40. [Concord]: State of New Hampshire, 1943.

Hanawalt, Barbara A. "Peasant Women's Contribution to the Home Economy in Late Medieval England." In Barbara A. Hanawalt, ed., *Women and Work in Preindustrial Europe,* 3–19. Bloomington: Indiana University Press, 1986.

Hanawalt, Barbara, ed. *Women and Work in Preindustrial Europe.* Bloomington: Indiana University Press, 1986.

Hartigan, Richard S. *The Forgotten Victim: A History of the Civilian.* Chicago: Precedent, 1982.

Hartmann, Heidi. "Capitalism, Patriarchy, and Job Segregation by Sex." *Signs: Journal of Women in Culture and Society* 1 (1976): 137–69.

Helly, Dorothy O., and Susan M. Reverby, eds. *Gendered Domains: Rethinking Public and Private in Women's History.* Ithaca: Cornell University Press, 1992.

Hemphill, C. Dallett. "Women in Court: Sex-Role Differentiation in Salem, Massachusetts, 1636–1683." *William and Mary Quarterly* 39 (1982): 164–75.

Henderson, Katherine U., and Barbara F. McManus. *Half Humankind: Contexts and Texts about Women in England, 1540–1640.* Urbana: University of Illinois Press, 1985.

Henretta, James. "The Transition to Capitalism in America." Paper presented to the Philadelphia Center for Early American Studies, 13 May 1988.

Herlihy, David. *Opera Muliebria: Women and Work in Medieval Europe.* New York: McGraw-Hill, 1990.

Herndon, Ruth W. "Warned Out in New England: Eighteenth-Century Tales of Trouble." Paper presented to the Philadelphia Center for Early American Studies, 22 September 1995.

Heyrman, Christine L. *Commerce and Culture: The Maritime Communities of Colonial Massachusetts, 1690–1750.* New York: Norton, 1984.

Higgins, Patricia. "The Reaction of Women, with Special Reference to Women Petitioners." In Brian Manning, ed., *Politics, Religion and the English Civil War,* 179–222. London: Edward Arnold, 1973.

Hill, Bridget. "Women's History: A Study in Change, Continuity, or Standing Still?" *Women's History Review* 2 (1993): 5–22.

———. *Women, Work, and Sexual Politics in Eighteenth-Century England.* Oxford: Blackwell, 1989.

Hill, Bridget, ed. *The First English Feminist: Reflections on Marriage and Other Writings by Mary Astell.* New York: St. Martin's Press, 1986.

Hill, Hamilton A. *History of the Old South Church, Boston, 1669–1884.* 2 vols. Boston: Houghton Mifflin, 1890.

Hill, John. *The Conduct of Married Life: Laid Down in a Series of Letters Written by the Honourable Juliana-Susannah Seymour to a Young Lady, her Relation, Lately Married.* 2d ed. London: R. Baldwin, 1754.

————. *On the Management and Education of Children* "by Juliana-Susannah Seymour." 1754. Reprint. New York: Garland, 1985.

Hitchcock, Enos. *Memoirs of the Bloomsgrove Family, in a Series of Letters to a Respectable Citizen of Philadelphia.* 2 vols. Boston: I. Thomas and E. T. Adams, 1790.

Hoff, Joan. *Law, Gender, and Injustice: A Legal History of U.S. Women.* New York: New York University Press, 1991.

Hopkins, Samuel. *Memoirs of the Life of Mrs. Sarah Osborn.* Catskill, N.Y.: N. Elliot, 1814.

Howard, George Elliott. *A History of Matrimonial Institutions, Chiefly in the United States and England.* 3 vols. Chicago: University of Chicago Press, 1904.

Howell, Martha C. "Citizenship and Gender: Women's Political Status in Northern Medieval Cities." In Mary Erler and Maryanne Kowaleski, eds., *Women and Power in the Middle Ages,* 37–60. Athens: University of Georgia Press, 1988.

————. "Women, the Family Economy, and the Structure of Market Production in Cities of Northern Europe during the Middle Ages." In Barbara Hanawalt, ed., *Women and Work in Preindustrial Europe,* 198–222. Bloomington: Indiana University Press, 1986.

Hubbard, William. *A General History of New England from the Discovery to 1680.* Massachusetts Historical Society Collections, 2d ser., vol. 5. Boston, 1848.

Hufton, Olwen. "Women, Work, and Family." In Natalie Z. Davis and Arlette Farge, eds., *A History of Women in the West,* vol. 3, *Renaissance and Enlightenment Paradoxes,* 15–45. Cambridge: Harvard University Press, 1993.

Hull, N. E. H. *Female Felons: Women and Serious Crime in Colonial Massachusetts.* Urbana: University of Illinois Press, 1987.

Hume, David. "Of Love and Marriage." In *Essays, Moral, Political, and Literary,* 552–57. London: Oxford University Press, 1963.

————. "Of the Rise and Progress of the Arts and Sciences." In *Essays, Moral, Political and Literary,* 112–38. London: Oxford University Press, 1963.

Hunnewell, James F., ed. *Records of the First Church in Charleston, Massachusetts, 1632–1789.* Boston, 1880.

Hunt, Lynn. *The Family Romance of the French Revolution.* Berkeley: University of California Press, 1992.

Jack, Dana C. *Silencing the Self: Women and Depression.* Cambridge: Harvard University Press, 1991.

Johnson, Penelope. "The Cloistering of Medieval Nuns: Release or Repression, Reality or Fantasy?" In Dorothy O. Helly and Susan M. Reverby, eds., *Gendered Domains: Rethinking Public and Private in Women's History,* 27–39. Ithaca: Cornell University Press, 1992.

Jones, Alice H. *American Colonial Wealth: Documents and Methods.* 3 vols. New York: Arno Press, 1978.

————. *Wealth of a Nation to Be: The American Colonies on the Eve of Revolution.* New York: Columbia University Press, 1980.

Jones, Douglas L. "The Strolling Poor: Transiency in Eighteenth-Century Massachu-

306 BIBLIOGRAPHY

setts." In James K. Martin, ed., *Interpreting Colonial America*, 285–308. New York: Harper and Row, 1978.

Jones, Howard M. "The Importation of French Books in Philadelphia, 1750–1800." *Modern Philology* 32 (1934–35): 157–77.

Juster, Susan. *Disorderly Women: Sexual Politics and Evangelicalism in Revolutionary New England*. Ithaca: Cornell University Press, 1994.

Karlsen, Carol F. *The Devil in the Shape of a Woman: Witchcraft in Colonial New England*. New York: Norton, 1987.

Kates, Gary. "'The Powers of Husband and Wife Must be Equal and Separate': The Cercle Social and the Rights of Women, 1790–1791." In Harriet B. Applewhite and Darline G. Levy, eds., *Women and Politics in the Age of the Democratic Revolution*, 163–80. Ann Arbor: University of Michigan Press, 1990.

Keller, Rosemary S. "New England Women: Ideology and Experience in First-Generation Puritanism." In Rosemary R. Ruether and Rosemary S. Keller, eds., *Women and Religion in America*, 2:132–92. San Francisco: Harper and Row, 1983.

Kelley, Mary. "Educating Women in Early America: Formal and Informal Systems." Paper presented at the conference entitled "Benjamin Franklin and Women," Franklin Institute, Philadelphia, 9 April 1994.

Kennedy, Roger G. *American Churches*. New York: Crossroad, 1982.

Kenrick, William. *The Whole Duty of Woman; or, A Guide to the Female Sex, Written by a Lady*. 1753. London: Dean and Munday, n.d.

Kerber, Linda K. "Separate Spheres, Female Worlds, Woman's Place: The Rhetoric of Women's History." *Journal of American History* 75 (1988–89): 9–39.

———. *Women of the Republic: Intellect and Ideology in Revolutionary America*. Chapel Hill: University of North Carolina Press, 1980.

Keyssar, Alexander. "Widowhood in Eighteenth-Century Massachusetts." *Perspectives in American History* 8 (1974): 83–119.

King, Margaret L. *Women of the Renaissance*. Chicago: University of Chicago Press, 1991.

Klapisch-Zuber, Christine. "Women Servants in Florence during the Fourteenth and Fifteenth Centuries." In Barbara Hanawalt, ed., *Women and Work in Preindustrial Europe*, 56–80. Bloomington: Indiana University Press, 1986.

Koehler, Lyle. *A Search for Power: The "Weaker Sex" in Seventeenth-Century New England*. Chicago: University of Illinois Press, 1980.

Konig, David. *Law and Authority in Puritan Massachusetts: Essex County, 1629–1692*. Chapel Hill: University of North Carolina Press, 1979.

Kowaleski, Maryanne. "Women's Work in a Market Town: Exeter in the Late Fourteenth Century." In Barbara Hanawalt, ed., *Women and Work in Preindustrial Europe*, 145–64. Bloomington: Indiana University Press, 1986.

Kowaleski, Maryanne, and Judith Bennett. "Crafts, Gilds, and Women in the Middle Ages: Fifty Years after Marian K. Dale." In Judith M. Bennett, Elizabeth A. Clark, Jean F. O'Barr, B. Anne Vilen, and Sarah Westphal-Wihl, eds., *Sisters and Workers in the Middle Ages*, 11–25. Chicago: University of Chicago Press, 1989.

Kujawa, Sheryl. "The Great Awakening of Sarah Osborn and the Female Society of the First Congregational Church in Newport." *Newport History* 65 (1994): 133–53.

Labaree, Leonard, et al., eds., *The Papers of Benjamin Franklin*. Vol 3. New Haven: Yale University Press, 1961.

Landes, Joan B. *Women and the Public Sphere in the Age of the French Revolution*. Ithaca: Cornell University Press, 1988.

Laurence, Anne. "A Priesthood of She-Believers: Women and Congregations in Mid-Seventeenth-Century England." In W. J. Shiels and Diana Wood, eds., *Women in the Church*, 345–63. Oxford: Blackwell, 1990.

Laws Respecting Women, The. London: J. Johnson, 1777. Reprint. Dobbs Ferry, N.Y.: Oceana, 1974.

Lechford, Thomas. *Plain Dealing; or, News from New England*. New York: Johnson Reprint Corp., 1969.

Legates, Marlene. "The Cult of Womanhood in Eighteenth-Century Thought." *Eighteenth-Century Studies* 10 (1976): 21–39.

Lerner, Gerda. *The Creation of Feminist Consciousness: From the Middle Ages to 1870*. New York: Oxford University Press, 1993.

———. *The Creation of Patriarchy*. New York: Oxford University Press, 1986.

Levy, Darline Gay, and Harriet B. Applewhite. "Women and Political Revolution in Paris." In Renate Bridenthal, Claudia Koonz, and Susan Stuard, eds., *Becoming Visible: Women in European History*, 279–306. Boston: Houghton Mifflin, 1987.

Lewis, Jan. "The Republican Wife: Virtue and Seduction in the Early Republic." *William and Mary Quarterly* 44 (1987): 689–721.

Locke, John. *Two Treatises of Government* [1690]. Ed. Peter Laslett. Cambridge: Cambridge University Press, 1960.

Lockridge, Kenneth A. *Literacy in Colonial New England: An Enquiry into the Social Context of Literacy in the Early Modern West*. New York: Norton, 1974.

Lothrop, Samuel. *A History of the Church in Brattle Street, Boston*. Boston, 1851.

Lougee, Carolyn. *The Paradis des Femmes: Women, Salons, and Social Stratification in Seventeenth-Century France*. Princeton: Princeton University Press, 1976.

Macaulay, Catherine S. "Letters on Education." in Moira Ferguson, ed., *First Feminists: British Women Writers, 1578–1799*, 400–411. Bloomington: Indiana University Press; Old Westbury, N.Y.: Feminist Press, 1985.

McCusker, John, and Russell R. Menard, *The Economy of British America, 1607–1789*. Chapel Hill: University of North Carolina Press, 1985.

Macfarlane, Alan. *Marriage and Love in England: Modes of Reproduction, 1300–1840*. Oxford: Blackwell, 1986.

Mack, Phyllis. "Women as Prophets during the English Civil War." *Feminist Studies* 8 (1982): 19–45.

McLoughlin, William G. *New England Dissent, 1630–1833: The Baptists and the Separation of Church and State*. 2 vols. Cambridge: Harvard University Press, 1971.

———. *Revivals, Awakenings, and Reform*. Chicago: University of Chicago Press, 1978.

McManus, Edgar J. *Law and Liberty in Early New England: Criminal Justice and Due Process, 1620–1692*. Amherst: University of Massachusetts Press, 1993.

McNamara, Jo Ann, and Suzanne Wemple. "The Power of Women through the Family in Medieval Europe, 500–1100." In Mary Erler and Maryanne Kowaleski, eds., *Women and Power in the Middle Ages*, 83–101. Athens: University of Georgia Press, 1988.

Main, Gloria L. "Gender, Work, and Wages in Colonial New England." *William and Mary Quarterly* 51 (1994): 39–66.

———. "Naming Children in Early New England, 1620–1795." Paper presented to the Philadelphia Center for Early American Studies, 7 April 1995.

———. *Tobacco Colony: Life in Maryland, 1650–1720.* Princeton: Princeton University Press, 1982.

Main, Jackson T. *The Social Structure of Revolutionary America.* Princeton: Princeton University Press, 1965.

———. *Society and Economy in Colonial Connecticut.* Princeton: Princeton University Press, 1985.

Makin, Bathsua. "An Essay to Revive the Antient Education of Gentlewomen." [1673]. In Moira Ferguson, ed., *First Feminists: British Women Writers, 1578–1799*, 128–42. Bloomington: Indiana University Press; Old Westbury, N.Y.: Feminist Press, 1985.

Mallary, Peter, and Tim Imrie. *New England Churches and Meetinghouses, 1680–1830.* New York: Vendome Press, 1985.

Manifesto Church, The: Records of the Church in Brattle Square, Boston, 1699–1872. Boston: Benevolent Fraternity of Churches, 1902.

Mann, Bruce. "The Formalization of Informal Law: Arbitration before the American Revolution." *New York University Law Review* 59 (1984): 443–81.

———. *Neighbors and Strangers: Law and Community in Early Connecticut.* Chapel Hill: University of North Carolina Press, 1987.

———. "Neighbors and Strangers: Legal Change and the Nature of Community in Connecticut, 1690–1760." Paper presented at the Organization of American Historians conference, 13 April 1986.

Marmontel, Jean François. *Moral Tales.* London: F. C. and J. Rivington, 1821.

Martin, John F. *Profits in the Wilderness: Entrepreneurship and the Founding of New England Towns in the Seventeenth Century.* Chapel Hill: University of North Carolina Press, 1991.

Mason, George C. *Annals of Trinity Church, Newport, Rhode Island, 1698–1821.* 2 vols. Newport, R.I.: Evans Printing House, 1890.

Mather, Cotton. *Ornaments for the Daughters of Zion.* 1692. Reprint. Delmar, N.Y.: Scholars' Facsimile and Reprints, 1978.

Matthaei, Julie A. *An Economic History of Women in America: Women's Work, the Sexual Division of Labor, and the Development of Capitalism.* New York: Schocken Books, 1982.

Mayhew, Jonathan. "A Discourse Concerning Unlimited Submission and Nonresistance to the Higher Powers" [1750]. In Bernard Bailyn, ed., *Pamphlets of the American Revolution*, 203–47. Cambridge: Harvard University Press, 1965.

Metcalf, Henry H., ed. *Probate Records of the Province of New Hampshire.* Provincial and State Papers Series, vols. 31 and 32. Bristol, N.H.: R. W. Musgrove, 1914.

Miller, Perry. *Errand into the Wilderness.* Cambridge: Harvard University Press, 1956, 1984.

Milton, John. *The Doctrine and Discipline of Divorce, Restor'd to the Good of Both Sexes.* London: T. P. and M. S., 1643.

Moller, Herbert. "Sex Composition and Correlated Culture Patterns of Colonial America." *William and Mary Quarterly* 2 (1945): 113–53.

Montaigne, Michel Eyquem de. "Of Friendship." In *The Essays; or, Morall, Politike and Militarie Discourses of Col. Michel de Montaigne: The First Book.* London, 1603.

Monter, William. "Protestant Wives, Catholic Saints, and the Devil's Handmaid: Women in the Age of the Reformation." In Renate Bridenthal, Claudia Koonz, and Susan Stuard, eds., *Becoming Visible: Women in European History,* 203–19. Boston: Houghton Mifflin, 1987.

Montesquieu, Charles-Louis de Secondat, baron de La Brède et de. *Spirit of the Laws* [1748]. Berkeley: University of California Press, 1977.

Moran, Gerald F. "'The Hidden Ones': Women and Religion in Puritan New England." In Richard Greaves, ed., *Triumph over Silence: Women in Protestant History,* 125–49. Westport, Conn.: Greenwood Press, 1985.

———. "'Sisters' in Christ: Women and the Church in Seventeenth-Century New England." In Janet W. James, ed., *Women in American Religion,* 47–67. Philadelphia: University of Pennsylvania Press, 1980.

Morgan, Edmund S. *The Gentle Puritan: A Life of Ezra Stiles.* Chapel Hill: University of North Carolina Press, 1962.

———. *The Puritan Family: Religion and Domestic Relations in Seventeenth-Century New England.* New York: Harper and Row, 1944, 1966.

Morris, Richard B. *Government and Labor in Early America.* 1946. Reprint. Boston: Northeastern University Press, 1981.

Moses, Clare G. "The Legacy of the Eighteenth Century: A Look at the Future." In Samia I. Spencer, ed., *French Women in the Age of Enlightenment,* 407–15. Bloomington: Indiana University Press, 1984.

Murray, Judith Sargent. *The Gleaner.* Schenectady, N.Y.: Union College Press, 1992.

———. "On the Equality of the Sexes." In Alice S. Rossi, ed., *The Feminist Papers,* 18–24. New York: Columbia University Press, 1973.

Nadelhaft, Jerome. "The Englishwoman's Sexual Civil War: Feminist Attitudes towards Men, Women, and Marriage, 1650-1740." *Journal of the History of Ideas* 43 (1982): 555–79.

Nash, Gary. *The Urban Crucible: Social Change, Political Consciousness, and the Origins of the American Revolution.* Cambridge: Harvard University Press, 1979. Abridged ed. *The Urban Crucible: The Northern Seaports and the Origins of the American Revolution.* Cambridge: Harvard University Press, 1986.

Nash, Margaret. "Rethinking Republican Motherhood: Benjamin Rush and the

Young Ladies' Academy of Philadelphia." *Journal of the Early Republic* 17 (1997): 171–91.

Neel, Carol. "The Origins of the Beguines." In Judith M. Bennett, Elizabeth A. Clark, Jean F. O'Barr, B. Anne Vilen, and Sarah Westphal-Wihl, eds., *Sisters and Workers in the Middle Ages*, 240–60. Chicago: University of Chicago Press, 1989.

Nelson, William. *Americanization of the Common Law: The Impact of Legal Change on Massachusetts Society, 1760–1830*. Cambridge: Harvard University Press, 1975.

New Hampshire. *Provincial and State Papers*. 40 vols. Concord, N.H., 1867–1943.

New Whole Duty of Man, The. London: John Hinton, 1766.

Noble, John, ed. *Massachusetts Colony Court of Assistants Records, 1630–1690*. 3 vols. Boston: Rockwell and Churchill Press, 1901–28.

Nobles, Gregory H. "Wages for Women in Seventeenth-Century Massachusetts: A Case Study of John Pynchon's Household Servants." Paper presented at the Fifth Berkshire Conference on the History of Women, 16–18 June 1981.

Norton, Mary Beth. "The Evolution of White Women's Experience in Early America." *American Historical Review* 89 (1984), 593–619.

———. *Founding Mothers and Fathers: Gendered Power and the Forming of American Society*. New York: Knopf, 1996.

———. "Gender and Defamation in Seventeenth-Century Maryland." *William and Mary Quarterly* 44 (1987): 3–39.

———. "'My Resting Reaping Time': Sarah Osborn's Defense of Her 'Unfeminine' Activities, 1767." *Signs: Journal of Women in Culture and Society* 2 (1976): 515–29.

———. "Women as Witnesses in Maryland Criminal Prosecutions, 1636–1683." Paper presented at the Seventh Berkshire Conference on the History of Women, 19 June 1987.

Notes Concerning the Channing Family. Collected by Edward Tyrrel Channing. Boston, 1895.

Oliver, Andrew, and James B. Peabody, eds. *The Records of Trinity Church, Boston*. 2 vols. Boston: Colonial Society of Massachusetts, 1980.

"On the Nature and End of Marriage, and the Means by Which the End Is to Be Obtained." In *The Matrimonial Preceptor; or, Instructive Hints to Those Who Are Like to Be Married: Gathered from the Works of the Most Classic Authors* [1755], 13–18. New Haven, Conn.: N. Whiting, 1829.

Ortner, Sherry. *Making Gender: The Politics and Erotics of Culture*. Boston: Beacon Press, 1996.

Otis, James. "The Rights of the British Colonies Asserted and Proved" [1764]. In Bernard Bailyn, ed., *Pamphlets of the American Revolution*, 408–82. Cambridge: Harvard University Press, 1965.

Ozment, Steven. *When Fathers Ruled: Family Life in Reformation Europe*. Cambridge: Harvard University Press, 1983.

Palmer, Henry. *Scripture and Reason Pleaded for Defensive Armes*. London, 1643.

Parker, Henry. *Jus Populi*. London, 1644.

Pateman, Carole. *The Sexual Contract*. Stanford: Stanford University Press, 1988.

Perdue, Theda. "Cherokee Women and the Trail of Tears." In Vicki L. Ruiz and Ellen C. DuBois, eds., *Unequal Sisters: A Multicultural Reader in U.S. Women's History*, 32–43. 2d ed. New York: Routledge, 1994.

Perlmann, Joel, and Dennis Shirley, "When Did New England Women Acquire Literacy?" *William and Mary Quarterly* 48 (1991): 50–67, 639–45.

Perry, Mary Elizabeth. *Gender and Disorder in Early Modern Seville.* Princeton: Princeton University Press, 1990.

Perry, Ruth. "Colonizing the Breast: Sexuality and Maternity in Eighteenth-Century England." In John C. Fout, ed., *Forbidden History: The State, Society, and the Regulation of Sexuality in Modern Europe*, 107–37. Chicago: University of Chicago Press, 1992.

Petiot, P. "La famille en France sous l'Ancien Régime." In *Sociologie comparée de la famille contemporaire, colloques du CNRS*, 1955.

Phillips, James D. *Salem in the Seventeenth Century.* Boston: Houghton Mifflin, 1933.

Pierce, Richard D., ed. *The Records of the First Church in Salem, Massachusetts, 1629–1736.* Salem, Mass.: Essex Institute, 1974.

———. *Records of the First Church of Boston, 1630–1868.* 3 vols. Boston: Colonial Society of Massachusetts, 1961.

Plutarch. "Conjugal Precepts." In *Plutarch's Essays and Miscellanies*, 2:486–507. New York: Colonial, 1905.

Plymouth Church Records, 1620–1859. Boston: Colonial Society of Massachusetts, 1920.

Pope, Alexander. "Epistle II, to a Lady: Of the Character of Women" [1735]. In Herbert Davis, ed., *Pope: Poetical Works*, 291–99. London: Oxford University Press, 1966.

Pope, Charles H., ed. *Records of the First Church at Dorchester in New England, 1636–1734.* Boston: G. H. Ellis, 1891.

Pope, Robert G., ed. *The Notebook of the Reverend John Fiske, 1644–1675.* Salem, Mass.: Essex Institute, 1974.

Poulain de La Barre, François. *The Equality of the Sexes.* 1673. Reprint. Manchester: Manchester University Press, 1990.

Powell, Chilton L. "Marriage in Early New England." *New England Quarterly* 1 (1928): 323–34.

Power, Eileen. *Medieval Women.* Cambridge: Cambridge University Press, 1975.

Prior, Mary. "Women and the Urban Economy: Oxford, 1500–1800." In Mary Prior, ed., *Women in English Society, 1500–1800*, 93–117. London: Methuen, 1985.

Probate Records of Essex County, Massachusetts, 1635–1681. 3 vols. Salem, Mass.: Essex Institute, 1916–20.

"Proceedings of Excommunication against Mistress Ann Hibbens of Boston (1640)." In John Demos, ed., *Remarkable Providences*, 222–39. New York: Braziller, 1972.

Pruitt, Bettye H. *The Massachusetts Tax Valuation List of 1771.* Boston: G. K. Hall, 1978.

Pufendorf, Samuel von. *De jure naturae et gentium.* 1672. Reprint. London: Walthoe, Wilkins, et al., 1729.

"Records of the Fifth Parish of Gloucester, Now Rockport." *Essex Institute Historical Collections* 21 (1884): 152–60, 225–40, 269–88.

"Records of the First Church in Marshfield, Massachusetts." *Mayflower Descendant* 11 (1909): 36–39, 121–23; 31 (1933): 117–24, 161–71; 32 (1934): 12–21.

Records of the Suffolk County Court, 1671–1680. In Publications of the Colonial Society of Massachusetts Collections, vols. 29 and 30. Boston: Colonial Society of Massachusetts, 1933.

Records Relating to the Early History of Boston. 39 vols. Boston: Rockwell and Churchill, 1876–1909. [Vols. 1–22 of this series were issued as *Report of the Records Commissioners*.]

Rediker, Marcus. *Between the Devil and the Deep Blue Sea: Merchant Seamen, Pirates, and the Anglo-American Maritime World, 1700–1750*. New York: Cambridge University Press, 1987.

Reyerson, Kathryn L. "Women in Business in Medieval Montpellier." In Barbara Hanawalt, ed., *Women and Work in Preindustrial Europe*, 117–44. Bloomington: Indiana University Press, 1986.

Rhode Island Court Records: Records of the Court of Trials of the Colony of Providence Plantations. 2 vols. Providence: Rhode Island Historical Society, 1922.

Rogers, Adrienne. "Women and Law." In Samia I. Spencer, ed., *French Women and the Age of Enlightenment*, 33–48. Bloomington: Indiana University Press, 1984.

Rogers, Horatio, et al., eds., *Early Records of the Town of Providence*. 21 vols. Providence, R.I.: Snow and Farnham, 1892–1915.

Rogers, Katharine. *Feminism in Eighteenth-Century England*. Urbana: University of Illinois Press, 1982.

Rogers, Kim L. "Relicts of the New World: Conditions of Widowhood in Seventeenth-Century New England." In Mary Kelley, ed., *Woman's Being, Woman's Place: Female Identity and Vocation in American History*. Boston: G. K. Hall, 1979.

Roper, Lyndal. *The Holy Household: Women and Morals in Reformation Augsburg*. Oxford: Clarendon Press, 1989.

Rosaldo, Michelle Z. "Women, Culture, and Society: A Theoretical Overview." In Michelle Z. Rosaldo and Louise Lamphere, eds., *Women, Culture, and Society*, 17–42. Stanford: Stanford University Press, 1974.

Rossi, Alice S., ed. *The Feminist Papers*. New York: Columbia University Press, 1973.

Rothman, David. *Discovery of the Asylum: Social Order and Disorder in the New Republic*. Boston: Little, Brown, 1971.

Rousseau, Jean-Jacques. *A Discourse on Inequality*. 1754. Reprint. New York: Viking Penguin, 1984.

———. *Emile*. 1762. London: Dent, 1911. Reprint. Rutland, Vt.: Tuttle, 1992.

Rowlands, Marie B. "Recusant Women, 1560–1640." In Mary Prior, ed., *Women in English Society, 1500–1800*, 149–80. London: Methuen, 1985.

Ruether, Rosemary R., and Rosemary S. Keller, eds. *Women and Religion in America*. 3 vols. San Francisco: Harper and Row, 1983.

Rush, Benjamin. "Of the Mode of Education Proper in a Republic." In *Essays Literary,*

Moral and Philosophical, 6–20. Philadelphia: Thomas and Samuel Bradford, 1798.

———. "Thoughts upon Female Education, Accomodated [*sic*] to the Present State of Society, Manners, and Government in the United States of America." In *Essays Literary, Moral and Philosophical*, 75–92. Philadelphia: Thomas and Samuel Bradford, 1798.

Salem Town Records. 3 vols. Salem, Mass.: Essex Institute, 1913, 1934.

Salmon, Marylynn. *Women and the Law of Property in Early America*. Chapel Hill: University of North Carolina Press, 1986.

Savile, George [Marquis of Halifax]. "The Lady's New Year's Gift; or, Advice to a Daughter." In *Miscellanies*, 1–84. London: Matt. Gillyflower, 1700.

Schochet, Gordon. *Patriarchalism in Political Thought*. Oxford: Blackwell, 1975.

Schulenburg, Jane T. "Female Sanctity: Public and Private Roles, ca. 500–1100." In Mary Erler and Maryanne Kowaleski, eds., *Women and Power in the Middle Ages*, 102–25. Athens: University of Georgia Press, 1988.

———. "Women's Monastic Communities, 500–1100: Patterns of Expansion and Decline." In Judith M. Bennett, Elizabeth A. Clark, Jean F. O'Barr, B. Anne Vilen, and Sarah Westphal-Wihl, eds., *Sisters and Workers in the Middle Ages*, 208–39. Chicago: University of Chicago Press, 1989.

"Scituate and Barnstable Church Records." In *New England Historical and Genealogical Register* 10 (1856): 37–43.

Shammas, Carole. "Anglo-American Household Government in Historical Perspective." *William and Mary Quarterly* 52 (1995): 104–44.

———. *The Pre-Industrial Consumer in England and America*. Oxford: Clarendon Press, 1990.

Shammas, Carole, Marylynn Salmon, and Michel Dahlin. *Inheritance in America from Colonial Times to the Present*. New Brunswick, N.J.: Rutgers University Press, 1987.

Shanley, M. L. "Marriage Contract and Social Contract in Seventeenth-Century English Political Thought." *Western Political Quarterly* 32 (1979): 79–91.

Sharples, Stephen P. *Records of the Church of Christ at Cambridge in New England, 1632–1830*. Boston: E. Putnam, 1906.

Shiels, Richard D. "The Feminization of American Congregationalism, 1730–1835." *American Quarterly* 33 (1981): 46–62.

Shorter, Edward. "Women's Work: What Difference Did Capitalism Make?" *Theory and Society* 111 (1976): 513–29.

Shurtleff, Nathaniel B., ed. *Records of the Governor and Company of the Massachusetts Bay in New England*. 6 vols. Boston: William White, 1853–54.

Silverman, Kenneth. *The Life and Times of Cotton Mather*. New York: Harper and Row, 1984.

Sinnott, Edmund W. *Meetinghouse and Church in Early New England*. New York: McGraw-Hill, 1963.

Sklar, Kathryn K. "The Founding of Mount Holyoke College." In Carol Berkin and

Mary Beth Norton, eds., *Women of America: A History,* 177–201. New York: Houghton Mifflin, 1979.

Smith, Barbara C. "Food Rioters and the American Revolution." *William and Mary Quarterly* 51 (1994): 3–38.

Smith, Billy G. *The "Lower Sort": Philadelphia's Laboring People, 1750–1800.* Ithaca: Cornell University Press, 1990.

Smith, Daniel Scott. "Female Householding in Late Eighteenth-Century America and the Problem of Poverty." *Journal of Social History* 28 (1994): 83–107.

Smith-Bannister, Scott. *Names and Naming Patterns in England 1538–1700.* New York: Oxford University Press, 1997.

Smith-Rosenberg, Carroll. "The Female World of Love and Ritual: Relations between Women in Nineteenth-Century America." *Signs: Journal of Women in Culture and Society* 1 (1975): 1–30.

Somerville, James K. "The Salem (Mass.) Woman in the Home, 1660-1770." *Eighteenth-Century Life* 1 (1974): 11–14.

Sonnet, Martine. "A Daughter to Educate." In Natalie Z. Davis and Arlette Farge, eds., *A History of Women in the West,* vol. 3, *Renaissance and Enlightenment Paradoxes,* 101–31. Cambridge: Harvard University Press, 1993.

Spectator, The. [By Addison, Steele, and others]. 4 vols. London: F. C. and J. Rivington, 1817.

Spencer, Samia I., "Women and Education." In Samia I. Spencer, ed., *French Women and the Age of Enlightenment,* 83–96. Bloomington: Indiana University Press, 1984.

Spencer, Samia, ed. *French Women and the Age of Enlightenment.* Bloomington: Indiana University Press, 1984.

Stabile, Susan. "'I Wou'd Wish Our Present Leaders Might Have a Three-Fold Dose, at the Dawn and Close of Every Day': Philadelphia Women Political Satirists as Moral Physicians." Paper presented to the Philadelphia Center for Early American Studies, 5 May 1995.

Stansell, Christine. *City of Women: Sex and Class in New York, 1784–1860.* New York: Knopf, 1986.

Staves, Susan. *Married Women's Separate Property in England, 1660–1833.* Cambridge: Harvard University Press, 1990.

Stiles, Ezra. *Extracts from the Itineraries and Other Miscellanies of Ezra Stiles, D.D., LL.D., 1755–1794.* Ed. Franklin B. Dexter. New Haven: Yale University Press, 1916, 1983.

———. *The Literary Diary of Ezra Stiles.* Ed. Franklin B. Dexter. 3 vols. New York: Scribners, 1901.

Stone, Lawrence. *The Family, Sex, and Marriage in England, 1500–1800.* New York: Harper and Row, 1979.

Stuard, Susan M. "The Dominion of Gender: Women's Fortunes in the High Middle Ages." In Renate Bridenthal, Claudia Koonz, and Susan Stuard, eds., *Becoming Visible: Women in European History,* 153–72. Boston: Houghton Mifflin, 1987.

Stuard, Susan M., ed. *Women in Medieval Society.* Philadelphia: University of Pennsylvania Press, 1976.

Suffolk County Wills: Abstracts of the Earliest Wills upon Record in the County of Suffolk, Massachusetts: From the New England Historical and Genealogical Register. Baltimore: Genealogical Publishing Co., 1984.

Taylor, Jeremy. *The Measures and Offices of Friendship.* London, 1657, 1662.

Taylor, Robert J., ed. *Massachusetts, Colony to Commonwealth: Documents on the Formation of Its Constitution, 1775–1780.* Chapel Hill: University of North Carolina Press, 1961.

Taylor, Robert J., et al., eds., *The Papers of John Adams.* 10 vols. Cambridge: Belknap Press of Harvard University Press, 1977–   .

Thomas, [Antoine-Léonard]. *Essay on the Character, Manners, and Genius of Women in Different Ages.* Paris: Moutard, 1772.

Thomas, Keith. "Women and the Civil War Sects." *Past and Present* 13 (1958): 42–62.

Thomas, M. Halsey, ed. *The Diary of Samuel Sewall.* 2 vols. New York: Farrar, Straus and Giroux, 1973.

Thompson, Roger. "Seventeenth-Century English and Colonial Sex Ratios: A Postscript." *Population Studies* 28 (1974): 153–65.

———. *Women in Stuart England and America.* London: Routledge and Kegan Paul, 1974, 1978.

Trenchard, John, and Thomas Gordon. *Cato's Letters; or, Essays on Liberty, Civil and Religious, and Other Important Subjects.* London: Russell and Russell, 1733.

"Truro Church Records." *Mayflower Descendant* 30 (1932): 28–36, 53–58, 105–9, 156–61.

Ulrich, Laurel T. "'Daughters of Liberty': Religious Women in Revolutionary New England." In Ronald Hoffman and Peter J. Albert, eds., *Women in the Age of the American Revolution,* 211–43. Charlottesville: University Press of Virginia, 1989.

———. *Good Wives: Image and Reality in the Lives of Women in Northern New England, 1650–1750.* New York: Knopf, 1982.

———. *A Midwife's Tale: The Life of Martha Ballard, Based on Her Diary, 1785–1812.* New York: Knopf, 1990.

Upham, William H., ed. "Beverly First Church Records." *Essex Institute Historical Collections* 35 (1899), 177–211.

Wabuda, Susan. "Shunamites and Nurses of the English Reformation: The Activities of Mary Glover, Niece of Hugh Latimer." In W. J. Shiels and Diana Wood, eds., *Women in the Church,* 335–44. Oxford: Blackwell, 1990.

Walton, Gary M., and James F. Shepherd. *The Economic Rise of Early America.* Cambridge: Cambridge University Press, 1979.

Warnicke, Retha M. *Women of the English Renaissance and Reformation.* Westport, Conn: Greenwood Press, 1983.

Watertown Records, Comprising East Congregational and Precinct Affairs, 1697–1737. Boston: Watertown Historical Society, 1906.

Weisberg, D. Kelly. "Under Great Temptations Here: Women and Divorce in Puritan Massachusetts." In D. Kelly Weisberg, ed., *Women and the Law: The Social Historical Perspective,* 2:117–31. 2 vols. Cambridge, Mass.: Schenkman, 1982.

Wells, Robert V. *The Population of the British Colonies in America before 1776: A Survey of Census Data.* Princeton: Princeton University Press, 1975.

Wemple, Suzanne. "Sanctity and Power: The Dual Pursuit of Early Medieval Women." In Renate Bridenthal, Claudia Koonz, and Susan Stuard, eds., *Becoming Visible: Women in European History,* 131–51. Boston: Houghton Mifflin, 1987.

Wertenbaker, Thomas J. *The Puritan Oligarchy: The Founding of American Civilization.* New York: Grosset and Dunlap, 1947.

White, Daniel A. *New England Congregationalism in Its Origin and Purity: Illustrated by the Foundation and Early Records of the First Church in Salem and Various Discussions Pertaining to the Subject.* Salem, Mass., 1861.

White, Deborah G. "Female Slaves: Sex Roles and Status in the Antebellum Plantation South." In Vicki L. Ruiz and Ellen C. DuBois, eds., *Unequal Sisters: A Multicultural Reader in U.S. Women's History,* 20–31. 2d ed. New York and London: Routledge, 1994.

Whitmore, William H., ed. *The Colonial Laws of Massachusetts: Reprinted from the Edition of 1672, with the Supplements through 1686.* Boston: S. Greene, 1887.

Wiesner, Merry E. *Women and Gender in Early Modern Europe.* Cambridge: Cambridge University Press, 1993.

Willen, Diane. "Women in the Public Sphere in Early Modern England: The Case of the Urban Working Poor." In Dorothy O. Helly and Susan M. Reverby, eds., *Gendered Domains: Rethinking Public and Private in Women's History,* 183–98. Ithaca: Cornell University Press, 1992.

Wilson, Joan Hoff. "The Illusion of Change: Women and the American Revolution." In Alfred A. Young, ed., *The American Revolution: Explorations in the History of American Radicalism.* DeKalb: Northern Illinois University Press, 1976.

Winthrop, John. *Winthrop's Journal: History of New England, 1630–1649.* Ed. James K. Hosmer. 2 vols. New York: Scribners, 1908.

Wollstonecraft, Mary. "A Vindication of the Rights of Woman." In Alice S. Rossi, ed., *The Feminist Papers,* 40–85. New York: Columbia University Press, 1973.

Wood, Gordon S. *The Radicalism of the American Revolution.* New York: Vintage Books, 1993.

Woodbridge, Linda. *Women and the English Renaissance: Literature and the Nature of Womankind, 1540–1620.* Urbana: University of Illinois Press, 1984.

Worthley, Harold T. *An Inventory of the Records of the Particular (Congregational) Churches of Massachusetts, Gathered 1620–1805.* Cambridge: Harvard University Press, 1970.

Yazawa, Melvin. *From Colonies to Commonwealth: Familial Ideology and the Beginnings of the American Republic.* Baltimore: Johns Hopkins University Press, 1985.

Young, Alfred F. "The Women of Boston: 'Persons of Consequence' in the Making of the American Revolution, 1765–76." In Harriet B. Applewhite and Darline G. Levy, eds., *Women and Politics in the Age of the Democratic Revolution,* 181–226. Ann Arbor: University of Michigan Press, 1990.

Young, Christine A. *From 'Good Order' to Glorious Revolution: Salem, Massachusetts, 1628–1689.* Ann Arbor: UMI Research Press, 1978, 1980.

Index

Abbott, Walter, 125

Abbott, Mrs., 125

Accounting: women displaced by professional accountants, 130

Adams, Abigail, 127, 219, 222, 229–30, 234, 289n30

Adams, Abigail (daughter of John and Abigail), 290n33

Adams, John, 217, 229–30, 234, 286n93, 289n30, 290n33

Adultery, 7, 187, 189, 190–92, 193, 197, 198, 201, 285n70. *See also* Fornication; Sexual behavior

African Americans: access of to courts, 146; in Boston, 19, 115; and cult of domesticity, 241; earning power of, 107, 120; education of, 54; in Essex, Mass., 76; and female-headed households, 17, 18; in New England meetinghouses, seating of, 61; in New York City, 246n2; in Newport, 10, 19–20, 54, 105, 113; in Philadelphia, 246; sex ratio of, 18–19; sexual promiscuity of women, alleged, 200; as subject to Anglo-American property law, 162; women's property ownership, 115. *See also* Slave trade; Slaves

Agriculture: shortage of labor in, 108; women workers in, 108

Ahaton, Sarah, 201

Ainsworth, Henry, 56

Alembert, Jean Le Rond d', 221

Alimony, 195

All, Samuel, 123

Allen, James, 66

Allison, Richard, 174

Almshouses, poorhouses, and workhouses, 119; in Boston, 112, 113, 115, 125, 185, 267n45; houses of correction and, 186; in Newport, 113, 117; in Portsmouth, 117; in Salem, 117;

Almy, Catherine, 93

Almy, Christopher, Jr., 205–6

Almy, Elizabeth, 205

Almy, Job, 206

American Revolution, 286n4; and family, 234; increase in divorces during era of, 191, 238; and oppression of women, 233; reduction of African Americans in Newport after, 19; and sex ratios in New England seaports, 12, 13–14; women, effect on, 6, 206–7, 212, 230, 243; women's role in, 235–36

Amory, Thomas, 127

Amsden, Susannah, 155–56

Andrews, Mrs., 116

Anglican church: marriage ceremony in, 188; in Newport, 72. *See also* Church of England

Anna (African American), 144

Anne, Queen, 235

Apprenticeships, 40–41, 123, 202–3. *See also* Binding out poor; Indentured servants; Putting-out system

Arbitration: in dispute resolution, 144, 151

Archaic state, development of, 4

Armitage, Goody, 177

Assoaske (Indian), 162

Astell, Mary, 211, 216, 233, 236

Austin, Mercy, 192

Auternote, Mary, 146

Awassomoag, Abigail, 163

Awassomoag, Thomas, 163

Topsfield, Mass., 65

Touzel, John, 126–27, 128

Towns: compared to rural areas, 5; importance of in America, 4; poor women an economic burden on, 176; urban problems in, 51. *See also* Seaports, New England; Urban settings

Townsend, Job, 136

Treby, Mehetabel, 129

Treby, Peter, 129, 149

Truro, Mass., 90

Trusler, Mrs. Thomas, 80

Tucker, Andrew, 125

Tucker, Mary, 125

Turner, Patience, 264

Turpin, Peter, 198

Tyler, Ann, 162

Ulrich, Laurel, 84–85, 126, 196–97, 269–70n69

Unmarried women: cohabiting with men, 188; inheritance of, 115; population of in Europe, 50; poverty of, 116, 135; sexual behavior of, 198; warned out in Rhode Island, 114. *See also* Poverty; Semi-married women

Upholstery, 104

Upshall, Goody, 180

Urban VIII, 57

Urban setting: opportunities for women in, 48–50; sex ratios in, 50. *See also* Seaports, New England; Towns

Ursulines, 28

Usher, Mary, 171

Vaughn, Mary, 87

Verin, Mercy, 80, 86–87

Verstilles, Peter, 132

Vibert, Widow, 89

Vicars, Elisabeth, 171

Visitors: women as, 78, 94

Vives, Juan Luis, 218

Voltaire, 233–34

Von Eyb, Albrecht, 223

Wages: in New England, 265; regulation of, 134–35, 184; room and board as benefits to women, 134–35. *See also* Earning power of women

Wain, William, 128

Waine, William, 104, 131

Walch, Gracy, 117

Walford, Jane, 45

Wanton, Ruth, 205–6

War: male casualties from, 12, 13, 50, 115; Indians' rules of, 147–48; rules of concerning women and children, 147–48; women's dependency greater during time of, 112

Ward, Benjamin, 156

Ward, Mary, 57–58, 156

Warnings out, 114, 199, 202

Washington, George, 240

Waterman, Ruth, 172

Watowswokotaus (Indian), 147

Watts, Thomas, 189

Webb, Mary, 186

Webb, Samuel, 128

Webb, Stephen, 122

Webber, Mrs., 116

Webster, John, 174–75

Webster, Rachel, 174–75

Welfare: in Boston, 112–14, 202, 267n45; in eighteenth century, 8, 49; in Newport, 186, 202–3; in Salem, 119, 186, 202; in seaports, 117; women as most likely recipients of, 112–14, 117–18. *See also* Almshouses, poorhouses, and workhouses; Poverty

Wells, Robert, 15, 18

Wenham, Mass., 66, 67, 75

West, Katherine, 185

West, Mary, 120

Westerly, R. I., 72

Weston, Francis, 21–22

Weston, Margret, 21–22, 80

Wharton, Mary, 80, 157

Wheeler, Elizabeth, 189

Whig interpretation of history: antithetical to female experience, 3

Whitamore, Hannah, 186

Whitwell, Samuel, 113

Widows: in Boston, 12, 13, 15, 16, 90; as converts to Protestantism, 30; in Eu-